Constitutional Conflicts
between Congress and
the President

Constitutional Conflicts between Congress and the President

LOUIS FISHER

PRINCETON UNIVERSITY PRESS

PRINCETON, NEW JERSEY

Published by Princeton University Press, 41 William Street,
Princeton, New Jersey 08540
In the United Kingdom: Princeton University Press,
Guildford, Surrey

Library of Congress Cataloging in Publication Data will
be found on the last printed page of this book

ISBN 0-691-07680-4   ISBN 0-691-02233-X (pbk.)

This book has been composed in Linotron Galliard

Clothbound editions of Princeton University Press books are
printed on acid-free paper, and binding materials are chosen for
strength and durability. Paperbacks, although satisfactory
for personal collections, are not usually suitable
for library rebinding

Printed in the United States of America by Princeton
University Press, Princeton, New Jersey

First published in 1978 by St. Martin's Press as *The
Constitution Between Friends: Congress, the President, and
the Law*. Princeton University Press edition extensively
revised, updated, and augmented by the author.

CONTENTS

CONTENTS

CONTENTS

10
Conclusions

PREFACE

The first edition of this book, published in 1978 under the title *The Constitution Between Friends: Congress, the President, and the Law*, bucked a strong tide of disinterest in public law among political scientists. The response to the book, justifying a second and expanded edition, has been both gratifying and reassuring. It provides welcome evidence that social scientists have become less willing to accept the artificial separation that divides law from politics.

The neglect of public law coincided with, and helped encourage, the belief that presidential power was our best hope for promoting the public good and should be unfettered by constitutional and statutory restrictions. That assumption was shattered, at least for a time, by the record in office of Lyndon Johnson and Richard Nixon. The subordination of constitutional principles to short-run political expediency is illustrated by President Johnson's ability in August 1964 to enlist the support of almost every member of Congress for his Gulf of Tonkin Resolution, granting him extraordinary powers over the military. Passage of the resolution put Congress in the back seat, legally, in determining the scope and direction of the Vietnam War. Johnson's use of the resolution, particularly as a "functional equivalent" to a declaration of war, seemed to many dismayed legislators a violation of congressional intent. But Johnson did not misread the statutory language, which represented a blanket and careless abdication of authority to the President. A few years later the Senate Foreign Relations Committee apologized for its part in this episode. It admitted that Congress, in adopting the resolution, committed the error of making a *personal* judgment about how a particular President would use the resolution. It should have made an *institutional* judgment about whether it was appropriate under the Constitution to grant such authority to *any* President.[1]

[1] S. Rept. No. 129, 91st Cong., 1st Sess. 23 (1969).

A tension runs throughout the American system of government. Statutory and constitutional restrictions are erected to keep the actions of the executive and legislative branches within legal boundaries. The drive for political power continually tests those boundaries, often stretching them to do what the law forbids. Because the demarcations between the branches are imprecise and subject to varying interpretations, periodic protests about "encroachments" and "usurpations" are to be expected. At any given time one branch may appear to be dominant, the other subordinate. Fortunes wax and wane; struggles for spheres of influence are inevitable.

A certain amount of friction is invited by the Constitution. Conflict between the branches serves the useful purpose of preventing an accumulation of power and the abuses that flow from unchecked power. Equally important, conflict develops public policies that have a broad base of support and understanding. However, as Attorney General Edward H. Levi has noted, the framers "did not envision a government in which each branch seeks out confrontation; they hoped the system of checks and balances would achieve a harmony of purposes differently fulfilled. The branches of government were not designed to be at war with one another. The relationship was not to be an adversary one, though to think of it that way has become fashionable."[2]

Conflict between the President and Congress can reach the point of stalemate, with each branch sensing that its vital powers and prerogatives are endangered. In such a climate, cooperation and good-faith efforts are scarce commodities. Reaction leads to overreaction, the pendulum of political balance swings unpredictably, and constitutional roles become confused. Instead of moving ahead with urgent public problems—energy, the environment, foreign policy, the economy—political leaders fill the air with mutual recriminations and countercharges. These paralyzing conflicts obviously result from something more basic than partisan bickering. What the country lacks is agreement on the

[2] Edward H. Levi, "Some Aspects of Separation of Powers," 76 Colum. L. Rev. 371, 391 (1976).

appropriate roles for the two branches, particularly on large policy questions such as national defense and budget.

Although the nature of government and our constitutional system call for some overlapping of functions, and to good effect, it should be possible to clarify the authorities and responsibilities of each branch. Clarification could reduce the frequency of head-on confrontations, contribute to accountability, and produce a more constructive relationship between political leaders. In a search for clarification, this book examines the central legal and constitutional conflicts between the President and Congress today.

Too often law and politics are viewed as isolated sectors of public policy. The Supreme Court reinforces this view by announcing on various occasions its unwillingness to decide "political questions"—a doctrine that survives on circular reasoning. Declared one federal judge in 1968, after refusing to decide a war-powers case: "Though it is not always a simple matter to define the meaning of the term 'political question,' it is generally used to encompass all questions outside the sphere of judicial power."[3] That definition does not push the frontiers of human knowledge very far. It is like the dictionary that explained: "violins are small cellos, and cellos are large violins."[4]

Today, as in Tocqueville's time more than a century ago, what begins as a political question often ripens into an issue appropriate for the courts. Regrettably, many citizens—including political scientists—cringe from informed debate on constitutional issues. Mere mention of a "legal" dimension seems to stifle further discussion. Why this is so I have never fully understood. Perhaps the technical presentation of court decisions presents a barrier, and yet federal judges often write with a flair, lucidity, and intelligibility rarely matched by offerings in the scholarly journals.

Part of the resistance, I believe, comes from the habit of associating political events with the real world while consigning legal matters to the realm of the remote and ethereal. This is a

[3] Velvel v. Johnson, 287 F.Supp. 846, 850 (D. Kans. 1968).
[4] John P. Roche, "Judicial Self-Restraint," 49 Am. Pol. Sci. Rev. 762, 768 (1955).

puzzling attitude, for constitutional and legal questions have their roots in tangible and concrete injuries. Someone suffers and seeks relief. Strong beliefs and deeply held feelings cause plaintiffs to take their grievances to the courts, often after being rebuffed by Congress and the executive branch. Great questions of constitutional law, Henry Steele Commager has remarked, are great "not because they are complicated legal or technical questions, but because they embody issues of high policy, of public good, of morality."[5]

Litigation is another form of politics. Plaintiffs unable to gain their objectives from Congress or the executive branch will turn to the courts, framing their arguments somewhat differently, using a vocabulary more attuned to the judiciary, but never wavering from the initial goal. Members of Congress are among these litigants, working independently or through the Senate Legal Counsel and the attorneys for the House of Representatives. Different combinations of legislators, executives, and private parties join forces to represent their interests in court, none of them at any time believing that the effort is any the less political.

The American Constitution is designed to protect individual liberties. That objective requires the consent and the understanding of the governed. When we shy away from constitutional issues, treating them as technical and abstract matters to be decided by legislators, executive officials, the courts, and a few academic specialists, democratic society suffers. A dependence on the people, Madison counseled in Federalist 51, is the primary control on the government. This book is written to encourage a broader public understanding of some central constitutional issues that we face today.

The book begins by discussing the basic elements of constitutional government, including the concepts of separation of powers and federalism. In addition to enumerated powers, the Constitution develops under the force of implied powers and custom. Broadly conceived, then, the meaning of the Constitu-

---

[5] "War Powers Legislation," hearings before the Senate Committee on Foreign Relations, 92d Cong., 1st Sess. 13 (1971).

tion is shaped not merely by judges but by legislators, executives, state officials, and private citizens.

Chapters 2 and 3 concern the structure of government: the creation of agencies and the appointment and removal of officers. Basic constitutional provisions have been supplemented over the years by statutory limitations, court decisions, and informal accommodations, producing a complex environment for executive-legislative action. Chapters 4 and 5 also complement one another, covering the nature of legislative power and the tools used to restrict it (vetoes of both presidential and legislative character). Important elements in this discussion are delegated powers, nonstatutory controls, and the legislative instruments available to the President: proclamations, executive orders, and the rulemaking process. Chapters 6 and 7 explore the powers used in the operation of government: congressional investigations, the power of contempt, impeachment, executive privilege, and the power of the purse. The final two chapters, 8 and 9, concentrate on international affairs: treaties, executive agreements, and the war power.

Each chapter represents a study of legal disputes within a political and historical context. Lower court rulings are reviewed along with Supreme Court decisions, as well as important legal opinions issued by other agencies of government, especially the Attorney General and the Comptroller General. The purpose is to leave with the reader a deeper understanding of the dynamics of government and the principles on which it operates.

ACKNOWLEDGMENTS

The manuscript for the first edition was read by three scholars who have made major contributions to the study of law and politics: Harold G. Maier of the Vanderbilt School of Law, Walter F. Murphy of Princeton University, and C. Herman Pritchett of the University of California at Santa Barbara. The profession is indebted to them for their leadership over the years.

Others who read parts of the manuscript for the first edition include Arthur S. Miller, formerly with the George Washington University National Law Center, and Harold C. Relyea of the Congressional Research Service. I keep in close contact with both scholars and continue to draw upon their advice and insight.

Most of the manuscript for the second edition was read carefully and thoughtfully by Morton Rosenberg of the American Law Division of the Congressional Research Service. Somehow he manages to balance with extraordinary skill and sensitivity the subjects of constitutional law, administrative law, and labor law (to name his major fields), with enough energy left in reserve to place legal developments in a historical and political context. I have relied extensively on his expert counsel and enthusiastic spirit.

Between the first and second editions it was my good fortune to become friends with Phillip J. Cooper of Georgia State University, author of a first-rate study entitled *Public Law and Public Administration* (1983). He too is an indefatigable explorer of law and politics, illuminating many areas of constitutional law and administrative law. His perceptive review of my draft helped upgrade a number of chapters.

I also want to express my appreciation to Sanford G. Thatcher of the Princeton University Press, who offered early interest and encouragement for this second edition. Having published *Presidential Spending Power* with him in 1975, I am happy to renew a relationship with a true professional and a very distinguished press. Elizabeth Gretz read the manuscript with great care, offering numerous suggestions to clarify passages, maintain consistency, and smooth the transition between chapters.

NOTE ON CITATIONS

All court citations refer to published volumes whenever available: *United States Reports* (U.S.) for Supreme Court decisions, *Federal Reporter* (F.2d) for appellate decisions, and *Federal Supplement* (F.Supp.) for district court decisions. For cases not yet reported, citations are either to the *United States Law Week* (U.S.L.W.), the *Supreme Court Reporter* (S.Ct.), or to the civil action number and date. There are also citations to *Opinions of the Attorney General* (Op. Att'y Gen.), *Decisions of the Comptroller General* (Comp. Gen.), and to *Opinions of the Office of Legal Counsel* (O.L.C.) in the Justice Department. Decisions that focus primarily on federal rules of civil and criminal procedure appear in *Federal Rules Decisions* (F.R.D.)

Several standard reference works are abbreviated in the footnotes by using the following system:

Elliot, Debates	Jonathan Elliot, ed., The Debates in the Several State Conventions, on the Adoption of the Federal Constitution (5 vols., Washington, D.C., 1836-1845).
Farrand, Records	Max Farrand, ed., The Records of the Federal Convention of 1787 (4 vols., New Haven: Yale University Press, 1937).
Richardson, Messages and Papers	James D. Richardson, ed., A Compilation of the Messages and Papers of the Presidents (20 vols., New York: Bureau of National Literature, 1897-1925).
Wkly Comp. Pres. Doc.	Weekly Compilation of Presidential Documents, published each week by the Government Printing Office since 1965.

Constitutional Conflicts
between Congress and
the President

1

THE CONSTITUTIONAL SETTING

Constitutional law texts have a disconcerting habit of avoiding any discussion about the meaning of "constitutionalism." With little introduction they plunge into an examination of individual court rulings. They provide few signposts to help the reader recognize the characteristics that distinguish a constitutional system from other forms of government.

Constitutionalism is more than a shorthand expression for a constitution and the case law that accompanies it. To be worthy of the name, a constitution embodies a philosophy of government, an understanding between public officials and the people. It promotes the commonweal while protecting individual rights, including those of the minority. Especially crucial is the right of the people to meet together, to express their opinions individually and through associations, and to participate in free elections. Constitutions that merely sanction the use of governmental power without limiting it—those of autocratic and totalitarian states—are hostile to the concept of constitutionalism.

The Elements of Constitutionalism

The main elements of constitutionalism are found in Bolingbroke's definition, written in 1733: "By constitution we mean, whenever we speak with propriety and exactness, that assemblage of laws, institutions and customs, derived from certain fixed principles of reason, directed to certain fixed objects of public good, that compose the general system, according to which the community hath agreed to be governed."[1] Governmental behavior is guided not only by laws but by institutions and customs, and legal principles must be set forth in a written document. Even the "unwritten" constitution of England—an amalgam of major enactments, minor statutes, judicial decisions, custom and con-

[1] Charles Howard McIlwain, Constitutionalism: Ancient and Modern 3 (1947).

vention, and parliamentary debates—is secured by publishing the fundamental principles for all to see: the Magna Carta, the Habeas Corpus Act, the Petition of Right, and the Act of Settlement.[2]

"Fixed principles of reason," Bolingbroke's second criterion, cannot be defined with any exact meaning and application. At the very least the concept eliminates political regimes that act in an arbitrary, irrational, and capricious manner. Constitutionalism cannot exist, even in the presence of a constitution, if the principles and standards of behavior are matters of whim for those in authority. Reason is also more than an exercise in logic or rational analysis. It must be tempered and tested by experience. As John Dickinson warned at the Philadelphia convention, "Experience must be our only guide. Reason may mislead us."[3]

The American concept of "due process of law" depends on reasonableness. Courts strike down statutes that exhibit the "vice of vagueness" (as in loyalty oaths). Citizens should not have to guess at the meaning of a law. Similarly, courts insist that legislative investigations relate to a legislative purpose. Questions during committee interrogations must be pertinent and relevant. When the judiciary finds that legislators have chosen a "rational basis" for carrying out, for example, the commerce power, the court's examination is at an end.[4]

Fixed principles of reason, as a constitutional standard, evokes the idea of natural law, "higher law," or *jus gentium*, which the Roman jurist Gaius called "that law which natural reason established among all mankind."[5] Natural law is given concrete meaning in a scene from Sophocles' *Antigone*. One of Antigone's brothers, Polyneices, joined in a military attack on the city of Thebes. Among the defenders was his brother. Both men, meeting face to face, died in battle. The regent of Thebes, Creon,

---

[2] H.R.G. Greaves, The British Constitution 15, 20-22 (1955); W. Ivor Jennings, The Law and the Constitution 32-40 (1943).

[3] Farrand, Records, II, 278.

[4] Katzenbach v. McClung, 379 U.S. 294, 303-04 (1964); Hodel v. Indiana, 452 U.S. 314, 323-24 (1981).

[5] Edward S. Corwin, The "Higher Law" Background of American Constitutional Law 17 (1955).

4

issued an edict ordering Polyneices' body left to rot on the battlefield, but Antigone defied the proclamation by burying her brother. When asked if she chose flagrantly to disobey the law, Antigone responds:

> Naturally! Since Zeus never promulgated
> Such a law. Nor will you find
> That Justice publishes such laws to man below.
> I never thought your edicts had such force
> They nullified the laws of heaven, which,
> Unwritten, not proclaimed, can boast
> A currency that everlastingly is valid;
> An origin beyond the birth of man.

Even Haemon, son of Creon, tells his father that he is "at loggerheads with open justice!" The chorus uses just eight words to define the issue of constitutionalism: "Where might is right there is no right."[6]

In one of the first examples of judicial review, in Dr. Bonham's Case of 1610, Justice Coke announced that when an act of Parliament was "against common right and reason, or repugnant, or impossible to be performed, the common law will controul it and adjudge such act to be void."[7] Common right and reason, Edward S. Corwin concluded, meant something fundamental and permanent: "it is higher law."[8]

The natural law doctrine enters American constitutionalism by way of John Locke's *Second Treatise on Civil Government* (1690). Locke believed that people living in the state of nature were governed by a law of nature, which obliged everyone to behave in a certain manner. Reason, "which is that law, teaches all mankind who will but consult it, that being all equal and independent, no one ought to harm another in his life, health, liberty or possessions." But humanity, biased and ignorant, failed to study the law of nature. When called upon to judge in their own cases, people punished others too harshly and excused their own

---

[6] Paul Roche, trans., The Oedipus Plays of Sophocles 179, 189, 194 (1958).
[7] Corwin, The "Higher Law" Background, at 44.
[8] Id. at 47.

transgressions. The result was that "inconveniences" (Locke's mild term) developed in the state of nature, creating the need for a common, unbiased judge to handle disputes.[9]

Although Locke regarded the legislative power as supreme, it could not be arbitrary. The purpose of the legislature was to preserve life, liberty, and fortune. If it became destructive of this end, people would find themselves in a condition worse than the state of nature. Under such circumstances the people were at liberty to dissolve the government and establish a new legislature.[10]

The Lockean influence carries over directly into the Declaration of Independence. The opening sentence explains that the rupture with England was necessary so that Americans might "assume among the Powers of the earth, the separate and equal station to which the Laws of Nature and of Nature's God entitle them." The idea of constitutionalism, emphasizing individual liberties and Locke's philosophy of government, appears in the very next paragraph:

> We hold these truths to be self-evident, that all men are created equal, that they are endowed by their Creator with certain unalienable Rights, that among these are Life, Liberty, and the pursuit of Happiness. That to secure these rights, Governments are instituted among Men, deriving their just powers from the consent of the governed; That whenever any Form of Government becomes destructive of these ends, it is the Right of the People to alter or to abolish it, and to institute new Government.

These sentiments lead to Bolingbroke's last two elements of constitutionalism: (1) government is directed to certain fixed objects of public good; and (2) the community gives its consent to be governed. Both points are consistent with Locke, who held that the legislature's power, "in the utmost bounds of it," was limited to the public good of the society. The executive's emer-

[9] John Locke, Second Treatise on Civil Government, §§ 4-6, 13, 124-25.
[10] Id. at §§ 135-37, 220-22.

gency power (the prerogative) was "nothing but the power of doing public good without a rule."[11]

The principle of public consent and popular control is implicit in Locke's belief that human rights existed prior to government. If government fails to protect those rights the people can change the government. In this sense the *public's* interpretation of natural law—as developed over a period of time—becomes the ultimate test of the legitimacy of civil law. The community can never agree to be governed by tyrannical or arbitrary regimes. It never loses control over the government it creates. Although regimes of that nature may exist, even supported by a written constitution, they are not constitutional forms of government.

The conviction that individuals retain certain rights, never to be surrendered to government, was basic to other political philosophers. Spinoza believed that no man's mind can possibly lie wholly at the disposition of another, for "no one can willingly transfer his natural right of free reason and judgment, or be compelled so to do." Any government attempting to control minds was, by definition, tyrannical. It was an abuse of sovereignty to seek to prescribe what was true or false, or what opinions should be held by men in their worship of God. "All these questions," to Spinoza, "fall within a man's natural right, which he cannot abdicate even with his own consent."[12]

Sutherland and Friedrich: Modern Views on Constitutionalism

These elements of constitutionalism, debated centuries ago, parallel the principles we discuss today. Arthur E. Sutherland, in a major study published in 1965, emphasized the "freedom of men, acting through an organized majority, to control their own political and economic fate."[13] This principle rejects hereditary rule, divine right of kings, and rule by elites. Sutherland also said that government, to remain righteous and just, must create institu-

[11] Id. at §§ 135, 166.
[12] The Philosophy of Spinoza 333 (Modern Library ed., 1954).
[13] Arthur E. Sutherland, Constitutionalism in America 2 (1965). Footnote omitted.

tions to correct its own injustices. Or, as Madison cautioned in Federalist 51: "In framing a government which is to be administered by men over men, the great difficulty lies in this: you must first enable the government to control the governed; and in the next place oblige it to control itself."

Sutherland recognized that his second principle jars with his first. Governmental action may be unjust even if willed by a majority of the people. Judicial officers, less vulnerable to majoritarian pressures, may declare invalid any governmental action that is inconsistent with standards of constitutional justice.[14] This proposition is not the same as "government by judiciary." Charles Evans Hughes reached too far with his injunction: "We are under a Constitution, but the Constitution is what the judges say it is . . . ."[15] The Supreme Court is a coequal, not superior, branch. In his inaugural address in 1861, President Lincoln denied that constitutional questions could be settled solely by Supreme Court rulings. If governmental policy on "vital questions affecting the whole people is to be irrevocably fixed by decisions of the Supreme Court . . . the people will have ceased to be their own rulers . . . ."[16] Constitutionalism is not entirely what the judges say it is.

In many instances the judiciary concludes that Congress is a more appropriate forum for reconciling conflicts between individual rights and governmental action. Supreme Court Justices recognize that members of Congress take the same oath as they do to uphold the Constitution and that deference to legislative judgment on constitutional questions is often an appropriate course.[17] In performing their assigned constitutional duties, "each branch of the Government must initially interpret the Constitution, and the interpretation of its powers by any branch is due great respect from the others."[18]

Moreover, Congress frequently passes legislation that has the

[14] Id. at 2-3..
[15] Charles Evans Hughes, Addresses and Papers 139 (1908).
[16] Richardson, Messages and Papers, VII, 3210.
[17] Rostker v. Goldberg, 453 U.S. 57 (1981), concerning male-only registration for military service.
[18] United States v. Nixon, 418 U.S. 683, 703 (1974).

effect of modifying a previous decision of a court. Because of the "political question" doctrine, many important constitutional issues are left to Congress and the President. Even when the courts intervene they often regard as authoritative a set of practices already established by legislators and executive officials.[19] Still other constitutional questions never reach the courts because of problems of jurisdiction, mootness, standing, ripeness, and other conditions for adjudication.

Sutherland points to three other criteria of constitutionalism. First, there must be fundamental equality before government. Although human beings are not identical, the standard of equality serves to eliminate artificial and arbitrary inequalities, such as discriminatory treatment on the basis of race, sex, or religion. Second, the fundamentals of the constitutional system must be reduced to a written statement, either a concise constitution, as in America, or the fragmented, cumulative written record of England. As a final element, Sutherland depends on structure to restrain government: dividing power between the nation and the states, and then again within the central government (creating separate executive, legislative, and judicial bodies).[20]

To Carl Friedrich this division of power cuts across two planes: functionally (separation of powers) and spatially (federalism). The doctrine of separated powers has been heavily attacked in the twentieth century, first for impeding the flow of power to public administrators (who supposedly possessed expertise not found among legislators), and secondly for interfering with the demand for centralized authority during World War II. Friedrich warns that "Many who today belittle the separation of powers seem unaware of the fact that their clamor for efficiency and expediency easily leads to dictatorship . . . ."[21]

[19] For legislative responsibility in shaping constitutional principles, see Donald G. Morgan, Congress and the Constitution (1966) and William G. Andrews, ed., Coordinate Magistrates: Constitutional Law by Congress and President (1969).

[20] Sutherland, Constitutionalism in America, at 4-7.

[21] Carl Friedrich, Constitutional Government and Democracy 175 (1946). See his "Constitutions and Constitutionalism," Int'l Encyc. Soc. Sci. (1968) and "Separation of Powers," Encyc. Soc. Sci., XIII, 664 (1935), as well as Charles H. Wilson, "The Separation of Powers under Democracy and Fascism," 52 Pol.

The Doctrine of Separated Powers

The abuse of power by recent Presidents, particularly Lyndon Johnson and Richard Nixon, generated some conventional and convenient arguments about the separation doctrine. Opponents of presidential power claimed that the framers distrusted government (especially the executive) and attempted to fashion an instrument of checks and balances to prevent tyranny. Although the framers did indeed construct a system designed to restrain power, that was only part of their intention. It would be inaccurate and a disservice to their labors at the Philadelphia convention to believe that they created a document primarily for the purpose of obstructing and hampering the operation of government.

It is important to understand the practical forces that led to the creation of separated branches. Our structure of government owes its existence to the experiences of the framers, not the theory of Montesquieu or precedents borrowed from England. The framers used Montesquieu selectively, adopting what they knew from their own experience to be useful and rejecting what they knew to be inapplicable. The product was more theirs than his. Having served in public life for many years, both in the colonies and in the fledgling republic, they knew firsthand the practical duties and problems of running a government. They were continuously and intimately involved in the mundane, down-to-earth matters of conducting a war and laying the foundation for a more perfect union. Their close familiarity with the classics in history and government, combined with the daily experience of public office, marked their special genius. They had vision without becoming visionaries.

British history, although valuable for the study of private and individual rights, is of marginal interest for the study of executive-legislative relationships in America. Questions of executive privilege, impoundment, and the war power cannot be resolved

Sci. Q. 481 (1937). Arthur T. Vanderbilt, in the introduction to his Doctrine of the Separation of Powers and Its Present-Day Significance (1953), has written that individual freedom and the progress of civilization were attainable only by adhering to the principles of the separation of powers.

by harkening back to British practices. The Supreme Court made this valid observation in 1850: "[I]n the distribution of political power between the great departments of government, there is such a wide difference between the power conferred on the President of the United States, and the authority and sovereignty which belongs to the English crown, that it would be altogether unsafe to reason from any supposed resemblance between them, either as regards conquest in war, or any other subject where the right and powers of the executive arm of the government are brought into question."[22]

It is said that powers are separated to preserve liberties. But separation can also destroy liberties. The French constitutions of 1791 and 1848 represented ambitious efforts to erect a rigid and dogmatic separation of powers. The first document produced the reign of Napoleon Bonaparte; the next effort led to the Second Empire.[23]

Instead of indiscriminately championing the virtues of the separation doctrine, we should remember that it can satisfy a number of objectives, not all of them worth seeking. The framers of the American Constitution did not want a political system so fragmented in structure, so divided in authority, that government could not function. Justice Story pointed out in his *Commentaries* that the framers adopted a separation of power but "endeavored to prove that a rigid adherence to it in all cases would be subversive of the efficiency of the government, and result in the destruction of the public liberties."[24] His observation has been underscored by others. Justice Jackson correctly identified the multiple goals that motivated the framers: "While the Constitution diffuses power the better to secure liberty, it also contemplates that the practice will integrate the dispersed powers into a workable government. It enjoins upon its branches separateness but interdependence, autonomy but reciprocity."[25]

Had this understanding prevailed in the 1960s and 1970s, we

[22] Fleming v. Page, 50 U.S. (9 How.) 602, 618 (1850).

[23] M.J.C. Vile, Constitutionalism and the Separation of Powers 176-211 (1967).

[24] Joseph Story, Commentaries on the Constitution of the United States, 5th ed., I, 396 (1905).

[25] Youngstown Co. v. Sawyer, 343 U.S. 579, 635 (1952).

might have been spared some of the stark, corrosive confrontations between President and Congress. More recently, in *Buckley* v. *Valeo* (1976), the Supreme Court noted that the framers recognized that a "hermetic sealing off of the three branches of Government from one another would preclude the establishment of a Nation capable of governing itself effectively."[26]

This conclusion is driven home by studying the political climate in which the framers produced their document. If they wanted weak government, if they wanted it shackled and ineffective, they could have retained the Articles of Confederation. They decided against this, with very good reason. The framers had labored under a weak government from 1774 to 1787, and deliberately rejected that model in favor of stronger central powers. Consciously, at the national level, they vested greater powers in an executive.

The distrust of executive power in 1776—against the king of England and the royal governors—was tempered by two developments in the following decade. Americans discovered that state legislative bodies could be as oppressive and capricious toward individual rights as executive bodies. Also, many delegates to the Continental Congress watched with growing apprehension as the Congress found itself incapable of discharging its duties and responsibilities. Support began to grow for an independent executive, in large part for the purpose of ensuring efficiency.

This interpretation challenges a famous dissent by Justice Brandeis, who claimed that the separation of powers doctrine was adopted *not* for efficiency but to preclude the exercise of arbitrary power.[27] His dictum, invoked regularly by those who urged legislative reassertion in the 1960s, is a half-truth. The historical record is clear and persuasive that the inefficiency of the Continental Congress convinced the framers of the need for a separate and independent executive.[28]

The practical source of the separation doctrine is generally overlooked or ignored. Much more satisfying, emotionally if not

[26] Buckley v. Valeo, 424 U.S. 1, 121 (1976).
[27] Myers v. United States, 272 U.S. 52, 293 (1926).
[28] See Louis Fisher, President and Congress 1-27, 241-70 (1972).

intellectually, is the belief that the Constitution was pounded into shape from abstract principles, with the name of Montesquieu leading the list of theorists. Gladstone reinforced this impression by describing the American Constitution as the most wonderful document ever "struck off at a given time" by the mind of man.[29] But the framers did not create out of whole cloth the document that guides us today. They were alert to the excesses and injustices committed by state legislators. They were sensitive, very sensitive, to the demonstrated ineptitude of the Continental Congress, which had to administer and adjudicate while trying to legislate. One branch of government performed all the tasks.

Because of the repeated failings of the Continental Congress, it soon began to delegate power—first to committees, then to boards staffed by people from outside the legislature, and finally, in 1781, to single executive officers.[30] These events occurred prior to the Philadelphia convention. The Constitution marked a continuity with political developments already under way. John Jay, after serving as Secretary of Foreign Affairs under the Continental Congress, remained in office in the Washington Administration until Thomas Jefferson could take his place. Henry Knox was Secretary of War under the Continental Congress and under President Washington. Because of this orderly transition it has been said that the Constitution did not create a system of separated powers; rather, a system of separated powers created the Constitution.[31]

Several delegates at the ratifying conventions objected to the fact that the branches of government—legislative, executive, and judicial—had been intermingled instead of being kept separate. "How is the executive?" demanded one irate delegate at Virginia's ratifying convention. "Contrary to the opinion of all the best writers, blended with the legislature. We have asked for bread,

[29] "Kin Beyond the Sea," North Am. Rev., vol. 127, no. 264 (September-October 1878), at 185.

[30] Fisher, President and Congress, at 6-14.

[31] Francis Wharton, The Revolutionary Diplomatic Correspondence of the United States, I, 663 (1889).

and they have given us a stone."[32] This outcry attracted some support, but not much. By the time of the Philadelphia convention the doctrine of separated powers had been modified to allow for checks and balances. One contemporary pamphleteer called the separation doctrine, in its pure form, a "hackneyed principle" and a "trite maxim."[33] Madison devoted several of his *Federalist* essays to the need for overlapping powers, claiming that the concept was superior to the impracticable partitioning of powers demanded by some of the Antifederalists.[34]

The system of checks and balances does not contradict the separation doctrine. Indeed, the two are complementary. Without the power to withstand encroachments by another branch, a department might find its powers drained to the point of extinction. The Constitution allocated separate functions to separate branches, but "parchment barriers" were not dependable. It was necessary, Madison concluded in Federalist 51, that "ambition must be made to counteract ambition," while in Federalist 48 he warned: "unless these departments be so far connected and blended as to give to each a constitutional control over the others, the degree of separation which the maxim requires, as essential to a free government, can never in practice be duly maintained."

The case for a strict separation of powers was tested in the form of an amendment to the Constitution. Three states—Virginia, North Carolina, and Pennsylvania—wanted to add a separation clause to the national bill of rights.[35] The proposed language read as follows: "The powers delegated by this constitution are appropriated to the departments to which they are respectively distributed: so that the legislative department shall never exercise the powers vested in the executive or judicial[,] nor the executive exercise the powers vested in the legislative or judicial, nor the judicial exercise the powers vested in the legislative or

---

[32] Quoted in Elliot, Debates, III, 280.

[33] Quoted in Vile, Constitutionalism and the Separation of Powers, at 153.

[34] Federalist 37 and 47 attempted to rebut some of the Antifederalist objections regarding blended powers. For the latter see Morton Borden, ed., The Antifederalist Papers (1965), papers 47, 48, 64, 67, 73, and 75.

[35] Elliot, Debates, III, 280, and IV, 116, 121; John Bach McMaster and Frederick D. Stone, eds., Pennsylvania and the Federal Constitution 475-77 (1888).

executive departments."[36] Congress rejected this proposal, as well as a substitute amendment to make the three departments "separate and distinct."[37]

Although powers are not separated in a pure sense, it does not help to characterize the federal government as a "blend of powers." The branches have distinctly different responsibilities, practices, and traditions. A certain distance between the branches is preserved by Article I, Section 6 of the Constitution, which prohibits members of either House from holding any other civil office.[38] Congress is prohibited from reducing the compensation of the President and members of the judiciary.[39] The Speech or Debate Clause was designed to protect legislators from executive or judicial harassment.[40] The purpose of this clause is to "preserve the constitutional structure of separate, coequal, and independent branches of government."[41]

Every occupant of the White House, after a short time in office, appreciates the degree to which an institutional separation exists, whether Congress is in the hands of the President's party or the opposition party. That is as it should be. The President does not share with Congress his pardoning power, nor does Congress share with the courts its taxing and appropriations powers (although the judiciary is participating in the outer fringes). In 1974 the Supreme Court highlighted the separation that exists in the federal government by stating that the judicial power vested in the federal courts by Article III of the Constitution "can no more be shared with the Executive Branch than the Chief Executive, for example, can share with the Judiciary the veto

[36] Edward Dumbauld, The Bill of Rights and What It Means Today 174-75, 183, 199 (1957).

[37] For the congressional debates, see Annals of Congress, I, 453-54 (June 8, 1789) and 789-90 (August 18, 1789). For action by the Senate, see U.S. Senate, Journals, 1789-1794, I, 64, 73-74 (1820).

[38] But see Schlesinger v. Reservists to Stop the War, 418 U.S. 208 (1974), in which the Supreme Court denied standing to plaintiffs who challenged the right of members of Congress to hold a commission in the armed forces reserves.

[39] For a recent case on judicial salaries and the no-diminution clause, see United States v. Will, 449 U.S. 200 (1980).

[40] United States v. Johnson, 383 U.S. 169, 177 (1966).

[41] United States v. Helstoski, 442 U.S. 477, 491 (1979).

15

power, or the Congress share with the Judiciary the power to override a Presidential veto."[42]

In administrative agencies that discharge executive, legislative, and judicial duties, those tasks are kept separate whenever the agency engages in adjudication. Agency employees involved in investigation or prosecution may not participate or advise in adjudicatory decisions except as witness or counsel.[43] In the case of informal rulemaking, agencies are not expected to follow the separation-of-functions requirement.[44] Agency officials may wear several hats, both as policymaker (legislator) and decisionmaker (administrator). In 1979 an appellate court upheld the right of Michael Pertschuk, chairman of the Federal Trade Commission (FTC), to speak out forcefully on issues that might later come to him for decision as a proposed rule.[45]

The Durability of the Doctrine

Has the balance among political institutions, as fashioned by the framers, failed to meet the test of time? Have events overtaken theory? Tocqueville, quoting with approval a passage from Jefferson, believed that the "tyranny of the legislature" in America would continue for a number of years before being replaced by a tyranny of the executive.[46] Yet presidential power, after cresting with Abraham Lincoln, subsided in the face of a determined and resurgent Congress. Writing in 1885, Woodrow Wilson be-

[42] United States v. Nixon, 418 U.S. 683, 704 (1974).

[43] 5 U.S.C. 554(d) (1976). See Kenneth Culp Davis, Administrative Law and Government 174-91 (1975). For conditions in which investigative and adjudicative functions can be combined in the same officer, see FTC v. Cement Institute, 333 U.S. 683, 701 (1948) and Withrow v. Larkin, 421 U.S. 35, 47, 58 (1975).

[44] Hercules, Inc. v. Environmental Protection Agency, 598 F.2d 91, 125 (D.C. Cir. 1978).

[45] Association of Nat. Advertisers, Inc. v. FTC, 627 F.2d 1151 (D.C. Cir. 1979), cert. denied, 447 U.S. 921 (1980). Although Pertschuk's dual role was upheld, he voluntarily withdrew from the pending case because the controversy over his involvement had diverted attention from the merits of the issue. Washington Post, January 8, 1980, at C1.

[46] Tocqueville, Democracy in America, I, 280 (1945 ed.).

lieved that Congress had become the dominant branch. He said that the Constitution of 1787 was a form of government in name rather than in reality, "the form of the Constitution being one of nicely adjusted, ideal balances, whilst the actual form of our present government is simply a scheme of congressional supremacy."[47]

Two decades later, glancing with covetous eyes at the White House, Wilson predicted that the President "must always, henceforth, be one of the great powers of the world. . . . We have but begun to see the presidential office in this light; but it is the light which will more and more beat upon it . . . ."[48] The new wellspring of presidential power, according to his analysis, was the burden of international responsibilities thrust upon the United States. The Great Depression of the 1930s, joined with the personal qualities of Franklin D. Roosevelt, gave further impetus to executive power.

The reputation of Congress plummeted with such swiftness that Samuel P. Huntington, in an influential study published in 1965, suggested that unless Congress drastically altered its operation it should abandon its legislative role and concentrate on serving constituents and overseeing the agencies.[49] The condition of Congress appeared to deteriorate even further, for in 1968 Philip B. Kurland charged that it did not have the "guts to stand up to its responsibilities." Congress was prostrate, the President transcendent. Kurland invited us to visit the "sickbed of another constitutional concept—the notion of separation of powers." Not only was the patient diseased, the affliction seemed terminal. Theoretically a cure was possible, but Kurland saw no grounds for optimism. The patient had lost the will to live.[50]

[47] Woodrow Wilson, Congressional Government 6 (1885).

[48] Woodrow Wilson, Constitutional Government in the United States 78 (1908).

[49] Samuel P. Huntington, "Congressional Responses to the Twentieth Century," in David B. Truman, ed., The Congress and America's Future 5-31 (1965). Writing a year later, however, Ralph K. Huitt argued that Congress played a more important part in legislation than its critics realized. See his "Congress, the Durable Partner," originally published in 1966 and reprinted in Ralph K. Huitt and Robert L. Peabody, Congress: Two Decades of Analysis 209-29 (1969).

[50] Philip B. Kurland, "The Impotence of Reticence," 1968 Duke L. J. 619, 621 (1968).

These dire predictions suggest that the imbalance between President and Congress is chronic and permanent. At no time, however, has either branch been as all-powerful or as defective as critics have claimed. Congress, though its particular life style may offend our tastes, is alive and well. The political system has shown a capacity for self-correction. Two Presidents, testing the limits of their power during the 1960s and 1970s, were driven from office. Congress, flexing its muscles during this time of reassertion, ran into barriers erected by the courts. In 1976 the Supreme Court ruled against the Federal Election Commission (FEC) because Congress had staked out a role for itself in the appointment of four of the commission's six members. The Court held this procedure contrary to the separation doctrine. Congress could not both legislate and enforce.[51]

The separation doctrine, subjected to ridicule for much of the twentieth century, still retains vitality. A longer view of American history provides room for confidence. Senator George Wharton Pepper offered this sound perspective: "[I]f the geometers of 1787 hoped for perfect peace and if the psychologists of that day feared disastrous conflicts, history, as so often happens, has proved that hopes were dupes and fears were liars. There has not been perfect peace; but the conflicts have not proved disastrous."[52]

Implied Powers

In civics courses we are taught that the American Constitution is one of limited and enumerated powers. This is satisfactory only if we stay within the classroom. Once we venture out and observe the actual workings of government, we must confront and resolve a perplexing array of powers that are not expressly stated. They parade under assorted names: implied and inherent, incidental and inferred, aggregate, powers created by custom and acquiescence, and delicate "penumbras," "interstices," "emana-

[51] Buckley v. Valeo, 424 U.S. 1 (1976).

[52] George Wharton Pepper, Family Quarrels: the President, the Senate, the House viii (1931).

18

tions," and "glosses" that add strange and new qualities to the Constitution. Whatever the name the result is identical: the conferral of a power that is neither expressly stated in the Constitution nor specifically granted by Congress.

The "genius and spirit of our institutions are hostile to the exercise of implied powers." Thus spake the Supreme Court in 1821. After making the appropriate gesture it proceeded to deal amicably with these hostile forces. It was utopian, said the Court, to believe that government could exist without allowing the exercise of discretion somewhere. In this particular case the Court recognized that Congress possessed powers not expressly granted by the Constitution: the power to issue warrants to compel a party's appearance, and the power to punish for contempt.[53]

If a constitution is intended to limit power and if we admit powers that are not expressly stated, can government be kept within bounds? Let the imagination run to far corners and the answer is No. Let experience be our guide (the framers' preference) and the prospect is more reassuring. The American Constitution cannot survive purely on the basis of express powers or "strict constructionism," a phrase made popular by the Nixon administration. Implied powers are required for any government. As Madison noted in Federalist 44: "No axiom is more clearly established in law, or in reason, than that whenever the end is required, the means are authorized; whenever a general power to do a thing is given, every particular power necessary for doing it is included."

The debate in 1789 on the Bill of Rights settled the need to grant implied powers to government. Members of the First Congress proposed that the Tenth Amendment be so worded that all powers not "expressly delegated" to the federal government would be reserved to the states. Madison immediately objected, insisting that it was impossible to limit a government to the exercise of express powers. There "must necessarily be admitted powers by implication, unless the Constitution descended to recount every minutiae." After elimination of "expressly" the Tenth Amendment was adopted with this language: "The powers not dele-

[53] Anderson v. Dunn, 6 Wheat. 204, 225 (1821).

gated to the United States by the Constitution, nor prohibited by it to the States, are reserved to the States respectively, or to the people."[54]

Chief Justice Marshall cited this debate when he ruled on the implied power of Congress to establish a national bank, even though not expressly permitted by the Constitution. Marshall observed that there was no phrase in the document which (like the Articles of Confederation) "excludes incidental or implied powers; and which requires that everything granted shall be expressly and minutely described."[55] A constitution represented a general structure, not a detailed instruction manual:

> A constitution, to contain an accurate detail of all the subdivisions of which its great powers will admit, and of all the means by which they may be carried into execution, would partake of the prolixity of a legal code, and could scarcely be embraced by the human mind. It would, probably, never be understood by the public. Its nature, therefore, requires, that only its great outlines should be marked, its important objects designated, and the minor ingredients which compose those objects, be deduced from the nature of the objects themselves.[56]

In interpreting the Constitution it is important to remember that government is created to carry out certain functions required for the people. A number of essential activities find no ready reference in the Constitution. As Marshall remarked: "All admit, that the government may, legitimately, punish any violation of its laws; and yet, this is not among the enumerated powers of Congress."[57]

The debate on implied powers is frequently sidetracked by partisan and policy motivations. It is interesting that Marshall upheld the U.S. Bank partly on the strength of Madison's reasoning on the Tenth Amendment. Madison strongly *opposed* the bank in 1791, this time speaking against implied powers and insisting

---

[54] Annals of Congress, I, 761 (August 18, 1789).
[55] McCulloch v. Maryland, 17 U.S. (4 Wheat.) 315, 404 (1819).
[56] Id. at 406.
[57] Id. at 415.

that the Constitution was not "a general grant, out of which particular powers are excepted; it is a grant of particular powers only, leaving the mass in other hands."[58] Despite Madison's opposition, the bill for a national bank passed the House of Representatives by a vote of 39 to 20.

Two years later Madison would again take a partisan stance on implied powers. After President Washington issued what is now known as the Neutrality Proclamation, his administration was subjected to bitter attacks from those who sympathized with France. Alexander Hamilton, writing under the pseudonym "Pacificus," denied that the proclamation had been issued without authority. Hamilton derived the power to issue proclamations from the general clause of Article II of the Constitution: "the executive Power shall be vested in a President of the United States of America." He believed that it was unsound to limit the executive power to the particular items enumerated in subsequent sections. They should not derogate from the "comprehensive grant" of power in the general clause, "further than as it may be coupled with express restrictions or limitations." With the exception of the Senate's participation in the appointment of officers and in the making of treaties, and Congress's power to declare war and to grant letters of marque and reprisal, all other executive powers were lodged solely in the President.[59]

Jefferson, outraged by this doctrine, wrote to Madison: "For God's sake, my dear Sir, take up your pen, select the most striking heresies and cut him to pieces in the face of the public."[60] Madison produced five articles under the name "Helvidius," charging that Hamilton's reading of the Constitution must be condemned "as no less vicious in theory than it would be dangerous in practice." The expansive interpretation of executive power would mean that "no citizen could any longer guess at the character of the government under which he lives; the most penetrating jurist would be unable to scan the extent of constructive prerogative."[61]

[58] Annals of Congress, II, 1945 (February 2, 1791).
[59] The Works of Alexander Hamilton (Lodge ed.), IV, 437-39.
[60] The Writings of Thomas Jefferson (Ford ed.), VI, 338.
[61] The Writings of James Madison (Hunt ed.), VI, 152.

Madison indulged in hyperbole, as did Hamilton. We could scarcely expect much else in the supercharged political atmosphere of 1793, heightened as it was by the intense rivalry between Hamilton and Jefferson in the Cabinet. But the issue they raised was to remain active. By the end of the nineteenth century the issue of implied powers for the President reached the Supreme Court in the case of *In re Neagle* (1890). Justice Stephen Field, serving as circuit justice in California, had his life threatened by two people he had sent to jail, David and Sarah Terry. David Neagle, a U.S. deputy marshal, was assigned to ride circuit to offer protection. One morning during breakfast, Field was assaulted by David Terry. Neagle, after identifying himself, shot and killed Terry. No statute authorized the President to appoint a deputy marshal for the purpose of protecting a Supreme Court Justice traveling in his circuit.

The Court, split 6 to 2, upheld the assignment of Neagle and his immunity from state law. His attorney acknowledged that there was no single specific statute making it a duty to furnish protection to a Supreme Court Justice. To the attorney, however, whatever was "necessarily implied is as much a part of the Constitution and statutes as if it were actually expressed therein."[62] Justice Miller, announcing the opinion for the Court, agreed: "In the view we take of the Constitution of the United States, any obligation fairly and properly inferrible from that instrument, or any duty of the marshal to be derived from the general scope of his duties under the laws of the United States, is 'a law' within the meaning of this phrase."[63]

The two dissenting Justices did not dispute the proposition that "whatever is necessarily implied in the Constitution and laws of the United States is as much a part of them as if it were actually expressed." Nor did they question the propriety of Neagle's action. But they related implied powers to the clause in Article I which augments the powers of Congress: "Congress shall have power . . . to make all laws which shall be necessary and proper for carrying into execution the foregoing powers, and

[62] In re Neagle, 135 U.S. 1, 27 (1890).
[63] Id. at 59.

22

all other powers vested by this Constitution in the government of the United States, or in any department or officer thereof." Finding no such law, and believing that the federal government was powerless to try and punish a man charged with murder in this offense, they would have had Neagle placed in the custody of the sheriff of San Joaquin, California, to be tried by the courts of that state.[64]

Theodore Roosevelt and William Howard Taft, debating the boundaries of presidential authority, appear to have held diametrically opposed positions on implied power. Roosevelt asserted that it was the President's right and duty to do "anything that the needs of the Nation demanded, unless such action was forbidden by the Constitution or by the laws."[65] His argument follows the one presented in Hamilton's "Pacificus" writings. Taft maintained that the President "can exercise no power which cannot be fairly and reasonably traced to some specific grant of power or justly implied and included within such express grant as proper and necessary to its exercise. Such specific grant must be either in the Federal Constitution or in an act of Congress passed in pursuance thereof."[66]

Use of the words "express" and "specific" appears to put Taft in the camp of those who believe in enumerated powers. But it is clear that he recognized the need for implied powers—powers that can be "fairly and reasonably traced" or "justly implied." He even adds to the Constitution a "necessary and proper" clause for the President. When Taft's study is read in full, it is evident that he believed in a generous interpretation of executive power: incidental powers to remove officers, inferable powers to protect the lives and property of American citizens living abroad, powers created by custom, and emergency powers (such as Lincoln's suspension of the writ of habeas corpus during the Civil War). Summing up, Taft said that executive power was limited "so far as it is possible to limit such a power consistent with that discretion and promptness of action that are essential to preserve the inter-

---

[64] Id. at 77-78, 83.

[65] The Works of Theodore Roosevelt, XX, 347 (1926).

[66] William Howard Taft, Our Chief Magistrate and His Powers 139-40 (1916), available in paperback under the title The President and His Powers (1967).

ests of the public in times of emergency, or legislative neglect or inaction."[67]

Custom and Acquiescence

The Supreme Court often discourages the idea that a precedent, even when repeated, represents an adequate basis for authority. In *Powell* v. *McCormack* (1969), the Court stated that because "an unconstitutional action has been taken before surely does not render that same action any less unconstitutional at a later date."[68] For example, "local tradition" is insufficient justification for the systematic exclusion of blacks or other minorities from jury service.[69]

Still, an action based on usage may acquire legitimacy. Practice and acquiescence for a number of years can be instrumental in fixing the meaning of the Constitution.[70] To the extent that an action is favorably exposed to popular judgment, custom does expand power. The Supreme Court, upholding the President's removal power in a 1903 decision, based its ruling largely on the "universal practice of the government for over a century."[71] Here constitutional law is made not by the courts but by the conduct of the executive and legislative branches.

William Howard Taft, often associated with a strict reading of the Constitution and presidential power, recognized that executive authority is based partly on custom: "so strong is the influence of custom that it seems almost to amend the Constitution."[72] A specific example dates from his own administration.

[67] For specific references in Taft's 1916 edition, see the following: pp. 56 and 76 on removal powers; p. 95 on inferable powers; p. 135 for powers created by custom; p. 147 for suspension of habeas corpus, and p. 156 for the need for executive discretion and promptness of action. A comparison between Roosevelt and Taft appears in Fisher, President and Congress, at 33-37.

[68] Powell v. McCormack, 395 U.S. 486, 546-47 (1969).

[69] Eubanks v. Louisiana, 356 U.S. 584 (1958).

[70] Stuart v. Laird, 5 U.S. (1 Cr.) 299, 309 (1803).

[71] Shurtleff v. United States, 189 U.S. 311, 316 (1903). Additional commentary on custom and acquiescence appears in American Jurisprudence, XVI, 264-70 (1964).

[72] Taft, Our Chief Executive and His Powers, at 135.

24

After Congress had opened public lands in the West to encourage oil exploration, settlers began to extract oil rapidly, fearing that entrepreneurs on adjacent lots might be tapping from the same source. Because of the limited supply of coal on the Pacific coast for the navy, it appeared that the federal government might have to purchase from the private sector the very oil it had given away.

Taft acted by issuing a proclamation that withdrew the affected lands from private exploration. A violation brought the case before the Supreme Court, where it was argued that the President could not suspend a statute or withdraw land that Congress had thrown open to acquisition. The Court declined to approach the controversy from the standpoint of abstract constitutional theory. The President's action, it said, was based upon and supported by years of precedents. Before 1910 there had been 99 executive orders establishing or enlarging Indian reservations, 109 executive orders establishing or enlarging military reservations, and 44 executive orders establishing bird reserves. Although it was true that the President had acted without statutory authority (and in fact had acted against it), the Court held that "nothing was more natural than to retain what the Government already owned. And in making such orders, which were thus useful to the public, no private interest was injured. . . . The President was in a position to know when the public interest required particular portions of the people's lands to be withdrawn from entry or location."[73] It was not until 1976 that Congress reversed this interpretation of presidential power.[74]

Justice Frankfurter described the cumulative impact of uncontested executive actions in these words: "A systematic, unbroken executive practice, long pursued to the knowledge of the Congress and never before questioned, engaged in by Presidents who have also sworn to uphold the Constitution, making as it were such exercise of power part of the structure of our government, may be treated as a gloss on 'executive Power' vested in the Pres-

[73] United States v. Midwest Oil Co., 236 U.S. 459, 469-71 (1915). Courts defer to agency interpretations consistently construed and made a repeated matter of public record; Udall v. Tallman, 380 U.S. 1 (1965).

[74] 90 Stat. 2792, sec. 704(a) (1976).

ident by §1 of Art. II."[75] In that same decision—the Steel Seizure Case of 1952—Justice Jackson spoke of a "zone of twilight" in which the distribution of power between Congress and the President is uncertain but "congressional inertia, indifference or quiescence may sometimes, at least as a practical matter, enable, if not invite, measures on independent presidential responsibility. In this area, any actual test of power is likely to depend on the imperatives of events and contemporary imponderables rather than on abstract theories of law."[76]

Under some circumstances, the failure of Congress to repeal or revise a grant of statutory authority in the face of administrative interpretation has been held by the courts as "persuasive evidence" that the interpretation was intended by Congress.[77] Custom is a source of executive power particularly when Congress fails to challenge and check.

Acquiescence has been part of Congress's record in permitting the war power to drift to the executive branch. In 1969 the Senate Foreign Relations Committee tried to explain this tendency by saying that Congress was unprepared for America's new role as a world power and the extraordinary demands placed upon the Constitution. An atmosphere of real or contrived urgency encouraged this legislative passivity. Congress was also overawed by the "cult of executive expertise." In addition, a legacy of guilt remained in the Senate after its rejection of the Covenant of the League of Nations in 1919. Senators practiced a form of penance that has "sometimes taken the form of overly hasty acquiescence in proposals for the acceptance of one form or another of international responsibility."[78]

Legislators are said to acquiesce because of the superior information and technical knowledge available to the executive branch. This attitude conceals a hidden motivation: an unwillingness to

---

[75] Youngstown Co. v. Sawyer, 343 U.S. 579, 610-11 (1952).

[76] Id. at 637. Footnote omitted.

[77] Zemel v. Rusk, 381 U.S. 1, 11 (1965). See Norwegian Nitrogen Co. v. United States, 288 U.S. 294, 313 (1933) and Costanzo v. Tillinghast, 287 U.S. 341, 345 (1932). Also on congressional acquiescence: Dames & Moore v. Regan, 453 U.S. 654, 678-88 (1981).

[78] S. Rept. No. 129, 91st Cong., 1st Sess. 15-16 (1969).

be held responsible for issues of national security and military preparedness. Delegation and acquiescence are natural by-products of the better-safe-than-sorry philosophy.

Some scholars resist "glosses" on the Constitution, believing that they invite usurpation of power. People with political ambitions and an impatience with legal niceties, instead of following the Constitution or attempting to amend it, might "adapt" it to their own narrow ends. This is indeed a risk, but to prohibit adaptation based on custom would require several hundred amendments to the Constitution and a willingness to keep it in a perpetual state of agitation and flux.[79]

The principles cited in this chapter provide the broad framework for the creation and protection of constitutional rights in America. The Constitution supplies a general structure for the three branches of government, assigns specific functions and responsibilities to each, and reserves certain rights to the people. Armed with powers of self-defense, the branches of government intersect in various patterns of cooperation and conflict. How these basic principles of law operate in practice is a question decided by experimentation, precedents, and constant adaptation and accommodation.

[79] See Robert G. Dixon, Jr., "Article V: The Comatose Article of Our Living Constitution?" 66 Mich. L. Rev. 931 (1968). For a critique of "adaptation by usage," see the testimony of Raoul Berger, "War Powers Legislation, 1973," hearings before the Senate Committee on Foreign Relations, 93d Cong., 1st Sess. 10 (1973).

2

APPOINTMENT POWERS

After Congress creates an office, three steps are required to fill it: nomination by the President, confirmation by the Senate, and commissioning of the appointee by the President. For lesser or "inferior officers," Congress may forego the confirmation requirement and place the power of appointment directly in the President, the courts, or departmental heads.

Nomination (at least in theory) is the President's prerogative. In practice it is shared with members of his own branch, with legislators and judges, and representatives from the private sector, all subject to various statutory limitations. After submitting a name the President may, and often does, withdraw it. Once the nomination has gone forward, the decision to advise and consent is a privilege reserved to each Senator, but many outside interests offer advice and try to influence the consent. Presidents also make recess and temporary appointments, opening up a vast range of discretionary action that Congress attempts to restrict with statutory guidelines.

Basic Principles

The British monarch not only appointed officers but created offices as well. The framers rejected this model by giving Congress the power to create offices and by joining the Senate with the executive in making appointments. The Constitution allows Congress to vest the appointment of "inferior officers" in the President alone, in the courts, or in department heads. For all other offices (except temporary appointments during Senate recess) the President nominates an individual and seeks the advice and consent of the Senate.

The initial draft presented at the Philadelphia convention (the Virginia Plan) lodged in Congress the responsibility for choosing an executive and the members of a national judiciary. The executive would have had the power "to appoint to offices in cases not otherwise provided for" by the Constitution. James Wilson, one of the ablest members of the convention, objected to the appointment of judges by a legislature: "Experience shewed the impropriety of such appointmts. by numerous bodies. Intrigue, partiality, and concealment were the necessary consequences. A principal reason for unity in the Executive was that officers might be appointed by a single, responsible person." To vest such power in a single person, others feared, would be "leaning too much toward Monarchy."[1]

James Madison proposed a compromise: let the Senate (not as numerous as the House, yet more numerous than the executive) appoint the judges. His plan was tentatively agreed to in mid-June. A month later delegates remained divided on the issue. Some worried that the executive, armed with the power to appoint, might favor one region of the country over another. Others, such as Luther Martin of Maryland, argued that the Senate would be "best informed of characters & most capable of making a fit choice." Madison modified his position by suggesting that the executive appoint judges with the concurrence of some fraction of the Senate. To him this had the advantage of uniting the responsibility of the executive with the security afforded by Senate opposition to "incautious or corrupt" nominations. On July 21, however, the convention voted to have judges appointed solely by the Senate. The delegates followed a different approach for appointments to the executive branch. The executive retained power "to appoint to offices in cases not otherwise provided for" in the Constitution.[2]

As the debate continued, the delegates moved away from the concept of a congressional choice over the President and judicial officers. The idea of three separate and distinct branches took shape, as well as the system of using electors from the states to choose the President.

In early September the convention gave the President authority to nominate and—by and with the advice and consent of the

[1] Farrand, Records, I, 21, 63, 119.
[2] Id. at I, 119-28, 232-33; II, 41-44, 80-83, 121.

Senate—appoint ambassadors, other public ministers and consuls, judges of the Supreme Court, and all other federal officers. A few days later the convention agreed to empower the President to fill all vacancies that "may happen" during the Senate's recess. It also added "and which shall be created by Law" (to prevent appointments to positions unauthorized by Congress) and reserved to Congress the right to vest the appointment of inferior officers in the President, the courts, or department heads.[3]

The President's appointment power under Article II extends to "Officers of the United States," a term construed by several court decisions. The Supreme Court has defined an office as "a public station, or employment, conferred by the appointment of government. The term embraces the ideas of tenure, duration, emolument, and duties." The duties of an officer are "continuing and permanent, not occasional or temporary."[4] Occasional or intermittent duties are carried out by agents, not officers.[5] Unless a person holds his position by virtue of a presidential appointment, or by an appointment from the courts or department heads as authorized by law, he is not an officer of the United States.[6] More recently the Supreme Court has held that any appointee exercising "significant authority" pursuant to a federal statute is an officer of the United States.[7]

To preserve the separation between the executive and legislative branches, the Constitution prohibits Senators and Representatives from being appointed to any federal office created—or to any federal office increased in salary—during their term of office (the Ineligibility Clause). Furthermore, no officer of the United States "shall be a Member of either House during his Continuance in Office" (the Incompatibility Clause).[8] These provisions reflect the framers' belief that elected officials in England had been corrupted through appointments to office by the Crown.[9]

---

[3] Id. at II, 498-99, 533, 539, 627-28.
[4] United States v. Hartwell, 73 U.S. (6 Wall.) 385, 393 (1868).
[5] United States v. Germaine, 99 U.S. (9 Otto.) 508, 511-12 (1879).
[6] United States v. Mouat, 124 U.S. 303, 307 (1888).
[7] Buckley v. Valeo, 424 U.S. 1, 126 (1976).
[8] Art. I, Sec. 6, Cl. 2.
[9] Reservists Committee to Stop the War v. Laird, 323 F. Supp. 833, 835-37

The Power to Nominate

In *Marbury* v. *Madison*, Chief Justice Marshall called the nomination process the "sole act of the president" and "completely voluntary."[10] Although Congress creates offices, it cannot, "by law, designate the person to fill those offices."[11] This principle was buttressed in 1871 by Attorney General Akerman, who reviewed a proposal that permitted a civil service board to designate a single person for appointment. To him it was "inadmissible" to have a method of selection that gave no room for the exercise of judgment and will by the President. To require the President to appoint a person judged by examiners as the fittest was no different in constitutional principle from insisting that "he shall appoint John Doe to that office."[12]

The Civil Service Act of 1883 recognized the President's prerogative over nominations by restricting appointments to those "among" the highest grades in competitive examinations. The first rules promulgated by President Arthur provided that four names would be considered for each vacancy. In 1888 the number was changed to three. Present law provides that a nominating or appointing official will be furnished at least three names from the top of the list of eligibles for each vacancy.[13]

In the case of the District of Columbia, over which Congress

(D.D.C. 1971), aff'd without published opinion, 495 F.2d 1075 (D.C. Cir. 1972), reversed and remanded, 418 U.S. 208 (1974). Efforts to litigate the Incompatibility Clause have been turned back by the courts on the ground of standing; Schlesinger v. Reservists to Stop the War, 418 U.S. 208 (1974). For additional information on incompatible offices, see Hinds' Precedents, I, ch. XVI; Cannon's Precedents, VI, ch. CLVIII; 40 Op. Att'y Gen. 301 (1943); and 1 O.L.C. 242 (1977).

The courts have done little to clarify the boundaries of the Ineligibility Clause, but see 33 Op. Att'y Gen. 88 (1922); Ex parte Levitt, 302 U.S. 633 (1937); 42 Op. Att'y Gen. 381 (1969); 119 Cong. Rec. 37688-90 (1973); and McClure v. Carter, 513 F.Supp. 265 (D. Idaho 1981), aff'd, 102 S.Ct. 559 (1981).

[10] Marbury v. Madison, 5 U.S. (1 Cr.) 137, 155 (1803).

[11] United States v. Ferreira, 54 U.S. (13 How.) 39, 50-51 (1852). See also Myers v. United States, 272 U.S. 52, 128 (1926).

[12] 13 Op. Att'y Gen. 516 (1871).

[13] 5 U.S.C. 3317-18 (1982). See 22 Stat. 404 (1883) and Civil Service Commission, Biography of an Ideal: A History of the Federal Civil Service 47 (1973).

has exclusive constitutional power to legislate, the President's prerogative to nominate may be completely circumvented. If the President within sixty days fails to nominate a judge from a list presented to him by the D.C. Judicial Nomination Commission, the commission shall nominate and, with the advice and consent of the Senate, appoint a person from the list.[14]

The President's authority to nominate has been curbed by a number of other developments. In creating an office, Congress may stipulate the qualifications of appointees. Justice Brandeis once prepared a long list of requirements that Congress had placed on the President's selection of nominees. These included citizenship; being a resident of the United States, a state, a particular state, a particular district, a particular territory, the District of Columbia, or a particular foreign country; specific professional attainments or occupational experience; test by examinations; requirements of age, sex, race, property, or habitual temperance in the use of intoxicating liquors; selection on a nonpartisan basis; and representation by industrial or geographic criteria.[15]

In 1974 President Ford objected to language in a bill that empowered the Commodity Futures Trading Commission to appoint an executive director, by and with the advice and consent of the Senate. He said that this provision raised "serious constitutional questions," allowing Congress to encroach upon the President, and urged Congress to pass remedial legislation to delete the request for Senate confirmation. Congress followed that advice four years later.[16]

The mere fact that the President sends forth a name for consideration does not obligate the Senate to act promptly. Particularly toward the end of a President's term, Congress may prefer to let his successor do the nominating. In 1976 dozens of nominations sent to Congress by President Ford were sidetracked in committee, left there to die quietly. The jobs included judges, U.S. attorneys, U.S. marshals, and regulatory commissioners.[17]

---

[14] P.L. 93-198, sec. 434(d)(1), 87 Stat. 798 (1973).

[15] Myers v. United States, 272 U.S. 52, 265-74 (1926) (dissenting opinion).

[16] Public Papers of the Presidents, 1974, at 462; P.L. 93-463, sec. 101 (1974); P.L. 95-405, sec. 2 (1978). See S. Rept. No. 850, 95th Cong., 2d Sess. 28 (1978).

[17] Washington Post, August 26, 1976, at A5, and October 3, 1976, at A8.

President Carter received the same treatment in 1980 when Republicans sensed (correctly) that they would soon have their own man in the White House.[18] Predictably, Democratic Senators in 1984 showed little interest in acting on nominations submitted by President Reagan.

Although there is some discretion on the part of the Senate, the President cannot decline to nominate. Once an office is authorized by Congress it must be filled. A President may frustrate this purpose for a time—as Franklin D. Roosevelt did in the 1930s by delaying the nomination of a Comptroller General—but at some point the name must go forward.

This principle was underscored in 1973 by a court decision against President Nixon. His budget recommended the rescission of $18 million in American Indian education funds.[19] The administration impounded money pending congressional action on the rescission request. Private parties brought suit to require the President to appoint members to the National Advisory Council on Indian Education. The Justice Department suggested that the action be dismissed because of the separation of powers doctrine, but District Judge June L. Green denied the motion. In her opinion she noted that implementation of the Indian Education Act would apparently be "impossible or impracticable unless the Council is constituted by the President."[20] She also stated that although the President "clearly has discretion to choose whom to appoint to the Council, he apparently has no discretion to decide if the Council should or should not be constituted." On May 5, 1973, about two weeks after Judge Green's opinion, President Nixon appointed fifteen individuals to the council. Further orders by the same judge forced the release of the $18 million and required the appointment of the Deputy Commissioner of Indian Education.[21]

In the Indian education example, Nixon's power to nominate

---

[18] Washington Post, October 16, 1980, at A4.

[19] Budget of the United States Government, Fiscal Year 1974, Appendix, at 1074.

[20] Minnesota Chippewa Tribe v. Carlucci, 358 F.Supp. 973, 975 (D.D.C. 1973). This was Civ. Action No. 175-73.

[21] Minnesota Chippewa Tribe v. Carlucci (Civ. Action No. 628-73, D.D.C. 1973), memorandum form.

had to be balanced against his constitutional duty under Article II to "take care that the laws be faithfully executed." Failure to appoint would have effectively nullified the law. But when an agency consists of several members at the top (as with commissioners of independent regulatory bodies), there are precedents for not filling every office. Although the Interstate Commerce Commission (ICC) was authorized eleven commissioners, President Jimmy Carter deliberately kept it to seven by not filling all the vacancies. The reduced size did not prevent the agency from functioning.

Several trucking companies filed a lawsuit, claiming that the ICC was illegally constituted and had taken actions without a quorum. In one of the contested actions only five commissioners voted, while in another decision only four commissioners voted. The trucking companies argued that the Interstate Commerce Act required six commissioners (a majority of the statutorily prescribed eleven). In 1980 an appellate court decided that a quorum under the act was a majority of the existing commission rather than a majority of the full complement of eleven. The companies also argued that the President had violated a nondiscretionary duty to appoint all eleven commissioners, but they did not bring a mandamus action and make the President a party defendant. The court expressed no opinion on the likelihood of success of such a mandamus action.[22] In 1982 Congress passed legislation to reduce the number of ICC commissioners to seven by January 1, 1983, and to five by January 1, 1986.[23]

The failure of a President to fill vacancies may reflect a bias against particular programs, based perhaps on a philosophy of anti-regulation or fiscal retrenchment. Unless the motivation is blatantly unconstitutional and capable of successful action in the courts, the Senate has no way of forcing the President to submit nominations. White House aides can always explain that they are recruiting as rapidly as possible but that a potential candidate has just turned down an offer because of the financial disclosure law

[22] Assure Comp. Transp., Inc. v. United States, 629 F.2d 467 (7th Cir. 1980), cert. denied, 449 U.S. 1124 (1981).

[23] P.L. 97-253, sec. 502 (1982).

enacted by Congress in 1978, or because the pay cap imposed by Congress discourages executives accustomed to higher-paying salaries in the private sector, or due to any number of equally plausible explanations. To pressure the White House, Congress would have to resort to selective sanctions against programs favored by the administration, or threaten inaction on legislative proposals and nominations wanted by the President.

Participants in the Nominating Process

The selection of a nominee is supposedly a presidential matter. As Alexander Hamilton stated in Federalist 66, there would be "no exertion of *choice* on the part of the Senate. They may defeat one choice of the Executive, and oblige him to make another; but they cannot themselves *choose*—they can only ratify or reject the choice of the President." But this is by no means the practice. Senators from the same party as the President often "nominate" judges, U.S. attorneys, and marshals who serve from their state. The President is then placed in the position of giving his "advice and consent." If he and his advisers object to a Senator's recommendation, they can offer suggestions in the hope of receiving a more acceptable name. Criteria can be established by executive officials to guide the Senate's choice. Teddy Roosevelt entered the White House declaring: "The Senators and Congressmen shall ordinarily name the *man*, but I shall name the *standard*; and the men have got to come up to it."[24]

Beginning with the Truman administration, the American Bar Association formalized its influence in selecting federal judges by setting up a special committee to determine the professional qualifications of judicial candidates. Acting only on names submitted by the Attorney General, the committee informs the chairman of the Senate Judiciary Committee whether in its judgment the candidate is "qualified," "well qualified," "exceptionally well qualified," or "not qualified."[25] In 1977 President Carter

[24] George H. Haynes, The Senate of the United States, II, 741 n. 1 (1938).

[25] Joel B. Grossman, Lawyers and Judges: The ABA and the Politics of Judicial Selection 62-81 (1965); Harold W. Chase, Federal Judges: The Appointing Process (1972).

sought greater independence from the Senate by establishing panels to recommend nominees to the appellate courts. The President's constitutional authority to nominate was protected by requiring the panels to recommend five candidates for each vacancy. This arrangement is politically feasible (with regard to the Senate's stake in the procedure) because appellate courts overlap several states. Nominations for district courts, located within a state, are still strongly influenced by individual Senators. When President Reagan took office he abolished the judicial nominating commissions for appellate judges.

Although many of these factors crowd upon the President's constitutional authority to nominate, some actions are plainly forbidden. Statutory qualifications may curb a President's discretion; they may not eliminate it altogether. In the words of Attorney General Akerman: "this right to prescribe qualifications is limited by the necessity of leaving scope for the judgment and will of the person or body in whom the Constitution vests the power of appointment." Nor may Congress, as the Supreme Court noted in 1947, violate the Bill of Rights by enacting legislation to provide that "no Republican, Jew or Negro shall be appointed to federal office."[26]

In 1976 the Supreme Court reviewed a lower court decision that upheld the power of Congress to appoint four members to the Federal Election Commission. All six voting members (including two nominated by the President) required confirmation by the majority of *both* Houses. The lower court reasoned that Congress possessed constitutional authority (by way of the "necessary and proper" clause) to appoint the members to carry out appropriate legislative functions, even though the commission performed "quasi-executive" and "quasi-judicial" functions as well.[27]

The Supreme Court reversed this judgment. Although it agreed that the "necessary and proper" clause empowered Congress to create the commission, the language could not be read so expan-

[26] 13 Op. Att'y Gen. 516, 520 (1871); United Public Workers v. Mitchell, 330 U.S. 75, 100 (1947).
[27] Buckley v. Valeo, 519 F.2d 821, 890-92 (D.C. Cir. 1975).

sively as to permit Congress to appoint its members. The clause had to be read in concert with other constitutional provisions. Congress could not, merely by concluding that a measure was "necessary and proper," pass a bill of attainder or an ex post facto law. Nor could it violate other portions of the Constitution, such as the Appointments Clause, especially when a commission created by Congress was designed to discharge more than legislative functions. The powers conferred upon the Federal Election Commission could be exercised only by "Officers of the United States," appointed pursuant to Article II, Section 2, Clause 2. For the Court this meant either one of two constitutional options: nomination by the President, subject to the advice and consent of the Senate; or vesting the appointment power in the President alone, in the courts of law, or in department heads. Congress chose the first option when it rewrote the act in 1976.[28]

Although Congress may not appoint agency officials, it can authorize private parties to select members of federal policymaking agencies. The Federal Open Market Committee, which exercises important powers over monetary policy, consists of seven members of the Board of Governors (presidential appointments) and five representatives of the Federal Reserve Banks. The latter are elected annually by the boards of directors of the Banks. Members of Congress, challenging the constitutionality of this procedure, have been denied standing by the courts to have their case heard.[29] Of course Congress at any time can rewrite the statute governing the appointment procedure.

Senate Advice and Consent

On the question of nominations and appointments, the President and the Senate were originally on completely equal footing. In an early communication to the Senate, President Washington stated that just as he had "a right to nominate without assigning his reasons, so has the Senate a right to dissent without giving theirs."

[28] Buckley v. Valeo, 424 U.S. 1, 134-43 (1976); 90 Stat. 475, sec. 101 (1976).

[29] Reuss v. Balles, 584 F.2d 461, 468 (D.C. Cir. 1978), cert. denied, 439 U.S. 997 (1978); Riegle v. Federal Open Market Committee, 656 F.2d 873 (D.C. Cir. 1981), cert. denied, 454 U.S. 1082 (1981).

Washington not only sought the advice of the Senate on nominations but also depended on the judgment of friends in other quarters. Recommendations by members of the House of Representatives, excluded by the Constitution in the appointments process, carried considerable weight.[30]

During the first year of Washington's administration, the Senate rejected Benjamin Fishbourn as naval officer at Savannah, Georgia. It was rumored that the two Senators from that state opposed the nomination because they had someone else in mind for the post. Washington, stung by this rebuff, advised the Senate that prior to voting down a nominee it should first inquire as to the qualifications and reasons in support of the nomination.[31]

In 1813 President Madison bridled at a Senate resolution that authorized a *committee* to confer with him on the nomination of a minister to Sweden. He declined to meet with it on the ground that the Constitution recognized only two types of action: the Senate could request information from the President or it could designate a committee to communicate with a department head. The appointment of a committee of the Senate "to confer immediately with the Executive himself appears to lose sight of the coordinate relation between the Executive and the Senate which the Constitution has established, and which ought therefore to be maintained."[32] Madison's successors have not reacted with such ruffled dignity at the thought of meeting with committees or individual Senators.

Senatorial Courtesy

It has become an accepted practice to defer to Senators' judgments about the merits of appointees from their own states. "Senatorial courtesy" is consistent with the expectation of the framers that Senators would be well suited to determine the fit-

[30] The Writings of Washington (Fitzpatrick ed.), XXX, 374. See Roy Swanstrom, The United States Senate, 1789-1801, S. Doc. No. 64, 87th Cong., 1st Sess. 93-95, 101-02 (1962), and also Dorothy Gansfield Fowler, "Congressional Dictation of Local Appointments," 7 J. Pol. 25 (1945).

[31] The Writings of Washington (Fitzpatrick ed.), XXX, 370-71.

[32] Richardson, Messages and Papers, II, 516 (July 6, 1813).

ness of a candidate from their constituency. Madison, in the First Congress, noted that Senators had been joined with the President in the appointment power because they were, "from their nature, better acquainted with the character of the candidates than an individual." A few weeks later Congressman Benjamin Goodhue drove home the same point by observing that it was "more probable that the Senate may be better acquainted with the characters of the officers that are nominated than the President himself."[33]

To come within the scope of senatorial courtesy, a nominee must be from the state of the Senator and the appointment must be to a position within that state rather than to a national office, such as the Cabinet. The custom is further refined by requiring that the objecting Senator be from the same party as the President. Although a number of nominations have been defeated on grounds of personal objection or because they are "personally offensive" to a Senator, senatorial courtesy has not prevailed in every instance.[34]

The reach of senatorial courtesy is broader than its formal dimensions. In 1970 Senator Barry Goldwater blocked an appointment to a national office (the State Department) that was not even subject to Senate advice and consent. Goldwater advised the Secretary of State that the individual, Arthur J. Olsen, was "personally obnoxious" because of an article he had written in 1964 linking Goldwater—at that time the Republican candidate for President—with right-wing elements in Germany. The Nixon administration, warned by Goldwater that there would be "trouble," withdrew the appointment.[35] Senators from the opposite party can also bargain for power over patronage. During the Nixon years, Senators Alan Cranston and John Tunney of California (both Democrats) were able to work out an agreement that gave every third federal judgeship in that state to a Democrat.[36]

---

[33] Annals of Congress, I, 380 (May 19, 1789) and 534 (June 18, 1789).

[34] Floyd Riddick, Senate Procedure: Precedents and Practices, S. Doc. No. 21, 93d Cong., 1st Sess. 563-64 (1974); see Joseph P. Harris, The Advice and Consent of the Senate 215-37 (1953).

[35] Washington Post, August 31, 1970, at A1, and September 1, 1970, at A2.

[36] Nina Totenberg, "Will Judges be Chosen Rationally?" 60 Judicature 93, 95

During the first year of the Reagan administration, Senator Jesse A. Helms of North Carolina put "holds" on four of the five key regional bureau jobs in the State Department. Operating from a position of strength as the third-ranking Republican member of the Senate Foreign Relations Committee, Helms also functioned as a guardian of conservative values for the Reagan administration and its foreign policy.

Supreme Court Nominees

The Senate is especially vigilant in reviewing nominations to the Supreme Court, rejecting approximately one out of five. Many of the rejections stem from partisan considerations, not individual qualifications.[37] Despite this record, the Senate's rejection of two of President Nixon's nominations to the Court seemed to many Senators a bold, if not unconstitutional, course of action. No matter how poorly the President may have made his selections, members of the Senate appeared uncertain and uncomfortable in exercising their prerogative. Acceptance of the third name submitted by President Nixon seemed inevitable. Why this uneasiness and sense of impropriety? A Senator is not obligated to vote for a nominee who appears unsuited for office.

A Senate study in 1976 tried to sharpen the criteria for Supreme Court nominees. The study regards lawyers with broad experience in their discipline, including political experience, as best suited to handle the responsibilities thrust upon members of the Court. Senators, for their part, are justified in considering not merely a nominee's political and constitutional philosophy but also other appointments by the President, particularly when the balance of views on the Court is at stake.[38]

(1976). See G. Calvin MacKenzie, The Politics of Presidential Appointments 121-24 (1981).

[37] Henry J. Abraham, Justices and Presidents 8 (1974) and William F. Swindler, "The Politics of 'Advice and Consent,' " 56 A.B.A.J. 533 (1970).

[38] Senate Committee on the Judiciary, "Advice and Consent on Supreme Court Nominations," 94th Cong., 2d Sess. (Comm. Print 1976); 121 Cong. Rec. 37650-52 (1975); and 117 Cong. Rec. 39778-83 (1971).

Executive Officials

More circumspect and deferential is the Senate's behavior toward Cabinet officers and other departmental positions. The doctrine that the President is entitled to a Cabinet of his own choice is broadly supported. Some Senators find this kind of submissive attitude offensive and degrading. Senator Charles McC. Mathias, Jr., asked in 1977:

> Does it simply mean that after the President has had an opportunity to exercise the broad and plenary power to choose from among 215 million Americans, that we then merely have to ascertain whether his choice is a convicted felon or a committed lunatic, and if we find that that is not the case, we then have to automatically grant confirmation?
> Well, I would say certainly not.[39]

The Senate's reluctance to contest presidential choices for department officials was anticipated by Alexander Hamilton, writing in Federalist 76: "as their dissent might cast a kind of stigma upon the individual rejected, and might have the appearance of a reflection upon the judgment of the Chief magistrate, it is not likely that their sanction would often be refused, where there were not special and strong reasons for the refusal." Joseph Story, one of the more distinguished commentators on the Constitution, correctly predicted that Senate rejections would be rare: "The more common error, (if there shall be any) will be too great a facility to yield to the executive wishes, as a means of personal, or popular favour."[40] If the nomination can be killed outright, Senators may encourage each other to mass for the attack. But a Senator may hesitate to step forward against a nominee who faces only minimal opposition. If the assault is likely to fall short, it may be prudent not to try. Better not to attack a bear at all than merely to wound it.

Only on rare occasions has the Senate rejected a Cabinet nomination, the most recent example being the disapproval of Lewis L. Strauss in 1959 to the position of Secretary of Commerce.

[39] 123 Cong. Rec. 2076 (1977).
[40] Joseph Story, Commentaries, III, §1526 (1833).

Prior to that time only seven other Cabinet nominees had been rejected, some of them several times. In 1843 the Senate rejected Caleb Cushing three straight times as Secretary of Treasury, the margin increasing against him with each vote. Charles B. Warren was turned down twice in 1925 for the post of Attorney General.[41]

Of eleven department heads submitted by President Carter in 1977, the Senate confirmed eight by voice vote. Rollcalls were taken only in the case of Attorney General Bell (75-21), Health, Education, and Welfare Secretary Califano (95-1), and Secretary of Labor Marshall (74-20). The Senate's perfunctory investigation and approval of Bert Lance to be Office of Management and Budget (OMB) Director, a position considered more powerful than any Cabinet office, became deeply embarrassing for the Senate when Lance resigned amidst serious charges about his past financial dealings. In 1981, rollcall votes were taken for all thirteen Cabinet nominees submitted by President Reagan. Five nominees were confirmed without a dissenting vote (Block, Lewis, Pierce, Regan, and Schweiker), and five other nominees received between one and three negative votes (Baldridge, Bell, Edwards, Smith, and Weinberger). Six Senators voted against Alexander Haig to be Secretary of State; twelve voted against James Watt to be Secretary of the Interior; and seventeen voted against Raymond Donovan to be Secretary of Labor.

The Senate periodically reexamines its responsibility for reviewing nominees to executive offices. To defer to the President, on the principle that he has a right to select his own assistants, makes a nullity of the Senate's advice-and-consent role. Department heads and their assistants are not mere staff support for the President. They are called upon to administer programs that Congress has enacted into law. A lack of interest by an administrator, or overt hostility to a legislative program, can undercut the policies that Congress has taken pains to announce as national goals. Administrators so disposed can shatter agency mo-

[41] Louis C. James, "Senatorial Rejections of Presidential Nominations to the Cabinet: A Study in Constitutional Custom," 3 Ariz. L. Rev. 232 (1961).

rale and create uncertainty for career personnel, who may not know whether they are supposed to implement or sabotage the statutory objectives.

The idea that political appointees are subordinate to congressional purposes was stressed long ago by Joseph Story. Offices in a republican government "are established, and are to be filled, not to gratify private interests and private attachments; not as a means of corrupt influence, or individual profit; not for cringing favourites, or court sycophants; but for purposes of the highest public good; to give dignity, strength, purity, and energy to the administration of the laws."[42] Roger Sherman, who had been a signer of the Declaration of Independence, member of the Continental Congress, and delegate to the Philadelphia convention, offered this advice in 1789 while serving as a Representative in the First Congress: "The executive magistrate is to execute the laws. The senate, being a branch of the legislature, will naturally incline to have them duly executed, and, therefore, will advise to such appointments as will best attain that end."[43]

Nevertheless, there is not even agreement at the present time that a nominee for a Cabinet post needs expertise or experience for the task about to be assumed. This issue arose in 1973 when the Senate considered the nomination of James T. Lynn (an attorney with very limited background in housing matters) to be Secretary of Housing and Urban Development. The issue reappeared in 1975 when Carla Anderson Hills was nominated to the same post. Some members objected to her lack of experience in the housing field, while others claimed that expertise might create a conflict of interest and suggested that inexperience might even be an asset.[44] Nor is there any agreement as to the right of the Senate to judge someone not simply on the basis of competence and integrity but also on philosophical grounds, particularly when there is doubt that the nominee's views and attitudes are in concert with the statutory mission.

---

[42] Story, Commentaries, III, §1524.
[43] The Works of John Adams (Charles Francis Adams ed.), VI, 440.
[44] 119 Cong. Rec. 2783-95 (1973); 121 Cong. Rec. 5263-69 (1975).

Although the record demonstrates that the Senate only infrequently rejects a nomination to an executive position, statistics do not reveal the candidates who are eliminated as a result of a preliminary canvass among Senators, people who decline an offer rather than submit to the glare of Senate publicity, those who are not even seriously considered by the executive branch because of the likelihood of Senate opposition, and the names withdrawn by the President after confirmation becomes hopeless.[45]

Ambassadors

The Constitution requires the Senate's advice and consent for two classes of public office: Justices of the Supreme Court and "Ambassadors, other public Ministers and Consuls."[46] Senate confirmation for all other officers depends on statutory conditions set by Congress.

The special attention accorded diplomatic officers flows from the Senate's responsibility in treaty matters. During the early years the act of confirming ambassadors often overlapped with substantive questions on treaties. Senators voted not merely on the fitness of a nominee but on the instructions he had received to negotiate with a foreign country.[47]

Diplomatic officers are distinctive for another reason. In two opinions in 1855 Attorney General Cushing concluded that ambassadors, public ministers, and consuls are officers created by the Constitution, not by acts of Congress. Even in the absence of statutory authority, a President (with the advice and consent of the Senate) may appoint diplomatic officers. Appropriations, however, are necessary to cover diplomatic expenses.[48] Presidents have also appointed agents and special envoys without submitting their names to the Senate. The claim is that they are temporary appointments and therefore technically not "officers," even though they discharge diplomatic duties.[49]

[45] See MacKenzie, The Politics of Presidential Appointments, at 174-81.
[46] Art. II, Sec. 2.
[47] Harris, The Advice and Consent of the Senate, at 281-84.
[48] 7 Op. Att'y Gen. 186, 242 (1855).
[49] Henry M. Wriston, "The Special Envoy," 38 Foreign Affairs 219 (1960).

In recent years the Senate has pushed for higher standards of professionalism for ambassadorial appointments. The Foreign Relations Authorization Act of 1975 provided the sense of Congress that the position of United States ambassador to a foreign country "should be accorded to men and women possessing clearly demonstrated competence to perform ambassadorial duties." No individual should be accorded the position of ambassador "primarily because of financial contributions to political campaigns." In 1976 the Senate voted to require that 75 percent of ambassadorial positions be filled by professionals from the Foreign Service. As enacted, however, this provision became a sense-of-Congress statement that a greater number of ambassadorial positions should be occupied by career Foreign Service personnel.[50] The Foreign Service Act of 1980 states that "positions as chiefs of mission should normally be accorded to career members of the [Foreign] Service" and that contributions to political campaigns should not be a factor in appointing chiefs of missions.[51]

Presidents Carter and Reagan engaged in a seesaw contest with Congress over ten American consulates that legislators wanted to keep open. Carter insisted that the President had implied powers under the Constitution to decide when and where an ambassador or consul should be appointed. He decided to treat statutory language—mandating that the consulates remain open—not as a requirement but rather as a recommendation.[52] When Congress later invoked its power of the purse to keep the consulates open, Carter proceeded to close seven of the consulates.[53] Reagan took a similar stand on his prerogatives. In 1982, while signing legislation requiring that the consulates be reopened and operated,

---

For distinctions between "officer" and "rank," see Wood v. United States, 15 Ct. Cl. 151 (1879), affirmed in Wood v. United States, 107 U.S. 414 (1882).

[50] 89 Stat. 757, sec. 104 (1975); 90 Stat. 829, sec. 120 (1976), and H. Rept. No. 1302, 94th Cong., 2d Sess. 37 (1976). See "The Senate Role in Foreign Affairs Appointments," prepared for the Senate Committee on Foreign Relations, 97th Cong., 2d Sess. (Comm. Print July 1982).

[51] 94 Stat. 2085, sec. 304(a) (1980).

[52] Public Papers of the Presidents, 1979, at 1434.

[53] 126 Cong. Rec. S4881-82 (daily ed. May 7, 1980); 126 Cong. Rec. S10984-85 (daily ed. August 6, 1980).

he advised Congress that he would treat the provision only as a recommendation.[54]

Regulatory Agencies

The record of regulatory appointments has been criticized for decades. Studies conducted by the Senate in 1976 and 1977 concluded that neither the White House nor the Senate had demonstrated a sustained commitment to high-quality appointments to regulatory agencies.[55] In the face of such evidence the Senate is adopting a more assertive attitude. In 1973, for the first time in more than two decades, it rejected by a recorded vote a nominee to a regulatory agency: Robert H. Morris to the Federal Power Commission. No one questioned Morris's ability or integrity. At issue was his close association with the industry he would have to regulate. A majority of the Senate believed that members on the commission were already too industry-oriented and insufficiently attentive to consumer interests.[56]

Since then the Senate Commerce Committee has refused to recommend the confirmation of several other nominees to regulatory agencies. The individuals, Senator Warren Magnuson said in 1976, "failed to meet minimum standards of qualifications for the post to which they were recommended." The committee adopted five reforms by (1) placing the background and financial statements submitted by nominees on the public record; (2) tightening the requirements for disclosing potential conflicts of interest; (3) reviewing the financial statements and biographies of nominees to identify potential conflicts of interest; (4) providing at least seven days' notice of hearings on nominees; and (5)

[54] Wkly Comp. Pres. Doc., XVIII, 1059-60 (August 24, 1982).

[55] "Appointments to the Regulatory Agencies," printed for the use of the Senate Committee on Commerce, 94th Cong., 2d Sess. (Comm. Print April 1976); "Study on Federal Regulations: The Regulatory Appointments Process" (Volume I), Senate Committee on Government Operations, 95th Cong., 1st Sess. (Comm. Print January 1977).

[56] 119 Cong. Rec. 19492-508 (1973). The previous month a number of Senators registered strong opposition to the nomination of William L. Springer to the Federal Power Commission (FPC); id. at 16265-81.

relying on written interrogatories to develop a record on the nominees' depth of knowledge, policy commitments, and regulatory philosophy.[57]

In 1981 the Senate Commerce Committee shelved the nomination of F. Keith Adkinson to the Federal Trade Commission. Adkinson, national director of Democrats for Reagan in the 1980 campaign, was accused of lying to the committee about a book contract he had signed while serving as a Senate staffer. With the committee prepared to vote against his appointment in March 1982, Reagan withdrew the nomination.[58]

The Senate's responsibility for confirming presidential nominees, although fixed firmly in the Constitution, remains unsettled in its application. The Senate was not meant to be a passive participant. Delegates to the Philadelphia convention believed that the Senate would be knowledgeable about nominees and capable of voting wisely. Yet for the most part it has acted cautiously, uncertain of the scope of its own constitutional power. The source of this uncertainty is not the Constitution. Nowhere in that document, or in its history, is there an obligation on the part of the Senate to approve a nomination. On the contrary, the burden should be on the President to select and submit a nominee with acceptable credentials.

Recess Appointments

The framers of the Constitution recognized that the Senate would not always be in session to give advice and consent to presidential nominations. To cover these periods the President is authorized to make recess appointments: "The President shall have Power to fill up all Vacancies that may happen during the Recess of the Senate, by granting Commissions which shall expire at the End of their next Session."[59] This provision was adopted at the Con-

[57] 122 Cong. Rec. 7310 (1976).
[58] Congressional Quarterly Weekly Report, December 19, 1981, at 2489; Washington Post, March 30, 1982, at D8.
[59] Art. II, Sec. 2, Cl. 3.

stitutional Convention without a dissenting vote[60] and with virtually no record to fix intent and scope.[61] A loose interpretation would jeopardize the Senate's role in the appointments process.

Two words have been most in dispute: *happen* and *recess*. Does happen mean "happen to take place" during the recess (the literal meaning)? A long list of opinions by Attorneys General has interpreted the language more broadly to mean "happen to exist" at the time of a recess, including vacancies that occur while the Senate is in session and available to give advice and consent. Attorney General Wirt claimed that the second meaning satisfied the reason, spirit, and purpose of the Constitution (which to Wirt was keeping offices filled).[62] Through various statutes, to be discussed, Congress has limited the reach of Wirt's opinion.

The word "recess" also requires interpretation. It means more than final adjournment at the end of a session or a Congress. A temporary recess of the Senate, "protracted enough to prevent that body from performing its functions of advising and consenting to executive nominations," permits the President to make recess appointments.[63] Senate adjournment from July 3 to August 8 in 1960 constituted a "Recess of the Senate" as interpreted by the Justice Department.[64] When the Senate temporarily adjourned in the middle of this session and reconvened, it continued the same session. It did not commence the "next session" in the meaning of the recess clause.[65] Short adjournments

[60] Farrand, Records, II, 540.

[61] Id. at 574, 600, 660; III, 421. Federalist 67, written by Hamilton, adds little to the intent of the recess clause.

[62] 1 Op. Att'y Gen. 631 (1823). For other Justice Department opinions along this line, see Taney at 2 Op. Att'y Gen. 525 (1832); Mason at 4 Op. Att'y Gen. 523 (1846); Bates at 10 Op. Att'y Gen. 356 (1862); Stanbery at 12 Op. Att'y Gen. 32, 38 (1866); Evarts at 12 Op. Att'y Gen. 455, 457 (1868); Devans at 16 Op. Att'y Gen. 522, 524 (1880); Brewster at 18 Op. Att'y Gen. 29 (1884); Miller at 19 Op. Att'y Gen. 261, 262 (1889); Gregory at 30 Op. Att'y Gen. 314, 315 (1914); Daugherty at 33 Op. Att'y Gen. 20, 23 (1921); and Walsh at 41 Op. Att'y Gen. 463, 465-66 (1960).

[63] 41 Op. Att'y Gen. 463, 466 (1960).

[64] Id. The Comptroller General had adopted a similar interpretation; 28 Comp. Gen. 30 (1948).

[65] 41 Op. Att'y Gen. 463, 477 (1960); see also 23 Op. Att'y Gen. 599, 604 (1901).

"for 5 or even 10 days" do not "constitute the recess intended by the Constitution," according to another Attorney General opinion.[66]

Statutory Restrictions

For more than a century, Congress has experimented with statutory restrictions on the power to make recess appointments. If Congress believes that the exercise of that power undermines the Senate's authority to confirm appointments, it can retaliate by withholding funds to pay the salaries of recess appointees. As Senator Fessenden remarked in 1863: "It may not be in our power to prevent the [recess] appointment, but it is in our power to prevent the payment; and when payment is prevented, I think that will probably put an end to the habit of making such appointments."[67]

Fessenden's comment came after the Senate had asked the Judiciary Committee to explore this question: did the practice of appointing officers to fill vacancies that existed *prior* to a recess, while the Senate was in session, conflict with the Constitution? The committee rejected Attorney General Wirt's position that a recess appointee can fill a vacancy that occurs during a session. To read the constitutional language "may happen during the Recess of the Senate" to include what happened before the recess seemed to the committee "a perversion of language." Such reasoning tilted the balance of power toward the President and placed excessive emphasis on the filling of a vacancy. Of equal importance was the need to protect the Senate's opportunity to pass judgment on the qualification of an officeholder. Unless Congress placed some constraint on the power to make recess appointments, an "ambitious, corrupt, or tyrannical executive" could nullify the Senate's constitutional function.[68]

Congress passed legislation in 1863 to prohibit the use of funds to pay the salary of anyone appointed during a Senate recess to

[66] 33 Op. Att'y Gen. 20, 25 (1921). See 3 O.L.C. 311, 314 (1979).

[67] Cong. Globe, 37th Cong., 3d Sess. 565 (1863).

[68] S. Rept. No. 80, 37th Cong., 3d Sess. (1863). Quotations from the report appear at pages 5 and 6.

fill a vacancy that existed "while the Senate was in session and is by law required to be filled by and with the advice and consent of the Senate, until such appointee shall have been confirmed by the Senate."[69] Under this statute an officer had to serve without pay (relying on savings or loans) until the Senate consented to the nomination.

The harshness of this law is illustrated by an example from the administration of Woodrow Wilson. George Rublee, nominated to the Federal Trade Commission in March 1915, served for more than a year as a recess appointee. After the Senate voted to reject him he continued to serve (at Wilson's request) the balance of his recess commission until September 1916, when Congress adjourned. Under the 1863 law, Rublee was not entitled to any remuneration. Congress had to pass a special appropriation that paid his salary for fourteen months, from the date his service began to the date the Senate rejected him.[70]

A House committee in 1940 concluded that the 1863 statute was excessively burdensome. It seemed particularly inequitable when a vacancy arose shortly before a recess, with insufficient time for Senate action, and when a session terminated before the Senate acted on a nomination that had been pending for months. The committee, supported by the Attorney General and the Budget Bureau, recommended changes to make the law "more flexible." The 1863 law was revised to permit three exceptions. First, payments may be made if a vacancy arises within thirty days before the end of the session of the Senate. Given the paucity of time, nominations submitted during this period are unlikely to receive the Senate's approval. Second, payments may be made if, at the end of the session, a nomination was pending before the Senate (other than for someone appointed during a preceding recess). This provision has two purposes: it protects the Senate from successive recess appointees and it protects nominees whose names went forward in timely manner. Third, payments may be made

---

[69] 12 Stat. 646 (1863). For the restrictive effect of this statute, see 16 Op. Att'y Gen. 522, 531 (1880), 26 Op. Att'y Gen. 234, 235 (1907), 32 Op. Att'y Gen. 271, 272 (1920), and 41 Op. Att'y Gen. 463, 473-74 (1960).

[70] 39 Stat. 801 (1916); see Haynes, The Senate of the United States, II, at 776-77.

if a nomination is rejected by the Senate within thirty days before the end of the session and an individual (other than the one rejected) receives a recess appointment. This exception takes care of possible cases of rejection on the eve of a recess. The statute also contains an important limitation: a nomination to fill a vacancy referred to in the three exceptions must be submitted to the Senate not later than forty days after the Senate's next session begins.[71] "Next session" has been interpreted in a nontechnical way to mean the return of the Senate from its recess, not the next session of Congress.[72]

Like other statutes, this one is not self-executing. It must be constantly monitored by Congress to prevent abuse. Presidents may let a position remain unfilled for months without submitting a name to the Senate and then, just before a recess, forward a name to be covered under the second exception. For example, the office of OMB Deputy Director became vacant on March 24, 1978. President Carter did not submit the name of John White until October 7, making it "pending" at the time of the recess and therefore within the guidelines of the law. By resubmitting White's name within forty days after the Senate reconvened, Carter stayed within the letter of the law, but his initial delay of six months helped circumvent the statutory requirement for Senate confirmation, which did not occur until April 10, 1979.

The scope of recess appointments is complicated by the presence of "holdover" clauses in federal statutes. For example, a member of the Federal Election Commission may serve after the expiration of his term "until his successor has taken office as a member of the Commission." The statute is ambiguous because it does not define *how* the successor takes office: by Senate confirmation (required for new members) or as a recess appointee.

The statute says that any vacancy in the membership of the commission "shall be filled in the same manner as in the case of the original appointment" (presumably by Senate confirmation). Nevertheless, on October 25, 1978, President Carter made John

---

[71] 54 Stat. 751 (1940), 5 U.S.C. 5503 (1982). For commentary on the hardship on appointees who had to serve without compensation, see 28 Comp. Gen. 30, 37 (1948) and 41 Op. Att'y Gen. 463, 479-80 (1960).

[72] 41 Op. Att'y Gen. 463, 477 (1960).

McGarry a recess appointee to the seat held by Neil Staebler, who was serving in holdover capacity. Staebler refused to leave office, arguing that McGarry had not been confirmed by the Senate and therefore no vacancy existed for Carter to fill.

A federal district judge, deciding against Staebler, pointed to many inconsistencies in the statute. If a vacancy existed only at the point of confirmation for a successor, this would place an almost unmanageable task on the President. How could he recruit someone for the office and submit a nomination if, in theory, no vacancy existed? Such a scheme would also disrupt the statutory design of staggered, six-year terms for the six commissioners. Under Staebler's interpretation, the statutory dates for these terms would constantly shift to take account of holdovers, creating a "baggage of peculiar practical difficulties."[73] The court could find no clear evidence that Congress tried to restrict the President's power to make recess appointments.[74] If the Senate wanted to protect its right to advise and consent, it could have rejected McGarry's nomination when Carter first sent it up on September 27, 1977 and then again on April 10, 1978. It was only after two sessions of Senate inaction that Carter made the recess appointment.[75]

The power to make recess appointments has been a major issue in the life of the Legal Services Corporation. On January 19, 1978, before the Senate reconvened for the second session of the 95th Congress, President Carter made several recess appointments to the LSC. Since the incumbents had not resigned and were protected by holdover clauses, there was a question whether vacancies existed for Carter to fill. Moreover, according to the statute creating the corporation, the members of the Board of Directors are not "officers" of the United States. Does this nullify the President's power to make recess appointments?[76]

President Reagan encountered the same issues when he made

---

[73] Staebler v. Carter, 464 F.Supp. 585, 589 (D.D.C. 1979). On appeal, the D.C. Circuit on May 17, 1979 dismissed the case as moot, remanding it to the district court.

[74] Id. at 592.

[75] Id. at 601. For the Senate's record on McGarry, see 587.

[76] 124 Cong. Rec. 7687-90 (1978).

recess appointments to the LSC. A case filed in federal court featured the "ins" (Reagan's recess appointees) against the "outs" (Carter's appointees in holdover status). The holdovers argued that they were not "officers" and therefore immune from Reagan's control. A district court ruled in 1982 that the Directors were "officers" because they performed significant governmental duties by determining funding eligibility pursuant to broad statutory standards. The court also pointed out that had Congress wanted to prevent the President from exercising his recess appointment power, it probably would not have made the Directors subject to presidential appointment with the advice and consent of the Senate. The court denied the holdovers' application for a temporary restraining order to prevent the Reagan appointees from meeting as Directors and conducting business.[77]

Later in 1982 the same court reviewed the holdovers' claim that the Reagan recess appointments were invalid. The court discovered nothing in the legislative history of the Legal Services Corporation Act to suggest that Congress intended to restrict the President's recess power. As to the alleged incompatibility between this power and the political independence of the LSC, the court noted that Presidents have made many recess appointments to the federal courts and to independent regulatory commissions.[78]

Congress can force a recess appointee to resign by rejecting the nomination. Because of language in a rider attached to the annual Treasury-Postal Service appropriations bill, a rejection has the effect of eliminating the appointee's compensation.[79] The language in the rider is as follows: "No part of any appropriation for the current fiscal year contained in this or any other Act shall be paid to any person for the filling of any position for which he or she has been nominated after the Senate has voted not to approve the nomination of said person."[80]

[77] Legal Services Corporation v. Dana, Civil Action No. 82-0542 (D.D.C. March 3, 1982).
[78] McCalpin v. Dana, Civil Action No. 82-542 (D.D.C. October 5, 1982).
[79] 3 O.L.C. 314, 317 (1979).
[80] E.g., 93 Stat. 574, sec. 604 (1979). When Congress fails to pass a Treasury-Postal Service appropriations bill, the rider on rejected nominees has been carried in the continuing appropriations bill.

Recess Appointments of Judges

The use of recess appointments for federal judges raises significant questions about judicial independence. The issue became pronounced in the 1950s when President Eisenhower placed three men on the Supreme Court after the Senate had recessed: Earl Warren, William J. Brennan, Jr., and Potter Stewart. All three joined the Court and participated in decisions before the Senate had an opportunity to review their credentials. The Senate confirmed them, but the experience convinced most Senators that the procedure was defective both for the Senate and for the judiciary.

In 1960 Senator Philip A. Hart introduced a resolution to discourage this practice. As a Senate resolution it would have no legally binding effect, but was meant to express the view of the Senate and to guide executive action. The Senate labored under unique difficulties when called upon to confirm a recess appointee who already sat on the Supreme Court. Should Senators take into account decisions rendered during that period? A negative vote by the Senate would represent more than the rejection of a nominee; it would remove a sitting Justice. Recess appointments conflicted with the principle of judicial independence. Justices might hedge their decisions to please the President or the Senate, leaving disappointed litigants wondering whether the outcome of their case turned on the incomplete status of recess appointees.

Opponents of Hart's resolution argued that the President needed to exercise his constitutional power to make recess appointments because of the heavy workload of the Court. They also objected to ambiguities in the language of the resolution and the fact that it had not been referred to the Department of Justice or the Judicial Conference for comment, nor had there been any hearings. The Senate passed the resolution 48 to 37, voting essentially along party lines.[81] The resolution, after a preamble that details the disadvantages of making recess appointments to the Supreme Court, reads as follows:

[81] 106 Cong. Rec. 18145 (1960).

Resolved, That it is the sense of the Senate that the making
of recess appointments to the Supreme Court of the United
States may not be wholly consistent with the best interests
of the Supreme Court, the nominee who may be involved,
the litigants before the Court, nor indeed the people of the
United States, and that such appointments, therefore, should
not be made except under unusual circumstances and for the
purpose of preventing or ending a demonstrable breakdown
in the administration of the Court's business.

Although legally nonbinding, the resolution had its intended effect. No President since Eisenhower has made a recess appointment to the Supreme Court.

The President's constitutional authority to make recess appointments to the federal courts was upheld by the Second Circuit in 1962.[82] However, in 1983 the Ninth Circuit held that
the President's constitutional power under Article II to make
recess appointments could not supplant the lifetime tenure guaranteed judges by Article III. Federal judges serving under a recess appointment lacked the independence required by the Constitution. A judge receiving his commission under the recess
appointment clause "may be called upon to make politically charged
decisions while his nomination awaits approval by popularly elected
officials. Such a judge will scarcely be oblivious to the effect his
decision may have on the vote of these officials."[83]

Temporary Appointments

In addition to the power to make recess appointments, Presidents make other temporary or interim appointments. When the
head of an executive department dies, resigns, or is sick or absent, the next in command may perform the duties until a successor is appointed or the absence ceases. As an alternative, the
President may direct someone else (previously appointed with
the advice and consent of the Senate) to perform the duties.

[82] United States v. Allocco, 305 F.2d 704 (2d Cir. 1962), cert. denied, 371
U.S. 964 (1963).
[83] United States v. Woodley, 726 F.2d 1328, 1330 (9th Cir. 1983).

These acting officials are restricted by law to a period not to exceed thirty days.[84] Actual practice is far more complicated. In May 1972, upon the death of FBI Director J. Edgar Hoover, L. Patrick Gray was named Acting Director and continued to serve in that capacity for almost a year. President Nixon did not submit Gray's name to the Senate for confirmation until February 21, 1973. With the Senate clearly opposed to Gray, Nixon withdrew the nomination on April 17 and Gray resigned shortly thereafter.[85]

Officials frequently serve in an acting capacity for more than the thirty days allowed under the Vacancy Act. This situation is routinely tolerated by Congress if the President has forwarded the name of the official to the Senate for confirmation. But when the President fails to send a name forward, Senate prerogatives are directly threatened. This was the situation in 1973 when President Nixon planned to dismantle the Office of Economic Opportunity (OEO). Instead of nominating a Director and seeking the advice and consent of the Senate, he appointed Howard J. Phillips as Acting Director. The administration asserted that the President had constitutional power to appoint officers temporarily without Senate confirmation, drawing that power from the President's obligation under Article II, Section 3 to "take Care that the Laws be faithfully executed." It was a bizarre argument: the administration ignored a number of laws in order to do what no law permitted.

A district court denied that the President possessed an inherent (or derivative) power to make interim appointments unless in an emergency, and the court found no emergency in this situation. The appointment was invalid because it did not satisfy the statute (requiring the Senate's advice and consent), nor was

[84] 5 U.S.C. 3345-3348 (1982). For earlier versions see 12 Stat. 656 (1863) and 15 Stat. 168 (1968). See also 2 O.L.C. 72 (1978).

[85] In a letter to Senator William Proxmire on February 22, 1973, Comptroller General Staats concluded that Gray was subject to the thirty-day limit in 5 U.S.C. 3348 and that his continued service was prohibited by law (B-150136). The Justice Department maintained that Gray became Acting Director under a different law (28 U.S.C. 508-510).

it made during a Senate recess.[86] As an emergency measure to permit OEO to function, the court allowed Phillips's successor, Alvin J. Arnett, to assume control as Acting Director. Arnett was later nominated, and confirmed, as OEO Director.

A different dilemma arose on February 15, 1972, when John Mitchell announced his resignation as Attorney General effective March 1, 1972. President Nixon submitted Deputy Attorney General Richard Kleindienst's name to Congress as his nominee for Attorney General. On March 1, 1972, Kleindienst assumed the duties; on June 8 he was confirmed. During this interim he authorized several wiretaps. The question was whether the wiretaps were valid, since Kleindienst had served for more than the thirty days permitted under the Vacancy Act. A district court upheld the wiretaps on the ground that Kleindienst had authority to act as he did. Important to the court was the fact that his name had been sent to the Senate for confirmation even before he assumed the duties of Attorney General: "Had the President been dilatory in sending a name to Congress, perhaps a different situation would be present."[87] In a separate decision, a district court held that Robert Bork became Acting Attorney General in 1973 under a statute other than the Vacancy Act and therefore was not subject to the thirty-day limit.[88]

As a way of covering the start-up period for new agencies, Congress has allowed the President to fill offices requiring Senate confirmation with interim appointees who had in the past been subject to advice and consent. This procedure permits acting officials to serve for more than the thirty days allowed under the Vacancy Act. In 1978 the Comptroller General of the General Accounting Office (GAO) concluded that four of the five interim appointees serving in the Department of Energy, under such an arrangement, had not been legally appointed because they had

[86] Williams v. Phillips, 360 F.Supp. 1363 (D.D.C. 1973). The D.C. Court of Appeals denied Phillips's motion for a stay, pending appeal, because he failed to show sufficient likelihood of success on the merits; Williams v. Phillips, 482 F.2d 669 (D.C. Cir. 1973).

[87] United States v. Lucido, 373 F.Supp. 1142, 1151 (E.D. Mich. 1974).

[88] United States v. Halmo, 386 F.Supp. 593, 595 (E.D. Wis. 1974).

never been confirmed by the Senate.[89] The Office of Legal Counsel in the Justice Department denied that the procedure in the Department of Energy Act established the exclusive manner of making interim appointments.[90] Robert J. Lipshutz, counsel to President Carter, described the GAO opinion as advisory "at best" and not binding on the executive branch. By the time the Comptroller General replied to Lipshutz regarding the GAO's authority, the four officials had been confirmed.[91]

Creating other problems with temporary appointees, Presidents have dispatched agents on diplomatic missions without seeking the advice and consent of the Senate.[92] Since the appointments were of a temporary nature, it could be argued that they did not satisfy the legal meaning of an "office," including such qualities as tenure and duration. But Congress can use its appropriations power to rein in appointments to non-ambassadorial posts. Teddy Roosevelt created a stir by appointing extralegal, unsalaried commissions to study social and economic issues. When he asked Congress for $25,000 to publish a commission study, Congress retaliated by prohibiting the appointment of commissions that lacked legislative authority. Although Roosevelt protested that Congress had no right to pass such restrictions and threatened to ignore the proscription, he had to seek private funds to publish the study.[93]

His cousin, Franklin D. Roosevelt, created agencies by executive order and used appropriations to finance agency activities that lacked legislative support. Congress passed the "Russell Rider" in 1944 to prohibit the use of any appropriation for an agency unless Congress specifically authorized it.[94] Toward the

[89] Comptroller General Decision B-150136 (May 16, 1978).

[90] 2 O.L.C. 405 (1978).

[91] Letter from Comptroller General Staats to Lipshutz, August 29, 1978 (B-150136). For the statutory procedure for the Department of Energy, see P.L. 95-91, sec. 902, 91 Stat. 612 (1977), 42 U.S.C. 7342 (Supp. IV 1980).

[92] The Constitution of the United States of America, S. Doc. No. 82, 92d Cong., 2d Sess. 521-23 (1973).

[93] The Works of Theodore Roosevelt, XX, 416-17; 35 Stat. 1027, sec. 9 (1909).

[94] 58 Stat. 387, sec. 213 (1944), codified at 31 U.S.C. 1347 (1982). See 90 Cong. Rec. 6021-39 for legislative history. The restriction applies to "action agencies" that perform governmental functions, not to advisory bodies; 3 O.L.C. 263 (1979).

end of the administration of Lyndon Johnson, Congress prohibited the use of funds for interdepartmental boards, commissions, councils, committees, or similar groups that did not have prior and specific congressional approval. This prohibition has been repeated each year in appropriations bills.[95]

The appointment power operates in a framework of studied ambiguity, its limits established for the most part not by court decisions but by imaginative accommodations between the executive and legislative branches. The actual power of nominating officials has been parceled out to interest groups, legislators, judges, and party leaders, with the White House trying to coordinate and centralize the decisions. For its part, the Senate is often hesitant in challenging and rejecting the names submitted by the President, especially his candidates for executive departments. Each Senator has widely different interpretations on the degree of deference that is appropriate. Largely uncharted is the realm of recess and temporary appointments, an area of vast presidential discretion. Congress polices the borders of this power by imposing statutory constraints and conditions, some of them of questionable constitutionality, but the result is a compromise that appears to meet the needs and interests of both branches.

[95] Action under Johnson had its origin in 1968; see S. Rept. No. 1275, 90th Cong., 2d Sess. 2-3 and H. Rept. No. 1348, 90th Cong., 2d Sess. 8. For contemporary language see 93 Stat. 575, sec. 608 (1979), attached to the Treasury-Postal Service appropriations bill for fiscal 1980. This bill was not enacted for fiscal years 1981 through 1984, but it is the practice to incorporate special provisions and limitations in the continuing appropriations bills that cover agencies without a regular appropriation.

3

THEORY IN A CRUCIBLE:
THE REMOVAL POWER

Occasionally a statement in the *Federalist Papers* is so wide of the mark, at such odds with events to come, that it has an abrupt and startling effect. So it is with the breezy claim of Alexander Hamilton, in Federalist 77, that the consent of the Senate "would be necessary to displace [public officials] as well as to approve."

The issue that Hamilton disposed of so nonchalantly produced deep divisions among the members of the First Congress. It overshadowed most of the matters that pressed upon the fledgling legislative body in 1789. From May 19 through June 24 the House of Representatives explored the removal power in all its nuances. The debate, occupying almost two hundred pages of the record, represents one of the most thorough expositions on the nature of implied powers. In contrast to many members of Congress today, who let constitutional issues slide by to be disposed of by the courts (if at all), the members of the First Congress faced the constitutional issue with a deep sense of responsibility.

For more than a century it has been the custom of attorneys and scholars, when discussing the removal issue in the First Congress, to write of four schools of thought: (1) the Senate, because of its role in appointments, must have equal participation; (2) removals may be made only by the constitutional process of impeachment; (3) Congress, since it creates an office, may attach to it any condition it decides proper for tenure and removal; (4) the power of removal belongs exclusively to the President as an incident of the executive power.[1]

Those four categories, although convenient for simplicity and tidiness, fail to do justice to the wide-ranging nature of the de-

---

[1] Ex parte Hennen, 13 Pet. 230, 233 (1839), argument of Mr. Coxe for plaintiff; George H. Haynes, The Senate of the United States, II, 786-87 (1938); Edward S. Corwin, The President 87 (1957).

bate, the complexity of the issues, or the shifting tide of opinion that advanced and receded each day as the deliberation continued. The debate merits close attention because of its instruction on constitutional power.[2]

The "Decision of 1789"

James Madison began the debate by proposing three executive departments: Foreign Affairs, Treasury, and War. At the head of each department would be a Secretary appointed by the President with the advice and consent of the Senate "and to be removable by the President." William Smith of South Carolina immediately objected to giving the President sole power of removal. Madison countered by saying that the removal power would make the President responsible for the conduct of department heads. His fellow Virginian, Theodorick Bland, wanted the removal power shared with the Senate to make it consistent with the Constitution's appointment process. If a department head were found unfit for his office "the person must remain there," Smith said, just like a member of Congress, unless guilty of some crime. But the House rejected Bland's motion to add the words "by and with the advice and consent of the Senate." John Vining, opposing the motion, pointed out that the Senate could not serve as an impartial judge in impeachment proceedings if it had already rendered a judgment in a removal case. As the first day's debate drew to a close, the House by a "considerable majority" declared that the removal power lay with the President.

Two days later the House considered a resolution to make the heads of the three executive departments "removable by the President." Eleven members, Madison among them, were appointed to draw up a bill. When the House took up the topic on June 16, William Smith clarified his position by identifying two choices: either the Constitution gave the President the power of removal

---

[2] The House debate in 1789, on all three executive departments, appears in the Annals of Congress, I, 368-83 (May 19), 384-96 (May 20), 396 (May 21), 455-79 (June 16), 479-512 (June 17), 512-52 (June 18), 552-77 (June 19), 578-85 (June 22), 590-92 (June 24), 592-607 (June 25), 611-14 (June 27), 614-15 (June 30), and 615 (July 1).

(in which case it was nugatory for Congress to repeat it) or else it was not given to him (and therefore improper for Congress to confer). He also cautioned that competent people would be reluctant to accept a position and risk their reputation if the President could remove them at will. Smith wanted the language eliminated and the question left to the judiciary. This represents a fifth school of thought on the removal issue and an early inclination, long before *Marbury* v. *Madison* (1803), of judicial review.

Madison, after taking a few days to reexamine the Constitution, conceded that it did not "perfectly correspond with the ideas I entertained of it from the first glance." Precisely how he had adjusted his opinion is not evident from his remarks. The Constitution, he said, vested the executive power in the President, subject to certain exceptions, such as the Senate's participation in the appointment process. He believed that Congress could not extend the exceptions or modify in any way the President's authority. Therefore it was improper to associate the Senate with the President in the removal process. Yet to strike the clause might imply that Congress doubted whether the President had the removal power. It was better, Madison concluded, to retain the language.

Other delegates objected to letting Congress amend the Constitution by statutory construction whenever the document was silent on a question. Congressman Samuel Livermore acknowledged that Congress had authority to create an office and to attach to it whatever limitations and restrictions it thought appropriate, but he thought it very improper to say that the power of giving birth to a creature permitted Congress to "bring forth a monster." Since he feared that a President might remove someone on mere caprice to make room for a favorite, he wanted every person "to have a hearing before he is punished." Here we have a sixth school: procedural due process.

On June 17 the House resumed debate on the motion to make the Secretary of Foreign Affairs "removable by the President." Thomas Hartley from Pennsylvania denied that officials had a property in their office and could be removed only for criminal conduct. That doctrine "may suit a nation which is strong in proportion to the number of dependents upon the Crown, but will be very pernicious in a Republic like ours." Some officers held their commissions during good behavior; others, like the Secretary, served at the pleasure of the President.

George Clymer of Pennsylvania had no doubt that the removal power belonged to the executive. Even if the Constitution had been silent on the power of appointment, he reasoned, the executive would have had that power as well. The Constitution mentioned appointment only to "give some further security against the introduction of improper men into office. But in cases of removal there is not such necessity for this check." One of the more active participants in the debate, Roger Sherman of Connecticut, said that an officer existed as a creature of Congress. Depending upon the statute creating the office, the person might hold office during good behavior, be elected every year, displaced for negligence of duty, or subjected to any other provision without calling upon the President or the Senate.

Madison abhorred this theory of government. He considered it fundamental that the Constitution vested the executive power in the President and required him to take care that the laws be faithfully executed. If the President wantonly removed a meritorious officer, that would "subject him to impeachment and removal from his own high trust." Madison wanted to protect the responsibility of the President: "Vest this power in the Senate jointly with the President, and you abolish at once that great principle of unity and responsibility in the Executive department, which was intended for the security of liberty and the public good."

Debate continued on June 18. The idea of deriving the removal power from the general nature of "executive power," as Madison had suggested, elicited a challenge from Alexander White of Virginia, who said that such a doctrine could be supported only by examples "brought from beyond the Atlantic." This is an amusing twist. Madison advanced essentially the same argument in 1793 while trying to refute Hamilton in the celebrated Pacificus-Helvidius exchange.

Still another Virginian, John Page, objected to joining the Senate with the President in the removal power. In nine cases out of

ten, he predicted, where the President was confident that someone must be removed, it would be impossible to produce the
necessary evidence. Could the Senate proceed without evidence?
If not, should such a man "be saddled upon the President, who
has been appointed for no other purpose but to aid the President
in performing certain duties?" James Jackson denied that the heads
of departments were necessarily dependent upon the President.
The Constitution itself "specifically points them out." Benjamin
Goodhue blunted the force of that argument. He explained that
while Senators played an important role in confirming an officer,
since they might be better acquainted with the nominee than the
President, the man's *performance in office* could be judged better
by the President. He would more likely learn of improper conduct by subordinates. To Livermore, Congress should not interfere with the executive departments by including language on
removals: "Leave them to do their duty, and let us do ours."

June 19 arrived and the House still did not know whether to
strike the words "to be removable by the President." Peter Silves-
ter of New York helped crystallize the issue: Congress had to
give its opinion either by declaration or by implication. If the
Constitution lodged the removal power in the President it was
useless for Congress to interfere by making an express declaration. If the Constitution did *not* leave the power with the President, could Congress give it? Although the Constitution did not
expressly grant the power, neither was there anything "in contra-
diction to it." The problem was compounded, Sherman added,
by the fact that the words "to be removable by the President"
might imply that the President lacked the removal power and
had to have it granted by law. The motion to strike the language
was rejected, 20 to 34.

By June 22 the House was headed in the direction of treating
the removal power by implication, not declaration. Benson moved
that the bill provide that the chief clerk (second in command in
the Foreign Affairs Department) take charge of all records whenever the Secretary "shall be removed from office" by the President. His motion avoided the problem in the phrase "to be removable by the President," which appeared to be a grant of power
by Congress. The new language displeased Smith, who preferred

that Congress express itself in "more candid and manly" terms by declaration, not implication, but Benson's motion carried, 30 to 18. Benson then moved to strike the phrase "to be removable by the President," to which the House agreed, 31 to 19.

When the Senate took up the bill and someone proposed to delete the President's power to remove the Secretary of Foreign Affairs, a tie vote (nine to nine) resulted. Vice President Adams broke the tie by voting against the motion.[3] A few days later, during House action on the bill to establish a War Department, Benson offered language to give the President removal power by implication. Although the identical principle and language were at issue, his motion carried by the smaller margin of 24 to 22. On a motion in the Senate to strike the President's power to remove the Secretary of War, the effort failed by the close vote of nine to ten.[4]

The Foreign Affairs and War Departments had been regarded as "executive departments," largely because of their origin and evolution during the Continental Congress. No such concession was made for Treasury.[5] One would have expected Congress, jealous of its control over finances during the preceding decade, to contest the President's power to remove the Secretary of the Treasury. The challenge came from the Senate, not the House. The Senate deleted the President's power to remove the Secretary. Later on a motion that the Senate recede from its position and accept the House language, another tie vote occurred, ten to ten. Vice President Adams cast the deciding vote for the motion.[6]

As a result of these actions, Congress passed legislation to adopt the same approach for the Departments of Foreign Affairs, War, and Treasury. The subordinate officers would have charge and custody of all records whenever the Secretary "shall be removed from office by the President of the United States."[7]

[3] Journal of the First Session of the Senate, I, 42 (1820). Vote occurred on July 18, 1789.

[4] Id. at 51 (August 4, 1789).

[5] Louis Fisher, President and Congress 86-87 (1972).

[6] Journal of the First Session of the Senate, I, 50, 62-63.

[7] 1 Stat. 29, 50, 67.

The fact that Congress recognized the President's freedom to remove department heads did not mean that the President could remove *all* administrative officials. Congress did not vest the entire removal power with him. When Madison turned his attention to the tenure of the Comptroller of the Treasury, he said that it was necessary "to consider the nature of this office." Its properties were not "purely of an Executive nature," he said. "It seems to me that they partake of a Judiciary quality as well as Executive; perhaps the latter obtains in the greatest degree." Because of the mixed nature of the office, "there may be strong reasons why an officer of this kind should not hold his office at the pleasure of the Executive branch of the Government."[8] Madison's insight would hold the attention of scholars and the courts more than a century later.

It is interesting to note that Hamilton retreated from his position in Federalist 77. In 1793, in his Pacificus essays, he offered a broad interpretation of executive power. With the exception of the Senate's participation in the appointment of officers and in the making of treaties, and the power of Congress to declare war and grant letters of marque and reprisal, Hamilton contended that "the *executive power* of the United States is completely lodged in the President. This mode of construing the Constitution has indeed been recognized by Congress in formal acts, upon full consideration and debate; of which the power of removal from office is an important instance."[9]

Controversies from Jackson to Cleveland

Congress has authority to create an office and specify the term of office. May it also specify the manner in which an incumbent is removed? This issue, offered here as an academic riddle, assumed solid form with Andrew Jackson in the White House.

Jackson's predecessors had used the removal power with restraint. The opportunity for removals, however, expanded con-

---

[8] Annals of Congress, I, 611-12 (June 27, 1789).
[9] The Works of Alexander Hamilton (Lodge ed.), IV, 439. Emphasis in original.

siderably in 1820 when Congress passed legislation that limited a large number of federal officers to a term of four years, stipulating that they would be "removable from office at pleasure."[10] Supported by this legislative authority and by his own philosophy favoring rotation of federal personnel, Jackson removed more officers than all of the Presidents who preceded him (252 for Jackson compared to 193 for his predecessors).[11] These numbers, though large, are less impressive as a proportion of the growing bureaucracy and do not constitute anything near the "clean sweep" suggested by some historians.[12]

Congressional opposition to Jackson's policy came to a head in 1833 when he removed the Secretary of the Treasury for refusing to carry out his policy toward the national bank. At issue was more than the removal power. Congress regarded Treasury with proprietary interest, often treating the Secretary as *its* agent. It had, for example, delegated to the Secretary—not the President—the responsibility for placing government funds either in national banks or state banks. The Senate responded to Jackson's action by passing a resolution of censure: "*Resolved*, That the President, in the late Executive proceedings in relation to the public revenue, has assumed upon himself authority and power not conferred by the Constitution and laws, but in derogation of both."

Jackson, outraged that the Senate should censure him on the basis of unspecified charges, without an opportunity to be heard and in circumvention of the formal constitutional procedure for impeachment, prepared a lengthy and impassioned protest. With great force he argued that the Constitution vested in the President the executive power, requiring him to take care that the laws be faithfully executed. That made him, he said, "responsible for the entire action of the executive department." Following this logic, the President had a right to employ agents of his own choice to aid him. When no longer willing to be responsible for

---

[10] 3 Stat. 582.

[11] Haynes, The Senate of the United States, II, at 793; Leonard D. White, The Jacksonians 317-21 (1954).

[12] Erik McKinley Eriksson, "The Federal Civil Service under President Jackson," 13 Miss. Valley Hist. Rev. 517 (1927).

their acts, he could remove them. Jackson regarded the Secretary of the Treasury as "wholly an executive officer."[13] Three years later the Senate ordered its resolution of censure expunged from the record.[14] Millard Fillmore, in his first annual message to Congress in 1850, suggested that in the case of "unfortunate" administrative appointments it would be proper for the President to exercise the power of removal.[15]

The removal power ripened into a poisonous dispute during the administration of Andrew Johnson. Even before he took office, Congress had begun to trench upon the President's removal power. Legislation in 1863 created a Comptroller of the Currency to hold office for the term of five years "unless sooner removed by the President, by and with the advice and consent of the Senate." Two years later Congress passed legislation to permit military and naval officers, upon dismissal by the President, to apply for a trial.[16]

Congress continued this policy in 1867 by passing the Tenure of Office Act. Every person holding civil office with the advice and consent of the Senate became entitled to hold office until the President appointed a successor, with the advice and consent of the Senate. The bill further provided that the Secretaries of State, Treasury, War, Navy, and Interior, the Postmaster General, and the Attorney General should hold office during the term of the President who appointed them, and for one month thereafter, "subject to removal by and with the advice and consent of the Senate." During Senate recess the President could suspend an official but would have to report to the Senate, upon its return, the evidence and reasons for the suspension. If the Senate concurred in his action the suspended officer would be removed.

[13] Richardson, Messages and Papers, III, 1288-1312. Jackson also rebuffed the Senate's effort to obtain "copies of the charges, if any," relating to the removal of a federal employee. He said that, in cases of this nature, the President possessed the "exclusive power of removal from office." Id. at 1352.

[14] Register of Debates, 24th Cong., 2d Sess. 379-418, 427-506 (1837); S. Journal, 24th Cong., 2d Sess. 123-24 (April 15, 1834).

[15] Richardson, Messages and Papers, VI, 2616 (Dec. 2, 1850).

[16] 12 Stat. 666 sec. 1 (1863); 13 Stat. 489, sec. 12 (1865).

If the Senate refused to concur, the suspended officer would resume the functions of his office.[17]

Here was a frontal challenge to presidential control over his own officers. Johnson vetoed the bill, claiming that it violated the Constitution and the construction placed upon it by the debate of 1789. His message was well reasoned and fully documented. But Congress, caught up in the fierce politics of that time, was not receptive to facts or argument. Both Houses promptly overrode his veto.[18]

Johnson had hoped that the disruptive voice in his Cabinet, Secretary of War Edwin M. Stanton, would resign. He did not. As the months rolled by and the political crisis deepened, Johnson decided to suspend Stanton. The Senate returned from its recess and refused to concur in the suspension. Johnson upped the ante by *removing* Stanton, with the expectation that the constitutionality of the Tenure of Office Act would be tested in the courts. Yet because of the actions of Ulysses S. Grant, whom Johnson had installed as War Secretary ad interim, and Lorenzo Thomas, Grant's successor, the tactic backfired. Stanton was able to regain his office. Johnson's strategy merely fanned the fire of impeachment that had been smoldering for a year, a movement that fell one vote short in the Senate.[19]

The political extravagance of Congress did not go unnoticed. President Grant, in his first annual message in 1869, recommended that Congress repeal the Tenure of Office Act. To him the law was inconsistent with efficient administration: "What faith can an Executive put in officials forced upon him, and those, too, whom he has suspended for reason?" Congress revised the act that year, softening the suspension section but retaining the Senate's involvement in the removal process.[20]

[17] 14 Stat. 430.

[18] Richardson, Messages and Papers, VIII, 3690-94 (March 2, 1867); 14 Stat. 430 (1867).

[19] Lately Thomas, The First President Johnson 484-618 (1968); Raoul Berger, Impeachment 252-96 (1973); Harold M. Hyman, "Johnson, Stanton, and Grant: A Reconsideration of the Army's Role in the Events Leading to Impeachment," 66 Am. Hist. Rev. 85 (1960).

[20] Richardson, Messages and Papers, IX, 3992; 16 Stat. 6 (1869).

Congress continued to expand the Senate's role. Legislation in 1872 required the Postmaster General and his three assistants to be appointed by the President, by and with the advice and consent of the Senate, and provided that they might be "removed in the same manner." In 1876 Congress required the Senate's advice and consent for the removal of all first-, second-, and third-class postmasters.[21]

A new confrontation between President and Congress occurred from 1885 to 1886, after Grover Cleveland suspended several hundred officials and refused to deliver certain papers and documents to the Senate. Cleveland declared that the power to remove or suspend executive officials was vested solely in the President by the Constitution, particularly by the "executive power" and "take care" clauses. He also noted that the law governing suspensions, as amended in 1869, did not justify the Senate's request for documents. Because of this dispute, Congress repealed the Tenure of Office Act in 1887.[22]

Court Interpretations: 1789 to 1926

Myers v. *United States* (1926) represents the first full-scale judicial decision on the removal power, but the issue had been explored by courts throughout the nineteenth century. In *Marbury* v. *Madison*, Chief Justice Marshall noted that the President had discretion over an office until an appointment is made. Thereafter "his power over the office is terminated in all cases, where by law the officer is not removable by him. The right to the office is *then* in the person appointed, and he has the absolute, unconditional power of accepting or rejecting it."[23] Marshall reasoned

[21] 17 Stat. 284, sec. 2; 19 Stat. 80, sec. 6.

[22] Richardson, Messages and Papers, X, 4960-68 (March 1, 1886); 16 Stat. 7, sec. 2 (1869); 24 Stat. 500 (1887). This incident is described in detail in Grover Cleveland, The Independence of the Executive 25-82 (1913), and Louis Fisher, "Grover Cleveland Against the Senate," 7 Cong. Studies 11 (1979).

[23] Marbury v. Madison, 5 U.S. (1 Cr.) 137, 162 (1803). Emphasis in original. In Myers v. United States, 272 U.S. 52, 139-42 (1926), Chief Justice Taft stated that the President's removal power was not before the court in *Marbury*. Justice McReynolds, dissenting in the Myers case, argued (at 201-02) that *Marbury* had expressly repudiated the claim that the President could remove officials contrary to congressional directives.

that since Congress had given Marbury's office a tenure of five years, he had a right to serve for that duration. This argument suggested that Congress could circumscribe the President's removal power by statute.

In 1839 the Supreme Court gave its first full attention to the nature of the removal power. *Ex parte Hennen* concerned the removal of a clerk by a new federal judge, who, although praising the clerk's record, wanted to give the office to a personal friend. Justice Thompson, speaking for a unanimous Court, said that the power to appoint a clerk had been vested exclusively in the lower court. The Supreme Court had no control over the appointment or removal, nor could it entertain any inquiry into the grounds for removal. If the judge had abused his power the plaintiff was advised to seek relief elsewhere—just how or where the Court did not say.[24]

In 1854 the Court ruled on President Pierce's authority to remove Aaron Goodrich as chief justice of the Supreme Court for the territory of Minnesota. The Attorney General had advised the President that he possessed the power to remove territorial judges "for any cause that may, in your judgment, require it."[25] Goodrich went to court to recover the pay for his unexpired term of office. Here was a novel and sensitive issue: the President's removal power directed against a sitting judge (not a potential member of the judiciary, as in *Marbury*). Still, it was not such a direct clash between the President and the judiciary. Territorial judges were not judges within Article III of the Constitution. Goodrich served as judge of a "legislative court," established to carry out Article I duties, not a constitutional court.

Although the attorneys who argued the case spent considerable time examining the nature of the removal power, Justice Daniel, delivering the opinion of the Court, rested his decision on narrower ground. The true question, he said, related neither to the tenure of the judicial office nor to the powers and functions of the President. Instead, it was a question whether a court could command the withdrawal of money from the Treasury to settle the claim. The particular facts of the case convinced the Court

[24] Ex parte Hennen, 13 Pet. 230 (1839).
[25] 5 Op. Att'y Gen. 288, 291 (1851).

that the administrative action was executive in nature, requiring judgment and discretion, and could not be reviewed and countermanded by the courts. Justice Curtis filed a separate opinion, joined by Justice Nelson, Grier, and Campbell, agreeing that a writ of mandamus to the Secretary of the Treasury was not an available remedy. He expressed no opinion on any other question argued by attorneys.[26]

Justice McLean dissented. He did not agree with the reasoning that gave the President removal power as an incident to the appointing power. Nevertheless, as applied to executive officers, he concluded that the removal power "has been, perhaps, too long established and exercised to be now questioned." But extending the President's removal power to judicial officers was another matter. The presidential duty to see that the laws are faithfully executed, and the President's responsibility over administrators, related to political, not judicial, officers of the government. The President's power to superintend the executive departments gave him no control over the actions of the judiciary. Justice McLean warned that whenever "any portion of the judicial power shall become subject to the executive, there will be an end to its independence and purity."[27] He regarded the payment of money to Goodrich as a ministerial act and therefore subject to mandamus proceedings.

Another removal case in 1886 involved the discharge of a naval cadet engineer who sued for his pay. The Court of Claims upheld his position without passing judgment on the President's removal power (the cadet had been removed by the Secretary of the Navy) or the authority of Congress to restrict that power. The court stated that when Congress, by law, vests the appointment of officers in the heads of departments, "it may limit and restrict the power of removal as it deems best for the public interest." Since the naval officer had not been found deficient at any examination and had not been dismissed for misconduct under the provisions of law, not sentenced by court-martial (also

26 United States v. Guthrie, 58 U.S. (17 How.) 284, 305.

27 Id. at 310. For a later decision upholding the right of the President to suspend a territorial judge and replace him with someone else, prior to the completion of his term of office, see McAllister v. United States, 141 U.S. 175 (1891).

pursuant to law), he was still in office and entitled to the pay attached to it. The Supreme Court unanimously affirmed the judgment of the Court of Claims.[28]

A decision in 1897, *Parsons* v. *United States*, involved President Cleveland's removal of a U.S. attorney. Parsons maintained that his commission for a four-year term had been illegally abridged by the President. The Supreme Court declined to answer the constitutional question. After reviewing many precedents, including the repeal of the Tenure of Office Act, it concluded in a unanimous decision that the President may remove an officer "when in his discretion he regards it for the public good, although the term of office may have been limited by the words of the statute creating the office."[29]

Another unanimous opinion by the Supreme Court, in *Shurtleff* v. *United States* (1903), dealt with President McKinley's removal of a customs official. Congress had specified "inefficiency, neglect of duty, or malfeasance in office" as the statutory grounds on which the President could remove such officers. McKinley did not act for any of these causes. The Court held that Congress could restrict the President to specified causes only if the statute clearly eliminated his general power of removal. The removal power inhered in the right to appoint, "unless limited by Constitution or statute. It requires plain language to take it away."[30]

In 1922 the Supreme Court decided *Wallace* v. *United States*, precipitated by President Wilson's dismissal of an officer from the Quartermaster Corps. The officer claimed that he had been wrongfully dismissed and applied unsuccessfully for trial by court-martial. He then brought suit in the Court of Claims to recover salary. Unsuccessful there, he turned to the Supreme Court. Chief

[28] United States v. Perkins, 116 U.S. 483, 485 (1886).

[29] Parsons v. United States, 167 U.S. 324, 343 (1897). For an earlier opinion by Attorney General Roger B. Taney, supporting the President's power to remove a district attorney, see 2 Op. Att'y Gen. 482, 489 (1831).

[30] Shurtleff v. United States, 189 U.S. 311, 316 (1903). Also regarding the right of Congress to limit presidential removals to causes prescribed by law: Reagan v. United States, 182 U.S. 419 (1901). Regarding other statutory restrictions on the removal power, see Blake v. United States, 103 U.S. (13 Otto.) 227 (1881) and Burnap v. United States, 252 U.S. 512 (1920).

Justice Taft, in a unanimous decision, reviewed the legislative restrictions that had been imposed upon the President's power to remove an army officer. He concluded that the restrictions did not apply since the President had submitted the name of another officer to take the place of the one dismissed and the Senate had given its consent. Taft presumed that the Senate knew that its confirmation would fill the legal complement of such officers and, to that extent, supported the President's removal.[31] This treatment allowed Taft to duck some central issues. Could Congress, by statute, restrict the President's removal power? If the President violated those restrictions, why was the Senate's participation in the violation legally significant? Within a few years Taft would have an opportunity to explore those questions more fully.

The Myers Case and Its Progeny

The Supreme Court's record on the removal power, though marked largely by unanimous holdings, contained many inconsistencies. The tension finally erupted in the celebrated case of *Myers* v. *United States* (1926). Since the litigation resulted from Woodrow Wilson's action, we need to review his earlier pronouncements on the removal power.

In 1920 Wilson opposed a section of the Budget and Accounting bill that reserved to Congress a role in the removal of the Comptroller General and the Assistant Comptroller General. They could be taken from office by impeachment, concurrent resolution, "and in no other manner." A concurrent resolution, which requires the consent of the House and Senate, is not sent to the President for his signature. Wilson vetoed the bill, expressing his conviction that Congress lacked constitutional power to "limit the appointing power and its incident, the power of removal derived from the Constitution."[32] Congress revised the bill to require a joint resolution (which does go to the President) and President Harding signed the bill into law. But even as modified, the bill allowed Congress to *initiate* a removal.[33]

[31] Wallace v. United States, 257 U.S. 541, 545-46 (1922).
[32] H. Doc. No. 805, 66th Cong., 2d Sess. (1920).
[33] 42 Stat. 24, sec. 303 (1921).

Wilson's dispute with the Supreme Court resulted from the appointment of Frank S. Myers, postmaster at Portland, Oregon, to a four-year term in 1917. Prior to the expiration of the term the Postmaster General removed him, an action concurred in by Wilson. This removal specifically violated the act of 1876, which required the Senate's advice and consent for the removal of all first-, second-, and third-class postmasters. Myers brought suit in the Court of Claims to recover his salary.

Attorneys for Myers, in their presentation to the Supreme Court, argued that the appointment of postmasters derived from a statute passed pursuant to a power granted Congress by the Constitution ("to establish post offices and post roads"). Congress could therefore attach to that office any conditions it desired. Solicitor General Beck, arguing for the administration, maintained that the law of 1876 could be held unconstitutional "without assuming the absolute power of the President to remove any executive officer."[34]

Chief Justice Taft, writing for a 6-to-3 majority, opted for a broader interpretation of presidential power—too broad, in fact, to withstand scholarly analysis and subsequent court holdings. Taft even parted company with his own reasonable position in *Wallace* (1922), where he had held that "*at least in absence of restrictive legislation*, the President, though he could not appoint without the consent of the Senate, could remove without such consent in the case of any officer whose tenure was not fixed by the Constitution."[35] Four years later Taft asserted that the President's power of removal was unrestricted, even in the presence of statutory limitations. From the congressional debates of 1789 he decided that there was not the "slightest doubt" that the power to remove officers appointed by the President and the Senate is "vested in the President alone."[36] This was a reckless conclusion, for the record in 1789 reveals deep divisions among members of the House and close votes on the Senate side. Moreover, many of the legislators supported presidential power because the office

---

[34] Myers v. United States, 272 U.S. 52, 61, 98 (1926).
[35] Wallace v. United States, 257 U.S. 541, 544 (1922). Emphasis added.
[36] Myers v. United States, 272 U.S. at 114.

in question was Secretary of Foreign Affairs, an agent of the President and executive in nature.

Taft recognized that the Court had, in the *Shurtleff* case, agreed that Congress might restrict the President's power by specifying causes for removal. He realized also that Congress, in establishing regulatory agencies (beginning with the Interstate Commerce Commission in 1887), had specified causes for removal: inefficiency, neglect of duty, or malfeasance in office. Still, he held that the postmaster law of 1876 was "in violation of the Constitution and invalid."[37]

Justice Holmes, in the first of three dissents, called the Chief Justice's arguments "spider's webs inadequate to control the dominant facts." Justice McReynolds's dissent identified many of the statutes that prescribed restrictions on removals. Protected by these restrictions were members of the Interstate Commerce Commission, the Board of General Appraisers, the Federal Reserve Board, the Federal Trade Commission, the Tariff Commission, and the Shipping Board, among others.[38]

The third dissenter, Justice Brandeis, conceded that the power to remove (or suspend) a high political officer "might conceivably be deemed indispensable to democratic government and, hence, inherent in the President." But he flatly denied that the President's ability to remove an inferior administrative officer, such as a postmaster, was essential to the workings of government.[39]

Taft's decision provoked immediate criticism from the academic community. The most devastating rebuke came from Edward S. Corwin, whose monograph, *The President's Removal Power Under the Constitution*, appeared in 1927. Corwin did not object too strongly to the proposition that when an executive officer is appointed by the President, with the advice and consent of the Senate, the removal power belongs to the President alone. Such a conclusion, although "decidedly vulnerable on both historical and logical grounds, is not improbably supported by practical considerations."[40]

[37] Id. at 171, 176.
[38] Id. at 177, 181.
[39] Id. at 241, 247.
[40] Edward S. Corwin. The President's Removal Power Under the Constitution vi (1927).

What Corwin found intolerable was the more sweeping prop-osition that *any* executive officer could be removed by the Pres-ident. Such a notion denied Congress any right to determine the tenure of an officer. A balance had to be reached, said Corwin, between the President's removal power and the power of Con-gress to create an office under the "necessary and proper" clause. To Corwin, this balance depended on the nature of the office involved. For example, he believed that a member of the Inter-state Commerce Commission did not exercise power that re-sulted from presidential authority, either constitutional or statu-tory. The commissioner's powers derived from a delegation by Congress of its own express power under the Constitution.[41] But this distinction does not resolve the issue; officers in the execu-tive departments also derive their powers and duties from Con-gress.

Corwin said that Presidents had been able to live with a num-ber of statutory restrictions on their removal power. Procedural safeguards existed for personnel in the classified civil service; they could not be removed "except for such cause as will promote the efficiency of said service and for reasons given in writing, and the person whose removal is sought shall have notice of the same and of any charges preferred against him." Federal employees had the right to join unions; no postal employee could be re-duced in rank or dismissed for joining such an organization. Civil service employees had the right to petition Congress without fear of removal. Congress had passed many other statutes to specify the causes for removal from regulatory commissions. Corwin's reading of the debates of 1789 led him to reject Taft's conclusion that a vast majority of the members of the House believed that removal was an incident of the executive power. Instead, Corwin said, Congress found that those who held to that theory "were a fraction of a fraction, a minority of a minority."[42] Somewhere between Corwin's and Taft's views on the debates of 1789 lies the truth.

Corwin could not delineate with any precision the boundaries

[41] Id. at v-viii; reproduced with little change as "Tenure of Office and the Removal Power Under the Constitution," 27 Colum. L. Rev. 353 (1927).

[42] Corwin, The President's Removal Power Under the Constitution, at 4, 22-23.

between executive-legislative prerogatives over the removal power. He asserted that the power of Congress was not absolute, any more than the President's, for it was "conditioned in each case by the nature of the office being dealt with as shown particularly by the source and nature of its powers."[43] But who decides "nature" and with what criteria?

This issue reached the Supreme Court in 1935 in *Humphrey's Executor* v. *United States*. William E. Humphrey, nominated by President Hoover for the Federal Trade Commission (FTC) in 1931, had been confirmed by the Senate. The FTC Act allowed the President to remove a commissioner for "inefficiency, neglect of duty, or malfeasance in office." On July 25, 1933, President Roosevelt asked Humphrey to resign, explaining that the "aims and purposes of the Administration with respect to the work of the Commission can be carried out most effectively with personnel of my own selection." The following month he wrote Humphrey: "I do not feel that your mind and my mind go along together on either the policies or the administering of the Federal Trade Commission." The bitterness of the conflict was foreshadowed by Humphrey's letter to Roosevelt, in which he described unnamed enemies who came with "slanderous and polluted lips and spew their putrid filth upon you under the pledge of secrecy." Humphrey railed against "mental perverts who glorify treachery and intellectual dishonesty."[44] After Humphrey refused to submit his resignation, Roosevelt removed him for policy reasons rather than those specified in the FTC Act.[45]

Justice Sutherland, delivering a unanimous opinion, described the FTC as charged with the enforcement of "no policy except the policy of the law. Its duties are neither political nor executive, but predominantly quasi-judicial and quasi-legislative." "Quasi," of course, is no more precise a term than Corwin's "nature," but Sutherland felt confident that a distinction could be drawn between the executive duties of a postmaster (the Myers case) and

[43] Id. at 66.

[44] William E. Leuchtenburg, "The Case of the Contentious Commissioner: Humphrey's Executor v. U.S.," in Harold M. Hyman and Leonard W. Levy, eds., *Freedom and Reform: Essays in Honor of Henry Steele Commager* 289 (1967).

[45] Humphrey's Executor v. United States, 295 U.S. 602, 618-19 (1935).

the duties of a Federal Trade Commissioner. The FTC "cannot in any proper sense be characterized as an arm or an eye of the executive."[46]

Corwin, although applauding the narrowing of Taft's holding, did not like Sutherland's classification of the FTC. If a Federal Trade Commissioner was not in the executive department, Corwin asked, "where is he? In the legislative department; or is he, forsooth, in the uncomfortable halfway situation of Mahomet's coffin, suspended 'twixt Heaven Earth?" Instead of conjuring up a fourth branch, floating independently, Corwin wanted to preserve the existing three branches of government. He regarded all nonjudicial agencies established to carry out the law as being "executive" in the sense of the Constitution.[47] Justice Jackson, in a later case, also voiced exasperation with the location of regulatory agencies in our tripartite system: "The mere retreat to the qualifying 'quasi' is implicit with confession that all recognized classifications have broken down, and 'quasi' is a smooth cover which we draw over our confusion as we might use a counterpane to conceal a disordered bed."[48]

In his closing paragraph, Sutherland admitted that there existed a "field of doubt" between *Myers* and *Humphrey's*: "we leave such cases as may fall within it for future consideration and determination as they may arise."[49] The "field of doubt" was soon in the courts because of a bitter, long-festering, and frustrating disagreement that threatened to paralyze the Tennessee Valley Authority (TVA). Arthur E. Morgan, chairman of the board of directors, was locked in a nasty feud with his fellow directors. He resisted President Roosevelt's effort to negotiate a settlement, claiming that Congress alone was the proper party to investigate the dispute. The President, after weeks of discussion, told Morgan either to withdraw publicly the charges he had made against his colleagues or to resign. When Morgan chose to do neither, Roosevelt removed him.[50]

[46] Id. at 624, 627-28.

[47] Corwin, The President, at 93, 378-79.

[48] FTC v. Ruberoid Co., 343 U.S. 470, 487-88 (1952).

[49] Humphrey's Executor 295 U.S. at 632.

[50] For background on Morgan's removal see C. Herman Pritchett, The Tennessee Valley Authority 203-15 (1943). A transcript of White House hearings,

The TVA Act required that appointments and promotions be made on the basis of "merit and efficiency." Any member of the Board of Directors found by the President "to be guilty of a violation of this section shall be removed from office by the President." The act also made board members subject to removal at any time by concurrent resolution. (Recall that Woodrow Wilson vetoed the Budget and Accounting Bill because it permitted removal by that very instrument.)

Morgan, seeking judicial relief, had his complaint dismissed by a district court. Although admitting that FDR's action was not specifically based on statutory considerations, the court did not find in the TVA Act a clear enough intent by Congress to limit the executive power over removals. Echoing the holding in the *Shurtleff* case, it stated that there had to be "plain language" in a statute to take away that power.[51]

The district court's opinion was upheld unanimously by an appellate court. Morgan's attorney argued that Congress deliberately intended to restrict the President's removal power by employing a concurrent (rather than joint) resolution for congressional removal. The court rejected this argument, and insisted that Congress, if that had been its intention, could have expressed its will in unequivocal terms. Also, during the time that the case was pending in the district court, Roosevelt sent to the Senate the name of James P. Pope to succeed Morgan and the Senate confirmed the appointment. Its action implied that at least one House of Congress did not oppose Morgan's removal. The appellate court also regarded the TVA as predominantly an administrative arm of the executive branch and therefore distinguishable from the regulatory commission involved in *Humphrey's*. The Supreme Court refused to review the case.[52]

---

conducted by President Roosevelt in the presence of Chairman Morgan and the other two directors of TVA, is reprinted in S. Doc. No. 155, 75th Cong., 3d Sess. (1938). Acting Attorney General Robert H. Jackson had advised FDR that the TVA was an executive agency and its members could be removed by the President; 39 Op. Att'y Gen. 145 (1938).

[51] Morgan v. TVA, 28 F.Supp. 732 (E.D. Tenn. 1939).

[52] Morgan v. TVA, 115 F.2d 990 (6th Cir. 1940), cert. denied, 312 U.S. 701 (1941). Arthur Larson, "Has the President an Inherent Power of Removal of his

More akin to the circumstances in *Humphrey's* was President Eisenhower's removal of a member of the War Claims Commission. The enabling statute, anticipating a short-lived agency, made no provision for removal. Eisenhower removed an official on the ground that the act should be administered "with personnel of my own selection." The Court of Claims dismissed the plaintiff's suit, but the Supreme court, in *Wiener* v. *United States* (1958), unanimously reversed this decision. It held that the President had no power under the Constitution or the statute to remove a member from the War Claims Commission. The agency's task, said the Court, had an "intrinsic judicial character." Congress had explicitly rejected a legislative option that would have placed responsibility with the administration. Congress could not, therefore, have wanted to hang over the head of the commission "the Damocles' sword of removal" for no other reason than that the President wanted his own man. By the time the commission went out of existence, the Senate still had not confirmed Eisenhower's nominee.[53]

Disloyalty Dismissals and Procedural Safeguards

As a result of congressional action and various executive orders, federal employees have been removed from office on the charge that they represented a security risk. One of the more flagrant legislative efforts came in 1943 when the chairman of the House Un-American Activities Committee announced that thirty-nine federal employees were "irresponsible, unrepresentative, crackpot radical bureaucrats" and affiliates of "Communist-front organizations." A special subcommittee, created to examine his sensational allegations, subsequently accused three of the employees of engaging in "subversive activity." By attaching an amendment

---

Non-Executive Appointees?" 16 Tenn. L. Rev. 259 (1940), did not agree that the TVA was a predominantly executive agency. He concluded that the members of the TVA, the Securities and Exchange Commission, the Federal Communications Commission, the Federal Power Commission, and the Employees Compensation Commission could not be removed by the President under any circumstances.

[53] Wiener v. United States, 357 U.S. 349 (1958)

to an appropriations bill, Congress prohibited the use of public funds for salaries to the three individuals. Counsel for Congress contended that congressional power over appropriations was plenary and not subject to judicial review.[54] In *United States* v. *Lovett* (1946), however, the Supreme Court struck down that use of legislative power because it inflicted punishment without a judicial trial and therefore violated the Constitution's prohibition against bills of attainder.[55]

Congressional use of purse strings to remove "disloyal" workers from federal employment was rebuffed again in 1982. Language in an appropriations bill stated that "None of the funds appropriated or otherwise made available by the Act may be used, pursuant to the Comprehensive Employment Training Act, for the participation of individuals who publicly advocate the violent overthrow of the Federal Government, or who have within the past five years, publicly advocated the violent overthrow of the Federal Government." This language, as amplified by the legislative history, was meant to exclude from the CETA program Dorothy Blitz, member of the Communist Workers Party. She challenged the language as a violation of her right of free speech under the First Amendment and a violation of the Bill of Attainder Clause. A federal court in 1982 agreed that the "Blitz Amendment" failed to draw a line between mere advocacy (protected by the Constitution) and advocacy that incites and is likely to produce violent action. Having found the statutory language contrary to the First Amendment, the court did not address the question of bill of attainder.[56]

Congress has adopted more general standards to regulate federal workers suspected of disloyalty. In 1950 it passed legislation to permit certain agencies to suspend civilian employees whenever "necessary in the interest of national security."[57] As later rewritten, the authority extended to the Departments of State, Commerce, Justice, and Defense; the military departments; the

[54] 89 Cong. Rec. 4583 (1943); United States v. Lovett, 328 U.S. 303, 306-07 (1946).

[55] 328 U.S. 303 (1946).

[56] Blitz v. Donovan, 538 F.Supp. 1119 (D.D.C. 1982).

[57] 64 Stat. 476 (1950).

Coast Guard; the Atomic Energy Commission (whose duties were later assigned to the Energy Department and to the Nuclear Regulatory Commission); the National Aeronautics and Space Administration; and any "such other agency of the Government of the United States as the President designates in the best interests of national security." If the agency head determines that the "interests of national security permit," he may notify the employee of the reasons for the suspension.[58]

Once suspended, an employee has access to procedural safeguards before being removed. An employee with a permanent or indefinite appointment, who has completed his probationary or trial period and who is a citizen of the United States, is entitled to these protections before removal: (1) a written statement of the charges within thirty days after suspension, stated as specifically as security considerations permit; (2) an opportunity to answer the charges and submit affidavits; (3) a hearing (at the employee's request) by an agency authority constituted for that purpose; (4) a review of the case by the agency head or designee before a decision adverse to the employee is made final; and (5) a written statement of the decision.

Administrative actions can be challenged in the courts. An appellate court decision in 1950 concerned the removal of Dorothy Bailey from her federal job on the ground of disloyalty. Although she was given notice, an opportunity for a hearing, and access to an appeal, the agency did not permit her to confront and cross-examine her secret accusers. The court rejected her plea for trial-type procedures, concluding that compliance with the Sixth Amendment was not a prerequisite for dismissing civil service employees. "Even in normal times," observed the court, "and as a matter of ordinary internal operation, the ability, integrity and loyalty of purely executive employees is exclusively for the executive branch of Government to determine, except in so far as the Congress has a constitutional voice in the matter." The court also noted that disloyalty in the government service "under present

---

[58] 64 Stat. 476 (1950), modified by 80 Stat. 529 (1966) and codified at 5 U.S.C. 7532 (1982).

circumstances" (the Cold War) was a matter of great public concern.[59]

Circuit Judge Edgerton, dissenting, demonstrated an appreciation for individual rights and procedural due process that would later find expression in Supreme Court rulings. He noted that Bailey occupied a "wholly nonsensitive position," that the informants had not been identified to her or even to the Regional Loyalty Board responsible for investigating her case, and that the informants did not make their statements under oath. In contrast, Bailey had denied under oath any membership in or relationship or sympathy with the Communist Party, any activities connected with it or with communism, and any affiliation with any organization that advocated the overthrow of the United States government. Judge Edgerton believed that the executive order that provided the standards for her dismissal required that employees should have an opportunity to cross-examine opposing witnesses. If secret accusers wanted to preserve their anonymity, the accused should be cleared or the proceedings dropped. Although Edgerton agreed that most dismissals from government employment were not punitive, did not require a judicial trial, and were within the authority of the executive, the dismissal of Dorothy Bailey constituted punishment—not for wrong conduct but for "wrong views." Dismissal for disloyalty was punitive in nature, as in the Lovett case, and the right of confrontation and cross-examination was essential for nonsensitive positions. The government had not demonstrated that the suspicion of the disloyalty indicated a security risk: *"Appellant's dismissal for wrong thoughts has nothing to do with protecting the security of the United States."*[60]

Corwin did not believe that federal employees dismissed for loyalty reasons were entitled to procedural safeguards. Even in cases of disloyalty it was "plausible doctrine that the President enjoys an overriding power of removal."[61] And what did Corwin

---

[59] Bailey v. Richardson, 182 F.2d 46, 51, 64 (D.C. Cir. 1950), aff'd per curiam by an equally divided Supreme Court, 341 U.S. 918 (1951).

[60] Bailey v. Richardson, 182 F.2d at 70. Emphasis in original.

[61] Corwin, The President, at 104, footnote omitted. Footnote 109, on page 385 of Corwin's work, refers to *Myers*, at 161.

use to document his position? None other than the majority opinion in the Myers case! The particular page of the decision cited by Corwin contains this statement by Chief Justice Taft: "The power to remove inferior executive officers, like that to remove superior executive officers, is an incident of the power to appoint them, and is in its nature an executive power." Corwin had excoriated the opinion when it first appeared. Why did he invoke it three decades later to support his argument? In his own value system the stigma of disloyalty did not have constitutional significance for the removal issue. To him it was a "unique proposition" that a court should stand in judgment against the determination of an executive official that someone is disloyal.[62] But why was it "unique" for a court to insist on procedural standards and constitutional rights for those accused of betraying their country?

Within a few years the Supreme Court began to place restrictions on administrative removals of so-called security risks. A leading case involved Kendrick Cole, removed from his position with the Department of Health, Education, and Welfare after an administrative investigation disclosed that he had associated with groups on the Attorney General's "subversive list." The Supreme Court in *Cole* v. *Young* (1956) decided that the term "national security," as used in the statute supporting the removal, related only to activities directly concerned with the nation's safety. Whereas the federal government could summarily suspend employees who occupied a "sensitive" position, this power did not extend to other positions. In view of the "stigma attached to persons dismissed on loyalty grounds," the need for procedural safeguards seemed even greater than in other cases.[63] The Court ruled that the administration's action did not conform to the governing statute and that Cole's discharge violated the procedures of the Veterans Preference Act (including the right to appeal to the Civil Service Commission).

Members of Congress tried to override the decision by specifically extending summary suspension powers to nonsensitive fed-

---

[62] Id. at 108, 110.
[63] 351 U.S. 536, 546 (1956).

eral jobs, but the effort failed. In other cases the Supreme Court insisted that individuals whose employment status had been jeopardized and injured by the federal government were entitled to confront and cross-examine their "faceless informers." When administrators felt legally unable to remove employees for loyalty reasons, they switched to grounds of "suitability" as established by civil service regulations.[64]

Through a series of holdings from the late 1960s to the early 1970s, the Supreme Court insisted that individuals could not be deprived of "property" or "liberty" without the protection of fundamental procedural safeguards, including notice and a hearing. This pattern was interrupted in 1974 by *Arnett* v. *Kennedy*, when a sharply divided (5 to 4) Court decided that a nonprobationary employee in the competitive civil service had been adequately protected by hearing procedures made available *after* his dismissal.[65]

The employee, Wayne Kennedy, claimed that the standards and procedures established by the Lloyd-LaFollette Act interfered with his freedom of expression and denied him procedural due process of law. Lloyd-LaFollette permits the removal of employees in the classified civil service "for such cause as will promote the efficiency of the service." An employee is entitled to reasons given in writing; notice of the action and of any charges preferred against her or him; a copy of the charges and reasonable time to file a written answer to them, with affidavits; and a written decision on the answer at the earliest practicable date.

[64] For congressional override efforts, see Walter F. Murphy, Congress and the Court 174-75, 218-19, 236 (1962). Other cases on employment rights: Service v. Dulles, 354 U.S. 363 (1957); Vitarelli v. Seaton, 359 U.S. 535 (1959); Greene v. McElroy, 360 U.S. 474 (1959); Cafeteria Workers v. McElroy, 367 U.S. 886 (1961). In Peters v. Hobby, 349 U.S. 331 (1955), the Court held that the Loyalty Review Board exceeded its delegated jurisdiction. For further discussion see C. Herman Pritchett, Congress Versus the Supreme Court 96-106 (1961). For "suitability" grounds, see H. Rept. No. 1637, 92d Cong., 2d. Sess. 61 (1973).

[65] Arnett v. Kennedy, 416 U.S. 134 (1974). For "property" and "liberty" issues, see Sniadach v. Family Finance Corp., 395 U.S. 337 (1969); Goldberg v. Kelly, 397 U.S. 254 (1970); Bell v. Burson, 402 U.S. 535 (1971); Lynch v. Household Finance Corp., 405 U.S. 538 (1972); and Perry v. Sindermann, 408 U.S. 593 (1972).

The act specifically states that the examination of witnesses, a trial, or a hearing, "is not required but may be provided in the discretion of the individual directing the removal or suspension without pay"[66] In addition to this statutory procedure, Kennedy had access to protections offered by Civil Service Commission and Office of Economic Opportunity regulations. Yet the Court decided that he could be removed prior to a hearing. If reinstated at some later date, he would receive full back pay.

A concurring opinion by Justice Powell, joined by Justice Blackmun, formed the 5-to-4 majority. Justice Powell balanced the government's interest against that of the employee, giving particular weight to the government's interest in removing employees whose conduct "hinders efficient operation and to do so with dispatch." Requirement of a prior evidentiary hearing, Powell said, "would impose additional administrative costs, create delay, and defer warranted discharges."[67]

The goal of government efficiency, used in this case to remove an employee, was later invoked by the Supreme Court to *protect* officeholders. Both of these later cases involved patronage dismissals at the local level. In *Elrod* v. *Burns* (1976), five members of the Court reached agreement only on one point: a public employee in a nonpolicymaking, nonconfidential position could not be fired solely on the ground of political belief or affiliation. Applying patronage removal to those with "limited responsibility" was inconsistent with First Amendment freedoms of speech and association. Moreover, the Court said that the wholesale replacement of public employees after each election would result in unwarranted inefficiency. The inability of the majority in *Elrod* to draw a clear line between policymaking and nonpolicymaking positions exposed the Court to criticism from dissenting Justices and scholars.[68] In *Branti* v. *Finkel* (1980), decided by a 6-to-3

[66] 37 Stat. 555, sec. 6 (1912), as amended by 62 Stat. 354 (1948), and codified at 5 U.S.C. 7501 (1976). Rewritten by the Civil Service Reform Act of 1978 and codified at 5 U.S.C. 7503 (1982).

[67] Arnett v. Kennedy, 416 U.S. at 168. See also Bishop v. Wood, 426 U.S. 341 (1976) for lack of a pretermination hearing.

[68] 427 U.S. 347, 369 (1976). See Leah M. Bishop "Patronage and the First Amendment After Elrod v. Burns," 78 Colum. L. Rev. 468 (1978); Kenneth J.

majority, the Court placed additional restrictions on patronage removals. The government had to demonstrate that party affiliation was an appropriate requirement for effective job performance.[69]

Public employees have a right under the First Amendment to comment upon matters "of public concern."[70] That right, however, does not prevent the removal of public employees who object to internal office conditions and attempt to organize opposition to superiors, even if the reasons for dismissal are alleged to be mistaken or unreasonable.[71]

Removal Actions from Nixon to Reagan

Although a large number of federal employees are formally protected from summary removal procedures, informal political pressures are sometimes used to force civil servants from office or place them in undesirable assignments. John M. McGee offended his superiors in the Navy Department during the late 1960s by talking about lax inspection procedures that permitted the theft of millions of gallons of fuel in Thailand. For his outspokenness the Navy reprimanded him and denied him an in-grade salary increase.[72]

The Air force meted out stiffer punishment to Ernest Fitzgerald, a procurement specialist. In response to Senator William Proxmire's question in 1968 about whether the C-5A cargo aircraft was running $2 billion above initial cost estimates, Fitzgerald called the figure "approximately right." The Pentagon, which had yet to acknowledge the cost overrun, took away Fitzgerald's civil service protection, assigned him menial tasks, searched into

Meier, "Ode to Patronage: A Critical Analysis of Two Recent Supreme Court Decisions," 41 Pub. Adm. Rev. 558 (1981).

[69] 445 U.S. 507 (1980).

[70] Pickering v. Board of Education, 391 U.S. 563 (1968).

[71] Connick v. Myers, 103 S.Ct. 1684 (1983).

[72] 115 Cong. Rec. 11045-48 (1969). See General Accounting Office, "Investigation in Thailand of the Systems for Distributing Petroleum, Oil, and Lubricants and for Processing Related Documentation," Report No. B-163928 (January 9, 1969).

his private life for incriminating evidence, and eventually fired him.[73] After more than a decade of arduous litigation, Fitzgerald won back his old job and, in 1982, was awarded legal fees and even gained a promotion. Former President Nixon, who in a taped White House conversation said of Fitzgerald "get rid of that son of a bitch," agreed in 1981 to pay Fitzgerald $142,000 to avoid a public trial.[74]

Fitzgerald's case has certain parallels with that of Gordon Rule, a naval procurement official who antagonized his superiors. In testimony before the Joint Economic Committee in 1972, he delivered his views with customary bluntness and spent the next day in bed recovering from laryngitis. There he received a visit from an admiral who asked him to sign a request for retirement. Rule, recipient of the Navy's highest civilian award the previous year, refused. His superiors tried to detail him to a training school to update its curriculum and had other pedestrian tasks in mind for him after that, but Rule fought successfully to retain his procurement responsibilities.[75]

The "Saturday Night Massacre" of 1973 catapulted the removal issue back into the courts. Archibald Cox, after pursuing presidential documents too assiduously for President Nixon's safety, was dismissed as Watergate special prosecutor. As an official in the executive branch, he would normally have been subject to presidential removal, but Nixon had relinquished that authority when the Justice Department released an order conferring an unusual degree of autonomy on the special prosecutor. The order gave Cox the "greatest degree of independence that is con-

[73] For more on the McGee and Fitzgerald incidents, see Senator William Proxmire, Report from Wasteland 25-47 (1970); "The Dismissal of A. Ernest Fitzgerald by the Department of Defense," hearings before the Joint Economic Committee, 91st Cong., 1st Sess. (1969).

[74] Washington Post, August 14, 1981, at A1, A11, and June 16, 1982, at A3; 128 Cong. Rec. S13392 (daily ed. October 1, 1982). In 1982 the Supreme Court held that Nixon, as a former President, was entitled to absolute immunity from damages related to the firing of Fitzgerald; Nixon v. Fitzgerald, 457 U.S. 731 (1982). For the extension of a qualified immunity to presidential aides involved in the Fitzgerald dismissal, see Harlow v. Fitzgerald, 457 U.S. 800 (1982).

[75] "The Acquisition of Weapons Systems" (Part 6), hearings before the Joint Economic Committee, 92d Cong., 2d Sess. 1821-1924, 2205-44 (1973).

sistent with the Attorney General's statutory accountability. . . .
The Attorney General will not countermand or interfere with the
Special Prosecutor's decisions or actions." According to the order from the Justice Department, the special prosecutor would
not be removed "except for extraordinary improprieties on his
part." Otherwise, he was to carry out his responsibilities "until
such time as, in his judgment, he has completed them or until a
date mutually agreed upon between the Attorney General and
himself."[76]

Ralph Nader and several members of Congress brought suit
against Robert Bork, Acting Attorney General, for discharging
Cox. The administration made no claim that Cox had been removed for "extraordinary improprieties." A district court did not
agree with Bork that the congressional plaintiffs lacked standing.
Nor was the controversy moot because Cox had returned to Har-
vard University and a new special prosecutor had been sworn in.
The issue was still alive. Legislation had been introduced relating
to Watergate and the new special prosecutor might be dismissed,
as the court noted, "if he presses too hard." The court held that
Cox had been illegally discharged from office.[77]

The Carter administration offered several proposals designed
to insulate the Justice Department from political pressures. One
idea was to prevent the removal of the Attorney General except
on a stated, rational basis. Carter's Attorney General, Griffin Bell,
explained in an interview: "We would like to put a system in
place where anybody that is Attorney General would have a feel-
ing of independence, even though he might not be completely
independent under the Constitution."[78] The Ethics Act of 1978
prohibits the removal of the special prosecutor except for extraordinary impropriety, physical disability, mental incapacity, or
"any other condition that substantially impairs the performance
of such special prosecutor's duties."[79]

After losing the contest over Archibald Cox, the Nixon administration was able to resist an effort by Congress to remove the

[76] 38 Fed. Reg. 14688 (1973).
[77] Nader v. Bork, 366 F. Supp. 104 (D.D.C 1973).
[78] Washington Post, Nov. 9, 1977, at A2:2.
[79] 92 Stat. 1869, sec. 596 (1978).

Director and Deputy Director of the Office of Management and Budget (Roy Ash and Frederick Malek). Congress wanted to abolish the two offices and to reestablish them subject to Senate confirmation. Nixon vetoed the bill in 1973 because it required "forced removal by an unconstitutional procedure." He did not dispute the authority of Congress to abolish an office, but said that the exercise of such power "cannot be used as a backdoor method of circumventing the President's power to remove." Congress, failing to override the veto, passed new legislation in 1974 that applied the confirmation process only to future OMB Directors and Deputy Directors.[80]

President Ford was able to ease out of office a member of a regulatory commission, the Civil Aeronautics Board (CAB). During June 1974 the chairman of the board, Robert D. Timm, spent a weekend in Bermuda as guest of the United Aircraft Corporation. Other guests included four airline executives whose firms had cases pending before the CAB. After the trip received publicity in the press and the House Commerce Committee conducted an investigation, Timm reimbursed United Aircraft for the expenses and disqualified himself from taking part in certain CAB proceedings. Additional congressional investigations revealed that he had made other trips with airline executives, often at their expense. By the end of the year the Ford administration announced that Timm would not be reappointed as chairman of the CAB.[81] The next question was whether he would remain on the board.

The issue picked up momentum in the fall of 1975 after Timm severely criticized the proposals of some members of the Ford administration. White House officials asked him to resign and planned a hearing to threaten removal and force his resignation. According to law, members of the CAB "may be removed by the

[80] 88 Stat. 11 (1974). Veto message: Public Papers of the Presidents, 1973, at 539. See Louis Fisher, Presidential Spending Power 51-55 (1975).

[81] The account in this paragraph is drawn from thirty-two newspaper and magazine articles, the more prominent ones being the Los Angeles Times, July 13, 1974, at 8; Wall Street Journal, August 21, 1974, at 13; New York Times, August 28, 1974, at 62; Washington Star-News, September 19, 1974, at A8; and Washington Star-News, December 20, 1974, at A1.

President for inefficiency, neglect of duty, or malfeasance in office." Timm regarded the hearing as unlawful, unauthorized, and a method of punishment for his positions on regulatory policy, particularly his opposition to administration policy. White House officials related the removal proceeding to Timm's "neglect of duty" and "inefficiency," in part stemming from the Bermuda trip. Although Timm denied all charges he resigned from office in December 1975.[82] In 1980 the U.S. Court of Claims rejected his argument that he was forced to resign and therefore entitled to back pay. Because he had had other courses of action, the court regarded his resignation as voluntary.[83]

The tension between Congress and the President on the removal power persisted under Presidents Carter and Reagan. In 1978 Carter objected to a bill that provided that "no person who is serving in an elected Federal, State, or local public office shall be eligible to serve or continue to serve" as a member of the Navajo and Hopi Indian Relocation Commission. Carter vetoed the bill because it "would oust incumbent members" of the commission if they happened to be these officials. Carter said the provision raised constitutional concerns "since it would allow for Congressional removal of officers in the Executive Branch." Interrupting the tenure of appointed officials by imposing new qualifications "should not be lightly undertaken." Congress could have sidestepped the constitutional issue by applying new qualifications only to future members of the commission. When Congress rewrote the bill, it deleted the section on qualifications.[84]

Also in 1978, Congress passed legislation requiring the President, when removing an Inspector General from office, to communicate his reasons to both Houses of Congress. The Office of Legal Counsel in the Justice Department considered this provision "an improper restriction on the President's exclusive power to remove Presidentially appointed executive officers."[85] In 1981

---

[82] Washington Star-News, September 9, 1975, at D7: 49 U.S.C. 1321(a) (2); Washington Post, December 11, 1975, at C1; Washington Star, December 11, 1975, at A3; Aviation Week & Space Technology, December 15, 1975, at 28.

[83] Timm v. United States, 223 Ct. Cl. 639 (1980).

[84] Public Papers of the Presidents, 1978, II, at 1925; 94 Stat. 929 (1980).

[85] 1 O.L.C. 18 (1977)

Reagan removed a dozen Inspectors General governed by the 1978 statute, but did not submit reasons to Congress other than a general desire to have nominees of his own choosing.[86]

Three other Reagan efforts were turned back by court action. In 1981 his removal of a member of the D.C. Judicial Nomination Commission was struck down by a federal judge, who ruled that the commission's sole function and duty is to exercise independent decisionmaking on merit qualifications. These duties are confined exclusively to local District of Columbia matters in which Congress, under the Constitution, has special supervisory responsibilities.[87] Reagan also tried to remove Democratic members of the U.S. Parole Commission but backed off after one member went to court and legislators from both Houses criticized his effort to interfere with the commission's independence.[88]

In 1983 President Reagan fired three Carter holdovers on the Commission on Civil Rights and nominated replacements who shared his positions on quotas, affirmative action, and busing. After a prolonged battle in the courts and in Congress, the commission was reconstituted to give the President authority for appointing only four of its eight members. The other four, including two of the Carter holdovers, would be named by Congress. Language was also added to allow the President to remove members "only for neglect of duty or malfeasance in office." The previous statute contained no provision for removal.[89]

Several other Reagan removals survived court challenges. Upon entering office, President Reagan imposed a hiring freeze on individuals who had been selected for federal jobs between November 5, 1980 and January 20, 1981. His order affected ap-

---

[86] 92 Stat. 1103, sec. 3(b) (1978); Wkly Comp. Pres. Doc., XVII, 27-28 (1981).

[87] Borders v. Reagan, 518 F. Supp. 250, 268 (D.D.C. 1981).

[88] Stephen Gettinger, "The Power Struggle Over Federal Parole," 8 Corrections Magazine 41 (1982).

[89] Berry v. Reagan, Civil Action No. 83-3182 (D.D.C. November 14, 1983); 97 Stat. 1301 (1983). See Dan Fagin, "In Winning the Battle for Rights Commission, Did Reagan Lose the War?," National Journal, December 17, 1983, at 2622-26.

proximately 20,000 people. Some had quit their former jobs in anticipation of a position with the federal government. An appellate court upheld his action by labeling most of the individuals "federal appointees" rather than federal employees. They therefore lacked the usual procedural safeguards provided against removal. In a few cases, individuals had access to possible remedies if their appointments had been improperly revoked.[90]

President Reagan triggered another court test in August 1981 through his response to a strike by the Professional Air Traffic Controllers Organization (PATCO). He announced that the controllers who failed to report for duty within forty-eight hours would forfeit their jobs. About 11,400 PATCO members were subsequently discharged and told they would not be rehired. The government's action found support in the courts, but the discharge can be interpreted not so much as an act of presidential discretion as an obligation to enforce anti-strike legislation passed by Congress.[91]

In a later case, Reagan's Secretary of Labor removed two members of the Benefits Review Board in 1982 without specifying his reasons or providing them with a hearing. Although the Board performed adjudicatory duties, it was not an Article III court entitled to life tenure. The statute establishing the board provided neither for the members' tenure nor for the terms of their removal. The Secretary's action was upheld by an appellate court on the ground that, in the face of statutory silence, the officers served at the discretion of the appointing officer.[92]

The Congressional Presence

As originally justified, the removal power was intended to protect the unity and responsibility of the executive. Because of the authority of Congress to create an office and attach conditions

[90] National Treasury Employees Union v. Reagan, 663 F.2d 239 (D.C. Cir. 1981).

[91] United States v. PATCO, 524 F. Supp. 160 (D.D.C. 1981).

[92] Kalaris v. Donovan, 697 F.2d 376 (D.C. Cir. 1983), cert. denied, 103 S.Ct. 3088 (1983).

to it—especially regarding tenure and cause for dismissal—the removal power has been sharply curtailed over the years.

Congress may remove an individual by abolishing the office. A term of office created by one statute can be reduced or eliminated by a subsequent statute requiring the discharge of a federal employee.[93] Congress has available a wide assortment of tools to force federal workers out of office, even at the top policymaking level. One scholar of executive-legislative relations estimated that congressional pressure is responsible for more firings and reassignments of executive branch personnel than presidential actions.[94]

Although the President remains theoretically responsible for the operation of the executive branch, this expectation has become increasingly unrealistic with the growth of the federal bureaucracy, the creation of agencies and commissions charged with legislative and judicial functions, civil service reform, and procedural safeguards imposed by the courts. With each development the President's removal power suffered some shrinkage until it now applies, in general, only to major officials on whom he depends to carry out his policies.[95]

Though members of Congress participate extensively in the removal power, Presidents draw the line on certain tactics. President Hoover repulsed the Senate's effort to remove members of the Federal Power Commission after the Senate had confirmed five commissioners. Finding fault with the decisions of the agency, the Senate voted to reconsider its confirmation of three of the commissioners and asked Hoover to return their nominations. Hoover insisted that the appointments had been constitutionally made and would not "admit the power in the Senate to encroach upon the Executive functions by removal of a duly appointed executive officer under the guise of reconsideration of his nomination." If the House of Representatives believed that the commissioners had been derelict in the performance of their duties,

[93] Crenshaw v. United States, 134 U.S. 99 (1890).

[94] Harold Seidman, Politics, Position, and Power 54 (1980).

[95] The courts continue to recognize the President's authority to remove purely executive officers; Martin v. Tobin, 451 F.2d 1335 (9th Cir. 1971); Martin v. Reagan, 525 F. Supp. 110 (D. Mass. 1981).

the "orderly and constitutional manner" of proceeding would be by impeachment.[96] The Senate proceeded to vote on the three commissioners, confirming two and rejecting George Otis Smith. It then instituted a court action to test Smith's right to hold office. In a unanimous decision the Supreme Court held that after the Senate confirms a nomination and the appointee takes the oath and enters into the duties of office, the Senate may not then reconsider and possibly reject the nomination.[97]

Congress, restricted in frontal attacks, has other methods of dislodging federal employees. Either House of Congress may pass a simple resolution, or both Houses may pass a concurrent resolution, expressing the sentiment that the President should remove an executive official. These resolutions are purely hortatory and have no legal effect, but they generate pressure for removal or resignation. In 1924 the Senate, after investigating the Teapot Dome scandal, passed a resolution stating that "it is the sense of the United States Senate that the President of the United States immediately request the resignation of Edwin Denby as Secretary of the Navy." On the day the resolution passed, President Coolidge announced that no official recognition could be given to it. The dismissal of an officer, "other than by impeachment, is exclusively an Executive function." Nevertheless, Denby offered his resignation several days later.[98]

Through the pressure of the investigative power, congressional committees can precipitate resignation or removal. In 1924 a special committee under Senator Burton K. Wheeler investigated the failure of Attorney General Harry Daugherty to prosecute people implicated in the Teapot Dome scandal. Daugherty resigned within a matter of weeks.[99] In 1958, after hearings by a House oversight subcommittee had publicized the financial operations of the Federal Communications Commission, FCC

[96] Public Papers of the Presidents, 1931, at 12, 15. Hoover's position had been supported by the Attorney General; 36 Op. Att'y Gen. 383 (1931).

[97] 74 Cong. Rec. 3939-40 (1931); United States v. Smith, 286 U.S. 6 (1932).

[98] Debate on Denby resolution appears at 65 Cong. Rec. 2223-45 (1924). Coolidge announcement: id. at 2335.

[99] Hasia Diner, "Teapot Dome, 1924," in Arthur M. Schlesinger, Jr., and Roger Bruns, eds., Congress Investigates 210-11 (1975).

Commissioner Richard A. Mack resigned.[100] Veterans Administration chief Robert P. Nimmo resigned in 1982 following detailed congressional investigations into his expenditure of funds.[101]

Congress also plays a positive role in the removal power: it intervenes to *protect* incumbents and ensure their tenure. It does this partly by specifying grounds for removal and by establishing procedural safeguards for federal employees facing dismissal or disciplinary action. In 1978, as part of the Civil Service Reform Act, Congress created a Special Counsel to protect the rights of whistleblowers. It has long been in the interest of Congress to prevent the top layer of the bureaucracy from penalizing federal employees who disclose agency wrongdoing or ineptitude. Congress depends on these employees to call attention to waste, corruption, and other practices that agencies like to conceal. Civil service employees who are fired for circulating a petition to Congress can be reinstated through court action.[102] But if their communications to Congress contain false or irresponsible information, protection from the judiciary may not be available.[103] Members of Congress resort to hearings, letters to agency heads, and other tactics to prevent an employee's removal or to press for reinstatement. Members intervene for reasons of simple justice and to keep open the channels of communication between agencies and Congress.

The case of Ernest Fitzgerald, a hero to liberal critics of military spending, has already been discussed. Members of Congress also defend agency employees identified with conservative causes. In 1963 the State Department informed Otto Otepka, a security officer, that he was being dismissed for giving classified information to the Senate Internal Security Subcommittee. Otepka found himself caught between conflicting loyalties. Departmental procedures restricted the disclosure of information; statutory provisions encouraged civil service employees to furnish information to Congress and its committees. After the subcommittee

[100] Congressional Quarterly Almanac, 1958, at 687-90.
[101] "Embattled VA Chief Steps Down," Washington Post, October 4, 1982, at A1.
[102] Steck v. Connally, 199 F.Supp. 104 (D.D.C. 1961).
[103] Turner v. Kennedy, 332 F.2d 304 (D.C. Cir. 1964).

held hearings on his dismissal and issued a lengthy report critical of the State Department, many of the initial charges against Otepka were dropped. Instead of dismissal he was demoted and reprimanded.[104]

Frances Knight, longtime director of the Passport Office, solidified her position over the years by forging close ties with Capitol Hill. Providing overnight passport service for Senators, Congressmen, and their constituents was one way to nurture congressional support. When Abba Schwartz, chief of the State Department's Bureau of Security and Consular Affairs from 1962 to 1966, tried to reorganize Knight out of a job, congressional defenders helped defeat the proposal. Within a few years Schwartz lost his own job through a reorganization plan; Knight remained head of the Passport Office until 1977.[105]

Because of a fundamental interest in program implementation, the operation of the civil service, and access to agency information, members of Congress will always have an interest in the suspension and removal of federal employees. Some past congressional techniques are off-limits today: allowing the Senate to act jointly with the President (as with the Tenure of Office Act); using the power of the purse to remove named employees; abolishing a position to put someone else on board; and requiring the President to return to the Senate for reconsideration the name of an official already confirmed and appointed. But Congress can abolish offices through reorganization and program cutbacks, provided it does not violate the Bill of Attainder Clause or First Amendment freedoms, and it can apply irresistible pressure both for and against agency employees through its investigative power.[106]

[104] "State Department Security—1963-65," a report of the Senate Committee on the Judiciary, 90th Cong., 1st Sess. (Comm. Print December 15, 1967). For congressional supporters of Otepka, see William J. Gill, The Ordeal of Otto Otepka (1969).

[105] Sanford J. Ungar, "J. Edgar Hoover Leaves the State Department," 28 Foreign Policy (1977), at 11-16 and "Frances Knight Ouster Tarnishes Carter Image," Human Events, July 16, 1977, at 1, 9-10.

[106] See Louis Fisher, "Congress and the Removal Power," 10 Congress & The Presidency 63 (1983).

4

LEGISLATIVE POWERS

Article I of the Constitution provides that "All legislative Powers herein granted shall be vested in a Congress of the United States." In one of the most restrictive opinions ever written on the President's role, Justice Black held that the Constitution "limits his functions in the lawmaking process to the recommending of laws he thinks wise and the vetoing of laws he thinks bad."[1] Black's theory, whatever its merits, ignores the vast scope of presidential legislative power that exists today and that prevailed even in much earlier periods.

The theory of constitutional limits—of powers enumerated and clearly defined—has lost ground to a number of stubborn forces. Even at the outset, two centuries ago, the lines between the three branches of the federal government were not crisp demarcations. Madison confided to Jefferson that the boundaries between the executive, legislative, and judicial powers, "though in general so strongly marked in themselves, consist in many instances of mere shades of difference."[2] In Federalist 37 Madison paused to acknowledge the inherent limitations of our language. Just as naturalists had difficulty in defining the exact line between vegetable life and the animal world, so was it an even greater task to draw the boundary between the departments of government, or "even the privileges and powers of the different legislative branches. Questions daily occur in the course of practice, which prove the obscurity which reigns in these subjects, and which puzzle the greatest adepts in political science."

Madison could not foresee the vast quantity of legislative power to be delegated to the President, to executive agencies, and later to independent regulatory commissions. The extent of this delegation has done much to undercut traditional notions of the separation of powers doctrine. Delegations are supposed to be ac-

[1] Youngstown Co. v. Sawyer, 343 U.S. 579, 587 (1952).
[2] The Writings of James Madison (Hunt ed.), V, 26.

companied by legislative standards that protect the essential lawmaking function of Congress, but standardless delegations are increasingly common. They survive court scrutiny because of procedural safeguards, guidelines that can be found in the legislative history of a statute, and various customs and traditions that help confine executive discretion.

In addition to statutory grants of powers, there are other forms of "administrative legislation": presidential proclamations, executive orders, agency regulations, and White House supervision of the rulemaking process. To retain some semblance of control, Congress has evolved a highly sophisticated set of tools, many of them of a nonstatutory nature. (An important statutory control, the legislative veto, is treated in the next chapter.)

Delegation

It is a fundamental principle of constitutional government that the legislature may not delegate its power to another branch. John Locke said that the legislature "cannot transfer the power of making laws to any other hands, for it being but a delegated power from the people, they who have it cannot pass it over to others."[3] This concept is embodied in the ancient maxim *delegata potestas non potest delegari* (delegated power cannot be delegated).[4]

Although Congress cannot surrender the basic legislative power entrusted to it by the Constitution, neither can it avoid delegating major pieces of discretionary authority to the executive branch and the independent regulatory commissions. The tension between these two competing values is relieved by some judicial tightrope walking. One author suggested this humorous but accurate syllogism: (1) *Major Premise*: Legislative power cannot be constitutionally delegated by Congress; (2) *Minor Premise*: It is essential that certain powers be delegated to administrative offi-

[3] John Locke, Second Treatise on Civil Government, §141.
[4] Patrick W. Duff and Horace E. Whiteside, "Delegata Potestas Non Potest Delegari: A Maxim of American Constitutional Law," 14 Corn. L. Q. 168 (1929); Horst P. Ehmke, " 'Delegata Potestas Non Potest Delegari,' A Maxim of American Constitutional Law," 47 Corn. L. Q. 50 (1961).

cers and regulatory commissions; (3) *Conclusion*: Therefore the powers thus delegated are not legislative powers.[5]

This kind of circular logic reappears in many decisions on delegation. Typically the Court declares that it would be a breach of the Constitution for Congress to transfer its legislative power to the President. After genuflecting to the theory of separated powers, the Justices regularly uphold the delegation in question.[6] Statutory language is sanctioned even when it is vague and ill-defined, such as general guidelines of "excessive profits," "reasonable rates," "unjust discrimination," and "in the public interest." The courts tolerate this kind of legislation not because the language is specific, which is far from the case, but because Congress supplies standards of due process to guide officials in administering the statute. Agencies are required by law to give notice and a hearing prior to issuing a rule or regulation. Findings of fact are supplied for the record; procedures exist for appeal. The Administrative Procedure Act of 1946 established various standards for agency rulemaking in order to guarantee fairness and equitable treatment. Through such procedural standards Congress tries to eliminate or minimize the opportunity for executive caprice and arbitrariness.

Vague and general grants of legislative power are criticized from various perspectives. Some critics insist that political accountability and democratic values depend on the establishment of clear guidelines for administrators.[7] Others point out that vague statutes make it difficult to conduct program evaluation, stressed in such recent statutes as the Legislative Reorganization Act of 1970 and the Congressional Budget and Impoundment Control Act of 1974.[8] How can Congress, assisted by the General Accounting Office and other staff support, determine whether programs are being carried out effectively unless the original legislative goals are clearly stated? Unless statutory standards exist,

---

[5] Robert E. Cushman, The Independent Regulatory Commissions 429 (1941).

[6] For example, Field v. Clark, 143 U.S. 649, 692 (1891) and Hampton & Co. v. United States, 276 U.S. 394, 406 (1928).

[7] Theodore J. Lowi, The End of Liberalism 298 (1969).

[8] 84 Stat. 1168, sec. 204 (1970); 88 Stat. 325, Title VII (1974).

how can courts judge whether agency actions are faithful to legislative intent?

The Impulse for Broad Delegation

From the first year of its existence, Congress has found it necessary to set general goals and to delegate to agents broad discretion in carrying out legislative policy. In 1789 the House of Representatives considered a bill to establish a permanent seat of government. The bill authorized the President to appoint a certain number of commissioners who would report recommendations for the best location and, with the President's advice, purchase the property and construct the necessary buildings for Congress and the rest of government.

Representative Tucker of South Carolina objected to the delegation as "totally inadmissible" because it gave a discretionary power "which no body of men ought to exercise but ourselves with the other branch of the Legislature. . . . Were we sent here to give such powers to any men?" Tucker proposed that the commissioners report to Congress, not the President, allowing Congress at a later session the opportunity to pass legislation for the nation's capital. His motion was defeated, 21 to 29. A year later Congress delegated this authority to the President and the commissioners.[9]

Part of Congress's hesitancy in writing explicit statutory language is rooted in a genuine dilemma: the problem of legislating for future events. William Blackstone, the eighteenth-century English jurist, observed that the "manner, time, and circumstances of putting laws in execution must frequently be left to the discretion of the executive magistrates."[10] Locke, despite his strictures against delegation, recognized that the legislature could not always be in session nor could it provide laws to cover every conceivable contingency: "It is not necessary—no, nor so much as convenient—that the legislative should be always in being; but

---

[9] Annals of Congress, 1st Cong., at 879 (September 5, 1789); 1 Stat. 130 (1790).

[10] William Blackstone, Commentaries, Book 1, *270.

absolutely necessary that the executive power should, because there is not always need of new laws to be made, but always need of execution of the laws that are made."[11]

Contingent (or conditional) legislation has had a long tradition in America. An early legal test involved a trade act directed against Britain. After the legislation lapsed in 1810, Congress let the President renew the trade restrictions at his discretion. When President Madison revived the act, a merchant complained in court that the President's proclamation had the force of law and was thus legislative in nature, violating the separation doctrine. The Supreme Court rejected this contention in *Brig Aurora*, affirming that Congress could legislate conditionally and leave to others the task of ascertaining the facts that bring its declared policy into operation.[12]

For more than a century, courts have recognized that it is essential to phrase statutes in general terms when events are "future and impossible to be fully known." Many subjects of government depend upon legislation that cannot be known to the lawmaking power "and must, therefore, be a subject of inquiry and determination outside of the halls of legislation."[13] Courts understand that the nature of government requires Congress to pass general legislation and leave to other branches the responsibility to "fill in the details."[14]

Toward the end of the nineteenth century and during the first part of the twentieth, administrative discretion became ever more familiar and widespread. Conditions in the economy requiring regulations were increasingly complex, interrelated, and in the process of rapid change. Administrators could not be expected to solve new problems while operating in a legislative strait jacket. They needed an opportunity to experiment and learn. Courts accepted broadness and generality in statutes as unavoidable qualities of legislation. Because of unique circumstances prevailing in different regions and localities, Congress need only declare

---

[11] Locke, Second Treatise on Civil Government, §153.
[12] Brig Aurora v. United States, 11 U.S. (7 Cr.) 382 (1813).
[13] Locke's Appeal, 72 Pa. St. 491, 498-99 (1873).
[14] Wayman v. Southard, 10 Wheat. 1, 46 (1825).

a general policy and leave to administrative officers the duty of applying the statute to particular circumstances.[15]

Especially in the case of the independent regulatory commission, the courts have sanctioned the use of vague and ill-defined statutory language. When Congress looked at the industries to be regulated after the Civil War and saw the turbulent, almost revolutionary changes in progress, it decided that commissions run by experts offered a more hopeful instrument than legislators periodically passing inflexible statutes. A commission, operating under a general charter, could respond more effectively to economic and technological change.

The judiciary has consistently rejected challenges to these broad delegations, upholding the power of the Interstate Commerce Commission to protect the "public interest," accepting the guideline of "unfair method of competition" for the Federal Trade Commission, the standard of "public convenience, interest, or necessity" for the Federal Communications Commission, and the ability of the Securities and Exchange Commission to ensure that corporations do not "unduly or unnecessarily complicate the structure" or "unfairly or inequitably distribute voting power among security holders."[16]

As a countervailing force to these loose standards, the commission form of government offers some built-in safeguards. Commissions operate on a multi-member (or collegial) basis, in contrast to executive departments headed by a single administrator. This structure creates a capacity for self-checking and self-correction, limiting the abuse of delegated power and placing the plural-member commissions more on the organizational scheme

[15] For example, Buttfield v. Stranahan, 192 U.S. 470, 496 (1904); Union Bridge Co. v. United States, 194 U.S. 364, 386 (1907); Monongahela Bridge Co. v. United States, 216 U.S. 177 (1910); and United States v. Grimaud, 220 U.S. 506, 516 (1911).

[16] For "public interest" guideline, see ICC v. Goodrich Transit Co., 224 U.S. 194, 214-15 (1912); Intermountain Rate Cases, 234 U.S. 476, 486-88 (1914); Avent v. United States, 266 U.S. 127, 130 (1924); N.Y. Central Securities Co. v. United States, 287 U.S. 12, 24-25 (1932). "Unfair method of competition": FTC v. Gratz, 253 U.S. 421, 427-28 (1920). "Public convenience" standard: FCC v. Pottsville Broadcasting Co., 309 U.S. 134, 137-38 (1940). For SEC: American Power Co. v. SEC, 329 U.S. 90, 104-06 (1946).

of appellate courts. The terms of commissioners are lengthy and staggered, insulating them somewhat from presidential transitions and the pressure of biennial elections. And finally, restrictions are placed on the number of commissioners who may belong to the same political party (although this safeguard is neutralized when the President selects nominal members of a political party or when members classify themselves as Independents).[17]

Broad delegations result from a number of other circumstances. Legislators and their staffs may lack the expertise needed to draft specific language for highly specialized subjects. Even experts in the agencies and the private sector find it difficult to develop strict standards that would be workable. When an assistant general counsel in the Department of Health, Education, and Welfare expressed misgivings about the lack of clarity in legislation being drafted for social services, his boss, HEW Secretary Wilbur Cohen, had little patience with the quest for legal precision. For those who worried about details and specificity he offered this advice: "Put it in regulations . . . do it later. I can't think of an answer."[18] Even later an agency may find it difficult to place in a regulation all of the factors needed to guide government action. In 1981 the Department of Justice cancelled a proposed rule after concluding that "it is impossible to foresee and enumerate all of the favorable or adverse factors which may be relevant and should be considered in the exercise of administrative discretion."[19]

These circumstances, faced by legislators and administrators alike, invite vague formulations of objectives. Furthermore, specificity of language may undermine the consensus needed to pass legislation. A ban on "sex discrimination" can attract a majority of votes in Congress. Working out precisely what the phrase means in terms of, say, father-son banquets or boy choirs might fracture the coalition required for passage.

[17] Louis Fisher, The Politics of Shared Power: Congress and the Executive 151-74 (1981).

[18] Martha Derthick, Uncontrollable Spending for Social Services Grants 8-9 (1975).

[19] 46 Fed. Reg. 9119 (1981).

Congress may also find a responsibility so vexing, so lacking in political rewards, that it tries to shift the chore elsewhere. General tariff-making exposed Congress to such ridicule that in time it delegated the bulk of that responsibility to the executive branch and the Tariff Commission (now the International Trade Commission). As one study concluded, "every favor which can be conferred is also a danger, because it must sometimes be refused. Responsibility involves blame. And, if the demands exceed what the congressman can effectively handle, then he may happily yield up a significant portion of his power. This is what happened with the tariff."[20]

As much as Congress tries to rid itself of unwanted tasks, it has difficulty breaking free entirely. In the case of international trade, industries and labor unions appealed to Congress for protection from foreign competition. Legislation soon appeared, providing federal assistance payments for dislocated industries and a variety of nontariff barriers. The Trade Act of 1974 marked a reassertion of Congress in this area.

A similar pattern is emerging with postal reform. In 1970 Congress established the Postal Service to make it "independent" of political pressures. The purpose was to convert the former Post Office into a modern, "businesslike" operation. Yet Congress would not surrender some sensitive political decisions, such as assuring rural delivery, providing subsidies for certain classes of mail, and continuing Saturday mail delivery.

The history of federal pay adjustments illustrates the frustration of trying to delegate an intrinsically political issue. Prior to 1967 Congress determined the rate of compensation for Senators and Representatives by a separate statute, setting forth the specific dollar amounts paid to legislators. In that year, as part of the Postal Revenue and Salary Act, Congress established a commission to recommend every four years the rates of compensation that should be paid to members of Congress, Justices of the Supreme Court, federal judges, and certain high-ranking

[20] Raymond P. Bauer et al., American Business and Public Policy 37 (1963). For delegation of tariff power see Louis Fisher, President and Congress 133-55 (1972).

106

government officials. The President, after receiving these recommendations, submitted to Congress his own proposals for salaries. They took effect within thirty days unless disapproved by either House or replaced by a different salary schedule enacted into law.

The issue is further complicated by another delegation included in the Federal Pay Comparability Act of 1970, which directed the President to have a report prepared each year to compare federal and private rates of pay. After considering this report, along with recommendations from the Advisory Committee on Federal Pay, the President proposed an adjustment in pay to satisfy the principle of comparability. He could also submit an alternative plan, taking into account national emergency or economic conditions. Unless either House vetoed his plan within thirty days, it would take effect.[21]

Through such mechanisms Congress hoped to remove "politics" from pay adjustments, but the issue continued to bounce around as a political football. Presidents, appealing to the country for spending restraints, repeatedly tried to delay federal salary increases or keep them below the line of comparability. In 1972 President Nixon, relying on an interpretation of the Economic Stabilization Act, refused to submit an alternative plan. An appellate court held that his action violated the law.[22] Members of Congress, responding to what they thought their constituents wanted, also helped frustrate the policy of pay comparability.

Congressman Larry Pressler asked the courts to declare unconstitutional the statutory procedure for setting legislative compensation. He claimed that the system, allowing salary adjustments without affirmative action by both Houses of Congress, violated the Constitution's Ascertainment Clause: "The Senators and Representatives shall receive a Compensation for their Services to be ascertained by law" (Article I, Section 6). A district court in 1976 decided that the meaning of "ascertains" was satisfied by

---

[21] 84 Stat. 1946 (1970).

[22] National Treasury Employees Union v. Nixon, 492 F.2d 587 (D.C. Cir. 1974). Earlier, in National Ass'n of Internal Revenue Employees v. Nixon, 349 F.Supp. 18 (D.D.C. 1972), a district court decided that it lacked jurisdiction.

the statutory procedure.[23] The record of federal pay since 1976 is one in which members of Congress continue to find themselves entangled in painful rollcall votes and deft parliamentary maneuvers, writhing again and again over their compensation and the salaries of executive and judicial officials.[24]

The Special Case of Foreign Affairs

A strong impulse for delegating legislative power draws its force from a distinction between domestic and foreign affairs. In *United States* v. *Curtiss-Wright Corp.* (1936), Justice Sutherland wrote eloquently about "this vast external realm, with its important, complicated, delicate and manifold problems." As a consequence, he said, legislation over the international field must often accord to the President "a degree of discretion and freedom from statutory restrictions which would not be admissible were domestic affairs alone involved."[25] *Curtiss-Wright* has become a justification not only for broad grants of legislative authority to the President but for the exercise of inherent presidential power. Because of the "very delicate, plenary and exclusive power of the President as the sole organ of the federal government in the field of international relations," the exercise of presidential power does not depend solely on an act of Congress.[26] Indeed, some of the powers are not even inherent in the Constitution, for Sutherland searched for powers outside the Constitution.[27]

Sutherland's remarks in *Curtiss-Wright* went far beyond the necessities of the case, echoing positions he had taken as a U.S. Senator and member of the Foreign Relations Committee. The decision closely tracks his article "The Internal and External Powers

[23] Pressler v. Simon, 428 F.Supp. 302 (D.D.C. 1976), vacated and remanded in light of intervening amendment to the Salary Act, 431 U.S. 169 (1977), but later affirmed, 434 U.S. 1028 (1978).

[24] Louis Fisher, "History of Pay Adjustments for Members of Congress," in Robert W. Hartman and Arnold R. Weber, eds., The Rewards of Public Service 25-52 (1980).

[25] 299 U.S. 304, 319, 320.

[26] Id. at 320.

[27] Louis Henkin, Foreign Affairs and the Constitution 22 (1972).

of the National Government" (printed as a Senate document in 1910) and his book, *Constitutional Power and World Affairs* (1919).[28] Every judge carries predilections to the bench, but few have an opportunity to use a Supreme Court case to disseminate a personal position written decades before and in an area not at all central to the issue being decided.

Sutherland believed that foreign and domestic affairs were different "both in respect of their origin and their nature" because the powers of external sovereignty "passed from the Crown not to the colonies severally, but to the colonies in their collective and corporate capacity as the United States of America."[29] Scholars, pointing out that the states in 1776 operated as sovereign entities and not as parts of a collective body, have repudiated Sutherland's thesis. The creation of the Continental Congress did not disturb the sovereign power of the states to make treaties, borrow money, solicit arms, lay embargoes, collect tariff duties, and conduct separate military campaigns.[30] The Supreme Court has recognized that the American colonies, upon their separation from England, acquired certain elements of sovereignty.[31]

Even if the power of external sovereignty had somehow passed intact from the Crown to the "United States," the Constitution divides that power between Congress and the President. The President and the Senate share the treaty power. The President receives ambassadors from other countries but U.S. ambassadors must be approved by the Senate. Congress has the power to declare war, to raise and support the military forces, to make rules for their regulation, to provide for calling up the militia to suppress insurrections and repel invasions, and to provide for the organization and disciplining of the militia. The Constitution

[28] S. Doc. No. 417, 61st Cong., 2d Sess. (1910); see Joel Francis Paschal, Mr. Justice Sutherland: A Man Against the State 93 (1951).

[29] 299 U.S. at 315-16.

[30] Charles Lofgren, *"United States* v. *Curtiss-Wright Export Corporation*: An Historical Reassessment," 83 Yale L. J. 1 (1973); David M. Levitan, "The Foreign Relations Power: An Analysis of Mr. Justice Sutherland's Theory," 55 Yale L. J. 467 (1946); Claude H. Van Tyne, "Sovereignty in the American Revolution: An Historical Study," 12 Am. Hist. Rev. 529 (1907).

[31] United States v. California, 332 U.S. 19, 31 (1947).

also explicitly grants to Congress the power to lay and collect duties on foreign trade, to regulate commerce with foreign nations, and to establish a uniform rule of naturalization. Moreover, world events since 1936 have increased the degree of overlap between foreign and domestic affairs.[32]

Nevertheless, the Supreme Court continues to look more sympathetically upon delegation that involves external affairs. Even Justice Rehnquist, the strongest advocate of the nondelegation doctrine on the Burger Court, holds to a different standard for international crises, "the nature of which Congress can hardly have been expected to anticipate in any detail."[33] He agrees that Congress "is permitted to legislate both with greater breadth and with greater flexibility" when a statute governs military affairs.[34] *Curtiss-Wright* is frequently cited to support broad delegations of legislative power to the President and even the existence of independent, implied, and inherent powers for the President.[35]

Subdelegation

The problem of delegation is compounded when the agent of Congress transfers the responsibility to a subordinate. The Supreme Court has been as lenient toward subdelegation as toward delegation, recognizing that the President and department heads cannot personally discharge all the statutory tasks assigned to them. For example, the Army Reorganization Act of 1920 provided for a classification of officers as a way of reducing their number while retaining the most competent. An officer who had been placed in a class that was not to be retained argued in court

[32] Bayless Manning, "The Congress, the Executive and 'Intermestic' Affairs: Three Proposals," 55 Foreign Affairs 306 (1977).

[33] Dames & Moore v. Regan, 453 U.S. 654, 669 (1981). See also his comment at 678.

[34] Rostker v. Goldberg, 453 U.S. 57, 66 (1981), quoting Parker v. Levy, 417 U.S. 733, 756 (1974).

[35] For broad-delegation arguments, see Ex parte Endo, 323 U.S. 283, 298 n.21 (1944); Zemel v. Rusk, 381 U.S. 1, 17 (1965); Goldwater v. Carter, 444 U.S. 996, 1000 n.1 (1979). Inherent powers discussed in United States v. Pink, 315 U.S. 203, 229 (1942); Knauff v. Shaughnessy, 338 U.S. 537, 542 (1950); United States v. Mazurie, 419 U.S. 544, 566-67 (1975).

that the statute imposed upon the President a personal, non-delegable duty to review the record of the Board of Final Classification. Instead, that task had been carried out by the Secretary of War. The Supreme Court decided that the officer's interpretation would place "a burdensome, if not impossible, personal duty upon the President" and could not be accepted as legislative intent unless Congress so stated.[36]

After World War II Congress enacted legislation that specifically recognized the President's need to subdelegate some of the functions invested in him by law. A survey disclosed that President Truman had to act, either expressly or by inference, under at least 1,100 statutes. In 1950, on the basis of that study, Congress authorized the President to subdelegate functions to his department heads or agency officials on the condition that the officer discharging these tasks be someone who had been confirmed by the Senate. In this way Congress hoped to maintain some system of accountability to elected representatives.[37]

Checks on Delegated Power

Not since 1935 has the Supreme Court struck down a delegation of power to the executive branch because of inadequate legislative guidelines. In that year delegations of power were twice overruled. Both decisions involved the National Industrial Recovery Act (NIRA), which placed upon industrial and trade associations the responsibility for drawing up codes to minimize competition, raise prices and restrict production. If the President

---

[36] French v. Weeks, 259 U.S. 326 (1922). The Supreme Court also said, in United States v. Chemical Foundation, 272 U.S. 1, 13 (1926), that "Obviously all the functions of his great office cannot be exercised by the President in person."

[37] 64 Stat. 419 (1950), codified at 3 U.S.C. 301 (1976). See Glendon A. Schubert, Jr., "Judicial Review of the Subdelegation of Presidential Power," 12 J. Pol. 668 (1950); Glendon A. Schubert, Jr., "The Presidential Subdelegation Act of 1950," 13 J. Pol. 647 (1951); Eli G. Nobleman, "The Delegation of Presidential Functions: Constitutional and Legal Aspects," 307 The Annals 134 (1956); and Nathan Grundstein, Presidential Delegation of Authority in Wartime (1961).

regarded the codes as unacceptable he could prescribe his own and enforce them by law.

The drafters of the NIRA, under heavy pressure from Roosevelt to produce a bill, gave little thought to constitutional questions of delegation or procedural safeguards. Congress, for its part, felt equally pressured to rush the bill to enactment. General Hugh Johnson, administrator of the National Recovery Administration (NRA), cared little for procedural niceties and his attorneys operated under absurdly tight deadlines. They processed hundreds of codes under the worst of conditions, including an array of industry and trade association talent that dominated the drafting sessions. A coherent strategy for litigation became impossible because of persistent conflicts between NRA attorneys and U.S. attorneys, Interior Department lawyers, and the Antitrust Division of the Justice Department.[38]

In the first of the two NRA cases, *Panama Refining*, the Court held that a section of the statute governing controls on petroleum production failed to establish "criterion to govern the President's course." It did not require any finding by the President as a condition of his action. The Court decided that Congress "has declared no policy, has established no standard, has laid down no rule."[39] Justice Cardozo, dissenting in the first case because he found that Congress had supplied adequate standards, exclaimed in the second (*Schechter*): "This is delegation running riot."[40]

The Court's decisions were handed down in a climate increasingly hostile to agency rulemaking. The scope of agency discretion and procedural irregularities were constant sore points. A Committee on Administrative Law, established by the American Bar Association in May 1933, viewed with anxiety the creation of the New Deal agencies, objected to the "haphazard bedlam"

[38] Peter H. Irons, The New Deal Lawyers 22-107 (1982).

[39] Panama Refining Co. v. Ryan, 293 U.S. 388, 415, 430 (1935).

[40] Schechter Corp. v. United States, 295 U.S. 495, 553 (1935). A year later an appellate court struck down an emergency appropriations bill because it unconstitutionally delegated legislative power to the President; Franklin Tp. in Somerset County, N.J. v. Tugwell, 85 F.2d 208, 218-20 (D.C. Cir. 1936).

112

of administrative practice, and advocated more uniformity and due process.[41]

The furious legislative pace of the Roosevelt administration exacerbated an administrative system which was already strained and deficient. FDR, in his first fifteen months in office, issued 674 executive orders. In its first year the NRA approved hundreds of codes and released 2,998 administrative orders that approved or modified the codes. Almost six thousand NRA press releases, some of them having a legislative effect, were issued during this period.[42] Department officials were sometimes unaware of their own regulations. As the Court discovered in *Panama Refining*, the government had brought an indictment and taken an appeal to the Court before discovering that the regulation on which the proceeding was based had been eliminated by an executive order.[43] These embarrassments led to the creation of a "Federal Register" to publish presidential and agency documents that were legislative in effect.

In neither NRA case did the Supreme Court object to delegation as a general principle. It acknowledged that the Constitution did not deny to Congress "the necessary resources of flexibility and practicality, which will enable it to perform its function in laying down policies and establishing standards—while leaving to selected instrumentalities the making of subordinate rules within prescribed limits and the determination of facts to which the policy as declared by the legislature is to apply."[44]

The "Schechter Rule," with its insistence on statutory standards, is rarely followed by either Congress or the courts. Standardless delegations have been upheld for many reasons, including the accumulated customs of a regulated industry and the practices developed by states that help narrow the discretion of a federal agency.[45] Standardless delegations have been considered acceptable when the legislative history leading to the enactment

[41] 58 A.B.A. Rep. 201 (1933).

[42] 59 A.B.A. Rep. 553-54 (1934).

[43] 293 U.S. at 412-13.

[44] 293 U.S. at 421; 295 U.S. at 529-30.

[45] Fahey v. Mallonee, 332 U.S. 245, 250, 253 (1947), concerning the Home Owners' Loan Act of 1933 and the Federal Home Loan Bank Board.

of a "facially standardless" statute supplies guidelines for administrative action.[46] The judiciary also recognizes that circumstances may require Congress to delegate broadly so that it can encompass those who might otherwise, through technicalities available in a statute, try to evade the purpose of federal regulation.[47]

A separate question concerns the right of Congress to delegate legislative power to *private* groups. In 1936 the Supreme Court struck down a statute in part because it delegated power to representatives of the coal industry to set up a code of mandatory regulations: "This is legislative delegation in its most obnoxious form; for it is not even delegation to an official or an official body, presumptively disinterested, but to private persons whose interests may be and often are adverse to the interests of others in the same business."[48] The Court considered such statutes an unconstitutional interference with personal liberty and private property and a denial of rights safeguarded by the due process clause of the Fifth Amendment.

A few years later, however, the Court allowed Congress to give farmers a veto power over marketing proposals made by the Secretary of Agriculture, and in subsequent years upheld the right of Congress to delegate legislative power to private associations that possess attributes of sovereignty over their members.[49]

The scope of contemporary delegation is underscored by the Economic Stabilization Act of 1970,.which authorized the President "to issue such orders and regulations as he may deem appropriate to stabilize prices, rents, wages, and salaries at levels not less than those prevailing on May 25, 1970." The remaining sections of the act failed to provide procedural safeguards—for

[46] Carl McGowan, "Congress, Court, and Control of Delegated Powers," 77 Colum. L. Rev. 1119, 1128 n. 33 (1977).

[47] Mourning v. Family Publications Service, Inc., 411 U.S. 356, 365-66, 371 (1973), concerning the Federal Reserve Board and the Truth in Lending Act.

[48] Carter v. Carter Coal Co., 298 U.S. 238, 311 (1936).

[49] Currin v. Wallace, 306 U.S. 1 (1939). United States v. Mazurie, 419 U.S. 544 (1975), permitted a delegation of legislative power to Indian tribal councils. For the broad scope of participation by private groups in the administration of federal laws, see George W. Liebmann, "Delegation to Private Parties in American Constitutional Law," 50 Ind. L. Rev. 650 (1975).

example, giving notice prior to issuing orders, providing a hearing for affected parties, and establishing machinery for judicial review.[50]

Because of President Nixon's public opposition to wage-price controls, Democratic members of Congress thought they could embarrass him and create an election-year issue. Each time the expiration date of the act drew near, Congress extended it. Nixon's refusal to use the authority permitted legislators to chastise him for inaction. Then, on August 15, 1971, Nixon stunned Congress by issuing Executive Order 11615, placing a ninety-day freeze on all prices, rents, wages, and salaries. In part he based his action on authority given him in the Economic Stabilization Act of 1970.[51] Congress had passed a domestic equivalent to the Gulf of Tonkin Resolution.

Private parties appealed to the courts to have the act struck down as an invalid delegation of legislative power. In one of the principal cases, a three-judge court upheld the legislation by noting that some of the legislative guidelines had been included in committee reports and the legislative history of the act: "Whether legislative purposes are to be obtained from committee reports, or are set forth in a separate section of the text of the law, is largely a matter of drafting style."[52] Yet is it more than that. Agencies are bound by law; they are not necessarily bound by nonstatutory controls (a point pursued in the next section). As for the 1970 act, Congress subsequently amended it to provide more explicit standards and guidelines.[53]

[50] 84 Stat. 799.
[51] 36 Fed. Reg. 15727 (1971).
[52] Amalgamated Meat Cutters & Butcher Work. v. Connelly, 337 F.Supp. 737, 750 (D.D.C. 1971) (three-judge court). See also California Teach. Ass'n v. Newport Mesa Unified Sch. Dist., 333 F.Supp. 436, 446 (C.D. Cal. 1971) and DeRieux v. Five Smiths, Inc., 499 F.2d 1321, 1329-30 (Temp. Emerg. Ct. of Appeals, 1974), as well as cases cited in note 11 of latter decision.
[53] The 1970 act was extended by 84 Stat. 1468, 85 Stat. 13, and 85 Stat. 38, before being fundamentally rewritten by legislation in 1971 (85 Stat. 743) which provided for more specific standards, procedural safeguards, and judicial review. For critiques of 1970 act see Stanley H. Friedelbaum, "The 1971 Wage-Price Freeze: Unchallenged Presidential Power," The Supreme Court Review, 1974, at 33-80, and Richard P. Carr and Robert P. Dutcher, "Phase V: The Cost-of-Living Council Reconsidered," 62 Geo. L. J. 1663 (1974).

The scope of delegated power was again at issue in 1975 when President Ford responded to the Arab oil embargo by placing a fee on imported oil. He issued Proclamation 4341 to promote energy conservation, encourage domestic production, and reduce dependence on foreign sources. The chief purpose, however, was to pressure Congress into passing the administration's energy bill. After an initial fee of a dollar per barrel, imposed on January 23, 1975, the plan called for additional dollar increases on March 1 and April 1. The Ford administration took the position that although taxes and tariffs were legislative prerogatives, requiring specific authorization by statute, a "fee" on imported material "may be set for non-revenue purposes and need not be legislated."[54]

Congressman Robert Drinan, joined by other parties in litigation, regarded the fee as a circumvention of the duty system established by the Constitution. However, a district judge decided that the fee program was one of several actions covered by the Trade Expansion Act, which permitted the President to "adjust imports." For those who criticized the statute as an undue delegation of legislative authority, the judge observed that the "non-delegation doctrine is almost a complete failure."[55]

An appellate court reversed this decision, holding that the Trade Expansion Act did not constitute authority for the fees imposed by President Ford. A review of previous trade legislation convinced the court that congressional delegations had been "narrow and explicit in order to effectuate well-defined goals." Also rejected was the administration's interpretation of a fee on imported materials. The Tariff Commission had called the license fee mechanism "substantially a duty system." Furthermore, the fee imposed by President Ford would have generated an estimated $4.8 billion a year, which exceeded the total amount of revenue derived from customs in 1974.[56]

The Supreme Court did not analyze the fee-duty distinction

[54] Algonquin Sng., Inc. v. FEA, 518 F.2d 1051, 1060 (D.C. Cir. 1975).

[55] Commonwealth of Massachusetts v. Simon, Civil Action No. 75-0129, and Algonquin Sng., Inc. v. Simon, Civil Action No. 75-0130 (D.D.C. February 21, 1975), reprinted at 518 F.2d at 1064.

[56] Algonquin Sng., Inc. v. FEA, 518 F.2d at 1056, 1061.

when it upheld the license fees. Writing for a unanimous Court, Justice Thurgood Marshall stated that the fees were within the scope of the Trade Expansion Act. The Court was not disturbed that the act delegated broadly, authorizing the President to "take such action, and for such time, as he deems necessary to adjust the imports of [the] article and its derivatives so that . . . imports [of the article] will not threaten to impair the national security." To Justice Marshall, the President's proclamation was authorized by the language of the Trade Expansion Act and its legislative history. He maintained that the legislative standards "are clearly sufficient to meet any delegation doctrine attack."[57]

In 1979 an appellate court upheld President Carter's Executive Order 12092 which had broad-ranging effects on federal procurement policy. It allowed the President to withhold federal contracts from companies that failed to follow the administration's wage-price standards. The order was based on a statutory requirement that procurement policy decisions be taken in consideration of "economy and efficiency."[58]

The Supreme Court has never discarded the nondelegation doctrine, but Justices who raise that banner do so usually in dissenting opinions, not for the majority. The majority uses the doctrine indirectly to restrict the reach of a statute until Congress deliberately, consciously, and explicitly expands its coverage. For example, in 1958 the Court decided that Congress had not intended in the Immigration and Nationality Act to give the Secretary of State the discretion he claimed: the power to deny passports to persons with alleged communist beliefs and associations. Referring to *Panama Refining*, the Court said it would "construe narrowly all delegated powers that curtail or dilute" such basic freedoms as the right to travel.[59]

A similar approach was used by the Court in 1980 to invalidate a safety standard promulgated by the Secretary of Labor.

---

[57] FEA v. Algonquin Sng. Inc., 426 U.S. 548, 559 (1976). See Thomas P. Preston, "National Security and Oil Import Regulation: The License Fee Approach," 15 Va. J. Int'l L. 400 (1975).

[58] American Federation of Labor, Etc. v. Kahn, 618 F.2d 784, 793 n. 51 (D.C. Cir. 1979). See dissent by Judge MacKinnon at 811-14.

[59] Kent v. Dulles, 357 U.S. 116, 129 (1958).

Justice Stevens, joined by Chief Justice Burger and Justice Stewart, agreed that the construction placed upon the statute by the government would have represented an unconstitutional delegation of legislative power. Justice Rehnquist, in a separate opinion, wrote an even stronger critique of the delegation.[60]

For the most part, the nondelegation doctrine appears in dissenting opinions. In a 1963 dissent, Justice Harlan (joined by Douglas and Stewart) cited *Schechter* and *Panama Refining* when he expressed constitutional doubts about the lack of standards to guide the Interior Secretary's power to apportion the waters of the Colorado River. A 1965 dissent by Justice Douglas objected to broad statutory authority that allowed the Secretary of State to restrict the right to travel. Justices Douglas and Brennan dissented in 1974 to excessive delegation of legislative power to the President.[61]

Instead of hoping for more stringent legislative standards, restrictions are more likely to come from the guides furnished by administrators who implement the programs. As agencies gain experience they should be able to generalize from this knowledge and announce rules for future actions.[62] Congress may also intervene to control administrative action by changing authorization language or by placing limitations in appropriations bills.[63] If the President issues an executive order pursuant to delegated authority and Congress wants to revoke the order, such action is well within its power.[64] Congress may decide to delegate with a

[60] Industrial Union v. American Petroleum, 448 U.S. 607, 646, 671-88 (1980). Justice Powell, joining the majority, withheld opinion on the delegation issue (at 664 n. 1). See National Cable Television Assn. v. United States, 415 U.S. 336, 341-42 (1974) and FPC v. New England Power Co., 415 U.S. 345 (1974), where the Court read narrowly a congressional statute to avoid constitutional problems of delegation.

[61] Arizona v. California, 373 U.S. 546, 624-27 (1963); Zemel v. Rusk, 381 U.S. 1, 21-22 (1965); California Bankers Assn. v. Shultz, 416 U.S. 21, 90-93 (1974). See McGautha v. California, 402 U.S. 183, 251-52 (1971).

[62] Henry J. Friendly, The Federal Administrative Agencies: The Need for Better Definition of Standards 14, 142-46 (1962); Kenneth Culp Davis, "A New Approach to Delegation," 36 U. Chi. L. Rev. 713 (1969); Kenneth Culp Davis, Discretionary Justice (1969).

[63] Eisenberg v. Corning, 179 F.2d 275 (D.C. Cir. 1949).

[64] Feliciano v. United States, 297 F.Supp. 1356, 1358 (D. Puerto Rico 1969), aff'd, 422 F.2d 943 (1st Cir. 1970), cert. denied, 400 U.S. 823 (1970).

shorter leash by including within a statute a termination date (so-called sunset or self-destruct provisions). This is especially likely after the Supreme Court's 1983 invalidation of the legislative veto (discussed in Chapter 5). One of the most effective checks on delegated authority results from the exercise of nonstatutory controls.

Nonstatutory Controls

Vagueness in legislation is remedied partially by details that appear in the legislative history, such as committee reports, committee hearings, floor debates, and correspondence from review committees. This material considerably narrows the range of agency discretion. For example, the energy appropriations act for fiscal 1984 contains what appears to be an extraordinary grant of power: a lump sum of $884 million for construction by the Corps of Engineers. But the two Houses of Congress had quite specific projects in mind in arriving at that sum. The projects appeared in the conference report, organized state by state so that each member knew the projects to be carried out.[65]

Nonstatutory controls meet the needs of both branches. Neither Congress nor the agencies are always certain of the specifics to be included in a statute. When judgments and predictions are wrong, the statute has to be rewritten. Putting guidelines and details in nonstatutory sources adds valuable flexibility to the legislative and administrative process. If an adjustment is necessary after a law is passed, committees and agencies can depart from the nonstatutory scheme without having to pass new legislation.

The system of nonstatutory controls is fragile. Much depends on a "keep the faith" attitude among agency officials. They must want to maintain the integrity of their budget presentations and preserve a relationship of trust and confidence with congressional committees. Violation of that trust may result in budget cutbacks, restrictive language in statutes, and line-item appropriations. The House Appropriations Committee has reminded the Defense Department that, regardless of the lump-sum nature of

---

[65] P.L. 98-50, 97 Stat. 247 (1983); H. Rept. No. 272, 98th Cong., 1st Sess. 14-18 (1983).

defense appropriations, the department is expected to spend funds in accordance with its detailed budget justifications:

> In a strictly legal sense, the Department of Defense could utilize the funds appropriated for whatever programs were included under the individual appropriation accounts; but the relationship with the Congress demands that the detailed justifications which are presented in support of budget requests be followed. To do otherwise would cause Congress to lose confidence in the requests made and probably result in reduced appropriations or line item appropriation bills.[66]

The evolution of nonstatutory controls is reflected in the history of "reprogramming" of funds by the Defense Department. Reprogramming consists of the shift of funds *within* an appropriation account (for example, within "Aircraft Procurement, Navy"). Shifts from one account to another (from "Aircraft Procurement, Navy" to "Weapons Procurement, Navy") is called a "transfer" and requires statutory authority. Reprogramming is essentially a nonstatutory development. Control is exercised for the most part through committee reports, agency directives, and a complicated set of understandings between the two branches.

Several decades ago the extent of legislative control over defense reprogramming consisted basically of review by two members from each of the appropriations committees: the chairman of the defense appropriations subcommittee and the ranking minority member. Often the review was by staff members. Gradually the subcommittee began to place restrictions in the committee reports. The Defense Department incorporated these restrictions in its directives and instructions to agency officials. Congressional review began to include a greater number of committee members (extending to the full subcommittee and sometimes the full committee) and eventually the authorization committees (Armed Services). On occasion the committees agreed that the decision was of such fundamental importance that it

---

[66] H. Rept. No. 662, 93d Cong., 1st Sess. 16 (1973). For a general treatment of nonstatutory controls, see Michael W. Kirst, Government Without Making Laws (1969).

should be made on the floor of Congress rather than worked out as an agency-subcommittee agreement.[67]

Although the procedure has worked well, members of Congress have uncovered attempts to circumvent the understandings. Particularly serious to Congress was a practice followed by some defense agencies. When funds for a program were not granted, other funds would be reprogrammed to it. This practice made a mockery of congressional action on the budget. After warnings were issued by the committees having jurisdiction (both Appropriations and Armed Services), a restriction was placed in the defense appropriations bill. For a number of years it has been the practice of Congress to insert this language: "No part of the funds in this Act shall be available to prepare or present a request to the Committees on Appropriations for the reprogramming of funds, unless for higher priority items, based on unforeseen military requirements, than those for which originally appropriated and in no case where the item for which reprogramming is requested has been denied by the Congress."[68] Congress included the clause concerning "higher priority items" to discourage agencies from applying surplus funds to marginal and low-priority programs.

The tenuous nature of nonstatutory controls is underscored by an incident that occurred in 1975. The conference report on the defense appropriations bill had directed the Navy Department to produce as its air combat fighter a derivative of the plane selected by the Air Force. The purpose was to increase commonality between the two services. Instead, the Navy picked an aircraft that was not a derivative. A contractor, who had bid on the expectation that the Navy would follow the understanding in the conference report, lodged a formal protest with the General Accounting Office, claiming that the contract was null and void. The contractor insisted that directives placed in a conference report were binding on an agency.

The GAO disagreed. The Comptroller General ruled that such directives had legal force only when some ambiguity in the lan-

---

[67] On the development of defense reprogramming, see Louis Fisher, Presidential Spending Power 80-98 (1975).

[68] E.g., P.L. 98-212, 97 Stat. 1445, sec. 736 (1983).

guage of a public law requires recourse to the legislative history. Otherwise, agencies follow nonstatutory controls for practical, not legal, reasons. Agencies may ignore nonstatutory controls but only "at the peril of strained relations with the Congress." To be legally binding, the directive on the Navy aircraft had to appear in the public law.[69]

Nonstatutory controls are weak when Congress sends contradictory signals, for example, adopting one policy in an authorization bill while expressing something else in a committee report that accompanies an appropriations bill. In 1978 the Supreme Court declined to give preference to the latter: "Expressions of committees dealing with requests for appropriations cannot be equated with statutes enacted by Congress, particularly not in the circumstances presented by this case."[70] Two years later an appellate court held that statements in a conference report, suggesting that Congress did not contemplate the use of certain statutory authority, cannot negate that authority when Congress grants it with unambiguous statutory language.[71] Executive departments have considerable leeway when contradictory instructions appear in reports from the authorization and appropriations committees, or when the House and the Senate cannot agree on consistent report language.[72]

Inconsistencies between nonstatutory controls and public law language could be eliminated by placing committee directives in the bill. Congressman John Dingell made this proposal in 1974, primarily to restrict the ability of the Appropriations Committees to "legislate" in their reports and infringe on the jurisdiction of authorization committees. His amendment to the House rules stated that a committee report accompanying an appropriations bill "shall not contain any directive or limitation with respect to

[69] 55 Comp. Gen. 307, 319, 325-26 (1975). See also 55 Comp. Gen. 812 (1976) and 1 O.L.C. 133 (1977).

[70] TVA v. Hill, 437 U.S. 153, 191 (1978). See also Demby v. Schweiker, 671 F.2d 507 (D.C. Cir. 1981), which favored statutory requirements over contrary instructions in a subsequent conference report and its legislative history.

[71] Nat'l Small Shipments v. CAB, 618 F.2d 819 (D.C. Cir. 1980).

[72] 128 Cong. Rec. H9830-31 (daily ed. December 15, 1982). Statements of Congressmen Nichols and Dickinson.

such appropriation unless such directive or limitation is set forth in the accompanying bill." After the chairman of the House Appropriations Committee objected that the amendment would impose an "intolerable burden upon everybody concerned" and add hundreds of pages to a public law, Dingell withdrew his amendment.[73]

Nonstatutory controls play an especially binding role in the annual authorization bill that covers the U.S. intelligence community. Instead of publicly disclosing the amounts spent for these agencies, the House committee report explains that a classified schedule ("directly incorporated into, and integral to, the bill itself") identifies the amounts of dollars and personnel ceilings for all programs included in the bill.[74] Failure by the administration to honor the numbers in the classified schedule would destroy the agreement between the executive and legislative branches to maintain secret budgets for the Central Intelligence Agency and other components of the intelligence establishment.

In case of litigation, an interpretation of a statute's legislative history can be decisive. But Congress and the public cannot enter the courts to resolve every grievance. Nonstatutory controls depend on good-faith efforts and a spirit of cooperation by agency officials. During the Nixon years, agencies demonstrated a studied contempt for nonstatutory controls, partly because of politicization in the top ranks of agencies and less influence by careerists. This record is largely an aberration, yet similar breakdowns in executive-legislative understandings have marred the history of other administrations. If some type of shift is under way, producing an attitude of agency independence and White House autonomy, Congress will have to depend more heavily on statutory provisions and sharper legislative guidelines.

Administrative Legislation

Presidents are obligated under the Constitution to take care that the laws be "faithfully executed." The often conflicting and am-

---

[73] 120 Cong. Rec. 34416-18 (1974).
[74] E.g., H. Rept. No. 486 (Part 1), 97th Cong., 2d Sess. 2 (1982).

biguous passages within a law must be interpreted by executive officials to construct the purpose and intent of Congress. As important as intent is the extent to which a law is carried out. President Taft once remarked: "Let any one make the laws of the country, if I can construe them."[75]

To carry out the laws, administrators must issue rules and regulations of their own. The courts long ago appreciated this need. The *Eliason* decision of 1842, concerning regulations issued by the Secretary of War, declared that rules and regulations "must be received as the acts of the executive, and as such, be binding upon all within the sphere of his legal and constitutional authority."[76] In a later decision the courts upheld regulations issued by the Treasury Department, partly because they were based upon general statutory authority given to executive departments to "prescribe regulations" for the conduct of their operations.[77] Current law authorizes the head of an executive department or military department to prescribe regulations "for the government of his department, the conduct of its employees, the distribution and performance of its business, and the custody, use, and preservation of its records, papers, and property."[78]

These duties, primarily of a "housekeeping" nature, relate only distantly to the citizenry. Many regulations, however, bear directly on the public. It is here that administrative legislation must be restricted in its scope and application. Regulations are not supposed to be a substitute for the general policymaking that Congress enacts in the form of a public law.[79] Although administrative regulations are entitled to respect, the authority to prescribe rules and regulations is not an independent source of power to make laws. Agency rulemaking must rest on authority granted directly or indirectly by Congress.[80]

[75] William Howard Taft, Our Chief Magistrate and His Powers 78 (1916).

[76] United States v. Eliason, 41 U.S. (16 Pet.) 291, 301 (1842).

[77] Boske v. Comingore, 177 U.S. 459 (1900).

[78] 5 U.S.C. 301 (1982).

[79] 6 Op. Att'y Gen. 10 (1853).

[80] Chrysler Corp. v. Brown, 441 U.S. 281, 306-08 (1979). See Lincoln Electric Co. v. Commissioner of Int. Rev., 190 F.2d 326, 330 (6th Cir. 1951); American Broadcasting Co. v. United States, 110 F.Supp. 374, 384 (S.D. N.Y. 1953), aff'd, 347 U.S. 284 (1954); and Independent Meat Packers Ass'n v. Butz, 526 F.2d 228, 234-36 (8th Cir. 1975), cert. denied, 424 U.S. 966 (1976).

Substantive policies must be published in the Federal Register or in the Code of Federal Regulations, not in internal agency manuals.[81] Unless agencies articulate and publish the standards and procedures that govern their decisions, the public is denied an opportunity for meaningful response and courts are unable to review the validity of agency actions.[82] Agencies may not legally ignore or depart from the policies and procedures that they promulgate.[83] They cannot violate their own regulations, although under certain circumstances (involving a criminal prosecution rather than an Administrative Procedure Act proceeding), evidence obtained in violation of an agency regulation is admissible at trial.[84]

In theory, agency regulations carry into effect the will of Congress as expressed in a statute: "A regulation which does not do this, but operates to create a rule out of harmony with the statute, is a mere nullity."[85] In practice, ambiguities and vagueness in statutes create opportunities, if not the necessity, for creative rulemaking by agencies. When a statute contains contradictory demands, the courts have sanctioned the adoption of rules that "harmonize" the competing provisions.[86]

Presidential Proclamations

Proclamations by the President take two forms. Some are merely declaratory in effect, such as those issued by President Carter during 1977 to designate Earth Week, Law Day, National Farm Safety Week, and other issues of general interest. Other proclamations have substantive impact.

A prime example of the latter was Nixon's "New Economic

---

[81] Morton v. Ruiz, 415 U.S. 199 (1974).

[82] Environmental Defense Fund v. Ruckelshaus, 439 F.2d 584, 598 (D.C. Cir. 1971); Historic Green Springs, Inc. v. Bergland, 497 F.Supp. 839, 854-57 (E.D. Va. 1980).

[83] Vitarelli v. Seaton, 359 U.S. 535 (1959); Note, "Violations by Agencies of Their Own Regulations," 87 Harv. L. Rev. 629 (1974).

[84] United States v. Caceres, 440 U.S. 741 (1979).

[85] Manhattan Co. v. Commissioner, 297 U.S. 129, 134 (1936). See Ernst & Ernst v. Hochfelder, 425 U.S. 185, 213-14 (1976) and Batterton v. Francis, 432 U.S. 416, 425 n. 9 (1977).

[86] Citizens to Save Spencer Cty. v. EPA, 600 F.2d 844 (D.C. Cir. 1979).

Policy" unveiled in 1971. In part it involved a 10 percent surcharge placed on articles imported into the United States. The stated purpose was to ensure that American products would not be at a disadvantage because of "unfair exchange rates."[87] The more immediate concern was a deterioration of the American balance of payments. A month later a study group of the Council of the General Agreement on Tariffs and Trade (GATT) called the surcharge incompatible with the GATT and an "inappropriate" remedy for the U.S. balance of payments deficit.[88]

Importers immediately filed appeals with the Customs Bureau. When their petitions proved unsuccessful they turned to the Customs Court for relief, contending that the surcharge went beyond the scope of any authority delegated to the President by Congress. The Customs Court, in 1974, agreed with the importers and declared the surcharge invalid. It said "the Proclamation, in fact, arrogated unto the President a power beyond the scope of any authority delegated to him by the Congress."[89] Had this decision stood, the federal government would have had to repay about $500 million it had collected.[90]

A year later, however, the Court of Customs and Patents Appeals reversed the decision. Although the appeals court subscribed to the theory that the President did not possess any undelegated power to regulate commerce or to set tariffs, and that no such inherent power existed for the President, it concluded that he had acted within the power delegated to him by the Trading With the Enemy Act (TWEA). Neither Proclamation 4074 nor the administration's legal defense (opinion of the General Counsel of the Treasury, September 29, 1971) had referred to the TWEA. Furthermore, nothing in the TWEA specifically

[87] Public Papers of the Presidents, 1971, at 889. Proclamation 4074, 36 Fed. Reg. 15724 (1971). The surcharge was terminated December 20, 1971; Proclamation 4098, 36 Fed. Reg. 24201 (1971).

[88] Philip C. Jones, "Attacks on the United States Import Surcharge Under Domestic and International Law: A Pragmatic Analysis," 6 J. Int'l L. & Econ. 269 (1971-72).

[89] Yoshida Int'l Inc. v. United States, 378 F.Supp. 1155, 1167 (Cust. Ct. 1974).

[90] Washington Post, July 9, 1974, at A1:5.

authorized or prohibited the imposition of a surcharge. The appeals court was not surprised that Congress "did not *specify* that the President could use a surcharge in a national emergency. Having left the battlefield, it would hardly do to dictate all the weapons to be used in the fight."

It was also "self-evident" to the court that the surcharge had overtones of foreign relations and foreign policy. Foreign exchange rates, international monetary reserves, balances of payments, and trade barriers had become increasingly intertwined. The court relied on *Curtiss-Wright* to argue that Congress could delegate more broadly in foreign affairs than in domestic affairs.[91] This reliance was misplaced. *Curtiss-Wright* involved a specific delegation of authority to prevent arms shipments to other regions. The Trading With the Enemy Act, as the court acknowledged, did not specifically delegate authority to impose a surcharge. Moreover, imposition of a surcharge is peculiarly within the province of Congress to levy tariffs and regulate foreign commerce.[92]

Less successful was Proclamation 4744, issued by President Carter in 1980 to impose a fee on imported oil. This action, which would have increased the price of gasoline by 10 cents a gallon, was meant to lower domestic gasoline consumption. A district court ruled that the proclamation "does not fall within the inherent powers of the President, is not sanctioned by the statutes cited by Defendants [the Department of Energy], and is contrary to manifest Congressional intent." At the time the court

[91] United States v. Yoshida Intern., Inc., 526 F.2d 560, 576, 580-82 (Ct. Cust. & Pat. App. 1975). See page 572 and note 13 for lack of inherent presidential power to regulate commerce or to set tariffs. In a separate action (Alcan Aluminum Corp. v. United States), challenging the appellate court decision in *Yoshida*, the Supreme Court denied certiorari; 429 U.S. 986 (1976). Background is provided by David Pollard and David A. Boillot, "The Import Surcharge of 1971: A Case Study of Executive Powers in Foreign Commerce," 7 Vand. J. Transnat'l L. 137 (1973).

[92] When a statute prescribes a specific procedure and the President elects to follow a different course, a proclamation by him is illegal and void. Schmidt Pritchard & Co. v. United States, 167 F.Supp. 272 (Cust. Ct. 1958); Carl Zeiss, Inc. v. United States, 76 F.2d 412 (Cust. & Pat. App. 1935).

handed down its decision, Congress was about to strip Carter of his authority to impose fees or quotas on imported oil.[93]

Executive Orders

A more far-reaching instrument for administrative legislation is the executive order. No one knows how many have been issued; in the early years they were not numbered. In 1907 the State Department began assigning each order a number and filing it in chronological order. By June 25, 1984, the numbered series had reached 12,483. This quantity is understated, since an administration—when it discovers executive orders from prior decades—has to shoehorn them into the existing series by using letters or fractions (for example, Executive Order 106½, Executive Order 103A). Estimates of the unnumbered executive orders range from 15,000 to as high as 50,000.[94]

In June 1941, before Pearl Harbor and America's entry into World War II, President Roosevelt resorted to executive orders to seize North American Aviation's plant in California. He based his action not on statutory authority but on the general powers vested in him "by the Constitution and laws of the United States, as President of the United States of America and Commander in Chief of the Army and Navy of the United States." He invoked these same powers when he seized shipbuilding companies, a cable company, a shell plant, and almost 4,000 coal companies.

[93] Independent Gasoline Marketers Council v. Duncan, 492 F.Supp. 614, 620-21 (D.D.C. 1980); "Oil Import Fees: The Administration of the Program and Its Impact," hearings before the House Committee on Ways and Means, 96th Cong., 2d Sess. (1980).

[94] On the numbering of executive orders see "Presidential Executive Orders," comp. by W.P.A. Historical Records Survey (2 vols., 1944), at viii. On the estimates, see "Executive Orders and Proclamations: A Study of a Use of Presidential Power," printed for the use of the House Committee on Government Operations, 85th Cong., 1st Sess. 37 (1957). A partial list of unnumbered orders appears in "List and Index of Presidential Executive Orders (Unnumbered Series), 1789-1941," New Jersey Historical Records Survey, Work Projects Administration (1943). Under Title 3 of the Code of Federal Regulations, five-year compilations are published containing the full text of all proclamations and executive orders issued from 1936 to the present.

128

Not until 1943 did Congress pass the War Labor Disputes Act to provide statutory authority for presidential seizure of plants, mines, and other facilities.[95] Congress invoked its power of the purse in 1944 to prevent Presidents from using appropriated funds to finance agencies created by executive order unless Congress appropriates specifically for the agency or specifically authorizes the expenditure of funds by it.[96]

Also beginning with Franklin Roosevelt, Presidents used executive orders to articulate and implement an antidiscrimination policy. Roosevelt threatened to withhold contracts from employers who failed to satisfy equal employment provisions in federal contracts. His executive order prohibited discrimination in the employment of workers in "defense industries or government because of race, creed, color, or national origin." Presidents Truman and Eisenhower continued this policy, and Kennedy threatened to cancel contracts as a means of forcing compliance with federal equal employment standards. Shortly after Kennedy issued his order, the Comptroller General stated that "So far as we are aware the propriety of [nondiscrimination] clauses ... has never been seriously questioned by any responsible administrative or judicial tribunal; nor has the Congress seen fit to proscribe the use of such clauses by appropriate legislation." Executive Order 11246, issued by President Johnson, established the administrative structure for carrying out the nondiscrimination clause.[97]

The principal constitutional issue is whether the implementation of Executive Order 11246 conflicts with statutory policy. In

[95] See 6 Fed. Reg. 2777 (1941) and John L. Blackmun, Jr., *Presidential Seizure in Labor Disputes* (1967).

[96] 58 Stat. 387, sec. 213 (1944); 31 U.S.C. 1347 (1982). This restriction applies to "action agencies" that exercise governmental power, not to advisory bodies; 3 O.L.C. 263 (1979).

[97] Executive Order (hereafter E.O.) 8802, 6 Fed. Reg. 3109 (1941); E.O. 10308, 16 Fed. Reg. 12303 (1951); E.O. 10479, 18 Fed. Reg. 4899 (1953); E.O. 10925, 26 Fed. Reg. 1977 (1961); E.O. 11246, 30 Fed. Reg. 12319 (1965). The Comptroller General's decision appears at 40 Comp. Gen. 593 (1961). See James E. Remmert, "Executive Order 11,246: Executive Encroachment," 55 Am. Bar Asso. J. 1037 (1969) and Ruth H. Morgan, *The President and Civil Rights: Policy-Making by Executive Order* (1970).

Title VII of the Civil Rights Act of 1964, Congress prohibited employment discrimination on the basis of race, color, religion, sex, or national origin, but did not require preferential treatment on those grounds. It created the Equal Employment Opportunity Commission (EEOC) to investigate claims of discrimination and propose remedies. The push for a preferential hiring system ("affirmative action") draws its force from Executive Order 11246. The responsibility for administering the order was vested in the Secretary of Labor, who relied on a newly-created Office of Federal Contract Compliance, later the Office of Federal Contract Compliance Programs (OFCCP). To the extent that Congress provides appropriations for the OFCCP, it sanctions or at least acquiesces in the affirmative action policy.

In 1969 the Comptroller General challenged the nondiscrimination policy of the Nixon administration. Under the "Philadelphia Plan" (promulgated pursuant to Executive Order 11246), contractors had to set specific goals for hiring members of minority groups as a condition for working on federally assisted projects. The Comptroller General decided that the plan conflicted with Title VII of the Civil Rights Act of 1964. To the Comptroller General it was immaterial whether the administration designated the hiring commitment a "goal" or "quota." Whatever the name, the practice violated the 1964 act.[98]

The Secretary of Labor disagreed. He said that interpretation of the Civil Rights Act had been vested by Congress in the Department of Justice, which had approved the plan as consistent with the act. The Secretary also claimed that the Comptroller General failed to recognize executive orders "as an independent source of law."[99] Various elements in Congress declared their opposition to the plan. A Senate subcommittee charged in 1971 that it was a "blatant case of usurpation of the legislative function by the executive branch."[100]

[98] 49 Comp. Gen. 59 (1969).
[99] 115 Cong. Rec. 23740 (1969); 42 Op. Att'y Gen. 402 (1969).
[100] See "Congressional Oversight of Administrative Agencies: The Philadelphia Plan," report of the Senate Judiciary Committee made by its Subcommittee on Separation of Powers, 92d Cong., 1st Sess. 13 (Comm. Print 1971).

Federal courts upheld the legality of the plan as well as the executive order that placed it in operation. This use of presidential power was supported partly by the chief executive's implied power—as it relates to economical procurement policy—to ensure that "the largest possible pool of qualified manpower be available for the accomplishment" of federal projects.[101] A number of decisions handed down since that time have circumscribed the reach of Executive Order 11246.[102]

Encroaching on Congress's prerogative of the purse was an executive order by President Kennedy in 1961 establishing the Peace Corps. Seven months went by before Congress appropriated funds for the agency. In the meantime, Kennedy financed the agency by drawing upon contingency funds made available by the Mutual Security Act.[103]

Another controversial executive order involved the Subversive Activities Control Board (SACB), established by President Truman in 1950 to investigate communist activities. The board had jurisdiction to identify and require the public registration of "communist-action" and "communist-front" organizations. Once

[101] Contractors Ass'n of Eastern Pa. v. Secretary of Labor, 442 F.2d 159, 171 (3d Cir. 1971), cert. denied, 404 U.S. 854 (1971). See also Contractors Ass'n of Eastern Pa. v. Secretary of Labor, 311 F.Supp. 1002 (E.D. Pa. 1970) and Robert P. Schuwerk, "The Philadelphia Plan: A Study in the Dynamics of Executive Power," 39 U. Chi. L. Rev. 723 (1972). Other courts find congressional support for Executive Order 11246 not only in procurement statutes but in Title VII of the Civil Rights Act of 1964 and the legislative history of the Equal Employment Opportunity Act of 1972, which amended Title VII; United States v. New Orleans Public Service, Inc., 553 F.2d 459, 466-67 (5th Cir. 1977), vacated and remanded on other grounds, 436 U.S. 942 (1978).

[102] United States v. East Texas Motor Fr. System, 564 F.2d 179 (5th Cir. 1977); Chrysler Corp. v. Brown, 441 U.S. 281 (1979); Liberty Mutual Insurance Co. v. Friedman, 639 F.2d 164 (4th Cir. 1981). See "Committee Analysis of Executive Order 11246 (The Affirmative Action Program)," prepared by the Senate Committee on Labor and Human Resources, 97th Cong., 2d Sess. (Comm. Print April 1982), and Andrée Kahn Blumstein, "Doing Good the Wrong Way: The Case for Delimiting Presidential Power Under Executive Order No. 11, 246," 33 Vand. L. Rev. 921 (1980).

[103] E.O. 10924, 26 Fed. Reg. 1789 (1961). Appropriation: 75 Stat. 721 (1961). See H. Rept. No. 1115, 87th Cong., 1st Sess. 66 (1961).

stigmatized in this fashion, members of such organizations became subject to various penalties. A series of court decisions held that the registration feature violated the Fifth Amendment prohibition against self-incrimination. Congress rejuvenated the board in 1968 by authorizing it to determine, through hearings, whether individuals and organizations were communist. The following year an appellate court declared that the new procedure violated the First Amendment freedom of association. After the Supreme Court refused to review this decision, the board faced extinction.[104]

The SACB gained a new lease on life in 1971 when President Nixon issued an executive order expanding the board's power and field of inquiry.[105] Senator Sam Ervin, challenging the order, introduced a resolution stating that the President had no power "to alter by Executive order the content or effect of legislation enacted by Congress." The Senate adopted Ervin's amendment to prohibit the use of appropriated funds to implement the executive order. Congressman Don Edwards attempted to instruct House conferees to accept the Ervin amendment, but his motion was tabled.[106]

The dispute continued the next year when the House passed a bill to legitimate the executive order. Senator Proxmire offered an amendment to delete $450,000 from the SACB (its entire budget). During debate on the amendment, Senator Ervin re-

[104] The SACB, created by 64 Stat. 997 (1950), was rejuvenated by 81 Stat. 765 (1968). For court cases on SACB, see Communist Party of the United States v. SACB, 367 U.S. 1 (1961); Albertson v. SACB, 382 U.S. 70 (1965); United States v. Robel, 389 U.S. 258 (1967); and Boorda v. SACB, 421 F.2d 1142 (D.C. Cir. 1969), cert. denied, 397 U.S. 1042 (1970).

[105] E.O. 11605, 36 Fed. Reg. 12831 (1971). A federal court, without deciding the issue, noted that there was no precedent for a President "delegating to an independent, quasi-judicial body far-reaching responsibilities different in form and effect from those specifically given that body when created by the Congress"; American Servicemen's Union v. Mitchell, 54 F.R.D. 14, 17 (D.D.C. 1972).

[106] Ervin: S. Res. 163, 92d Cong., 1st Sess. (1971) and 117 Cong. Rec. 30248 (1971). Adoption of his amendment: 117 Cong. Rec. 25898-902 (1971). Edwards: id. at 27305-312. A Proxmire amendment, to delete $450,000 for the SACB, was rejected 41-47; id. at 25888-98.

marked that the board had held hearings on 111 cases the previous year, devoting about 48 seconds to each case. "That is all they did last year," Ervin said, "except draw their breath and their salaries."[107] After the Senate adopted the Proxmire amendment, House and Senate conferees compromised by providing the board with $350,000 but expressly prohibited it from using any of the funds to carry out the executive order.[108] Beginning with the fiscal 1974 budget, the administration did not even bother to request funds for the SACB.

Executive orders are a source of law only when they draw upon the constitutional powers of the President or powers expressly delegated by Congress. Actions that exceed those bounds have been struck down by the courts. When executive orders lack statutory support, they have been held by the courts to be without the force and effect of law. Executive orders may not supercede a statute or override contradictory congressional expressions.[109]

The major example of the judiciary striking down an executive order is the Steel Seizure Case of 1952, which held that President Truman's attempt to seize the steel mills of the nation had no basis in statute or in the Constitution.[110] When departmental policies are contrary to due process they have been held invalid, as in *Cole* v. *Young* (1956), where the Supreme Court decided that the standard prescribed by an executive order—directed against "disloyal" civilian employees in the Department of Health, Ed-

[107] House passage: 118 Cong. Rec. 19075-103 (1972). Proxmire amendment: id. at 21053-74. Ervin remark: id. at 21063-64.

[108] 86 Stat. 1131, 1134 (1972). See "President Nixon's Executive Order 11605 Relating to the Subversive Activities Control Board," hearing before the Senate Committee on the Judiciary, 92d Cong., 1st Sess. (1971).

[109] Lack of statutory support: Manhattan-Bronx Postal Union v. Gronouski, 350 F.2d 451 (D.C. Cir. 1965), cert. denied, 382 U.S. 978 (1966); Stevens v. Carey, 483 F.2d 188 (7th Cir. 1973); Independent Meat Packers Ass'n v. Butz, 526 F.2d 228, 234-36 (8th Cir. 1975), cert. denied, 424 U.S. 966 (1976). Conflicts with statutory policy: Marks v. CIA, 590 F.2d 997, 1003 (D.C. Cir. 1978); Weber v. Kaiser Aluminum & Chemical Corp., 563 F.2d 216, 227 (5th Cir. 1977), rev'd on other grounds, Steelworkers v. Weber, 443 U.S. 193 (1979).

[110] Youngstown Co. v. Sawyer, 343 U.S. 579 (1952).

ucation, and Welfare—did not conform to statutory provisions.[111]

Procedural Controls

Because of the ubiquity and necessity of administrative regulations, they must be reconciled to the rule of law. Agencies are not, like legislatures, representative bodies. They are not created to formulate and express a will. It is their duty to carry out the will announced by the legislative body. Agency officials should have greater expertise than legislators because of their opportunity to specialize, but this capability introduces a weakness to the administrative process: narrowness of view. Procedures are needed to bring forth, in systematic fashion, the full information and facts required for fair and intelligent rulemaking.[112]

Procedural safeguards are basic to the maintenance of a legal system. Yet throughout the nineteenth century and well into the twentieth, due process in administrative matters depended on voluntary agency actions and scattered statutory directives. It is remarkable that not until recent decades were administrative regulations required to be published in a central document. The House Judiciary Committee in 1935 spoke of "utter chaos" regarding the publication and distribution of administrative rules and pronouncements.[113]

Congress passed legislation in 1935 to provide for the custody of federal documents and their publication in a Federal Register. Included among the documents to be published are all presidential proclamations and executive orders that have general applicability and legal effect, and all documents or orders that prescribe

[111] Cole v. Young, 351 U.S. 536, 555 (1956). Other executive orders were struck down in Little v. Barreme, 2 Cr. 170 (1804); United States v. Symonds, 120 U.S. 46 (1887); Panama Refining Co. v. Ryan, 293 U.S. 388, 433 (1935); Schechter Corp. v. United States, 295 U.S. 495, 525-26 (1935); and Kaplan v. Johnson, 409 F.Supp. 190, 206 (N.D. Ill. 1976).

[112] "Report of the Attorney General's Committee on Administrative Procedure," S. Doc. No. 8, 77th Cong., 1st Sess. 101-102 (1941).

[113] H. Rept. No. 280, 74th Cong., 1st Sess. 1-2 (1935). See Erwin N. Griswold, "Government in Ignorance of the Law—A Plea for Better Publication of Executive Legislation," 48 Harv. L. Rev. 198 (1934).

a penalty. Based partly on the statutory authority vested in him by the Federal Register Act, President Roosevelt issued an executive order in 1936 that centered in the Bureau of the Budget (now the Office of Management and Budget) the responsibility for reviewing all proposed executive orders and proclamations.[114]

Additional steps were needed to improve the process for drafting rules. In a major study published in 1937 for the Brownlow Committee, James Hart supported the use of advisory committees as one way to put before administrators the views of organized (and unorganized) interests. Other basic procedural safeguards to be used in the formulation of regulations were notice of a proposed regulation, formal hearings, publication of draft regulations, informal conferences with groups affected, and progression from voluntary to mandatory standards.[115] The Walter-Logan Bill, vetoed by President Roosevelt in 1940, represented the first general legislative effort to impose a uniform standard of procedures for administrative agencies. Roosevelt vetoed it partly because he believed that legislation should await the report of the Attorney General's Committee on Administrative Procedure, which was released in 1941.

These studies, reinforced by congressional hearings, culminated in the Administrative Procedure Act (APA) of 1946, a landmark effort to guarantee fairness by establishing procedures and uniform standards for rulemaking. Some of the major features of the act include adequate notice to the parties concerned, an opportunity for interested persons to participate in rulemaking by submitting material, and publication of the rule not less than thirty days prior to its effective date. The APA relies on the doctrine of separated powers by prohibiting investigative or prosecuting personnel from participating in the agency's decision. Judicial review is available. Courts may hold unlawful any agency action found to be "arbitrary, capricious, an abuse of dis-

[114] 49 Stat. 500, sec. 5 (1935). Roosevelt's Executive Order 7298, February 18, 1936, appeared too early for the first volume of the Federal Register. It is reprinted in James Hart, "The Exercise of Rule-Making Power," The President's Committee on Administrative Management 355 (1937).

[115] Hart, President's Committee, at 339-342.

cretion, or otherwise not in accordance with law" and "contrary to constitutional right, power, privilege, or immunity."[116] Agencies may circumvent the notice-and-comment requirement of the APA by issuing "interpretive rules" and "general statements of policy," but these actions lack the force and effect of law.[117]

Critics of the APA claimed that it mistakenly tried to apply an adversary model to administrative procedures. By placing agency activity in a "judicialized strait jacket," they said, the act "sabotaged" the administrative process.[118] But agencies have managed to live with the act without serious disability. For four decades it has survived with little change.

Although this system has improved the visibility and accountability of administrative legislation, Presidents can circumvent the publication of executive orders and proclamations in the Federal Register by changing the name of the document to a national security directive, memorandum, letter, military order, or some other designation.[119] Furthermore, although executive orders and proclamations are published in the Federal Register, it is not expected that their announcement will be preceded by formal notice, hearing, or other APA procedures required for agency regulations.[120] Draft copies are sometimes made available to Congress and the public for notice and comment, but such initiatives are usually voluntary on the part of the President.[121] Re-

[116] 60 Stat. 237, sec. 10(e) (1946); 5 U.S.C. 500-706 (1982). See "Administrative Procedure Act: Legislative History," S. Doc. No. 248, 79th Cong., 2d Sess. (1946).

[117] Chrysler Corp. v. Brown, 441 U.S. 281, 313-15 (1979).

[118] Frederick A. Blachly and Miriam E. Oatman, "Sabotage of the Administrative Process," 6 Pub. Adm. Rev. 213 (1946) and Foster H. Sherwood, "The Federal Administrative Procedure Act," 41 Am. Pol. Sci. Rev. 271 (1947).

[119] Glenn E. Fuller, "The National Emergency Dilemma: Balancing the Executive's Crisis Powers with the Need for Accountability," 52 S. Cal. L. Rev. 1453, 1466 (1979); S. Rept. No. 922, 94th Cong., 2d Sess. 16-18 (1976).

[120] Metzenbaum v. Edwards, 510 F.Supp. 609, 611 (D.D.C. 1981). See Harold H. Bruff, "Judicial Review and the President's Statutory Powers," 68 Va. L. Rev. 1, 18-24 (1982).

[121] A rare, if not unprecedented, example of an executive order published in draft form in the Federal Register for notice and comment is an order by President Carter to improve federal regulations, first printed at 42 Fed. Reg. 59740 (1977) and published in final form as Executive Order 12044 four months later, 43 Fed. Reg. 12661 (1978), including an analysis of public comments.

cent case law strongly suggests that Congress can impose notice-and-comment requirements on presidential proclamations and executive orders when issued to implement statutory policy, provided Congress does so explicitly.[122]

The APA did not provide for ongoing studies to improve and modify administrative rulemaking. This deficiency was corrected in 1954 when President Eisenhower established an administrative conference to study the changes needed in administrative procedures. President Kennedy formed another temporary conference in 1961. Finally, in 1964 President Johnson created a permanent body called the Administrative Conference of the United States to study and make recommendations on the "efficiency, adequacy, and fairness of the administrative procedure used by administrative agencies in carrying out administrative programs." The conference has since offered a number of recommendations to improve the administrative process.[123]

Presidential Control of Rulemaking

Beginning with the Brownlow Committee in 1937, study commissions and a number of scholars have recommended that the rulemaking functions of all agencies (including the independent regulatory commissions) be placed directly under the President. The Hoover Commission made the same proposal in 1949, as did the Ash Council in 1971, Lloyd Cutler and David Johnson

---

[122] In *United States v. Wayte*, 549 F.Supp. 1376, 1389-91 (C.D. Cal. 1982), a district judge held that President Carter's Proclamation 4771 on draft registration was invalid for failure to comply with notice-and-comment requirements of the Military Selective Service Act. Although reversed in *United States v. Wayte*, 710 F.2d 1385, 1388-89 (9th Cir. 1983), both decisions recognize the authority of Congress to make such a requirement. In *United States v. Martin*, 557 F.Supp. 681 (N.D. Iowa 1982), concerning the same issue, another district judge said that statutes enacted by Congress "are not subjected to notice and comment periods and no reason appears why the same should not be true for presidential proclamations" (at 690). This analogy ignores the constitutional grant of legislative power to Congress and the checks that operate on that power, including bicameralism and the presidential veto, which are not available to constrain presidential proclamations and executive orders.

[123] 78 Stat. 616, sec. 6 (1964). See Randy H. Hamilton and Judy Kelsey, "The Administrative Conference of the U.S.," 29 Pub. Adm. Rev. 286 (1969).

in 1975, and a study commission of the American Bar Association in 1979.[124] Congress has consistently refused to delegate to the President a general supervisory function over all federal regulations.

Lacking this statutory authority, Presidents Ford, Carter, and Reagan established procedures within the White House and the OMB to monitor federal regulations that impose heavy costs on businesses and consumers. These efforts, under the banner of regulatory reform or "deregulation," led to the creation of the Council on Wage and Price Stability (COWPS) and the Regulatory Analysis Review Group (RARG).[125]

Of far greater significance was Executive Order 12291, issued by President Reagan in 1981. It authorized the OMB to review "major" regulations and subject them to cost-benefit analysis. By making the OMB the central clearinghouse and arming it with a vague cost-benefit weapon, the order opened the door to ex parte contacts between industry spokesmen and federal officials and allowed the OMB to use the cost-benefit concept as a way to delay or kill regulations the administration did not want. The unrecorded communications between White House and agency officials and between executive officials and industry representatives raised serious questions of due process and deprived the rulemaking docket of information needed for judicial review.[126]

[124] Brownlow: The President's Committee on Administrative Management, "Administrative Management in the Government of the United States," at 37 (1937); Hoover Commission, Concluding Report (May 1949), at 9, 72; President's Advisory Council on Executive Reorganization, "A New Regulatory Framework: Report on Selected Independent Regulatory Agencies (1971); Lloyd N. Cutler and David R. Johnson, "Regulation and the Political Process, 84 Yale L. J. 1395, 1414-17 (1975); Commission on Law and the Economy of the American Bar Association, "Federal Regulation: Roads to Reform," Final Report 1979, With Recommendations, at 79-82, 88-91.

[125] "Executive Branch Review of Environmental Regulations," hearings before the Senate Committee on Environment and Public Works, 96th Cong., 1st Sess. (1979).

[126] Morton Rosenberg, "Beyond the Limits of Executive Power: Presidential Control of Agency Rulemaking Under Executive Order 12,291," 80 Mich. L. Rev. 193 (1981). For a recent exploration of presidential involvement in agency rulemaking and questions of ex parte influence, see Sierra Club v. Costle, 657 F.2d 298 (D.C. Cir. 1981).

Innocent-sounding procedures became a vehicle for pursuing substantive goals of the White House.

Executive Order 12291 applied only to executive departments and agencies, not to the independent regulatory commissions. However, the latter were subject to OMB's control under the Paperwork Reduction Act of 1980. The OMB puts a control number on federal requests for information from the private sector. Without a control number, agency requests for information can be ignored. By using cost-benefit policy and paperwork review procedures, the OMB was able to pursue Reagan's policy of substituting free market controls for federal regulation.[127]

The ambiguity of our system of "enumerated" and "separated" powers is nowhere more evident than in the assignment of the legislative power. Much of the original legislative power vested in Congress is now exercised, as a practical matter, by executive agencies, independent commissions, and the courts. The President's legislative power, invoked on rare occasions in the early decades, is now discharged on a regular basis throughout the year in the form of executive orders, proclamations, and other instruments of executive lawmaking. In self-defense, Congress has developed a complex system that depends on procedural guidelines for agency action, judicial review, committee and subcommittee oversight, and a constantly evolving structure of informal, nonstatutory controls.

[127] See Issues of "Inside O.M.B.," July 3, 1982, at 7-8; October 22, 1982, at 2-3; November 5, 1982, at 1-2; December 3, 1982, at 7; and "Inside the Administration," January 14, 1983, at 13-14.

5

VETOES: PRESIDENTIAL AND
LEGISLATIVE

It has become customary to associate the veto with the executive. Historically, however, the veto has played a more general role in government. Roman tribunes uttered "veto" to protect the plebs from injustice at the hands of the patricians.[1] In the seventeenth century Poland adopted a *liberum veto*, permitting a single deputy of the legislature to exclaim "I disapprove." During the time of Alexander Hamilton, the New York constitution lodged the veto power in a Council of Revision consisting of the governor, chancellor, and judges of the supreme court.[2] The Articles of Confederation (1777) granted to each state a veto over any amendment to that charter. The framers of the American Constitution gave serious consideration to the idea of a joint revisionary power, to be shared between the President and the Supreme Court. They thought that joining the executive and the judiciary for this purpose would help preserve their independence against Congress.[3]

The veto, as an instrument to prevent or postpone governmental action, is exercised today on many fronts: the executive veto provided in the Constitution, the ability of courts to strike down legislative and executive actions as invalid, statutes that vest in governors and private parties a veto power, and Senate vetoes of treaties and appointments. A "legislative veto" was available to Congress until the Supreme Court declared it unconstitutional in 1983. However, functional equivalents to the legislative veto will be used in the future.

---

[1] Charles J. Zinn, The Veto Power of the President 1 (1951), a committee print for the use of the House Committee on the Judiciary.

[2] Federalist 73, and Charles C. Thach, Jr., The Creation of the Presidency 35-41 (1923).

[3] Farrand, Records, I, 105, 108, 139; II, 77.

The Presidential Veto

The framers of the Constitution gave short shrift to the proposal for an absolute executive veto. They had only to recall the very first charge leveled against King George III in the Declaration of Independence: "He has refused his Assent to Laws, the most wholesome and necessary for the common good." James Wilson and Alexander Hamilton maintained that an absolute veto was acceptable for the American Presidency, since there was little danger it would be "too much exercised," but delegates at the Philadelphia convention rejected such speculation. The proposal was turned down, ten states voting against it and not a single one in favor. The President received a qualified veto, subject to an override by a two-thirds majority of each House of Congress.[4]

Some of the Antifederalists, espousing a literalist view of the separation doctrine, regarded the executive veto as an encroachment upon the legislature. One critic of the Constitution called it "a political error of the greatest magnitude, to allow the executive power a negative, or in fact any kind of control over the proceedings of the legislature."[5] To this kind of criticism Hamilton replied, in Federalist 73, that the veto was necessary to protect the President against the "depredations" of the legislature: "He might gradually be stripped of his authorities by successive resolutions or annihilated by a single vote. And in the one mode or the other, the legislative and executive powers might speedily come to be blended in the same hands."

The Purpose of the Veto

Hamilton identified one of the principal objectives of the veto: to protect the executive from legislative encroachment. Use of

---

[4] Farrand, Records, I, 96-104. George Reed of Delaware later proposed that the President be given an absolute veto; his motion was rejected, 1 to 9 (id. at II, 200). The delegates voted on August 15 to require a three-fourths majority for an override, voting 6 to 4 (id. at II, 301), but reversed themselves on September 12 by an identical vote in support of the two-thirds requirement (id. at II, 582-583, 585-587).

[5] Anonymous "William Penn" writing in the (Philadelphia) Independent Gaz-

the veto for other reasons has produced periodic waves of hysteria. As recently as the administration of Gerald Ford, critics claimed that he had used the veto unconstitutionally. Edward Pessen, professor of history at Baruch College, concluded that the veto power exercised by Ford, Nixon, Johnson, and almost all Presidents since Andrew Jackson has been "utterly at odds" with the intentions of the framers. According to Pessen, the veto should be rarely exercised. Madison and Hamilton, he said, believed that the veto would be used for limited purposes: "protection of the integrity of the Presidential office and rejection of flagrantly unconstitutional legislation."[6]

Charles L. Black, Jr., professor of law at Yale University, also insisted that President Ford misused the veto. This power may be applied "only rarely, and certainly not as a means of systematic policy control over the legislative branch, on matters constitutionally indifferent and not menacing the President's independence."[7] According to Black, the early vetoes mainly protected the integrity of the President's office. Should the veto be used sparingly? Should it be used primarily to protect the President's office? Neither assertion is well founded.

As to the frequency of vetoes, the framers could not have anticipated the vast range of activities to be carried out by the federal government, the outpouring of legislation that resulted, and the great mass of private bills. On a single day in 1886 President Cleveland received nearly 240 private bills granting new pensions for veterans, increasing their benefits, or restoring old names to the list. Many of the bills were so indefensible that they invited a veto.[8] Congress adopted the practice of keeping separate lists of public and private bills. Although congressional efforts to

etteer, January 3, 1788, cited by Morton Borden, ed., The Antifederalist Papers 210 (1965).

[6] Edward Pessen, "The Arrogant Veto," The Nation, August 30, 1975, at 133-37.

[7] Charles L. Black, Jr., "Some Thoughts on the Veto," 40 Law & Contemp. Prob. 87, 90 (1976).

[8] Richardson, Messages and Papers, X, 5001-02 (May 8, 1886) and 5020-40 (June 21-23, 1886).

override vetoes of public bills are common, Congress generally concedes vetoes of private bills without a vote.[9]

Nor did the framers foresee the emergence of party politics, the possibility that different parties could control Congress and the White House, and the encouragement this would give to vetoes. Congress has also provoked numerous vetoes by passing hundreds of measures in the closing days of a session.[10] A favorite device used by Congress to enhance its power consists of tacking irrelevant amendments ("riders") onto appropriations bills. Since appropriations are necessary for the operation of the government, members hope to gain safe passage for a legislative idea that might not survive on its own merits. Rutherford B. Hayes vigorously opposed this tactic, which he regarded as a coercive measure designed to strip him of the veto power.[11] After a series of vetoes he prevailed, but Presidents continue to receive omnibus bills that are amalgams of disparate elements. These are some of the factors that explain the growth of presidential vetoes.

What of the second proposition: that vetoes should be used primarily to protect the President's office? Justice White, in a 1976 opinion, claimed that the veto's principal aim was not to provide "another check against poor legislation" but rather to protect the executive against legislative encroachments.[12] Some delegates to the Philadelphia convention, including Elbridge Gerry, did regard the veto primarily as an instrument to defend the executive branch, not the general interest. But Madison viewed the power in more generous terms. The veto existed "to restrain the Legislature from encroaching on the other co-ordinate Departments, or on the rights of the people at large; or from passing laws unwise in their principle, or incorrect in their form . . . ."[13]

[9] Clarence A. Berdahl, "The President's Veto of Private Bills," 52 Pol. Sci. Q. 505 (1937).

[10] John D. Long, "The Use and Abuse of the Veto Power," 4 The Forum 253 (1887).

[11] Richardson, Messages and Papers, IX, 4475, 4488, 4494 (April 29, May 29, and June 23, 1879); T. Harry Williams, ed., Hayes: The Diary of a President 193-234 (1964).

[12] Buckley v. Valeo, 424 U.S. 1, 285 (1976).

[13] Farrand, Records, II, 586; I, 139. See also II, 74, 587, and IV, 81.

Hamilton, in Federalist 73, defended the veto as necessary not only to protect the President but also to furnish "an additional security against the enaction of improper laws. It establishes a salutary check upon the legislative body, calculated to guard the community against the effects of faction, precipitancy, or of any impulse unfriendly to the public good, which may happen to influence a majority of that body." The veto would protect the community from the passage of "bad laws, through haste, inadvertence, or design." This larger view of Madison and Hamilton prevailed.

It is interesting that Gerald Ford's critics placed such heavy emphasis on the use of the veto to protect the President's office. The historical record is quite to the contrary. George Washington vetoed two bills—the first on constitutional grounds (an apportionment bill) and the second because he thought the bill so carelessly drafted and so unwise in substance that it should not become law.[14] Neither bill affected the President's office. Professor Black suggested that the second bill, involving the military, "may have been seen as a dangerous weakening of the country's military force, connected with the Commander-in-Chief power, so that the veto may well be thought to fall within the category of defense of the presidential office . . . ."[15] This supposition depends on too many "mays." The evidence is straightforward: Washington thought it a bad bill.

John Adams and Thomas Jefferson did not use the veto power. The next President, James Madison, relied on it five times for regular (as opposed to pocket) vetoes. Four were for constitutional reasons (one involving trials in district courts, one having to do with internal improvements, and two concerning church-state separation). The fifth bill, which regarded the national bank, seemed to Madison too poorly designed to accomplish its purpose.[16] Professor Black states that Madison vetoed the bank bill because it failed to provide adequately for circulating money in time of war: "Perhaps, without stretching too much, such a veto

[14] Richardson, Messages and Papers, I, 116, 203.
[15] Black, "Some Thoughts on the Veto," at 90.
[16] Richardson, Messages and Papers, II, 496, 569, 474, 475, 540 (in order of my discussion).

may (like Washington's second veto) be connected with protection of the President's role as Commander-in-Chief, and with the effective execution of that power."[17] Again, too much stretching.

During this initial period of twenty-eight years, covering four Presidents and seven administrations, there were seven regular vetoes, five of them for constitutional reasons. Only one affected the independence of the executive: the district courts bill, which Madison vetoed in part because he thought it usurped his appointment powers.[18]

Ironically, the critics of the Ford administration borrowed unwittingly from Whig theories of the nineteenth century. Increased use of the veto by Presidents Jackson and Tyler had produced three basic complaints: (1) since the veto was rarely overridden it amounted to an absolute veto, contrary to the framers' intent; (2) the veto was originally granted to bolster a weak executive, who was now able to defend himself by other means; and (3) the veto's limited purpose (to defend the Constitution) had been ignored by Presidents. Members of Congress tried to reduce the vote needed for an override from two-thirds to a simple majority. All such proposals failed.[19]

During this period a number of chief executives recorded their philosophy on the veto power. In 1841 President William Henry Harrison recommended a restrained use of the veto, for it was "preposterous" to believe that the President could better understand the wishes of the people than their own representatives. He conceded that Presidents were more independent of sectional pulls, however, and might have to veto legislation of a strongly local nature. Harrison justified vetoes to protect the Constitution, to defend the people from hasty legislation, and to preserve the rights of minorities from the effects of combinations.[20]

Harrison's successor, John Tyler, exercised the veto too frequently for his opponents in Congress, who introduced a resolution to impeach him. Among the grounds was this: "I charge him with the high crime and misdemeanor of withholding his

[17] Black, "Some Thoughts on the Veto," at 90-91.
[18] Richardson, Messages and Papers, II, 496.
[19] Edward Campbell Mason, The Veto Power 133-137 (1890).
[20] Richardson, Messages and Papers, III, 1866.

assent to laws undispensable [*sic*] to the just operations of government, which involved no constitutional difficulty on his part . . . ."[21]

The Democratic party held a less restricted view of the veto power. President Polk, in a detailed analysis in 1848, denied that the obligations of the President were "in any degree lessened by the prevalence of views different from his own in one or both Houses of Congress." The President had to do more than check hasty and inconsiderate legislation. If Congress, after full deliberation, agreed to measures which the President regarded as "subversive of the Constitution or of the vital interests of the country, it is his solemn duty to stand in the breach and resist them."[22] The Democratic platforms of 1844, 1848, 1852, and 1856 placed the party on record as being "decidedly opposed" to taking from the President his qualified veto power to suspend the passage of bills that lacked a two-thirds majority in each House. The veto power, claimed the platforms, had saved the American people from the "corrupt and tyrannical domination" of the United States Bank and the "corrupting system of general interest improvements."[23]

Zachary Taylor, who followed Polk in the White House, adhered to the Whig interpretation. He viewed the veto as "an extreme measure, to be resorted to only in extraordinary cases, as where it may become necessary to defend the executive against the encroachments of the legislative power or to prevent hasty and inconsiderate or unconstitutional legislation."[24] The personal opinion of the President "ought not to control the action of Congress upon questions of Domestic policy; nor ought his opinion & objections to be interposed when questions of Constitutional power have been settled by the various Departments of government and acquiesced in by the people." On such subjects as the tariff, the currency, and internal improvements "the will of the people as expressed through their Representatives in

[21] Cong. Globe, 27th Cong., 3d Sess. 144 (1843).

[22] Richardson, Messages and Papers, VI, 2512 (December 5, 1848).

[23] Kirk H. Porter and Donald Bruce Johnson, National Party Platforms 4, 11, 17, 24 (1956).

[24] Richardson, Messages and Papers, VI, 2561 (December 4, 1849).

Congress ought to be . . . carried out and respected by the Executive."[25] In essence, this is the position of Democrats who criticized Ford's veto record. How chagrined they would be to know that they walk in the footsteps of Zachary Taylor.

Constitutional Procedures

If the President decides to withhold his signature from a bill, he is directed by Article I, Section 7, of the the Constitution to return it, "with his Objections to that House in which it shall have originated, who shall enter the Objections at large on their Journal, and proceed to reconsider it." If "two thirds of that House" agree to pass the bill, it is reconsidered by the other House "and if approved by two thirds of that House, it shall become a Law."

The ambiguities of this language were later clarified by legislative precedents and judicial decisions. What was meant by "two thirds of that House"—two-thirds of the total membership of each House, or merely two-thirds of a majority of its members? The House of Representatives decided on two-thirds of the members present, provided they formed a quorum.[26] This ruling was liberalized in 1912 when Speaker Clark held that an override required two-thirds of the members present *and voting*. On this particular override attempt there were 174 yeas, 80 nays, and 10 present. The 174 did not represent two-thirds of the 264 present, but it did constitute two-thirds of the 254 voting. The override therefore carried.[27]

In 1919 the Supreme Court, referring to precedents established by Congress, decided that two-thirds of a quorum sufficed for an override. Two-thirds of "that House" meant a House organized and entitled to exert legislative power (a quorum).[28] The

---

[25] Taylor's first "Allison letter," April 22, 1848, to his brother-in-law, John Stadler Allison, reprinted in Arthur M. Schlesinger, Jr., ed., History of American Presidential Elections, II, 913-914 (1971).

[26] Hinds' Precedents, IV, §3537-38 n. 2.

[27] Id. at VII, §1111.

[28] Missouri Pac. Ry. Co. v. Kansas, 248 U.S. 276 (1919).

practice of Congress has been to require two-thirds of the members present and voting.

Another issue: can a President sign a bill after Congress has recessed? If presidential approval of a bill is not strictly an executive function, being legislative in nature, must approval occur only when both Houses are actually sitting for legislative functions? The Court in 1899 refused to accept that construction. If a President decides to sign a bill, no further action by Congress is required and therefore there is no need for it to sit.[29]

Taking this a step further, can a President sign a bill after the final adjournment of Congress? Two Attorneys General had argued that he could.[30] In 1932 the Supreme Court agreed. Important for the Court was the constitutional right of the President to take up to ten days (Sundays excepted) to consider the merits of bills presented to him. The Court pointed out that during the last twenty-four hours of the 71st Congress, 184 bills were presented to President Hoover, placing upon him a burden that required the full ten days to act responsibly. Furthermore, the holding of the Court in 1899 (that no action by Congress was required for the signing of a bill after a recess) applied equally well to final adjournment.[31]

A remaining question concerned the meaning of "presentation." The Constitution provides that any bill not returned by the President within the ten-day period "after it shall have been presented to him" shall be a law, as if he had signed it, unless a congressional adjournment prevented its return. Must Congress present the bill to him personally ("presented to him") or may it leave the bill with an agent at the White House? If the President is traveling outside Washington, D.C., but within the United States, presentation to the White House has been considered adequate. But what if the President is traveling abroad?

This issue was decided by the Court of Claims in 1964. Congress had delivered a bill to the White House on August 31,

---

[29] La Abra Silver Mining Co. v. United States, 175 U.S. 423, 451-55 (1899).

[30] 32 Op. Att'y Gen. 225 (1920) and 36 Op. Att'y Gen. 403 (1931). See Lindsay Rogers, "The Power of the President to Sign Bills After Congress Has Adjourned," 30 Yale L. J. 1 (1920).

[31] Edwards v. United States, 286 U.S. 482 (1932).

1959, after President Eisenhower had departed for a trip to Europe. He did not return until September 7 and vetoed the bill on September 14. Congress did not attempt an override. Had he acted within the ten-day period? The Court of Claims held that a President about to travel abroad had three choices. He could demand that Congress personally present bills to him abroad, ask that they be delayed until his return, or direct that bills be accepted at the White House as though he were present. If Congress dislikes the second option, it may send the bill abroad and present it to the President ("who has to make himself reasonably available for that purpose").[32] In this case Eisenhower had advised Congress that he was selecting the second option and Congress had acquiesced. The veto was therefore valid.

Most of the controversies over the veto power have remained within the political arena. James Monroe alarmed some members of Congress in 1817 by signaling in advance his opposition to contemplated legislation. He announced his "settled conviction" that Congress lacked constitutional authority to appropriate money for internal improvements. A House committee, established to review his message, reacted with indignation. The committee's report said that the President's message should not be permitted to have any influence on Congress's disposition to legislate on the subject. Nothing should restrain the ability of Congress to express its will. If Congress, deferring to the President's opinion, refrained from action, "it might happen that the opinion of the President would prevent the enaction of a law, even though there should be the Constitutional majority of two-thirds of both Houses in its favor." Such a practice should not go uncontested, for otherwise the presidential veto "would acquire a force unknown to the Constitution, and the legislative body would be shorn of its power from a want of confidence in its strength, or from indisposition to exert it."[33] Today such "interference" by the President is commonplace.

---

[32] Eber Bros. Wine & Liquor Corporation v. United States, 337 F.2d 624, 630 (Ct. Cl. 1964), cert. denied, 380 U.S. 950 (1965). See 2 O.L.C. 383 (1977).

[33] Annals of Congress, 15th Cong., 1st Sess. 451-52 (1817). For Monroe announcement, see id. at 18.

Other practices broadened the scope of presidential action. The Constitution provides for three forms of action: the President may sign a bill, veto it, or allow it to lapse by using a "pocket veto." Custom soon extended the range of choice, such as letting a bill become law without the President's signature. Grover Cleveland took this course in 1894 to dissociate himself from the Wilson-Gorman Tariff Act. To veto the bill would have offended his party (in control of both Houses and therefore responsible for the measure) and yet Cleveland did not want his name on the bill. To him it contained provisions "which are not in line with honest tariff reform, and it contains inconsistencies and crudities which ought not to appear in tariff laws or laws of any kind."[34]

Pocket Vetoes

The Constitution provides that any bill not returned by the President "within ten Days (Sundays excepted)" shall become law "unless the Congress by their Adjournment prevent its Return, in which Case it shall not be a Law." This instrument, known as the "pocket veto," was first used in 1812 by President Madison. From Madison through Andrew Johnson, Presidents who used the pocket veto generally prepared a memorandum giving the reasons for their disapproval. This practice lapsed from Grant through Hoover but was reinstated by Franklin D. Roosevelt.[35]

Uncertainty over the meaning of the Constitution led to the Pocket Veto Case of 1929. A bill had been presented to President Coolidge less than ten days before Congress adjourned at the end of a first session. The adjournment lasted from July to December. The Supreme Court unanimously upheld the pocket veto, concluding that the adjournment prevented the President from returning the bill. The critical issue was not whether an adjournment was final or interim but whether it "prevented" the bill's return. The Court also decided that "ten Days" meant calendar days, not legislative days.[36]

[34] Robert McElroy, Grover Cleveland, II, 116 (1923).
[35] Clement E. Vose, "The Memorandum Pocket Veto," 26 J. Pol. 397 (1964).
[36] The Pocket Veto Case, 279 U.S. 644 (1929). See Abram R. Serven, "The Constitution and the 'Pocket Veto,'" 7 N.Y.U.L. Q. Rev. 495 (1919).

Other questions were resolved by *Wright* v. *United States* (1938). In this controversy the Congress did not adjourn. The Senate alone had recessed for three days, a period the Supreme Court considered so short that the Senate could act with "reasonable promptitude" on the veto. Also, the Secretary of the Senate functioned during the recess and was able to receive (and did receive) the bill. As a more general point the Court noted that the veto procedure served two fundamental purposes: (1) to give the President an opportunity to consider a bill presented to him and (2) to give Congress an opportunity to consider his objections and override them. Both objectives required protection. To allow the concept of a pocket veto to expand without limit would create a kind of absolute veto emphatically rejected by the framers.[37]

There the matter rested until December 14, 1970, when the Family Practice of Medicine Bill was presented to President Nixon. It had passed by such overwhelming majorities (64 to 1 in the Senate and 346 to 2 in the House) that a veto would have met an almost certain override. Both Houses adjourned on December 22 for the Christmas holidays. The Senate returned December 28, the House the following day. Not counting December 27 (a Sunday), the Senate was absent for four days and the House for five. Despite the shortness of that interval and the fact that the Senate had designated an officer to receive messages from the President, Nixon pocket vetoed the bill on December 26.[38]

Unlike the 1929 case, Nixon's action involved a short adjournment *during* a session rather than a lengthy adjournment at the end of a session. This distinction was of pivotal importance to the judiciary. In 1973 a district court held that the Christmas adjournment had not prevented Nixon from returning the bill to Congress as a regular veto. The bill therefore became law, said the court, on December 25, 1970.[39]

The manner in which an appellate court upheld this decision the next year cast doubt on pocket vetoes during *any* intrasession

---

[37] Wright v. United States, 302 U.S. 583, 589-590, 596-597 (1938). For an Attorney General's opinion upholding a pocket veto after Congress had adjourned in 1943 for two months, see 40 Op. Att'y Gen. 274 (1943).

[38] Public Papers of the Presidents, 1970, at 1156.

[39] Kennedy v. Sampson, 364 F.Supp. 1075, 1087 (D.D.C. 1973).

adjournment, no matter how long. An intrasession adjournment of Congress "does not prevent the President from returning a bill which he disapproves so long as appropriate arrangements are made for the receipt of presidential messages during the adjournment."[40] This reasoning could be carried a step further. Because of the brief interval between the first and second sessions (which can be shorter than an intrasession adjournment), it is logical to prohibit *inter*session pocket vetoes as well. This reasoning would restrict the use of the pocket veto to one occasion: final adjournment at the end of the second session.

The Nixon administration did not carry this case to the Supreme Court.[41] What was left hanging as a legal issue was soon resolved by a political accommodation. The Ford administration, communicating its views through House Minority Leader John Rhodes, decided not to use the pocket veto during intersession adjournments. In 1975 Rhodes announced: "he will either sign it or veto it in the ordinary way, which would preserve the right of this House and of the other body to either sustain or override those vetoes when we come back after the sine die adjournment."[42]

The determination of Senator Edward Kennedy to settle the matter in the courts resulted in an announcement from the Justice Department on April 13, 1976. It stated that President Ford would use the return veto rather than the pocket veto during intrasession and intersession recesses and adjournments of Congress, provided that the House of Congress to which the bill was returned had specifically authorized an officer or other agent to receive return vetoes during the period.[43]

The Family Practice of Medicine Act is remembered for its legal significance, not for its impact on programs. It was printed as a public law in 1975 (P.L. 91-696) and backdated to Decem-

---

[40] Kennedy v. Sampson, 511 F.2d 430, 437 (D.C. Cir. 1974). See also Public Papers of the Presidents, 1970, at 441, and the final paragraph at 442; Kennedy v. Jones, 412 F.Supp. 353 (D.D.C. 1976).

[41] Arthur John Keeffe, with John Harry Jorgenson, "Solicitor General Pocket Vetoes the Pocket Veto," 61 Am. Bar Assn. J. 755 (1975).

[42] 121 Cong. Rec. 41884 (1975).

[43] 122 Cong. Rec. 11202 (1976).

ber 25, 1970—the expiration of the ten-day period. Congress had appropriated the token sum of $100,000 for the program, but the money was impounded during the litigation. After the administration decided against an appeal, it released the money for obligation. But officials at the Department of Health, Education, and Welfare estimated that it would cost $300,000 to set up the administrative machinery called for by the act. With the concurrence of the appropriations committees, HEW reprogrammed the $100,000 to a similar activity under Title VII of the Public Health Services Act.[44]

The accommodation announced by the Ford administration on the pocket veto was honored by President Carter. On January 5, 1981, at the start of the 97th Congress, the House of Representatives changed its rules to reflect *Kennedy* v. *Sampson* by authorizing its Clerk "to receive messages from the President and from the Senate at any time that the House is not in session."[45] Nevertheless, after Congress had adjourned at the end of the first session of the 97th Congress (to return in about six weeks), President Reagan pocket vetoed a special relief bill for a bankrupt Florida firm. The company went to court to contest his action.[46]

At the end of the first session of the 98th Congress, Reagan again exercised his pocket veto power. On November 30, 1983, he pocket vetoed a bill to require certification of human rights practices in El Salvador as a precondition for sending military aid. The House had adjourned sine die on November 18 and did not return until January 23, 1984—nine weeks later. A bipartisan group of thirty-three members of the House of Representatives filed suit to require that the bill be published as a public law.

---

[44] Interview with HEW budget official. The $100,000 had been made available in a supplemental appropriations bill in 1973 (P.L. 93-50, 87 Stat. 106). The impoundment was reported as D75-87 in 1974; H. Doc. No. 386, 93d Cong., 2d Sess.

[45] House Rule III, Clause 5; H. Doc. No. 398, 96th Cong., 2d Sess. 310-11 (1981).

[46] Wkly Comp. Pres. Doc., XVII, 1429 (December 29, 1981); "Briefing," Washington Post, September 29, 1982, at B8. President Reagan abided by *Kennedy* v. *Sampson* to the extent that he did not exercise the pocket veto during intrasessions; Wkly Comp. Pres. Doc., XX, 1196-97 (August 29, 1984).

On March 9, 1984, a district judge upheld President Reagan's action. The judge reasoned that the case most pertinent was the Pocket Veto Case of 1929, which also involved a multi-month sine die adjournment between the first and second sessions. Although the decision in 1929 had been somewhat shaken by *Wright* in 1938 and the *Kennedy* cases, the judge felt obliged to follow the single holding of the Supreme Court that seemed to him most relevant.[47]

The Pocket Veto Case of 1929 stands on a fragile foundation. It has been the practice of each House of Congress to authorize an official to receive messages from the President at any time that House is not in session. The President is therefore not "prevented" from returning a bill. Congressional recesses and adjournments are of much shorter duration than in 1929. More importantly, upholding Reagan's pocket veto would give the President an absolute veto that the framers had deliberately withheld. This result is tolerable if it can be shown that a multi-month sine die adjournment between sessions somehow threatens fundamental powers of the President. However, even while Congress is in session it is constitutionally permissible for Congress to wait months before attempting to override a presidential veto. The reasoning in *Wright* and *Kennedy* seems more persuasive than the Pocket Veto Case of 1929. The veto procedure must serve two purposes: giving the President an opportunity to consider a bill presented to him, and giving Congress an opportunity to consider his objections and vote to override. Until the issue is finally resolved, Congress can avoid pocket vetoes by remaining in session for ten days, excluding Sundays, after presenting the last bill of the first session to the President, or by delaying presentment of the bill until the beginning of the next session.

The Item Veto

Given the omnibus nature of modern legislation, should Presidents be allowed to veto individual items of a bill? Although the

---

[47] Barnes v. Carmen, 582 F.Supp. 163 (D.D.C. 1984). The district judge was overturned by the D.C. Circuit on August 29, 1984.

courts have never decided the question, Presidents have exercised this power on many occasions.

Andrew Jackson sparked a controversy in 1830 when he signed a bill and simultaneously sent to Congress a message that restricted the reach of the statute.[48] The House, which had recessed, was powerless to act on the message. A House report later interpreted his action as constituting, in effect, an item veto of one of the bill's provisions.[49] President Tyler continued the custom by advising the House in 1842 that, after signing a bill, he had deposited with the Secretary of State "an exposition of my reasons for giving to it my sanction." He expressed misgivings about the constitutionality and policy of the entire act.[50] A select committee of the House issued a spirited protest, claiming that the Constitution gave the President only three options upon receiving a bill: a signature, a veto, or a pocket veto. To sign a bill and add extraneous matter in a separate document could be regarded "in no other light than a defacement of the public records and archives."[51]

A more obvious form of item veto developed with public works legislation when Presidents decided to carry out certain projects while ignoring others. Senator Stephen Douglas of Illinois explained how an appropriations act of 1857 had failed to benefit his state. President Buchanan, after quarreling with Congressmen from Illinois, penalized them by withholding funds from their districts. The funds had been scheduled for post offices and other public buildings.[52] In 1876, while signing a river and harbor bill, President Grant objected to particular projects and announced that he would refuse to spend funds on projects that were "of purely private or local interest."[53]

This selective enforcement of laws received support from influential legislators. In 1896 Senator John Sherman, second-ranking Republican on the Finance Committee, expressed regret that

---

[48] Richardson, Messages and Papers, III, 1046 (May 30, 1830).
[49] H. Rept. No. 909, 27th Cong., 2d Sess. 5-6 (1842).
[50] Richardson, Messages and Papers, V, 2012 (June 25, 1842).
[51] H. Rept. No. 909, 27th Cong., 2d Sess. (1842).
[52] Cong. Globe, 36th Cong., 2d Sess. 1177 (1861).
[53] Richardson, Messages and Papers, IX, 4331 (August 14, 1876).

Cleveland had vetoed a river and harbor bill. Sherman regarded the appropriations bill as permissive in nature: "If the President of the United States should see proper to say, 'That object of appropriation is not a wise one; I do not concur that the money ought to be expended,' that is the end of it. There is no occasion for the veto power in a case of that kind."[54]

The practice of impounding funds, which gained momentum under Franklin D. Roosevelt, allowed Presidents to negate part of an appropriations act. Most of the impoundments by Roosevelt, Truman, Eisenhower, and Kennedy were directed at military programs. Lyndon Johnson moved against domestic programs, but only temporarily, for he backtracked in the face of opposition from Congress and the states. The spate of Nixon's impoundments caused Congress to pass the Impoundment Control Act of 1974. The statute directs the President to report two types of impoundments: a permanent cancellation of funds (rescission), which requires the approval of both Houses of Congress within forty-five days of continuous session; and a temporary withholding of funds (deferral), which can be disapproved by either House at any time.[55] Because of the Supreme Court's decision in *INS* v. *Chadha* (1983), the one-House legislative veto over deferrals is no longer available. But Presidents may still submit deferrals as well as proposed rescissions.

There are substantial differences between item-veto authority and the Impoundment Control Act. A constitutional amendment is needed for the former; statutory action satisfies the latter. Second, most constitutional proposals require a two-thirds majority in each House to override an item veto, as with any presidential veto. Congressional action on impoundment took the form of a one-House veto (for deferrals) or support by both Houses within forty-five days of continuous session (for rescission proposals). Third, item vetoes would be exercised at the time a bill is presented to the President. Impoundment occurs weeks and months after a bill becomes law.

[54] 28 Cong. Rec. 6031 (1896).
[55] 88 Stat. 332-39 (1974). See Louis Fisher, Presidential Spending Power 147-201 (1975).

In addition to impoundment actions, Presidents have discriminated against sections of authorization bills. Woodrow Wilson signed a merchant marine bill in 1920, ignoring one section that he found unconstitutional. On the basis of advice from the State Department, Wilson refused to carry out the provisions of the section:

The action sought to be imposed upon the Executive would amount to nothing less than the breach or violation of said treaties, which are thirty-two in number and cover every point of contact and mutual dependence which constitute the modern relations between friendly States. Such a course would be wholly irreconcilable with the historical respect which the United States has shown for its international engagements and would falsify every profession of our belief in the binding force and the reciprocal obligation of treaties in general.[56]

President Nixon, upon signing a military authorization bill in 1971, said that one of the sections (the "Mansfield Amendment" dealing with Southeast Asia) did not represent the policy of his administration. He regarded the section as "without binding force or effect."[57] A federal court in 1972 disputed his position: "No executive statement denying efficacy to the legislation could have either validity or effect." Nixon's statement, said the court, was "very unfortunate."[58] In 1976 President Ford signed a defense appropriations bill which required, for certain executive actions, the approval of the Appropriations and Armed Services Committees of both Houses. Characterizing the procedure as a legislative encroachment upon the constitutional powers of the executive branch, Ford said that he would treat it "as a complete nullity." He adopted the same position toward a one-House veto provision in a veteran's bill: he severed a provision from the balance of the bill.[59] Presidents Carter and Reagan also singled out

[56] Richardson, Messages and Papers, XVII, 8871-72 (September 24, 1920).
[57] Public Papers of the Presidents, 1971, at 1114.
[58] DaCosta v. Nixon, 55 F.R.D. 145, 146 (E.D. N.Y. 1972).
[59] Wkly Comp. Pres. Doc., XII, 172 (February 10, 1976), and id. at 1519 (October 15, 1976). See also Wkly Comp. Pres. Doc., XII, 1104 (July 1, 1976).

specific provisions that they found constitutionally defective, and "severed" or altered their substance while signing bills into law.[60]

How do these actions square with the Constitution? Some writers argue that a separate veto of a rider might be upheld in the courts if the rider bore no relationship to the legislation. A crucial question is what constitutes a "bill" under Article I, Section 7 of the Constitution, which empowers the President to sign or return with his objections "every bill which shall have passed the House of Representatives and the Senate." If Congress tried to attach a reapportionment measure to a foreign assistance act (actually attempted in 1964), would the President be faced with one bill or two? May he sign the basic legislation and veto the rider? Some scholars answer Yes. Others maintain that such a power might undermine the policy-setting role of Congress and violate the separation of powers doctrine.[61]

Legislation has been introduced over the years to grant the President an item veto. Generally the proposals are limited to disapproval of an appropriation; occasionally they cover provisions (riders) in an appropriations bill and also items in an authorization bill. Scholars have argued that this power could be extended to the President by mere statute, simply by defining "bill," although most commentators agree that a constitutional amendment would be required. A combination is possible: a constitutional amendment to permit Congress, by statute, to vest the power in the President. This would allow Congress to withdraw the power by statutory action rather than to initiate another constitutional amendment.

These are intriguing questions and worthy of debate, but it is extremely unlikely that Congress will ever consent to item-veto authority. The idea does have wide public support, since it appears to offer hope for increased economy and efficiency in gov-

[60] For example, Wkly Comp. Pres. Doc., XIII, 1940-41 (December 28, 1977); XV, 1434 (August 15, 1979); XVI, 1592 (August 29, 1980); XVII, 1428 (December 29, 1981).

[61] For a supporting view see Richard A. Givens, "The Validity of a Separate Veto of Nongermane Riders to Legislation," 39 Temp. L. Q. 60 (1965); in opposition is Richard A. Riggs, "Separation of Powers: Congressional Riders and the Veto Power," 6 U. Mich. J. L. Reform 735 (1973).

ernment, and it appears to be ideally suited to combat "logroll-ing" and "pork-barrel" politics in Congress. In his State of the Union Message in 1984, President Reagan appealed for line-item authority as "a powerful tool against wasteful or extravagant spending."[62] Closer examination, however, drains much of the emotional support from the item veto.

First, President Reagan pointed out that most states have granted their governors an item veto: "It works in 43 States. Let's put it to work in Washington for all the people." This argument carries weight if Congress wants to pattern itself after state legislatures and if presidential power can be equated with gubernatorial power. Yet the parallels in each case are weak. Governors were granted item vetoes because state legislatures were in session for only brief periods of the year, sometimes meeting once every other year. This part-time status placed a heavy pre-mium on responsible action by the governor and substantial del-egation of budget authority to him. Item vetoes were also used to comply with balanced budget requirements in state constitu-tions. Neither condition applies to the federal government. Moreover, governors exercise item vetoes over territories that are smaller and more cohesive than those faced by Presidents. Gov-ernors have a familiarity with local needs that cannot be expected of Presidents and their assistants.[63] In 1983 Senator Chiles drew this comparison between governors and Presidents:

> . . . I think we can say that the States tend to have much
> stronger executives, much stronger Governors. In fact, I think
> that was one of the problems when a Governor of Georgia
> came up here, and became President of the United States.
> He did not have any idea what he was running into with
> Congress because he had been dealing only with the Geor-

[62] Wkly Comp. Pres. Doc., XX, 90 (January 25, 1984).

[63] See remarks by Senator Stevens in "Review of the Congressional Budget and Impoundment Control Act of 1974," hearings before the Senate Committee on Governmental Affairs, 97th Cong., 1st Sess. 109 (1981) and dialogue be-tween Senators Chiles and Long at 129 Cong. Rec. S14941 (daily ed. October 29, 1983).

gia legislature. . . . just because something works in the States is no reason for us to adopt it.[64]

Second, it is widely assumed that logrolling is a peculiar trait of the legislature, yet it is no less characteristic of the executive branch. The Blue Ribbon Defense Panel, in its report to President Nixon in 1970, concluded that the frequent unanimity of the Joint Chiefs could not be interpreted simply as subjugation of particular service views. Such unanimity could just as "cogently support a conclusion that the basis of such recommendations and advice is mutual accommodation of all Service views, known in some forums as 'log rolling,' and a submergence and avoidance of significant issues or facets of issues on which accommodations of conflicting Services views are not possible."[65] It is naive to think that the executive branch is uniquely blessed with a penchant for economy.

Third, allowing the President to veto a portion of a bill may upset the original design of the legislation. Deletion of some sections may make the remainder contrary to legislative intent, in terms of not only technical and substantive questions but political balance (tradeoffs and compromises) as well.

Fourth, who would define "item"? Would it embrace restrictive language and provisos or only dollar amounts? Would it apply to entire appropriation accounts or also to earmarking of specific programs within an account? It is a misconception to think that a President could delete individual construction projects in a bill (so-called pork-barrel projects). Those details are usually found only in the accompanying committee reports or other parts of the legislative history. The bill presented to the President contains a lump-sum amount.

Fifth, Congress could easily neutralize the theoretical advantage of the item veto. State legislatures have become adroit at combining within a single item a program the governor dislikes with one that he supports. The availability of an item veto would

[64] 129 Cong. Rec. S14940 (daily ed. October 29, 1983).

[65] Report to the President and the Secretary of Defense on the Department of Defense by the Blue Ribbon Defense Panel 33 (July 1, 1970).

trigger a new round of budgetary legerdemain and political un-accountability.

Sixth, an item veto might make Congress more irresponsible. To satisfy constituent demands, even of the most indefensible nature, a member need only add extraneous material to a bill with the understanding among his colleagues that the President will probably strike the offending amendment. Instead of adopting a reform to control logrolling, the problem would be exacerbated.

Seventh, the item veto would magnify the stature of the President's budget. When first initiated under the Budget and Accounting Act of 1921, the executive budget was nothing more than a proposal to be amended (up or down) as Congress decided. The final judgment lay with Congress, subject to presidential veto. But the President, armed with an item veto, could strike from an appropriations bill the programs that Congress had added or augmented. Rarely could Congress attract a two-thirds majority in each House to override him. Administration officials who advocate item-veto authority are very candid in admitting that congressional initiatives and add-ons would be vulnerable. Budget Director Percival Brundage told the House Judiciary Committee in 1957 that the authority to veto an appropriation item "would include authority to reduce an appropriation—but only to the extent necessary to permit the disapproval of amounts added by Congress for unbudgeted programs or projects, or of increases by Congress of amounts included in the budget."[66] The President's budget should be a starting point, not a fixed ceiling, for congressional action (as will be discussed in Chapter 7).

Eighth, item vetoes would rarely be exercised by the President, other than in a formal sense. White House aides and OMB analysts would become involved in the political decisions, immersing themselves in agency details and depriving executive departments and independent commissions of their line operating responsibilities.

Ninth, Presidents and White House aides could easily use item-

---

[66] "Item Veto," hearings before the House Committee on the Judiciary, 85th Cong., 1st Sess. 24 (1957).

veto authority to control the votes of members of Congress. A particular project in a member's district or state could be held hostage in return for the member's support for a nominee or some other objective of the White House.[67] Coercion could be quite subtle. A presidential aide advises a member that the OMB is questioning a project in a bill before the President and then asks, as an aside, how the member plans to vote on the administration's bill scheduled for a vote next week.

After the Supreme Court struck down the legislative veto in 1983, some officials in the Reagan administration suggested a constitutional amendment that would return to Congress the legislative veto while at the same time giving the President the item veto. For reasons stated in the section, such a trade is highly unlikely.

The Legislative Veto

The legislative veto emerged in the 1930s as an effort to reconcile two conflicting needs. Executive officials wanted to broaden their discretionary authority; Congress insisted on a control mechanism without passing another public law. The resulting accommodation permitted Presidents and administrators to make proposals which would become law unless Congress disapproved by simple resolution of either House (a one-House legislative veto) or by concurrent resolution (a two-House veto). Neither resolution went to the President for his signature or veto. As it evolved, the legislative veto included requirements for congressional approval as well as disapproval and vested some of the controls in congressional committees.

This procedure obviously departs from the customary route of having Congress pass a bill and present it to the President. Article I, Section 7, of the Constitution provides that "Every Order, Resolution, or Vote to which the Concurrence of the Senate and House of Representatives may be necessary (except on a

---

[67] Id. at 94 (statement by Senator Paul H. Douglas). See also the objections against the line item veto by Congressman Clarence Cannon; 106 Cong. Rec. 9767-68 (1960).

question of Adjournment)" shall be presented to the President. The legislative veto reversed the normal order. Under its procedure the President presented proposals subject to the veto of Congress.

Even before the 1930s, the Constitution permitted some exceptions to the Presentation Clause. Congress adopted constitutional amendments in the form of resolutions and referred them directly to the states (rather than through the President) for ratification. This procedure, sanctioned by Article V of the Constitution, was upheld by the Supreme Court in 1798.[68]

From an early date Congress also passed simple resolutions and concurrent resolutions for internal housekeeping matters. Since these were not regarded as "legislative in effect," there was no need to present them to the President. Many of them were adopted pursuant to congressional powers under Article I to determine procedural rules and to punish or expel members. A Senate report in 1897 concluded that "legislative in effect" depended not on the mere form of a resolution but on its substance. If it contained matter that was "legislative in its character and effect," it had to be presented to the President.[69]

Nevertheless, simple and concurrent resolutions gradually evolved into instruments for controlling executive actions. An important conceptual breakthrough occurred in the nineteenth century when executive officials realized that the legislative effect of such resolutions could be changed fundamentally by having their use sanctioned in a public law. In 1854 Attorney General Cushing stated that a simple resolution could not coerce a department head "unless in some particular in which a law, duly enacted, has subjected him to the direct action of each; and in such case it is to be intended, that, by approving the law, the President has consented to the exercise of such coerciveness on the part of either House."[70] Specific examples were not long in coming. In 1905 Congress relied on concurrent resolutions to direct the Secretary of War to make investigations in rivers and

[68] Hollingsworth v. Virginia, 3 Dall. 378 (1798).
[69] S. Rept. No. 1335, 54th Cong., 2d Sess. 8 (1897).
[70] 6 Op. Att'y Gen. 680, 683 (1854).

harbors matters. Two years earlier Congress had resorted to simple resolutions to direct the Secretary of Commerce to make investigations and to issue reports.[71]

Reorganization Authority

Although in recent decades the legislative veto has been attacked as a congressional usurpation of executive duties, initially it favored the President. In 1932 Congress gave President Hoover authority to reorganize the executive branch. His plans would become law within sixty days unless either House disapproved. In the midst of economic depression, Hoover had advocated reorganization powers as an "economy and efficiency" measure and hoped to use this authority to cut federal spending. In December, after being defeated overwhelmingly for reelection, he issued eleven executive orders consolidating some fifty-eight governmental activities. With a single vote, the House of Representatives rejected all of his initiatives.[72]

Despite this rebuff, the procedure clearly favored the President. Hoover did not have to secure the support of both Houses, as would have been necessary through the regular legislative process. Instead, the burden was placed on Congress to prevent his plans from taking effect. Other expedited features also benefited the President. The executive orders to reorganize could not be buried in committee, filibustered, or altered by Congress, either in committee or on the floor.

Constitutional doubts were raised about the legislative veto. Hoover's Attorney General, William Mitchell, viewed legislative vetoes as intrusions by Congress on the President's administrative duties.[73] Partly on the basis of that opinion but also because

[71] 33 Stat. 1147, sec. 2 (1905); 32 Stat. 829, sec. 8 (1903). See Hinds' Precedents, II, §§1593-94.

[72] 76 Cong. Rec. 2125-26 (1933). For details on the history of reorganization authority, see Louis Fisher and Ronald C. Moe, "Delegating With Ambivalence: The Legislative Veto and Reorganization Authority," in "Studies on the Legislative Veto," House Committee on Rules, 96th Cong., 2d Sess. 164-247 (Comm. Print February 1980).

[73] 37 Op. Att'y Gen. 56 (1933).

of greater trust in the new President, Congress in 1933 granted Franklin D. Roosevelt broad-ranging powers of reorganization without the check of a legislative veto. His authority lasted two years.[74] This unconditional delegation of reorganization authority to the President also reflected the skepticism of members of Congress about their own institution. Senator Vandenberg remarked: "let us confront the precise situation and the realities. We now face the necessity for drastic retrenchment and reorganization of the bureaus, departments, and so forth. We have just witnessed the impossibility of achieving even an incidental step in that direction by presidential order so long as Congress, with its diverse interests, retains the veto."[75]

In 1937 Roosevelt asked Congress to renew the authority to reorganize the executive branch, subject to a joint resolution of disapproval (a form of legislative action that must be submitted to the President for his signature). He advised Congress in 1938 that any action short of a bill or joint resolution, such as by simple resolution or concurrent resolution, was merely "an expression of congressional sentiment" and could not "repeal Executive action taken in pursuance of a law."[76] The Senate passed a bill incorporating his principles.

Although Roosevelt said that he would "in the overwhelming majority of cases" sign a joint resolution disapproving his reorganization proposals, members of the House of Representatives were not satisfied. They disliked the prospect of having to locate a two-thirds majority in each House if the President exercised his veto power. In effect, they would have delegated authority by majority vote but could retrieve it only with an extraordinary majority. Realizing that his proposal was dead in the House of Representatives, Roosevelt reversed his constitutional principles within a matter of days. The administration then supported an amendment to allow Congress to reject any executive order by a majority vote of both Houses (a concurrent resolution).

Arguments were offered to justify the administration's switch.

---

[74] 47 Stat. 1518, sec. 403(c); 48 Stat. 16 (1933).
[75] 76 Cong. Rec. 2587 (1933).
[76] 83 Cong. Rec. 4487 (1938).

The President would be acting as an "agent" of Congress, subject to the conditions established by the legislative branch. The legislative veto would be the vehicle by which Congress would announce that the President had violated or misused his power of agency. Moreover, administration supporters distinguished between the use of a concurrent resolution applied to past laws (which would have been unconstitutional) and those applied to laws "in the making" (constitutionally acceptable).[77]

By 1939 both branches agreed that any grant of reorganization authority to the President would be accompanied by a two-House veto. The House Select Committee on Government Organization defended the concurrent resolution procedure by pointing to a recent Supreme Court decision, *Currin* v. *Wallace*, which had upheld a delegation of authority to the Secretary of Agriculture to designate tobacco markets. No market could be designated unless two-thirds of the growers voting in a referendum favored it.[78] To the committee it seemed absurd "to believe that the effectiveness of action legislative in character may be conditioned upon a vote of farmers but may not be conditioned on a vote of the two legislative bodies of the Congress."[79]

As passed in 1939, the Reorganization Act authorized the President to submit plans for executive reorganization. The plans would take effect after sixty days unless Congress, within that time, disapproved them by concurrent resolution. Extension of the authority in 1949 permitted disapproval by a single House. Congress renewed the President's reorganization authority periodically until 1973, when it lapsed because of opposition to President Nixon. Congress restored the authority in 1977, but only after a major challenge from Congressman Jack Brooks, who believed that the constitutional process required Congress to vote affirmatively on each reorganization plan. As passed, however, the legislation retained the one-House veto.[80] Brooks described

[77] Id. at 5004-05.
[78] 49 Stat. 732, sec. 5 (1935); Currin v. Wallace, 306 U.S. 1 (1939).
[79] H. Rept. No. 120, 76th Cong., 1st Sess. 6 (1939).
[80] 53 Stat. 561 (1939); 63 Stat. 203 (1949); and 91 Stat. 29 (1977). See remarks of Congressman Brooks at 123 Cong. Rec. 9344 (1977).

the measure as the "best unconstitutional bill you could draw up."[81]

The Justice Department, having objected to previous legislative vetoes on the ground that they trespassed upon presidential authority, made an exception for reorganization authority. Attorney General Griffin Bell argued that since the decision to present a plan lay solely with the President, this freedom not to act was equivalent to a presidential veto.[82] Judging from the record of the executive branch on reorganization authority—proposing a joint resolution in 1938, acceding to a concurrent resolution the next year and a simple resolution a decade later—it appeared that the Justice Department could construct whatever argument was necessary to obtain reorganization authority for the President.

The debate in 1977 was not characterized by analytic rigor. Attorney General Bell claimed that the reorganization statute "does not affect the rights of citizens or subject them to any greater governmental authority than before. It deals only with the internal organization of the executive branch, a matter in which the President has a peculiar interest and special responsibility."[83] His statement was wholly unrealistic. When the House Committee on Government Operations reported the bill, it acknowledged the substantive impact of reorganization on the people. It recommended that "appropriate means should be provided by the President for citizen advice and participation in executive reorganization. This intention recognizes the vital role that citizens and the public (those ultimately most affected) should play in Government reorganization."[84] But if the issue is "vital," why should Congress not go on record by an affirmative vote?

For many members of Congress it was sufficient that Jimmy Carter had promised during the 1976 campaign to reorganize the federal government. To deny him that authority, they reasoned, would torpedo a solemn pledge to the people. Still, a campaign promise should not relieve legislators of the responsi-

[81] H. Rept. No. 105, 95th Cong., 1st Sess. 43 (1977).
[82] 43 Op. Att'y Gen. No. 10 (January 31, 1977).
[83] Id.
[84] H. Rept. No. 105, 95th Cong., 1st Sess. 6, 11 (1977).

bility for deciding whether a delegation of authority is constitutional or prudent. Members used other arguments to evade the constitutional question. They said that the issue was already in the courts and would be resolved there. But the courts might be unable to decide the matter, or might decide it in a manner unsatisfactory to Congress. Members have a duty to express their own views regarding the constitutionality of their actions. Each member of Congress takes an oath of office that reads: "I do solemnly swear (or affirm) that I will support and defend the Constitution of the United States against all enemies, foreign and domestic; that I will bear true faith and allegiance to the same; that I take this obligation freely, without any mental reservation or purpose of evasion, and that I will well and faithfully discharge the duties of the office on which I am about to enter." This duty cannot be set aside lightly by legislators who say they are not lawyers, or, if lawyers, not constitutional scholars. To swear to defend a document and then to claim ignorance of its contents is a pointless exercise.

The reorganization authority given Carter in 1977 was extended for a year before expiring in April 1981. The Reagan administration, perhaps to maintain a consistent policy against *all* legislative vetoes, did not push hard for the renewal of reorganization authority. The advantages of this delegation had been oversold by its proponents and deserved closer scrutiny by scholars.[85] Reorganization continued, but through the regular legislative process.

The Spirit of Accommodation

Whatever legal misgivings Presidents have had about the legislative veto in reorganization acts, they have acquiesced in this type of conditional legislation. They realized that Congress would not delegate such authority without attaching strings to it. By this reasoning a constitutional issue was reduced to practical proportions. Presidents who wanted the authority had to take the

[85] See Louis Fisher and Ronald C. Moe, "Presidential Reorganization Authority: Is It Worth the Cost?" 96 Pol. Sci. Q. 301 (1981).

conditions that went with it. The Nixon administration never uttered a word of protest when the Impoundment Control Act of 1974 authorized the President to defer the spending of funds subject to a one-House veto. It wanted the authority and accepted the condition. No one in the Ford, Carter, or Reagan administrations suggested that the one-House veto over deferrals was in any way unconstitutional.

President Roosevelt regarded the Lend Lease Act of 1941 as unconstitutional because Congress reserved to itself the opportunity to terminate the President's authority by concurrent resolution. The political situation, however, did not permit him to disclose his position. Long-standing political enemies had already opposed the concurrent resolution as unconstitutional; to reveal his attitude would associate the President with the wrong group. His Attorney General, Robert H. Jackson, later explained: "to make public his views at that time would confirm and delight his opposition and let down his friends. It might seriously alienate some of his congressional support at a time when he would need to call on it frequently."[86]

Congress incorporated a legislative veto in the War Powers Resolution of 1973. It had been unable to stop the Vietnam War that spring, even though a majority in each House opposed the President's policy. A majority was not enough, Congress discovered. Each effort by Congress to end the war encountered a veto from President Nixon. A lower court concluded that the failure of Congress to override the President should not be taken as legislative authority to continue the war. Said Judge Judd: "It cannot be the rule that the President needs a vote of only one-third plus one of either House in order to conduct a war, but this would be the consequence of holding that Congress must override a Presidential veto in order to terminate hostilities which it has not authorized."[87] To insist that every legislative action must be presented to the President and made subject to his veto

[86] Robert H. Jackson, "A Presidential Legal Opinion," 66 Harv. L. Rev. 1353, 1356-1357 (1953).

[87] Holtzman v. Schlesinger, 361 F.Supp. 553, 565 (E.D. N.Y. 1973), reversed by Holtzman v. Schlesinger, 484 F.2d 1307 (2d Cir. 1973) after stays by the Supreme Court, 414 U.S. 1304, 1321 (1973).

would allow the President to conduct a war with minority backing. That cannot be the intention of the Constitution.

The War Powers Resolution, passed over Nixon's veto, allowed Congress by concurrent resolution to direct the President to disengage from military operations. Congress never exercised this veto and legal advisers in the executive branch testified that a President need not honor the legislative veto when his constitutional responsibilities were at stake. But both branches recognized that the legislative veto helped bridge a subject that is not exclusively executive or legislative (see Chapter 9).

Arms sales, subject to a two-House veto, was another area that relied on a legislative veto to accommodate the competing interests of Congress and the President. During a briefing in 1978, Attorney General Bell was asked if President Carter would feel himself bound if Congress, by concurrent resolution, vetoed his Mideast arms sales package. Bell replied: "He would not be bound in our view, but we have to have comity between the branches of government, just as we have between nations. And under a spirit of comity, we could abide by it, and there would be nothing wrong with abiding by it. We don't have to have a confrontation every time we can." White House adviser Stuart Eizenstat added: "I think the point the Judge is making is that we don't concede the constitutionality of any of [the legislative vetoes] yet, but that as a matter of comity with certain of these issues where we think the Congress has a legitimate interest, such as the War Powers Act, as a matter of comity, we are willing to forego the specific legal challenge and abide by that judgment because we think it is such an overriding issue."[88]

Committee Vetoes

A committee veto obligates an executive agency to submit its program to designated committees before placing the program in operation. Committee vetoes actually predate the legislative

---

[88] Office of the White House Secretary, Briefing by Attorney General Griffin B. Bell, Stuart E. Eizenstat, Assistant to the President for Domestic Affairs and Policy, and John Harmon, Office of Legal Counsel, June 21, 1978, at 4.

vetoes of the reorganization acts. Legislation in 1867 placed the following restriction on appropriations for public buildings and grounds: "To pay for completing the repairs and furnishing the executive mansion, thirty-five thousand dollars: *Provided*, That no further payments shall be made on any accounts for repairs and furnishing the executive mansion until such accounts shall have been submitted to a joint committee of Congress, and approved by such committee."[89] Such were the sad straits of Andrew Johnson.

President Wilson vetoed a bill in 1920 because it provided that no government publication could be printed, issued, or discontinued unless authorized under regulations prescribed by the Joint Committee on Printing. Wilson said that Congress had no right to endow a joint committee or a committee of either House "with power to prescribe 'regulations' under which executive departments may operate."[90]

The executive branch continued to object to committee involvement in administrative matters. In 1933 Attorney General Mitchell regarded as unconstitutional a bill that authorized the Joint Committee on Internal Revenue Taxation to make the final decision on any tax refund that exceeded $20,000.[91] Previous legislation had allowed the committee to decide all tax refunds over $75,000. Apparently executive officials had lived with that requirement without objection. By lowering the dollar threshold, an acceptable procedure was transformed into unconstitutional "meddling" with executive detail.[92] At what point on the continuum between $75,000 and $20,000 did the constitutional violation occur? The joint committee presently conducts a review (in effect a veto) of tax refunds in excess of $200,000.[93]

Many of the committee vetoes date back to the 1940s as a response to emergency conditions during World War II. Because of the volume of wartime construction it was impracticable to follow the customary practice of having Congress authorize each

[89] 14 Stat. 469 (1867).
[90] H. Doc. No. 764, 66th Cong., 2d Sess. 2 (1920).
[91] 37 Op. Att'y Gen. 56 (1933).
[92] See 76 Cong. Rec. 2448 (1933).
[93] 26 U.S.C. 6405 (1982).

defense installation or public works project. Beginning with an informal system in 1942, all proposals for acquisitions of land and leases were submitted in advance to the Naval Affairs Committees for their approval. On the basis of that informal understanding, Congress agreed to pass general authorization statutes in lump sum without specifying individual projects. Two years later Congress incorporated that understanding into law. Additional "coming into agreement" provisions were added in 1949 and 1951, requiring the approval of the Armed Services Committees for acquisition of land and real estate transactions.[94]

Every President from Truman to Reagan has expressed opposition to committee vetoes. Frequently Presidents have signed bills with the statement that they would not abide by a committee-veto provision. Nevertheless, the committee veto has become a fixture in an increasing number of statutes. During the Eisenhower administration, Attorney General Herbert Brownell advised that the committee veto represented an unconstitutional infringement on executive duties.[95] Undaunted, Congress created another procedure that yielded precisely the same control. A bill was drafted to prohibit appropriations for certain real estate transactions unless the Public Works Committees first approved the contracts. Eisenhower signed the bill after Brownell assured him that this procedure—based on the authorization-appropriation distinction—was within Congress's power.[96] The form had changed; the committee veto remained.

In addition to committee vetoes provided by statute, Congress has evolved a complex set of committee and subcommittee vetoes that are described in nonstatutory sources, chiefly committee reports and department directives and instructions. Most activity in this area consists of agency proposals to reprogram funds within an appropriation account. Depending on the amount of money

[94] See Virginia A. McMurtry, "Legislative Vetoes Relating to Public Works and Buildings," in "Studies on the Legislative Veto," House Committee on Rules, 96th Cong., 2d Sess. 432-514.

[95] 41 Op. Att'y Gen. 230 (1955), reprinted in 60 Dick. L. Rev. 1 (1955). See also 41 Op. Att'y Gen. 300 (1957).

[96] Joseph P. Harris, Congressional Control of Administration 230-31 (1964).

involved and the nature of the transaction, prior approval by committees and subcommittees may be required.[97]

Legislative Veto of Regulations

Rulemaking represents a fusion of two qualities. It is both legislative (agency regulations have the force of law) and executive (agencies carry out the laws passed by Congress). The extent of lawmaking by federal agencies prompted Congress in the Legislative Reorganization Act of 1946 to make its celebrated plea that each standing committee exercise "continuous watchfulness" over the execution of laws. Senator Robert LaFollette remarked that when Congress "yields up that rulemaking power and delegates it to an executive agency, it is part of the responsibility of Congress to keep informed as to whether the power is being exercised as it intended it should be."[98]

Criticism of agency rulemaking, a constant issue over the next few decades, reached a shrill pitch in the 1970s. Constituents reported various "horror stories" of administrative regulations that seemed to them a product of agency confusion, caprice, and plain harassment. Members of Congress vented this frustration by introducing legislation to control the regulatory process. Some of the proposals called for a legislative veto over agency regulations.

In 1976 the House of Representatives voted 265 to 135 in favor of the Administrative Rulemaking Reform Act. Although far in excess of a majority, the vote fell short of the two-thirds needed under the parliamentary procedure used (suspension of the rules). The legislation would have permitted Congress, by concurrent resolution, to disapprove agency rules.[99] Subsequent efforts to apply the legislative veto to agency rulemaking were delayed either in the House Judiciary Committee or by a refusal on the part of the House Rules Committee to allow floor action

[97] Fisher, Presidential Spending Power, at 75-98.
[98] 92 Cong. Rec. 6446 (1946); 60 Stat. 832, sec. 136 (1946).
[99] 122 Cong. Rec. 31668 (1976).

on the regulatory reform bill. However, in 1982 the Senate voted 65 to 27 for a two-House veto over agency regulations.[100]

Although Congress failed to pass a generic legislative veto to cover all agency rulemaking, it applied that control selectively to individual agencies. In 1974 it adopted a one-House veto over General Services Administration (GSA) regulations on Nixon's papers, a two-House veto over regulations issued by the Commissioner of Education, a two-House veto over passenger restraint rules by the National Highway Traffic Safety Administration, and a one-House veto over FEC regulations.[101] In 1978 it chose a one-House veto to disapprove incremental pricing regulations proposed by the Federal Energy Regulatory Commission (FERC). In 1980 it decided on a two-House veto for FTC rules and renewed that legislative veto two years later.[102]

Officials in the Reagan administration initially suggested that they would not object to legislative vetoes aimed at the independent regulatory commissions. They reasoned that since the President has limited control over these agencies, a legislative veto might serve to curb unnecessary regulations.[103] But later the administration opposed every form of legislative veto.

Court Challenges

Some of the early decisions by federal courts upheld legislative vetoes and found others unconstitutional, but the courts approached the controversy with great caution and circumspection. They limited their holdings to the specific statute before them and often avoided, on procedural grounds, any decision at all.

The constitutionality of legislative vetoes reached the Supreme

[100] 128 Cong. Rec. S2572-2605 (daily ed. March 23, 1982). The bill, containing the two-House veto, passed the Senate 94 to 0; 128 Cong. Rec. S2713 (daily ed. March 24, 1982).

[101] GSA: 88 Stat. 1697, sec. 104(b) (1974). Education: 88 Stat. 566, sec. 509 (1974). NHTSA: 88 Stat. 1482, sec. 109 (1974). FEC: 88 Stat. 1287, sec. 209 (1974) and 90 Stat. 486, sec. 110 (1976).

[102] FERC: 92 Stat. 3372, sec. 202(c) (1978). FTC: 94 Stat. 393, sec. 21(a) (1980) and 96 Stat. 1870 (1982).

[103] Washington Star, April 2, 1981, at C1; Washington Post, May 8, 1981, at D1.

Court obliquely in 1976. The Federal Election Campaign Act had been challenged on a number of grounds, especially the limitations placed on private campaign contributions and the participation by Congress in the appointment of members to the Federal Election Commission. The statute also allowed either House of Congress to veto regulations proposed by the FEC. Having struck down the manner in which the commission was appointed (and therefore its ability to issue rules as constituted), the Court declined to pass judgment on the legislative veto.[104] Justice White, however, suggested in a separate opinion that the legislative veto had constitutional support. The one-House veto, he said, "no more invades the President's powers than does a regulation not required to be laid before Congress." Although congressional influence over the substantive content of agency regulations might be enhanced by this procedure, he did not view "the power of either House to disapprove as equivalent to legislation or to an order, resolution or vote requiring the concurrence of both Houses." White did indicate that legislative vetoes might be invalid if Congress tried to usurp "the functions of law enforcement, to control the outcome of particular adjudications, or to pre-empt the President's appointment power."[105]

Several decisions appeared in 1977. An appellate court ruled that the issue of a one-House legislative veto over FEC regulations was not ripe for judicial determination because Congress had yet to exercise the veto.[106] In that same year the Court of Claims considered a challenge to the one-House veto in the Federal Salary Act. After the Senate had disapproved a pay raise for federal employees, 140 judges objected that the statute violated the constitutional procedure for enacting legislation (including passage by both Houses and submission to the President). The court held that the President had an opportunity to exercise his veto when the bill containing the legislative veto was first presented to him. Under the court's ruling, Congress had a right to delegate conditionally and, if it exercised its disapproval power

[104] Buckley v. Valeo, 424 U.S. 1, 140 n.176 (1976).
[105] Id. at 284-85, 285-86.
[106] Clark v. Valeo, 559 F.2d 642 (D.C. Cir. 1977), aff'd sub nom. Clark v. Kimmitt, 431 U.S. 950 (1977).

to keep federal salaries as before, no further participation by the President was required.[107]

In a third decision in 1977 the Supreme Court reviewed a statute that allowed either House of Congress to disapprove regulations issued by the General Services Administrator concerning President Nixon's tape recordings and other materials. Although not squarely ruling on the legislative veto, the Court offered this judgment: "whatever are the future possibilities for constitutional conflict in the promulgation of regulations respecting public access to particular documents, nothing in the Act renders it unduly disruptive of the Executive Branch and, therefore, unconstitutional on its face."[108]

The courts in 1977 approached the legislative veto with great circumspection. In the FEC case, the appellate court warned that the "question of legislative review of Executive and administrative agency actions is a sweeping subject to be treated in gingerly fashion by the courts." Judicial review "ought at an absolute minimum be informed by experience and not depend solely on abstract analysis or speculation."[109] In the federal salary case, the Court of Claims remarked that "[w]e are not to consider, and do not consider, the general question of whether a one-House veto is valid as an abstract proposition, in all instances, across-the-board, or even in most cases." It was imperative for courts to consider a specific mechanism in a specific statute, and concentrate on "how it works, what it involves, what values and interests are implicated—not on an overarching attempt to cover the entire problem of the so-called legislative veto, or even a large segment of it."[110]

The same caution appears in a decision by the Ninth Circuit in 1980, striking down a legislative veto in a deportation case. Acting under statutory authority, the House of Representatives disapproved six out of 340 requests by the Attorney General to suspend the deportation of aliens. The Ninth Circuit held that

---

[107] Atkins v. United States, 556 F.2d 1028, 1063-65 (Ct. Cl. 1977), cert. denied, 424 U.S. 1009 (1978).

[108] Nixon v. Administrator of General Services, 433 U.S. 425, 444-45 (1977).

[109] 559 F.2d at 650 n.10.

[110] 556 F.2d at 1059.

the legislative veto violated the doctrine of separated powers and intruded impermissibly upon the executive and judicial branches. Not only did Congress disapprove the judgment of an executive officer (the Attorney General), it had set aside the decisions of an Immigration Judge and the Board of Immigration Appeals. The Ninth Circuit viewed the process for suspending deportation as adjudicatory (trial-like) in nature.[111]

Still, the Ninth Circuit was careful to circumscribe the reach of its decision, which was directed against legislative vetoes affecting individual, adjudicative-type determinations. The court emphasized that it was not faced with a legislative veto used in situations in which "the unforeseeability of future circumstances" (as with the Nuclear Nonproliferation Act and its two-House veto) or "the broad scope and complexity" of an agency's rulemaking authority prevented Congress from establishing specific statutory guidelines.[112]

The incremental, case-by-case approach to legislative vetoes stopped abruptly in 1982 when the D.C. Court of Appeals struck down a one-House veto of FERC regulations, a two-House veto of FTC regulations, and a committee veto of HUD reorganizations. The broad basis of these rulings implied that all legislative vetoes, of whatever character, were unconstitutional because they failed to follow the established course for lawmaking.[113]

The argument for the D.C. Court of Appeals is set forth most comprehensively in the FERC case, where the court held that the legislative veto enabled Congress "to expand its role from one of oversight, with an eye to legislative revision, to one of shared administration." This increase in congressional power, said the court, "contravenes the fundamental purpose of the separation of powers doctrine." The court contradicted itself a few sentences later when it observed that legislative vetoes do not necessarily increase congressional power. Because of the presence of the veto, a "rulemaking agency is given greater power than Con-

---

[111] Chadha v. INS, 634 F.2d 408 (9th Cir. 1980).

[112] Id. at 433.

[113] Consumer Energy Council of America v. FERC, 673 F.2d 425 (D.C. Cir. 1982); Consumers Union, Inc. v. FTC, 691 F.2d 575 (D.C. Cir. 1982); AFGE v. Pierce, 697 F.2d 303 (D.C. Cir. 1982).

gress might otherwise delegate . . . ."[114] The proscription on "shared administration" was also overstated, as we shall see.

Chadha and Beyond

The immigration case decided by the Ninth Circuit in 1980 was argued twice before the Supreme Court on February 22 and December 7, 1982. Attorneys representing the House and the Senate explained that this legislative veto originated during the FDR administration to accommodate the interests of both Congress and the President. Many aliens had been subjected to mandatory deportation from the United States, with relief available only in the form of private bills passed by Congress. Because of the hardship on aliens of good character and the desire on the part of the Roosevelt administration for discretionary authority, Congress amended the law in 1940 to allow the Attorney General to suspend deportations. But in delegating that authority Congress reserved to itself the right to disapprove individual suspensions by a two-House veto.[115] By 1952 Congress decided to impose a concurrent resolution of approval on certain categories of aliens and a one-House disapproval on others.

In announcing *INS* v. *Chadha* on June 23, 1983, the Supreme Court decided that the one-House legislative veto in the Immigration and Nationality Act was unconstitutional because it violated both the principle of bicameralism and the Presentation Clause of the Constitution. Chief Justice Burger, joined by five Justices, wrote the opinion for the Court. He said that whenever congressional action has the "purpose and effect of altering the legal rights, duties and relations of persons" outside the legislative branch, Congress must act through both Houses in a bill presented to the President.[116] Justice Powell concurred in the judgment, but stated his preference for a more narrowly drawn holding. Justice White delivered a lengthy dissent dissecting the majority's reasoning. Justice Rehnquist also dissented, but only

[114] 673 F.2d at 474.

[115] Harvey C. Mansfield, "The Legislative Veto and the Deportation of Aliens," 1 Pub. Adm. Rev. 281 (1940).

[116] INS v. Chadha, 103 S.Ct. 2764, 2784 (1983).

on the question of severability. The legislative history seemed persuasive to Rehnquist that Congress delegated the authority to suspend deportations only on the condition that it retain a one-House veto. If the legislative veto fell so should the Attorney General's authority, for they were inseverable. The majority held that it was possible to strike down the legislative veto and retain the delegated authority.

The majority's opinion raises a host of questions. It decided that the legislative veto was severable from the immigration statute, despite clear evidence of a quid pro quo between Congress and the President. If severability can be discovered by the Court from this legislative history, presumably it can be found in almost every other statute. The result gives the executive branch a one-sided advantage in an accommodation that was meant to be a careful balancing of executive and legislative interests.

Second, the Court claimed that the mere fact that a law or procedure is "efficient, convenient, and useful in facilitating functions of government, standing alone, will not save it if it is contrary to the Constitution. Convenience and efficiency are not the primary objectives—or the hallmarks—of democratic government . . . ." Later in the decision the Court said that although the legislative veto may be a "convenient shortcut" and an "appealing compromise," it is "crystal clear from the records of the Convention, contemporaneous writings and debates, that the Framers ranked other values higher than efficiency."[117]

Here the Court played fast and free with history, for efficiency was highly valued by the framers. The decade prior to the Philadelphia convention represented an anxious and persistent search for a form of government that would perform more efficiently than that set up by the Articles of Confederation. In deciding the *Chadha* case, the Ninth Circuit treated the efficiency issue more responsibly and with better balance.[118]

Third, the Court described the purpose of the Presentment Clause as a means of giving the President the power of self-defense against an encroaching Congress. The President's veto

---

[117] Id. at 2780-81, 2788.
[118] 634 F.2d at 420-25.

would check "oppressive, improvident, or ill-considered measures."[119] This argument is misleading because it suggests that the legislative veto, by evading the President's veto, threatened the independence of the executive branch and invited ill-considered measures. In fact, the legislative veto was directed only against those measures submitted by the President. He sent them up and retained total control over their contents. Congress could not amend them; members had to vote yes or no. Even if exercised, a legislative veto simply restored the status quo. For example, if either House defeated a reorganization plan the structure of government remained as before. The President did not need his veto for purposes of "self-defense."

Fourth, the Court said that the framers wanted congressional power exercised "in accord with a single, finely wrought and exhaustively considered, procedure." The records of the Convention and debates in the states preceding ratification provide "unmistakable expression of a determination that legislation by the national Congress be a step-by-step, deliberate and deliberative process."[120] But both Houses of Congress regularly use "shortcut" methods that pose no problems under *Chadha*: suspending the rules, asking for unanimous consent, placing legislative riders on appropriations bills, and even passing bills that have never been sent to committee.

Fifth, it is not self-evident that the House of Representatives altered the legal rights of Jagdish Rai Chadha when it disapproved the Attorney General's recommendation for suspended deportation. The Attorney General, acting through the Immigration and Naturalization Service, did not have exclusive authority to determine suspensions. By statute, that authority was conditioned on the availability of a one-House veto.

Sixth, each House of Congress may alter the legal rights and duties of persons outside the legislative branch without resorting to bicameral action and presentment to the President. Each House may command witnesses to appear before congressional committees and may apply sanctions to those who refuse to cooperate.

[119] INS v. Chadha, 103 S.Ct. at 2782.
[120] Id. at 2784, 2788.

Seventh, note 18 of the majority opinion states that there is no provision "allowing Congress to repeal or amend laws by other than legislative means pursuant to Art. I." In adopting a one-House veto, Congress was not repealing or amending the immigration law. It was fulfilling it. The law was effectively amended when the Supreme Court (without any participation by the other two branches) deleted the legislative veto and allowed the balance of the statute to remain in force.

Eighth, the ability to "make law" through unilateral executive orders and presidential proclamations is all the more extraordinary in view of the Court's decision in *Chadha* that congressional lawmaking must follow the comprehensive route set forth in the Constitution: action by both Houses and presentation of a bill or joint resolution to the President. Under *Chadha*, legislative shortcuts are available now only for the President, not for Congress.

The Court's misreading of history and congressional procedures will yield some strange results. Its theory of government is too much at odds with the practices developed over a period of decades by the political branches. Neither administrators nor congressmen want the static model proffered by the Court. The conditions that spawned the legislative veto a half century ago have not disappeared. Executive officials still want substantial latitude in administering delegated authority; legislators still insist on maintaining control without having to pass another law.

Without access to the legislative veto, the executive and legislative branches will develop substitutes to serve as the functional equivalent of the legislative veto. Forms will change, but not necessarily power relationships and the need for a quid pro quo.

Instead of a one-House veto over executive reorganization, Congress is likely to select a joint resolution of approval. This device satisfies the twin tests of bicameralism and presentment, but will require the President to obtain the support of both Houses within a specified number of days. If one House withholds support, the effect is a one-House veto. The burden is also reversed, placing responsibility on the President to cultivate support in both Houses.

No one should underestimate the ingenuity of Congress to

think up devices that will be more cumbersome for the President than the legislative veto. Without a one-House veto to control impoundment deferrals, Congress could require that whenever the President proposes to defer appropriations for a particular program, the funds must be released unless Congress within forty-five days completes action on a bill approving all or part of the proposed deferral.[121] No constitutional problem exists, since Congress would act through the regular legislative process. Yet the President ends up with essentially a one-House veto that is more onerous than before. Under the Impoundment Control Act, one House had to take the initiative to overturn a deferral. Under the statutory procedure described above, one House could succeed through inaction.

Now that the legislative veto has been declared invalid, the temptation will be strong for Congress to grant powers for shorter periods, forcing the President to return to Congress for extensions. Of course either House, by inaction, could deny him the authority.

Internal House and Senate rules offer another option. Congress can require that funds be appropriated only after an authorizing committee has passed a resolution of approval. This is essentially a committee veto, but the Justice Department may acquiesce and reason that the process relies on Congress's distinction between authorization and appropriation and that the committee resolution is directed at a stage within Congress rather than outside.

If an agency adopts a regulation that offends Congress, legislators can attach language to an appropriations bill denying the use of funds to implement the regulation. No constitutional issue arises concerning the right of Congress to do this, although riders to appropriations bills are far from the ideal way to make law. They are added without the hearings, careful consideration, and substantive knowledge that was more likely with the legislative veto process.[122] Since a President would rarely veto an

[121] For example, see 95 Stat. 1466, sec. 406 (1981).

[122] Appropriations riders and other techniques are carefully examined by Frederick M. Kaiser, "Congressional Action to Overturn Agency Rules: Alternatives to the 'Legislative Veto,'" 32 Admin. L. Rev. 667 (1980).

appropriations bill because of an objectionable rider, the practical effect is at least a two-House veto. Because of House-Senate comity, the effect in many instances will be a one-House veto.

Statutes can require that selected committees be notified before an agency implements a program. Notification does not raise a constitutional issue, since it falls within the report-and-wait category already sanctioned by court rulings.[123] But "notification" in a statute can become a code word for committee prior-approval. Only in highly unusual circumstances would an agency defy the expressed wishes of an oversight committee.

After *Chadha*, Congress will continue to use informal and nonstatutory methods to control the executive branch. Agencies are allowed to shift funds within an appropriations account if they obtain committee approval for major changes. Agencies comply because they want to retain this administrative flexibility. Since these "gentlemen's agreements" are not placed in statutes, they are unaffected by the Court's decision. They are not legal in effect. They are, however, in effect legal.

With or without the legislative veto, Congress will remain a partner in "shared administration." It is inconceivable that any court or any President can prevent it. Call it supervision, intervention, interference, or just plain meddling, Congress will find a way.[124] And government is not the worse off for it. For the most part, statutes can define only the broad contours of public policy. The specific application of funds will remain a joint enterprise between executive agencies and congressional committees. Contrary to the Court's doctrine, future legislative control will not be exercised solely through public laws. We should not be too surprised or disconcerted if, after the Court has closed the door to the legislative veto, we hear a number of windows being raised and perhaps new doors constructed, making the executive-legislative structure as accommodating as before for shared power.

[123] Sibbach v. Wilson & Co., 312 U.S. 1, 14-15 (1941).

[124] Louis Fisher, "Congress and the President in the Administrative Process: The Uneasy Alliance," in Hugh Heclo and Lester M. Salamon, eds., The Illusion of Presidential Government 21-43 (1981).

6

POWER OVER KNOWLEDGE:
SEEKING AND WITHHOLDING
INFORMATION

The Constitution does not explicitly grant Congress the power to investigate; neither does it give the President the privilege of withholding information. Yet the Supreme Court has held that the exercise of both powers, when essential for the proper functioning of each branch, is implied in the Constitution. The Court announced in 1927 that a legislative body "cannot legislate wisely or effectively in the absence of information respecting the conditions which the legislation is intended to affect or change . . . ."[1] Investigation is a prerequisite for intelligent lawmaking. In 1974 the Court decided that the President's interest in withholding information for the purpose of confidentiality is implied in the Constitution: "to the extent this interest relates to the effective discharge of a President's powers, it is constitutionally based."[2]

These implied powers meet head-on whenever Congress, in an attempt to carry out its investigative function, is denied information by a President who invokes executive privilege. Which power should yield? It would be satisfying to discover a formula that is both unequivocal and trustworthy, but too much depends on individual circumstances. To subordinate one branch to another would destroy their coequal status and disrupt the system of separated powers. We are left with a search for general boundaries and guideposts that satisfy constitutional principles as well as practical realities.

Congressional Investigations

Congress uses its investigative power for four main purposes: to enact legislation, to oversee the administration of programs, to

---

[1] McGrain v. Daugherty, 273 U.S. 135, 175 (1927).
[2] United States v. Nixon, 418 U.S. 683, 711 (1974).

inform the public, and to protect its integrity, dignity, reputation, and privileges. To enforce these essential duties, Congress possesses an inherent power to punish for contempt.

A study of court cases necessarily distorts the record of Congress and its investigative power. The cases test the outer limits of the power to probe and place Congress in its most unfavorable light. By their very nature, these cases are exceptional. The vast majority of congressional investigations proceed without the need for litigation and without jeopardizing either individual liberties or the separation of powers. Moreover, the investigative power of Congress has often enhanced individual liberties by curbing executive abuses.

Early Precedents

The House ordered its first major investigation on March 27, 1792. It appointed a committee to inquire into the ill-fated expedition of Major General St. Clair, whose troops had suffered disastrous losses to the Indians. The committee was empowered "to call for such persons, papers, and records, as may be necessary to assist their inquiries." According to the account of Thomas Jefferson, President Washington convened his Cabinet to consider the extent to which the House could call for papers. The Cabinet considered and agreed

> first, that the House was an inquest, and therefore might institute inquiries. Second, that it might call for papers generally. Third, that the Executive ought to communicate such papers as the public good would permit, and ought to refuse those, the disclosure of which would injure the public: consequently were to exercise a discretion. Fourth, that neither the committee nor House had a right to call on the Head of a Department, who and whose papers were under the President alone; but that the committee should instruct their chairman to move the House to address the President.

The Cabinet concluded that there was not a paper "which might not be properly produced." The committee examined papers furnished by the executive branch, listened to explanations from department heads and other witnesses, and received a written statement from General St. Clair.[3] Yet the potential for executive privilege had been established. The President could refuse papers "the disclosure of which would injure the public."

The first use of the investigative power to protect the dignity of the House occurred in 1795. William Smith, a Representative from South Carolina, told the House that a Robert Randall had confided to him a plan to obtain from Congress a grant of some twenty million acres, to be divided into forty shares. More than half would be set aside for members of Congress who supported the scheme. Congressman William Murphy had also been approached by Randall on the attempted bribery. One of Randall's associates, Charles Whitney, contacted Congressman Daniel Buck to curry his favor. The House adopted a resolution to direct the Sergeant at Arms, upon the order of the Speaker, to apprehend Randall and Whitney.[4]

On January 6, 1796, the House passed a resolution stating that Randall had been guilty of contempt and a breach of House privileges by attempting to corrupt the integrity of its members. He was brought to the bar, reprimanded by the Speaker, and recommitted to custody. The case against Whitney was handled differently, since he had attempted to bribe a member-elect. The House discharged Whitney from custody without charging him with contempt, and a week later voted to release Randall.[5]

The first committee witness punished for contempt of the House was Nathaniel Rounsavell, a newspaper editor charged in 1812 with divulging sensitive information to the press. Although he admitted to a select committee that he was the source of a published account that concerned secret House debates on a proposed embargo, and that he had derived part of it from a conversation between members of the House, he refused to identify the members or say where the conversation had occurred. Placed in the custody of the Sergeant at Arms and brought before the bar of the House to be interrogated, he once again declined to identify the legislators.

[3] The Writings of Thomas Jefferson (Mem. Ed. 1903), I, 303-05. See Annals of Congress, 2d Cong., 1-2 Sess. 493-94, 1113.

[4] Annals of Congress, 4th Cong., 1st Sess. 155-70.

[5] Id. at 171-245, passim. For further details on Congress's power to punish for contempt, see Hinds' Precedents, II, §§1597-1640.

On the following day, still in custody, Rounsavell prepared a letter in which he disclaimed any intention of showing disrespect to the House. He described the conversation of the members as inadvertent and explained that he had withheld information from the committee only because it might incriminate those who had committed no crime. Only with prior knowledge, obtained from other sources, had he been aware that the subject under discussion was an embargo. At that point John Smilie of Pennsylvania rose to identify himself as the member from whom Rounsavell had obtained the information. Smilie considered the published information "of no importance." If the House wanted a victim, he said, he offered himself for Rounsavell.

Some means had to be found to discharge Rounsavell without compromising the rights and dignity of the House. The Speaker put to him the question: "Are you willing to answer such question as shall be propounded to you by order of the House?" Rounsavell answered in the affirmative. The House then moved that the editor, having purged himself of contempt, be discharged from confinement. The motion carried without opposition.[6]

Judicial Review and the Contempt Power

The British Parliament regarded the contempt power and its determination of legislative privileges as wholly immune from the review of the courts. Not so with Congress. The authority of Congress to punish citizens for contempt of its authority or for a breach of its privileges, the Supreme Court has ruled, "can derive no support from the precedents and practices of the two Houses of the English Parliament, nor from the adjudged cases in which the English courts have upheld these practices."[7]

The power of Congress to investigate became the subject of judicial scrutiny in *Anderson* v. *Dunn* (1821). The controversy

[6] Annals of Congress, 12th Cong., 1st Sess. 1255-74. Additional cases where the House punished witnesses for contempt are described in Hinds' Precedents, III, §§1666-1701.

[7] Kilbourn v. Thompson, 103 U.S. 168, 189 (1881). See also Marshall v. Gordon, 243 U.S. 521, 533-41 (1917) and Watkins v. United States, 354 U.S. 178, 192 (1957).

arose when Congressman Lewis Williams advised the House that a Colonel John Anderson had offered him $500 in return for certain favors and considerations. The House issued a warrant directing the Sergeant at Arms to take Anderson into custody. After being brought to the bar and interrogated by the Speaker, Anderson was declared guilty of contempt and in violation of the privileges of the House. The Speaker reprimanded him and discharged him from custody.[8]

Three questions were placed before the Supreme Court. Did the House have authority to issue the warrant? Was issuance of a warrant exclusively a judicial power? Did the Constitution require a jury trial for all crimes? The Court upheld the action of the House as a valid exercise in self-preservation. Without the power to punish for contempt, the House would be left "exposed to every indignity and interruption that rudeness, caprice, or even conspiracy, may meditate against it."[9] However, the power to punish for contempt was limited: the House had to exercise the least possible power adequate to the end proposed (in this case the power of imprisonment) and the duration of punishment could not exceed the life of the legislative body (that is, imprisonment had to terminate with adjournment).

Because of this latter restriction, an individual could violate the dignity of the House in the closing days of a Congress and be punished only during that period. Partly for that reason, as well as a desire to delegate such matters to the courts, Congress passed legislation in 1857 to enforce the attendance of witnesses on the summons of either House. Failure to appear or refusal to answer pertinent questions could lead to indictment as a misdemeanor in the courts.[10]

[8] Annals of Congress, 15th Cong., 1st Sess. 580-83, 592-609, 777-90 (1818).

[9] Anderson v. Dunn, 6 Wheat. 204, 228 (1821). The Senate, a continuing body, is not limited by the expiration of a Congress; McGrain v. Daugherty, 273 U.S. 135, 181-82 (1927).

[10] 11 Stat. 155 (1857), amended by 12 Stat. 333 (1862). For legislative history and the use of this statute see Allen B. Morehead, "Congressional Investigations and Private Persons," 40 So. Cal. L. Rev. 189, 203-11 (1967). The 1857 law, as amended, was upheld by the Supreme Court; In re Chapman, 166 U.S. 661 (1897). The 1857 law, amended in 1938 (52 Stat. 942), is codified at 2 U.S.C. 192-94 (1982).

The contempt power was narrowed by *Kilbourn* v. *Thompson* (1881). The House of Representatives had summoned Hallet Kilbourn to answer certain questions and produce papers relating to a real estate partnership. For refusing to comply with the congressional directive he was judged guilty of contempt and imprisoned for forty-five days. The Supreme Court recognized that Congress possessed a number of judicial powers. It could punish its members for disorderly behavior or for failure to attend its sessions. The House could also decide cases of contested elections and determine the qualifications of its members. It exercised the sole power of impeachment of officers of the government and in some cases might even fine or imprison a contumacious witness. But neither House possessed a general power to punish for contempt.[11] The constitutional right of a person to life, liberty, or property, unless taken by due process of law, meant "a trial in which the rights of the party shall be decided by a tribunal appointed by law, which tribunal is to be governed by rules of law previously established."[12] In this case the congressional investigation involved a matter pending in the courts and was thus judicial, not legislative, in nature. The scope of *Kilbourn* has been narrowed by subsequent holdings, to be discussed.

McGrain v. *Daugherty* (1927) adopted a more generous view of investigations used to obtain information for a legislative function. A Senate committee, investigating the Teapot Dome scandal, issued a subpoena commanding Mally S. Daugherty to give testimony and bring certain records. He refused to appear for either purpose. The Supreme Court faced this issue: did either House of Congress have the power to compel a private individual to appear before it, or one of its committees, to give testimony needed for the exercise of its legislative function? The Court decided that the Senate had ordered the investigation for a legitimate object; that the witness had wrongfully refused to appear and testify; and that the Senate was entitled to have him give

---

[11] Kilbourn v. Thompson, 103 U.S. at 190.

[12] Id. at 182. A 1917 decision held that a letter written to a House committee chairman, although ill-tempered in content, was not of such character to threaten the ability of the House to carry out its legislative authority; Marshall v. Gordon, 243 U.S. 521, 545-46 (1917).

testimony pertinent to the inquiry, either at its bar or before a committee.[13] Two years later the Court unanimously supported another phase of the Senate's investigation of the Teapot Dome scandal, this time concerning the president of the Mammoth Oil Company.[14]

Prior to 1978, Congress had only two methods of enforcing compliance with its power to investigate and to issue subpoenas: an inherent power to punish for civil contempt and the statutory mechanism (adopted in 1857) to punish for criminal contempt. The two methods differ fundamentally in purpose and scope.

Under the first procedure, a witness who refuses to testify can be committed to the Sergeant at Arms of the respective House until he is willing to purge himself by supplying the requested information or otherwise satisfying Congress. The objective is to force compliance with the congressional will. Once an individual purges himself the punishment ends. In any event, punishment may not extend beyond that session of Congress.

Under the second procedure, the objective is to punish rather than coerce. Once convicted for criminal contempt, an individual forfeits the opportunity to purge himself and escape further punishment. Moreover, punishment may continue beyond that session of Congress (including a fine of not more than $1,000 nor less than $100 and imprisonment for not less than one month nor more than twelve months).[15]

In 1978 Congress adopted a third approach. If an individual refuses, or threatens to refuse, to comply with a Senate subpoena, the Senate may request a court order requiring the individual to comply with the subpoena. Failure to obey a court order may result in a citation for civil contempt. Sanctions imposed under this procedure "shall not abate upon adjournment sine die by the Senate at the end of a Congress if the Senate or the committee or subcommittee of the Senate which issued the

[13] McGrain v. Daugherty, 273 U.S. at 180.

[14] Sinclair v. United States, 279 U.S. 263 (1929).

[15] For the distinction between civil and criminal contempt in congressional investigation cases, see United States v. Fort, 443 F.2d 670, 676-77 (D.C. Cir. 1970), cert. denied, 403 U.S. 932 (1971), and Wright, Federal Practice and Procedure: Criminal 2d §704.

subpena or order certifies to the court that it maintains its interest in securing the documents, answers, or testimony during such adjournment."[16] But since the purpose is to coerce rather than to punish, sanctions are lifted once the individual complies with the Senate's request.[17]

Protection of Individual Rights

The investigative power is interpreted broadly by the courts to permit Congress to carry out its legislative functions. Zealous or careless investigations, however, can violate individual freedoms protected by the Constitution. In 1957 the Supreme Court declared that the Bill of Rights is applicable to congressional investigations: "Witnesses cannot be compelled to give evidence against themselves. They cannot be subjected to unreasonable search and seizure. Nor can the First Amendment freedoms of speech, press, religion, or political belief and association be abridged." Strong words, yet later in the same decision the court used meeker language to warn that Congress cannot "unjustifiably encroach" upon First Amendment rights.[18] How far can Congress go?

The Supreme Court has tried to circumscribe the reach of congressional investigations. In *Kilbourn* (1881) the Court stated that congressional investigations must relate to some legislative purpose. Congress could not conduct "fruitless" investigations into the personal affairs of individuals (fruitless in the sense that the investigation "could result in no valid legislation on the subject to which the inquiry referred"). Later the Court rendered a more sympathetic judgment by adopting a presumption in favor of a legislative purpose. Thus, *McGrain* (1927) decided that a

[16] 28 U.S.C. 1364 (1982).

[17] Application of U.S. Senate Perm. Subcom. on Invest., 655 F.2d 1232 (D.C. Cir. 1981), cert. denied, 454 U.S. 1084 (1981).

[18] Watkins v. United States, 354 U.S. 178, 188, 198-99. For an earlier decision, sustaining an abridgment of First Amendment rights by the House Committee on Un-American Activities, see Barsky v. United States, 167 U.S. 241 (D.C. Cir. 1948), cert. denied, 334 U.S. 843 (1948). In 1953 the D.C. Circuit held that a search and seizure by a Senate committee violated the Fourth Amendment; Nelson v. United States, 208 F.2d 505 (D.C. Cir. 1953), cert. denied, 346 U.S. 827 (1953).

"potential" for legislation is sufficient. It is enough that the subject is one on which Congress can legislate and "would be materially aided by the information which the investigation was calculated to elicit."[19]

Even the "potential" theory is too narrow a test for congressional investigations. The courts recognize that committee efforts devoted to overseeing executive agencies may take researchers up "blind alleys" and into nonproductive enterprises: "To be a valid legislative inquiry there need be no predictable end result."[20]

One way to circumscribe congressional investigations is to require proper authorization. When a resolution defines the scope of an investigation, a committee may not go beyond the legislative instruction.[21] Inquiries must be properly authorized by a committee before it invokes criminal sanctions to punish a witness for refusing to cooperate.[22]

Congressional investigations must respect the Fifth Amendment right that protects individuals against self-incrimination. In the *Quinn* and *Emspak* decisions in 1955 the Supreme Court reversed the convictions of individuals who had refused to testify before a House committee regarding their alleged membership in the Communist Party. The Court ruled that even indirect and ambiguous references to the Fifth Amendment will afford witnesses the privilege against self-incrimination.[23] But Congress may, through a majority vote of either House or a two-thirds vote of a committee or subcommittee, request a federal court to issue an order that compels witnesses to testify. By surrendering the Fifth Amendment right witnesses are given partial immunity (their testimony may not be used against them in any criminal case).[24]

[19] Kilbourn v. Thompson, 103 U.S. at 194-95 and McGrain v. Daugherty, 273 U.S. at 177.

[20] Eastland v. United States Servicemen's Fund, 421 U.S. 491, 509 (1975).

[21] United States v. Rumely, 345 U.S. 41 (1953).

[22] Gojack v. United States, 384 U.S. 702 (1966).

[23] Quinn v. United States, 349 U.S. 155 (1955); Emspak v. United States, 349 U.S. 190 (1955).

[24] For immunity procedure see 18 U.S.C. 6001-05 (1982). It use as a substitute for the Fifth Amendment has been upheld in Ullmann v. United States, 350 U.S. 422 (1956), which supported the Immunity Act of 1954 (68 Stat. 745); Kastigar v. United States, 406 U.S. 441 (1972); and Application of U.S. Senate Select Com. on Pres. Cam. Act., 361 F.Supp. 1270 (D.D.C. 1973).

By the early 1950s it was evident that the investigative process had taken a turn for the worse. Most frequently attacked for violating individual rights and freedoms were the House Un-American Activities Committee (HUAC) and the Senate Permanent Investigations Subcommittee, chaired by Joseph R. McCarthy. Members of Congress, bar associations, and civic and political action groups drafted codes of fair procedure. Beginning in 1953 the House Rules Committee held hearings on suggested codes of rules for the committees, and in 1955 the House adopted a set of procedures for committee investigations.[25] Those procedures are now part of the House rules.

Each committee may fix the number of its members to constitute a quorum for the purpose of taking testimony and receiving evidence, but the number cannot be less than two. The Supreme Court had earlier held that testimony received from a witness before a committee without a quorum could not be regarded as perjury. Under such circumstances the committee is not a "competent tribunal."[26] In the Senate, one-member committees (or subcommittees) may constitute a quorum for the purpose of receiving testimony and even taking sworn testimony, but committees that adopt special rules permitting a one-man quorum must publish the rule in the Congressional Record within thirty days.[27]

Due process was at issue in *Watkins* v. *United States* (1957). John Watkins, a labor organizer, described for HUAC his past participation with the Communist Party. He even agreed to identify current members of the party, but he objected to committee questions about those who had left the movement. Instead of "taking the Fifth," Watkins considered such questions irrelevant to the committee's work. He believed that the committee had no right to expose people publicly because of their

[25] "Legislative Procedure," hearings before the House Committee on Rules, 83d Cong., 2d Sess. (1953). See Edward J. Heubel, "Congressional Resistance to Reform: The House Adopts a Code for Investigating Committees," 1 Midwest J. Pol. Sci. 313 (1957).

[26] Christoffel v. United States, 338 U.S. 84 (1949). On committee quorums see House Rule XI, cl. 2(h) and Senate Rule XXVI, para. 7(a)(2).

[27] United States v. Reinecke, 524 F.2d 435 (D.C. Cir. 1975).

past activities. His refusal to answer certain questions led to his conviction for contempt.

The Supreme Court, in a 6-to-1 decision, sided with Watkins. Fundamental fairness demanded that a witness be given adequate guidance in deciding the pertinency of questions. Whether in the resolution authorizing the investigation, in the remarks of the chairman or members of the committee, or in the nature of the proceeding, a witness had to have an opportunity to make a reasonable judgment about a question's pertinence. The Court ruled that, unless the subject matter appears with "undisputable clarity, it is the duty of the investigative body, upon objection of the witness on grounds of pertinency, to state for the record the subject under inquiry at that time and the manner in which the propounded questions are pertinent thereto." Because HUAC failed to do that, Watkins's conviction violated the due process clause of the Fifth Amendment.[28]

The tone of the decision, containing reprimands aimed at Congress—together with other decisions handed down during that period—produced a groundswell of opposition from legislators. Various bills were introduced to curb the Court.[29] In the face of this political pressure the Supreme Court, two years later, retreated from its position.

Lloyd Barenblatt, a college professor, refused to answer certain questions put to him by a subcommittee of HUAC. He maintained that (1) the compelling of testimony by the subcommittee was neither legislatively authorized nor constitutionally permissible because of vagueness in the character of the authority given to the parent committee; (2) he had not been adequately apprised of the pertinency of the subcommittee's questions; and (3) the questions he refused to answer infringed on rights protected by the First Amendment. He expressly disclaimed reliance on the Fifth Amendment privilege against self-incrimination.

---

[28] Watkins v. United States, 354 U.S. 178, 214-15 (1957). In 1927 the Court had held, on the basis of prior decisions, that a witness "rightfully may refuse to answer where the bounds of the power are exceeded or the questions are not pertinent to the matter under inquiry"; McGrain v. Daugherty, 273 U.S. at 176.

[29] For this period see Walter F. Murphy, Congress and the Court (1962) and C. Herman Pritchett, Congress Versus the Supreme Court (1961).

The Supreme Court, sharply divided in a 5-to-4 vote, rejected all three contentions. Borrowing language from the *Watkins* case, the Court decided that pertinency had been made to appear with "undisputable clarity." As to the constitutional question, the Court acknowledged that in some circumstances the First Amendment protects an individual from being compelled to disclose his associational relationships. But the judiciary chose to balance competing private and public interests. In this case the Court struck the balance in favor of the government's interest in self-preservation. Justice Black, in a biting dissent, objected to the "balancing test" because the interest of a solitary individual is not likely to outweigh the alleged interest of the government. To him the real interest in an individual's right to remain silent is the "interest of the people as a whole in being able to join organizations, advocate causes and make political 'mistakes' without later being subjected to governmental penalties for having dared to think for themselves."[30]

The Court remained divided in two 1961 cases that upheld the right of HUAC to question individuals suspected of Communist Party ties. Frank Wilkinson, after traveling to Atlanta to oppose the work of HUAC, was summoned to testify before the committee. Asked whether he was then a member of the Communist Party, he refused to answer on the basis of his First Amendment rights and his belief that the committee lacked authority for its investigations. His refusal led to conviction and a sentence of one year in prison. Five members of the Court upheld the committee, while four members dissented. The dissenters were especially disturbed by the ability of HUAC to use the contempt power as a weapon against those who dared criticize it.[31]

When the activities of an organization do not raise questions of subversion, at least directly, the rights of association are more

---

[30] Barenblatt v. United States, 360 U.S. 109, 144 (1959). Contemporary law provides that individuals summoned to testify before Congress shall be deemed guilty of a misdemeanor when they refuse to answer "any question pertinent to the question under inquiry . . . ." 2 U.S.C. 192 (1982).

[31] Wilkinson v. United States, 365 U.S. 399 (1961). A companion case, Braden v. United States, 365 U.S. 431 (1961), also upheld HUAC on a 5-4 vote.

likely to find protection in the courts. This is the teaching of *NAACP* v. *Alabama* (1958). Although the case occurred at the state level and involved an attempt by the state's attorney general (not a legislature) to obtain an organization's membership list, the principles announced give greater support to the rights to freedom of speech, assembly, and association. Balancing still occurs, but here the individual is on firmer ground.[32]

Committees may not intervene in a pending adjudicatory proceeding by focusing on the process used by agency officials to reach a decision. In such cases Congress would be interfering not in an agency's "*legislative* function, but rather, in its *judicial* function."[33] Congressional inquiries into the legislative (rule-making) function of an agency are more permissible, but even here a member of Congress may not force an executive official to take into account considerations that Congress had not intended.[34]

For the most part, however, courts assume that agency officials possess the necessary "backbone" to withstand searching inquiries by congressional committees.[35] Even when pressure during a congressional hearing becomes the direct impetus for a change in agency policy, courts treat such influence as "part of the give and take of democratic government."[36]

The Speech or Debate Clause

Congressional investigations play an important part in protecting individual liberties, especially by uncovering executive abuses. But

[32] NAACP v. Alabama, 357 U.S. 449 (1958). See also Gibson v. Florida Legislative Investigation Committee, 372 U.S. 539 (1963).

[33] Pillsbury Co. v. FTC, 354 F.2d 952, 954 (5th Cir. 1966). Emphasis in original. In Koniag, Inc. v. Kleppe, 405 F.Supp. 1360, 1372 (D.D.C. 1975), a federal court characterized hearings by a House committee as "an impermissible congressional interference with the administrative process," but this part of the decision was reversed by Koniag, Inc., Village of Uyak v. Andrus, 580 F.2d 601, 610-11 (D.C. Cir. 1978).

[34] D.C. Federation of Civic Associations v. Volpe, 459 F.2d 1231, 1247 (D.C. Cir. 1972), cert. denied, 405 U.S. 1030 (1972).

[35] Gulf Oil Corp. v. FPC, 563 F.2d 588, 610-12 (3d Cir. 1977).

[36] United States ex rel. Parco v. Morris, 426 F.Supp. 976, 982 (E.D. Pa. 1977).

individual rights may also be jeopardized whenever legislators and their aides argue that the Constitution grants an absolute immunity for their actions.

Article I, Section 6, of the Constitution provides that "for any Speech or Debate in either House," Senators and Representatives "shall not be questioned in any other Place." This clause, adopted at the Constitutional Convention without discussion and without opposition, is almost verbatim from the Articles of Confederation and closely follows language in the English Bill of Rights of 1689.[37] The courts have consistently held that the immunities of the Speech or Debate Clause exist not simply for the personal or private benefit of members "but to protect the integrity of the legislative process by insuring the independence of individual legislators."[38]

How much can be done under the shield of this clause to violate civil liberties? In *Kilbourn* v. *Thompson* (1881), the first case to interpret the Speech or Debate Clause, the Supreme Court read it broadly to include not only "words spoken in debate" but anything "generally done in a session of the House by one of its members in relation to the business before it."[39] The clause protects members for remarks made in the course of committee hearings or in committee reports. Speeches printed in the Congressional Record are covered, whether delivered or not. The acquisition of information by congressional staff, obtained formally or informally, is a necessary stage of legislative conduct generally protected by the Speech or Debate Clause.[40]

A number of other activities, which the courts call "political" rather than "legislative," are not protected: contacts with executive agencies, assistance to individuals who seek federal contracts,

---

[37] United States v. Johnson, 383 U.S. 169, 177 (1966).

[38] United States v. Brewster, 408 U.S. 501, 507 (1972).

[39] Kilbourn v. Thompson, 103 U.S. 168, 204 (1881). For early decisions on the Speech or Debate Clause as supportive of a far-reaching legislative investigation power, see Tenney v. Brandhove, 341 U.S. 367 (1951) and Nelson v. United States, 208 F.2d 505 (D.C. Cir. 1953), cert. denied, 346 U.S. 827 (1953).

[40] Committee hearings and reports: Doe v. McMillan, 412 U.S. 306, 311-13 (1973); Congressional Record: Hutchinson v. Proxmire, 433 U.S. 111, 116 n.3 (1979); legislative staff: Tavoulareas v. Piro, 527 F.Supp. 676, 680 (D.D.C. 1981).

preparing news releases and newsletters for constituents, and speeches delivered outside the Congress.[41] Nor is there any legislative immunity when disseminating documents and information outside Congress.[42]

In some early cases the courts afforded legislators more protection under the Speech or Debate Clause than their aides.[43] *Gravel* (1972), however, treated members of Congress and their aides "as one" when an aide carries out a task that would have been a legislative act if performed personally by the member. When performing these tasks, aides become members' "alter egos."[44] But even in the case of legislative acts the Speech or Debate Clause does not extend a privilege to members or aides who "violate an otherwise valid criminal law in preparing for or implementing legislative acts."[45] The courts may require aides to testify before grand juries and subject them to other pressures of a lawsuit.[46]

How this principle works in practice can be seen from the *Eastland* and *McSurely* decisions. In the first, the Supreme Court in 1975 upheld an investigation by a Senate subcommittee that threatened an organization's First Amendment freedom of the press and its right of association. The majority opinion concluded that the actions of the subcommittee, the individual Senators, and the chief counsel of the subcommittee were protected by the Speech or Debate Clause and therefore immune from judicial interference. The balancing test, even though it tilts easily in the government's favor, did not even come into play. When-

[41] United States v. Brewster, 408 U.S. at 513; Hutchinson v. Proxmire, 443 U.S. at 130-33.

[42] Doe v. McMillan, 412 U.S. at 314-17; Gravel v. United States, 408 U.S. 606, 625-26 (1972).

[43] Dombrowski v. Eastland, 387 U.S. 82, 84-85 (1967).

[44] Gravel v. United States, 408 U.S. at 616-17. See Doe v. McMillan, 412 U.S. at 312.

[45] Gravel v. United States, 408 U.S. at 626.

[46] Id. at 626-27; Benford v. American Broadcasting Companies, 502 F.Supp. 1148 (D. Md. 1980), aff'd, 661 F.2d 917 (4th Cir. 1981), cert. denied, 454 U.S. 1060 (1981); Benford v. American Broadcasting Companies, Civil Action No. N-79-2386 (D. Md. December 22, 1982); Tavoulareas v. Piro, 527 F.Supp. 676 (D.D.C. 1981).

ever the courts are faced with a situation where an activity by Congress is within its "legitimate legislative sphere, balancing plays no part."[47] This holding surpassed even the *Barenblatt* doctrine. Justice Douglas wrote a dissenting opinion. Three members of the Court (Marshall, Brennan, and Stewart) concurred in the judgment but rejected its sweeping interpretation of the Speech or Debate Clause.

In the second case, spanning more than a decade, Alan and Margaret McSurely won a damage suit against Senator John McClellan, two of his aides, and a rural Kentucky prosecutor. The couple, convicted of contempt of Congress in 1970 for refusing to surrender certain documents to a Senate subcommittee, successfully challenged the conviction on the ground that the subcommittee had violated their Fourth Amendment right to be free of unreasonable searches and seizures. During oral argument in 1978, the government told the Supreme Court that congressional investigators could "probably" break into a private home and take papers from a locked drawer or safe, and even commit murder with impunity, if they sought information for a legislative purpose.[48] Instead of endorsing this position (which the government conceded was not "intuitively appealing"), the Court let stand a lower court ruling that members of Congress and their aides are not immune from liability in a suit for damages involving illegal search and seizure. In 1983 a jury awarded the McSurelys $1.6 million in damages because of the illegal search and the violations to their First Amendment right to free speech.[49]

Members of Congress and their aides insist that they have total immunity for their actions both under the Speech or Debate Clause and the common law (inherent) doctrine of official immunity. To narrow that protection to qualified immunity, they argue, would defeat the underlying purpose of legislative inde-

---

[47] Eastland v. United States Servicemen's Fund, 421 U.S. 491, 501, 510 n.16 (1975).

[48] McAdams v. McSurely, oral argument before the Supreme Court, No. 76-1621, March 1, 1978, at 14-15.

[49] Washington Post, January 8, 1983, at A1. See McSurely v. McClellan, 521 F.2d 1024 (D.C. Cir. 1975); McSurely v. McClellan, 553 F.2d 1277 (D.C. Cir. 1976), cert. denied, 438 U.S. 189 (1978).

pendence. The courts are comfortable with absolute immunity only when restricted to a core area of legislative acts. To grant Congress absolute immunity for all acts—legislative and investigative, with or without authorization, within the halls of Congress and outside, by members as well as by aides—would jeopardize the individual rights of free speech, free association, due process, Fourth Amendment freedoms, and other basic liberties protected by the Constitution.

Impeachment

The investigative power, in its most solemn form, is invoked during the impeachment process. The Constitution provides that the President, Vice President and all civil officers of the United States shall be removed from office upon "Impeachment for, and Conviction of, Treason, Bribery, or other high Crimes and Misdemeanors." The House impeaches by a majority vote; a two-thirds vote of the Senate is needed for conviction.

The grounds for removal remain unresolved. Treason does not present much of a problem, for it is defined in Article III, Section 3 of the Constitution. Bribery, although not defined in the Constitution, is generally understood to mean the giving, offering, or taking of rewards as payment for favors. But what of "other high Crimes and Misdemeanors"? Does impeachment apply only to actions indictable in the courts (statutory offenses) or does it extend to abuses of office and "political crimes" against the government? A separate issue is whether courts may review an impeachment and conviction by Congress. On all such questions the authorities disagree.

"What, then, is an impeachable offense?" asked Minority Leader Gerald Ford in 1970, during the attempted impeachment of Justice Douglas. The only "honest answer," he said, "is that an impeachable offense is whatever a majority of the House of Representatives considers it to be at a given moment in history; conviction results from whatever offense or offenses two-thirds of the other body considers to be sufficiently serious to require the removal of the accused from office."[50] This kind of open-ended definition parallels the vague grounds that James Madison so quickly and successfully opposed at the Philadelphia convention.

Madison did not disagree on the need for an impeachment provision. He believed it was indispenable that there be some way to defend the community against the "incapacity, negligence or perfidy of the chief Magistrate." The President might "pervert his administration into a scheme of peculation or oppression. He might betray his trust to foreign powers." But later in the convention, when George Mason moved to add "maladministration" as a basis for impeachment because treason and bribery might be insufficient to reach other "great and dangerous offenses," Madison objected. He said that ill-defined and loose terms would be equivalent to having the President serve at the pleasure of Congress. Mason withdrew the language and substituted "other high crimes & misdemeanors," which passed by a vote of eight to three.[51]

During subsequent impeachment proceedings it has been characteristic for counsel of the accused to contend that the phrase "other high crimes and misdemeanors" refers only to an indictable offense.[52] Although it is correct that the framers rejected vague grounds ("maladministration"), it would be an error in the opposite direction to claim that they insisted on specific statutory offenses. In Federalist 65, Alexander Hamilton called the object of impeachment "those offenses which proceed from the misconduct of public men, or, in other words, from the abuse or violation of some public trust. They are of a nature which may with peculiar propriety be denominated POLITICAL, as they relate chiefly to injuries done immediately to the society itself." Hamilton conceded in the same essay that there is danger that the decision to impeach will be regulated "more by the comparative strength of parties than by the real demonstrations of

[50] 116 Cong. Rec. 11913 (1970).

[51] Farrand, Records, II, 65-66, 550.

[52] For example, see the position of President Nixon's attorneys, "An Analysis of the Constitutional Standards for Presidential Impeachment," Wkly Comp. Pres. Doc., X, 270-83 (February 28, 1974).

innocence or guilt." The framers chose to live with the risk of unwarranted impeachments. The alternative (which they rejected) is to permit an unfit person to remain in office, to the detriment of the government and the people, because the grounds for removal are too narrowly drawn.

James Madison later reinforced the view that impeachment covers abuses of office. In the First Congress he argued that the removal power of the President would make him responsible for the conduct of department heads "and subject him to impeachment himself, if he suffers them to perpetrate with impunity high crimes and misdemeanors against the United States, or neglects to superintend their conduct, so as to check their excesses."[53]

To insist on an indictable offense contradicts this record. Moreover, the emphasis on statutory crimes does not automatically yield the advantage claimed by supporters. Congress, by rewriting the criminal code, could subject Presidents to impeachment for minor infractions. Even if unrevised, the criminal code contains actions of insufficient stature to merit impeachment. Impeachment is a political, not a judicial, act. The purpose is to remove someone from office, not to punish for a crime. Impeachable conduct need not be criminal.[54]

Both Irving Brant and Raoul Berger, authors of two leading works on impeachment, rely on British precedents. Although the language in the United States Constitution is lifted from English history, care must be taken not to borrow too much. The English Parliament has far greater power to punish than its American counterpart; the American President has more independence and coequal status than the British prime minister; and the American

[53] Annals of Congress, I, 372-73 (May 19, 1789).

[54] This is also the conclusion reached by the staff of the House Committee on the Judiciary, in preparation for the impeachment of President Nixon. "Constitutional Grounds for Presidential Impeachment," Report by the Staff of the Impeachment Inquiry, House Committee on the Judiciary, 93d Cong., 2d Sess. (Comm. Print February 1974). Even Irving Brant, who repudiated Gerald Ford's position and insisted on a narrow definition of the grounds needed for impeachment, did not go so far as to insist on statutory offenses alone. He believed that a President or judge could be impeached for violating the oath of office (such as by gross and willful neglect of duty); Irving Brant, Impeachment 20-23, 67, 73 (1972).

202

system of separated branches differs fundamentally from the close executive-legislative linkage that exists in England. After the development of ministerial responsibility to Parliament, impeachment in England became an anachronism. It remains a necessary check in America.

Is there a need for judicial review? The question turns in large part on what constitutes an impeachable offense—statutory offenses or political abuses. If the latter, the court is an inappropriate forum. Raoul Berger, relying heavily on *Powell* v. *McCormack* (1969), concludes that the courts may review impeachment and conviction. But *Powell* involved explicit criteria for the qualifications of members of Congress: age, citizenship, and residence in the state from which they are chosen. The standards for impeachable activity are not spelled out in the Constitution with the same precision.[55]

It is possible to conceive of circumstances where courts might play a role. There could be blatant procedural irregularities, such as providing inadequate time for the accused to prepare a defense or denying the accused an opportunity to cross-examine. Treason is defined in the Constitution; Congress cannot apply the term loosely. Some of the grounds for impeachment might be of a frivolous nature. For example, Article X against Andrew Johnson charged that he attempted to disgrace Congress by making and delivering "with a loud voice certain intemperate, inflammatory, and scandalous harangues . . . amid the cries, jeers, and laughter of the multitudes." Such thin-skinned reactions from Congress obviously fall short of describing an impeachable offense. Also, Article VII charged him with violating the Tenure of Office Act of 1867, which I believe (but a majority of Congress then did not) was itself an unconstitutional limitation on the President's control over his Secretary of War.

If Congress decides that an officeholder has committed "high crimes and misdemeanors," even if unindictable in the courts, and builds a record to demonstrate that the individual acted in a manner harmful to the political system and must be removed,

---

[55] Powell v. McCormack, 395 U.S. 486 (1969); Raoul Berger, Impeachment 103-21 (1973).

there is no recourse to the judiciary. Congress acts essentially as a political body when it impeaches and convicts. Courts lack jurisdiction to review these decisions entrusted to legislators.[56]

Executive Privilege

The claim of executive privilege sets the stage for a confrontation between two "absolutes": the power of Congress to investigate and the power of a President to withhold information. Although these prerogatives are often cast in unqualified and unconditional terms, generally there are opportunities to negotiate a settlement that is satisfactory to both branches. If the two branches cannot agree, the matter may find its way into the courts. Based on political and legal controversies over the past two centuries, it is possible to identify broad areas where control is exclusive and where it is shared.

Access by Congress

The House of Representatives has the "sole Power of Impeachment." It cannot discharge that constitutional responsibility unless it has full access to materials needed for an investigation. When President Washington refused to share with the House certain papers regarding the Jay Treaty, he did so because the House is constitutionally excluded from the treaty-making process. Had the House sought the papers as part of an impeachment, Washington suggested, the information would have been made available.[57] The power of impeachment, said President Polk, gives to the House of Representatives

the right to investigate the conduct of all public officers under the Government. This is cheerfully admitted. In such a case the safety of the Republic would be the supreme law, and the power of the House in the pursuit of this object would penetrate into the most secret recesses of the Execu-

[56] Ritter v. United States, 84 Ct. Cl. 293 (1936), cert. denied, 300 U.S. 668 (1937).

[57] Richardson, Messages and Papers, I, 187 (March 30, 1796).

tive Departments. It could command the attendance of any and every agent of the Government, and compel them to produce all papers, public or private, official or unofficial, and to testify on oath to all facts within their knowledge.[58]

Even short of impeachment, executive privilege is inappropriate when there are charges of administrative malfeasance. President Jackson, a jealous defender of executive prerogatives, told Congress that if it could "point to any case where there is the slightest reason to suspect corruption or abuse of trust, no obstacle which I can remove shall be interposed to prevent the fullest scrutiny by all legal means. The offices of all the departments will be opened to you, and every proper facility furnished for this purpose."[59] In the *Watkins* case, in 1957, the Supreme Court noted that the power of Congress to conduct investigations "comprehends probes into departments of the Federal Government to expose corruption, inefficiency or waste."[60]

Attorney General William French Smith, although upholding a very broad theory of executive privilege in 1982, admitted that he would not try "to shield documents [from Congress] which contain evidence of criminal or unethical conduct by agency officials from proper review."[61] During a news conference in 1983, President Reagan said "we will never invoke executive privilege to cover up wrongdoing."[62]

Several barriers stand in the way of full disclosure to Congress. The Supreme Court noted in 1959 that Congress "cannot inquire into matters which are within the exclusive province of one of the other branches of the Government."[63] Were Congress to seek information concerning a pardon, the President could decline on the ground that the matter is solely executive in nature and of no concern to Congress (unless the pardon required ap-

---

[58] Id. at V, 2284 (April 20, 1846).

[59] Cong. Debates, 24th Cong., 2d Sess., Vol. 13, Pt. 2, Appendix, at 202, but see entire discussion at 188-225.

[60] Watkins v. United States, 354 U.S. at 187.

[61] Letter of November 30, 1982, to Congressman John Dingell, reprinted in H. Rept. No. 968, 97th Cong., 2d Sess. 41 (1982).

[62] Wkly Comp. Pres. Doc., XIX, 244 (February 16, 1983).

[63] Barenblatt v. United States, 360 U.S. at 112.

propriations for an amnesty program). The President need not disclose to anyone in Congress the details of a treaty being negotiated. He may do so to enlist the support of legislators, but the invitation is voluntary on his part. He does so for political, not constitutional, reasons. Nor is the President under any obligation to share with members of Congress the plans of tactical military operations.[64]

Similarly, until the President submits to the Senate the name of a nominee, Congress has no grounds for gaining access to the applicant's file. Requests for personnel and medical files might also be regarded by the President as an unwarranted intrusion into personal privacy.[65] The removal power over executive officials is strongly attached to the President's office. Grover Cleveland once withheld from the Senate various papers and documents that pertained to a suspended official. The power to remove, he said, was solely an executive prerogative and could not be shared or compromised with the Senate.[66]

Investigatory files in the executive branch may enjoy a protected status. Whereas the judicial process calls for strict rules of evidence and procedural safeguards to protect the accused, looser standards prevail during congressional investigations. The President may therefore feel an obligation to protect an individual against the disclosure of allegations and hearsay. It is possible to extend this argument to the protection of security files for federal employees (except for confirmation purposes). In 1950, President Truman wrote to Senator Millard E. Tydings that he was denying his request for investigative files relating to federal employees charged with disloyalty. Release of these investigative

[64] Legislation adopted in 1974 requires the President to report to designated committees of Congress concerning covert military operations by the Central Intelligence Agency; 88 Stat. 1804, sec. 32.

[65] Such files are specifically exempted under the Freedom of Information Act (Exemption 6); 5 U.S.C. 552(b)(6) (1982). This exemption limits the public, not Congress, but subsequent discussion in this chapter shows that this distinction does not always survive in practice.

[66] Louis Fisher, "Grover Cleveland Against the Senate," 7 Cong. Stud. 11 (1979); Grover Cleveland, The Independence of the Executive 48-82 (1913). President Jackson, also operating on the theory that the removal power lay exclusively with the President, refused the Senate information concerning a dismissed official; Richardson, Messages and Papers, III, 1352.

files, he said, might prejudice the effectiveness of FBI investigations, embarrass and endanger confidential informants, and injure innocent individuals accused by malicious or misinformed people.[67]

Formulation of a policy requires trust and confidentiality among presidential aides. No one in Congress is entitled to the preparatory materials that led up to the Camp David accords under President Carter, or to the early drafts within the Reagan administration proposing the sale of military aircraft (AWACS) to Saudi Arabia. When a witness before a congressional committee in 1971 commented that the President's first draft of a message was none of Congress's business, Senator William Fulbright replied: "Sure. What did he say to Mr. Kissinger this morning before breakfast? I think that is out."[68] Congressional committees recognize that advisers to the President need not disclose to Congress discussions of a confidential nature.[69]

Congressional investigations into matters pending in the courts have unique hurdles to overcome. The Senate Watergate Committee failed in its attempt to obtain certain documents and tapes directly from President Nixon. Stymied in this effort, the committee appealed to the judiciary, only to be told by a district court that it lacked jurisdiction. Congress passed a special statute to confer jurisdiction, but this time the lower courts held that the release of material to the committee created undue risk of pretrial publicity in the pending Watergate prosecutions.[70] The courts also concluded that the Senate had failed to demonstrate an immediate need for the tapes, partly because the House Judiciary Committee already possessed copies of the tapes, acquired during its impeachment investigation.[71]

[67] Public Papers of the Presidents, 1950, at 229-32, 240-41. See Op. Att'y Gen. 45 (1941) and Archibald Cox, "Executive Privilege," 122 U. Pa. L. Rev. 1383, 1427 (1974).

[68] "Transmittal of Executive Agreements to Congress," hearings before the Senate Committee on Foreign Relations, 92d Cong., 1st Sess. 31, 33 (1971).

[69] Donald G. Morgan, Congress and the Constitution 16-21 (1966).

[70] Senate Select Com. on Pres. Campaign Activities v. Nixon, 366 F.Supp. 51 (D.D.C. 1973); 87 Stat. 736 (1973).

[71] Senate Select Com. on Pres. Campaign Activities v. Nixon, 370 F.Supp. 521 (D.D.C. 1974), aff'd, Senate Select Com. on Pres. Campaign Activities v. Nixon, 498 F.2d 725, 732, 734 (D.C. Cir. 1974).

The existence of an impeachment effort underscores the extraordinary circumstances surrounding this case. On other occasions the spirit between the branches has been more cooperative. In order not to interfere with the government's prosecution of a criminal case, congressional committees often decide to defer their investigation until completion of the criminal trial. For example, after Senator Harrison A. Williams, Jr., was indicted on several counts for criminal conduct, the Senate suspended its own investigation until he was found guilty in 1981. Facing an almost certain expulsion vote later that year, he resigned.[72]

Kilbourn and other early decisions suggested that a congressional investigation could not interfere with matters pending before a court. Under that doctrine, however, legislative inquiries could be frustrated for years while awaiting the outcome of a lawsuit. Congress is free to investigate a matter even if it results in publicity that is prejudicial to a defendant. In such situations a court may find it necessary to postpone a trial until the prejudice has been removed.[73] When Congress seeks a document that it could have had in the absence of a lawsuit, the mere existence of a suit or a grand jury action is inadequate reason to withhold information from Congress.[74]

Executive officials sometimes claim that they cannot share information with Congress without it being leaked to the public. For example, Congressman John E. Moss sought information on a company's reserve estimates for all of its natural gas leases and contracts. This information is protected by Exemption 4 of the Freedom of Information Act, which exempts "trade secrets and commercial or financial information obtained from a person and privileged or confidential." However, Moss requested the information not as a member of the public but in his capacity as subcommittee chairman. Another argument used to withhold the information from him relied on language in the Federal Trade

---

[72] S. Rept. No. 187, 97th Cong., 1st Sess. 2 (1981).

[73] Delaney v. United States, 199 F.2d 107, 114-15 (1st Cir. 1952). See also Hutcheson v. United States, 369 U.S. 599, 612-13, 623-25 (1962) and Sinclair v. United States, 279 U.S. 263, 295 (1929).

[74] In re Hearings before the Committee on Banking and Currency of the United States Senate, 19 F.R.D. 410, 412 (N.D. Ill. 1956).

Commission Act, which empowers the commission to release information "except trade secrets and the names of customers." The company maintained that the restriction also applied to Congress, implying that what was shared with Congress would soon find its way to the public domain. Two courts refused to conclude that the transfer of information from the FTC to the subcommittee would lead "inexorably to either public dissemination" or disclosure to the company's competitors. Judges presume that congressional committees will exercise their powers responsibly.[75]

When executive officials refuse to comply with a congressional request for information, one of the instruments for coercion is the contempt power. A 1975 tug of war between the branches, with Congress the eventual victor, concerned Arab boycott reports compiled by the Department of Commerce. Secretary Rogers Morton initially refused to comply with a committee subpoena. After facing contempt proceedings, however, he bowed to the will of Congress and released the material. In 1980 President Carter threatened to withhold documents concerning his oil import fee. Secretary Charles W. Duncan, Jr., with a contempt citation hanging over his head, yielded the documents to a House subcommittee. A year later Energy Secretary James B. Edwards narrowly escaped a contempt citation by agreeing to provide information on the synthetic fuels program to a House committee.[76]

This pattern of conflict continued with two members of the Reagan Cabinet: Interior Secretary James Watt and Environmental Protection Agency (EPA) Administrator Anne (Gorsuch) Burford. Watt withheld documents from a House subcommittee in 1981, provoking a committee subpoena for the documents

[75] Ashland Oil, Inc. v. FTC, 409 F.Supp. 297, 308 (D.D.C. 1976), aff'd, 548 F.2d 977 (D.C. Cir. 1976). See also Exxon Corp. v. FTC, 589 F.2d 582, 589-91 (D.C. Cir. 1978), cert. denied, 441 U.S. 943 (1979).

[76] "Contempt Proceedings Against Secretary of Commerce, Rogers C. B. Morton," hearings before the House Committee on Interstate and Foreign Commerce, 94th Cong., 1st Sess. (1975) and 121 Cong. Rec. 40768-69 (1975); Duncan: Cong. Q. Wkly Rept., May 17, 1980, at 1352; Edwards: Washington Post, July 30, 1981, at A2.

and a recommendation by the Committee on Energy and Commerce that he be cited for contempt. Several weeks later Watt made the documents available to the subcommittee. The documents were to be delivered to a secure room on Capitol Hill and reviewed only by subcommittee members. The technical assistance of subcommittee staff would not be available. Moreover, the members could not photocopy the documents, but could take notes. Some of the subcommittee members were particularly distressed by the exclusion of staff, who are a necessary extension and "alter ego" of members of Congress.[77]

In an early phase of the Watt confrontation, Attorney General William French Smith advised President Reagan to invoke executive privilege in response to the subcommittee subpoena. Smith's opinion displayed an extraordinary misconception about the legislative branch. First, he said that "the interest of Congress in obtaining information for oversight purposes is, I believe, considerably weaker than its interest when specific legislative proposals are in question."[78] But the courts have consistently held that the investigative power is available not merely to legislate, or when a "potential" for legislation exists, but even for pursuits down blind alleys. Even if there were some basis for Smith's argument (and there is none), Congress could easily neutralize it by introducing a bill whenever it had oversight in mind.

Smith also claimed that "[a]ll of the documents in issue are either necessary and fundamental to the deliberative process presently ongoing in the Executive Branch or relate to sensitive foreign policy considerations."[79] The dispute with Watt concerned the impact of Canadian investment and energy policies on American commerce, an issue clearly within the enumerated constitutional power of Congress to "regulate Commerce with foreign Nations" and its authority to oversee the particular statute that

[77] "Contempt of Congress," hearings before the House Committee on Energy and Commerce, 97th Cong. 385-94 (1982).

[78] "Executive Privilege: Legal Opinions Regarding Claim of President Ronald Reagan in Response to a Subpoena Issued to James G. Watt, Secretary of the Interior," prepared for the use of the House Committee on Energy and Commerce, 97th Cong., 1st Sess. 3 (Comm. Print November 1981).

[79] Id. at 2.

established the nation's policy on foreign investments. Moreover, the record demonstrates that the documents were not of "fundamental" importance to the deliberative process. They could have been, and eventually were, shared with the committee.[80]

The accommodation over the Watt documents should have formed a foundation for better executive-legislative relationships. Indeed, when the oversight subcommittee of the House Public Works Committee sought documents on the EPA's enforcement of the "Superfund" program, it was advised by the agency that there would be no objection "so long as the confidentiality of the information in those files was maintained."[81] The subcommittee had been investigating the $1.6 billion program established by Congress to clean up hazardous-waste sites and to prosecute companies responsible for illegal dumping.

Shortly thereafter the Reagan administration decided that Congress could not see documents in active litigation files. The reversal appeared to be triggered by requests from other committees. Another oversight panel from the House Energy and Commerce Committee wanted access to the same type of information. The administration expressed concern that executive branch control would be undermined by these multiple requests.[82] Both oversight subcommittees had reason to suspect that the major chemical companies were not paying their full share of the costs, leaving the balance to be picked up by taxpayers.

EPA Administrator Gorsuch, acting under instructions from President Reagan, refused to turn over "sensitive documents found in open law enforcement files." Reagan's memorandum to her, dated November 30, 1982, claimed that those documents represented "internal deliberative materials containing enforcement strategy and statements of the Government's position on various legal issues which may be raised in enforcement actions relative to the various hazardous waste sites" by the EPA or the Depart-

---

[80] "Contempt of Congress," hearings before the House Committee on Energy and Commerce, 97th Cong., 2d Sess. 385-94 (1982); H. Rept. No. 898, 97th Cong., 2d Sess. (1982).

[81] H. Rept. No. 968, 97th Cong., 2d Sess. 11 (1982).

[82] Id. at 15, 21.

ment of Justice.[83] The administration's initial position in the Watt dispute had not changed; it assumed that since documents shared with Congress might find their way into the public realm, they should not be shared at all. Following this logic, congressional oversight would have to be put on hold for years until the government completed its enforcement actions.

After the Public Works Committee held Gorsuch in contempt, the House of Representatives voted 259 to 105 to support the contempt citation. Although partisan overtones were present, 55 Republicans joined 204 Democrats to build the top-heavy majority.[84] Pursuant to the statutory procedure for contempt citations, the Speaker certified the facts and referred them to the U.S. Attorney for presentation to a grand jury. Instead, the administration asked a district court to declare the House action an unconstitutional intrusion into the President's authority to withhold information from Congress. In 1983 the court dismissed the government's suit on the ground that judicial intervention in executive-legislative disputes "should be delayed until all possibilities for settlement have been exhausted."[85] The court urged both parties to devote their energies to compromise and cooperation, not confrontation.

The Reagan administration agreed to release "enforcement sensitive" documents to Congress, but only in a series of steps, beginning with briefings and edited versions and eventually ending with the unedited documents.[86] Congress then moved to clarify the duty of the U.S. Attorney to bring contempt actions before the grand jury. Legislation under consideration would make that duty nondiscretionary, to be carried out not later than sixty days after a contempt citation had been certified.[87]

One of the casualties of this confrontation was former EPA official Rita M. Lavelle, sentenced in 1984 to six months in prison,

[83] H. Rept. No. 968, 97th Cong., 2d Sess. 76 (1982); id. at 42.

[84] 128 Cong. Rec. H10033-61 (daily ed. December 16, 1982).

[85] United States v. House of Representatives, 556 F.Supp. 150, 152 (D.D.C. 1983).

[86] H. Rept. No. 323, 98th Cong., 1st Sess. 18-40 (1983).

[87] H.R. 3456, 98th Cong., 1st Sess. (1983); 129 Cong. Rec. H6441-47 (daily ed. August 3, 1983).

five years' probation, and a fine of $10,000 for lying to Congress about her management of the Superfund program. She was the only EPA official indicted in the scandal. More than twenty top officials, including Anne Burford, left the EPA amid allegations of perjury, conflict of interest, and political manipulation of the agency.[88]

Access by the Courts

Efforts to withhold information may have to give ground in case of criminal prosecution. When government prosecutors attempt to withhold from the judiciary sensitive materials needed for a trial (statements by witnesses for the government, an informer's identity, and the like), the courts offer prosecutors a choice: either produce the information or drop the charges.[89] Congress passed legislation to empower federal judges to inspect sensitive materials *in camera* (in the privacy of their chambers). If the government decides not to comply with this procedure, the courts may strike from the record the testimony of the government's witness or else declare a mistrial.[90]

A brief for President Nixon during his impeachment process acknowledged that executive privilege "cannot be claimed to shield executive officers from prosecution for crime." But Nixon believed that the President, not the courts, should determine whether information fell within the scope of the privilege. The brief concluded that the "public interest in a conviction, important though it is, must yield to the public interest in preserving the confidentiality of the President's office."[91] In a subsequent brief, Nixon maintained that the only constitutional recourse against a Presi-

[88] Washington Post, January 10, 1984, at A2.

[89] Roviaro v. United States, 353 U.S. 53 (1957) and Jencks v. United States, 353 U.S. 657 (1957).

[90] 71 Stat. 595 (1957). See also Alderman v. United States, 394 U.S. 165, 181 (1969) and Giordano v. United States, 394 U.S. 310 (1969).

[91] Wkly Comp. Pres. Doc., IX, 968-969 (August 7, 1973). The brief also stated that "Executive privilege does not vanish because the grand jury is looking into charges of criminal conduct." Id. at 967.

213

dent in matters of executive privilege "is by impeachment and through the electoral process."[92]

In its unanimous decision in *United States* v. *Nixon* (1974), the Supreme Court required Nixon to produce certain Watergate tape recordings and documents relating to his conversations with aides. A federal grand jury had returned an indictment charging seven men—employed either by the White House or by the Committee for the Re-Election of the President—with a number of offenses, including conspiracy to defraud the United States and to obstruct justice. To permit an absolute, unqualified executive privilege would have prevented the judiciary from carrying out its duties under the Constitution. The adversary nature of the American judicial system requires access to information in order to establish guilt or innocence. "The ends of criminal justice," said the Court, "would be defeated if judgments were to be founded on a partial or speculative presentation of the facts." The integrity of the judicial system depends on the compulsory process of producing evidence needed by the prosecution or defense.[93]

A prosecutor had to persuade the trial court that the materials sought were relevant, admissible as evidence, and specific. Once this had been done, the trial judge could inspect the requested materials *in camera*, determining which portions were required for the trial. Of central importance was the conclusion that the courts, not the President, would decide the scope of executive privilege. Also significant was the first recognition by the Supreme Court that executive privilege has its source in the Constitution. The President's privilege regarding communications with his aides is "fundamental to the operation of government and inextricably rooted in the separation of powers under the Constitution." The question of what would happen when evidence is needed for *civil* litigation was left for another day.[94]

In this particular instance the President's general privilege of confidentiality in communications did not prevail against the needs

[92] Id. at X, 662 (June 21, 1974).

[93] United States v. Nixon, 418 U.S. 683, 709 (1974). President Nixon also lost two lower court tests: In re Subpoena to Nixon, 360 F.Supp. 1 (D.D.C. 1973) and Nixon v. Sirica, 487 F.2d 700 (D.C. Cir. 1973).

[94] United States v. Nixon, 418 U.S. at 708, 712 n.19.

of criminal justice. The presumptive confidentiality of presidential communications was narrowed again in 1977, when the Supreme Court (dividing 7 to 2) upheld a statute that gave custody of Nixon's public papers and tapes to Congress and the head of the General Services Administration. Although agreeing that executive privilege survives a President's tenure, the Court held that the expectation of the confidentiality of executive communications "has always been limited and subject to erosion over time after an administration leaves office."[95] The Court concluded that the screening process contemplated by the statute, which required archivists to segregate public papers from personal and private documents, did not constitute any greater intrusion into presidential confidentiality than the *in camera* inspections by courts approved in *United States* v. *Nixon*.[96]

Since the statute applied only to Nixon, singling him out for special treatment, he claimed that the act violated the Bill of Attainder Clause. Nixon's resignation, his acceptance of a pardon for offenses committed while in office, and the judgment of Congress that he was an unreliable custodian of his papers, already distinguished him as a unique category. The Court further noted that at the time Congress passed the legislation, only Nixon's materials demanded immediate attention. Presidential papers from Hoover to Johnson were housed in presidential libraries. Moreover, Nixon alone had entered into a depository agreement (with GSA Administrator Sampson) calling for the destruction of certain materials. For these reasons the Court held that Nixon constituted "a legitimate class of one."[97]

National Security and Foreign Affairs

Even more privileged than executive confidentiality in communications, according to the Court in *Nixon* (1974), is the President's "need to protect military, diplomatic or sensitive national

---

[95] Nixon v. Administrator of General Services, 433 U.S. 425, 451 (1977). See also 448-50.

[96] Id. at 455.

[97] Id. at 472. In Allen v. Carmen, 578 F.Supp. 951 (D.D.C. 1983), a federal judge blocked access to Nixon's papers because of the presence of a legislative veto in the enabling act.

security secrets."[98] This is consistent with previous decisions that defer to presidential responsibilities in military and diplomatic matters. In 1948 the Supreme Court said that it would be "intolerable that courts, without the relevant information, should review and perhaps nullify actions of the Executive taken on information properly held secret. Nor can courts sit *in camera* in order to be taken into executive confidences. But even if courts could require full disclosure, the very nature of executive decisions as to foreign policy is political, not judicial."[99]

What happens when "secret" information is needed for a trial? In *Reynolds* v. *United States* (1952), three women tried to recover damages as widows of civilians killed in the crash of a military aircraft. To support their claim they requested certain documents from the Air Force. A lower court ruled that the government's claim of privilege—withholding evidence required for a pending lawsuit—involved a justiciable question, "traditionally within the competence of the courts." The Supreme Court reversed the judgment by a 6-to-3 vote. Although the Court noted that judicial control over the evidence of a case cannot be "abdicated to the caprice of executive officers," it also held that the judiciary "should not jeopardize the security which the privilege is meant to protect by insisting upon an examination of the evidence, even by the judge alone, in chambers." To add weight to its judgment the Court noted (in the climate of the Korean war) that "this is a time of vigorous preparation for national defense."[100] In essence, then, the Court did indeed abdicate its role to executive officers. If courts are unwilling to examine national security evidence *in camera*, they cannot know whether administration officials are acting capriciously.

Since the early 1950s the courts have been drawn into several disputes involving secret information. The concept of "national security," used on occasion as an umbrella term to justify any number of executive actions, brings into play many competing sections of the Constitution. The Nixon administration, for ex-

---

[98] United States v. Nixon, 418 U.S. at 706.

[99] C. & S. Air Lines v. Waterman Corp., 333 U.S. 103, 111 (1948).

[100] United States v. Reynolds, 345 U.S. 1, 9-10 (1952). For lower court case see Reynolds v. United States, 192 F.2d 987, 997 (3d Cir. 1951).

ample, attempted to have the courts enjoin two newspapers from publishing the Pentagon Papers, a secret study on the origins and conduct of the Vietnam War. The Supreme Court held against the administration. The word "security," said Justice Black, "is a broad, vague generality whose contours should not be invoked to abrogate the fundamental law embodied in the First Amendment. The guarding of military and diplomatic secrets at the expense of informed representative government provides no real security for our Republic."[101] This decision has limited application to executive privilege. The Pentagon Papers were leaked to the press. The question was therefore one of prior restraint on the press—a First Amendment test an administration would find difficult to meet.

Most instances of executive privilege involve documents over which the administration has retained control. Access to this material is regulated in part by the Freedom of Information (FOI) Act. As written in 1966, the FOI Act directed agencies to make information available to the public, subject to nine exemptions. The first consisted of matters "specifically required by Executive order to be kept secret in the interest of the national defense or foreign policy." The exemptions were supposed to limit access to information by the *public*, not Congress. The act explicitly states that the exemptions do not constitute authority "to withhold information from Congress."[102]

Nevertheless, the FOI Act has been used to withhold infor-

---

[101] New York Times Co. v. United States, 403 U.S. 713, 719 (1971). United States v. Marchetti, 466 F.2d 1309 (4th Cir. 1972), cert. denied, 409 U.S. 1063 (1972), required an author to submit to the Central Intelligence Agency—prior to publication—any writing relating to the agency. The CIA could excise from the manuscript any passage that contained undisclosed classified information. In part the decision was based on the President's constitutional responsibility in foreign affairs and national security to prevent disclosure of classified materials (executive privilege), but the court also cited statutory grounds for agency censorship (delegated power). Snepp v. United States, 444 U.S. 507 (1980) also upheld the CIA's prepublication review, but appeared based on statutory authority (see note 3 at 509 and also 512).

[102] Originally enacted in 1966 (80 Stat. 250), the FOI Act was codified the following year with some changes (81 Stat. 54) and amended in 1974 (88 Stat. 1561) and 1976 (90 Stat. 1241). It is codified at 5 U.S.C. 552.

217

mation from individual members of Congress. In 1971, thirty-three members of the House of Representatives attempted to obtain documents prepared for President Nixon concerning an underground nuclear test scheduled for Amchitka Island, Alaska. The Supreme Court in the *Mink* case (1973) decided it had no authority to examine the documents *in camera* to sift out "non-secret components" for their release.[103] Executive privilege was not at issue, since the information had been withheld on statutory grounds (Exemption 1 of the FOI Act). The Court's interpretation prompted Congress to rewrite the Freedom of Information Act in 1974. Congress required that material withheld under Exemption 1 be "properly classified" pursuant to an executive order. This provision, coupled with a clarification of court review, overrode the holding in *Mink*. Federal courts are now clearly authorized to examine executive records in judges' chambers as part of a determination of the nine categories of exemptions under FOI.[104] This authority brings the courts a long way in terms of attitude, procedures, and capability in passing judgment on national-security withholdings. The new doctrine contrasts sharply with the rulings in *C. & S. Air Lines* (1948) and *Reynolds* (1952).

Although it may be proper for the courts on some occasions to defer to the President on national security grounds, the same attitude should not be taken by Congress. Unlike the courts, Congress has explicit responsibilities under the Constitution to declare war, provide for the common defense, raise and support armies, and provide and maintain a navy. Legislative expertise exists in the Armed Services Committees, the defense appropriations subcommittees, the Budget Committees, and a number of other congressional panels. By 1977 both Houses had established select committees on intelligence to receive classified information from the CIA and other elements of the U.S. intelligence community. Deference by the courts, therefore, need not mean deference by Congress. In *C. & S. Air Lines*, the Supreme Court declined to settle an issue on the ground that foreign pol-

[103] EPA v. Mink, 410 U.S. 73 (1973).
[104] 88 Stat. 1562, sec. 4 (B). See H. Rept. No. 1380, 93d Cong., 2d Sess. 8-9, 11-12 (1974).

icy decisions "are wholly confided by our Constitution to the political departments of the government, Executive *and Legislative*."[105]

This joint responsibility is illustrated by a recent confrontation. Congressman John Moss, acting through his subcommittee, issued a subpoena to obtain from the American Telephone & Telegraph Company information on "national security" wiretaps by the administration. A district court, after balancing the investigative power of Congress against the President's executive privilege in foreign affairs, announced in 1976 that "if a final determination as to the need to maintain the secrecy of this material, or as to what constitutes an acceptable risk of disclosure, must be made, it should be made by the constituent branch of government to which the primary role in these areas is entrusted. In the areas of national security and foreign policy, that role is given to the Executive." An appellate court remanded this decision five months later. The election of Jimmy Carter had created new possibilities for resolving the matter out of court. The appellate court returned the case to the lower court with the recommendation that Congress and the executive branch attempt to negotiate a settlement: "A compromise worked out between the branches is most likely to meet their essential needs and the country's constitutional balance."[106]

Additional guidance was needed from the appellate court to break the deadlock between the two branches. Judge Harold Leventhal put pressure on both parties to clarify their major concerns and reach an accommodation. The case was dismissed on December 21, 1978, after the Justice Department and the subcommittee amicably resolved their differences.[107]

---

[105] C. & S. Air Lines v. Waterman Corp., 333 U.S. 103, 111 (1948). Emphasis added.

[106] United States v. American Tel. & Tel. Co., 551 F.2d 384, 394 (D.C. Cir. 1976). See United States v. American Tel. & Tel. Co., 419 F.Supp. 454, 461 (D.D.C. 1976).

[107] United States v. American Tel. & Tel. Co., 567 F.2d 121 (D.C. Cir. 1977). For settlement, see "Court Proceedings and Actions of Vital Interest to the Congress, Current to December 31, 1978," prepared by the House Select Committee on Congressional Operations, 95th Cong., 2d Sess. 50 (1978).

In discussing executive privilege, there is a temptation to cede to the President broad scope in military, diplomatic, or national security affairs. This is too great a concession. Generalizations of this order should be avoided. A fundamental basis for executive privilege—the need to protect communications between high government officials—cuts across foreign and domestic policy-making. Many of the justifications cited in this chapter, involving pardons, removals, and formulation of policy, apply equally well to the foreign and the domestic areas. And as illustrated by the James Watt dispute, what appears to be "foreign policy" to the President may seem with equal clarity "foreign commerce" to Congress. Although the judiciary may decide to yield to presidential initiatives in military, diplomatic, and national security affairs, no such acquiescence should be expected of Congress.

The scope of executive privilege remains in a state of tension because of three competing demands: the integrity of the judicial process requires evidence; the executive branch needs a measure of confidentiality in its deliberations; and Congress depends on information to carry out its responsibilities. If the three branches of government are coequal in status and have a right to preserve their independence and influence, it would be contrary to the Constitution for one branch to subordinate its interests to another. Accommodations by all parties are essential. The Supreme Court may claim to be the final arbiter in disputes involving executive privilege, but it can exercise that role only selectively and discreetly. It cannot (except at severe cost) referee every collision between Congress and the President.

7

THE POWER OF THE PURSE

Based primarily on its power to appropriate funds and its unique status as a representative body, Congress with good reason considers itself the "First Branch of Government." The power of the purse, James Madison noted in Federalist 58, represents the "most complete and effectual weapon with which any constitution can arm the immediate representatives of the people, for obtaining a redress of every grievance, and for carrying into effect every just and salutary measure." Article I, Section 9 of the Constitution places this weapon squarely in the hands of Congress: "No Money shall be drawn from the Treasury, but in Consequence of Appropriations made by Law." Using pithier language in Federalist 48, Madison said that "the legislative department alone has access to the pockets of the people."

Constitutional Limitations

The appropriations power, while broad, is restricted by other provisions in the Constitution. Congress cannot lawfully use its funding power to establish a religion,[1] diminish the compensation of members of the federal judiciary,[2] or take other actions specifically proscribed by the Constitution. Congress may not impose unconstitutional conditions on recipients of federal funds.[3] Where statutory directives conflict with constitutional rights, the

---

[1] Flast v. Cohen, 392 U.S. 83, 104-05 (1968). However, the courts may deny plaintiffs standing to challenge federal assistance to religious institutions. Valley Forge College v. Americans United, 454 U.S. 464 (1982). In this 5-to-4 decision, the dissenters disagreed sharply with the Court's paper-thin distinction between the Spending Clause (*Flast*) and the Property Clause (*Valley Forge*).

[2] United States v. Will, 449 U.S. 200 (1980); Booth v. United States, 291 U.S. 339 (1934); O'Donoghue v. United States, 289 U.S. 516 (1933).

[3] Comments, "The Federal Conditional Spending Power: A Search for Limits," 70 Nw. U. L. Rev. 293 (1975). See also Smith v. Ehrlich, 430 F.Supp. 818 (D.D.C. 1976), although in this instance the condition was upheld.

courts are available to police the boundaries. The flow of federal money is not "the final arbiter of constitutionally protected rights."[4]

A celebrated example of judicial supervision concerned a rider to an appropriations bill in 1943 that prohibited the payment of federal salaries to three named "subversives." The section was struck down by the courts because it represented a bill of attainder proscribed by Article III, Sectiton 3, of the Constitution.[5] When a proviso in an appropriations act collides with the President's power to pardon and attempts to prescribe to the judiciary the effect of the pardon, the proviso cannot stand.[6] In 1977 Congress raised a constitutional issue by including in two appropriations bills a proviso that denied funds to President Carter to implement his pardon order.[7] By the time the provisos became law some portions had no practical effect, but Carter objected to one feature (regarding entry of aliens) as an unconstitutional interference with his pardon order, a bill of attainder, and a denial of due process.[8]

In recent years the courts have reviewed the constitutionality of provisions in appropriations bills that deny public funds to indigent women seeking an abortion. In 1976 a district court struck down the following language in an appropriations act: "None of the funds contained in this Act shall be used to perform abortions except where the life of the mother would be endangered if the fetus were carried to term."[9] The same court, in 1980, held unconstitutional a congressional restriction (the Hyde Amendment) on the use of federal funds for abortion.[10] In response, 238 members of Congress signed an amicus curiae brief instructing the Supreme Court that the district court had violated the appropriations power of Congress. Claiming that

[4] Clark v. Board of Education of Little Rock Sch. Dist., 374 F.2d 569, 571 (8th Cir. 1967). See Califano v. Westcott, 443 U.S. 76, 92-93 (1979).

[5] United States v. Lovett, 328 U.S. 303 (1946). See also Blitz v. Donovan, 538 F.Supp. 1119 (D.D.C. 1982).

[6] United States v. Klein, 13 Wall. 128 (1872); Hart v. United States, 118 U.S. 62 (1886).

[7] 91 Stat. 114, sec. 306, and 91 Stat. 444, sec. 706.

[8] Wkly Comp. Pres. Doc., XIII, 1164 (August 3, 1977).

[9] McRae v. Mathews, 421 F.Supp. 533 (E.D. N.Y. 1976).

[10] McRae v. Califano, 491 F.Supp. 630, 728-31 (E.D. N.Y. 1980).

the "appropriation and expenditure of tax funds is inherently a political question," the brief argued that the Supreme Court "has never taken the position that the judiciary may oversee the appropriations process or set itself up as the ultimate arbiter of federal fiscal policy."[11] Overstated, to be sure, but later that year the Court upheld the Hyde Amendment. It refused to extend the constitutional freedom of choice to have an abortion to a right of federal financial support. The latter was "a question for Congress to answer, not a matter of constitutional entitlement."[12]

The Constitution prohibits the appropriation of funds to raise and support armies for a term of more than two years. Yet Congress, supported by opinions of the Attorney General, has been able to provide funds to the Defense Department for longer periods—even providing "no-year" funds for defense procurement and research and development (making funds available until expended). This practice came to an end in 1970 when Congress appropriated on a two-year basis for research and development, adopted three years for procurement, and five years for shipbuilding. Congress changed for policy, not constitutional, reasons.[13]

The legal justification for appropriating funds to the Defense Department for more than a two-year term relies on the following distinction: "raising and supporting" (subject to the two-year limit) and "equipping" (which is not). The drafts of the Constitution offer some support for this interpretation. The verb "equip" was initially applied to the Navy, as in "raise armies, ⟨& equip Fleets.⟩"; "raising a military Land Force—and of equiping a Navy—"; or "raise Armies; to build and equip Fleets." When the draft was completed, the Constitution used "raise and support" for the Army and "provide and maintain" for the Navy. The two-year limit applied to armies, not navies. The framers, primarily concerned about a standing army, were less concerned that funds might remain available over a period of years for the construction of vessels. Taking this reasoning a step further, it can be argued

[11] 126 Cong. Rec. H2011 (daily ed. March 19, 1980).
[12] Harris v. McRae, 448 U.S. 297, 318 (1980).
[13] Louis Fisher, Presidential Spending Power 127-30 (1975).

that the two-year limit does not apply to a construction item that takes years to produce, even if for the Army, Air Force, or Marine Corps.[14]

These topics have been of recurrent interest throughout America's constitutional history, flaring up at times to present major controversies. Of more permanent concern, and forming the heart of this chapter, are two issues unresolved since 1789: (1) the establishment of budget priorities by Congress and the President, and (2) reliance on confidential and secret funds.

The Budget and Accounting Act of 1921 attempted to pull together the scattered parts of a process that had become fragmented and uncoordinated over the years. Neither branch, prior to the act, could be said to have exercised financial control. The legislation remained faithful to constitutional principles by making the President responsible for budget estimates and giving Congress final control over appropriated levels. The two branches were supposed to work in tandem, each carrying out distinct and specific duties.

This assignment of functions has begun to unravel in recent years. The lines of responsibility established by law and the Constitution are becoming blurred by actions on the part of both branches. Congress has passed a number of statutes that restrict the President's ability to put together a budget he can defend. No longer is he responsible for some of the budget estimates he submits to Congress; he is forbidden by law to alter them. On the other hand, when administrations resort to impoundment they negate Congress's power to control the final level of funding.

Presidential Responsibility for Estimates

The President formulates budget estimates and submits them to Congress in accordance with the Budget and Accounting Act of 1921. Although this is the statutory source, the authority for submitting such estimates can also be found in the Constitution.

[14] Farrand, Records, II, 143, 158, 168, 182. See 25 Op. Att'y Gen. 105 (1904) and 40 Op. Att'y Gen. 55 (1948).

Under Article II, Section 3, of the Constitution, the President "shall from time to time give to the Congress Information of the State of the Union, and recommend to their Consideration such Measures as he shall judge necessary and expedient." The President does not have to await statutory authority to submit a budget. Indeed, President Taft submitted a budget in 1912 despite opposition from Congress.

The dispute about Taft's budget originated in 1910 when Congress appropriated $100,000 to finance a study into more efficient and economical ways of conducting the public business. Taft used the money to set up a five-member Commission on Economy and Efficiency. In June 1912 he released the commission's report, which called for a national budget initiated by the President and for which the President would be held responsible. In that same month Taft ordered department heads to prepare two sets of estimates: one for the customary "Book of Estimates" (a loosely organized report consisting of unrelated bureau estimates) and one for the national budget recommended by the commission. Congress tried to stop Taft by passing legislation that directed executive officials to prepare estimates only in the customary manner.[15]

Treating the statute as unconstitutional, Taft reiterated to department heads his determination to have two sets of estimates:

Under the constitution the President is intrusted with the executive power and is responsible for the acts of heads of departments and their subordinates as his agents, and he can use them to assist him in his constitutional duties, one of which is to recommend measures to Congress and to advise it as [to] the existing conditions and their betterment. . . . If the President is to assume a responsibility for either the manner in which business of the government is transacted or results obtained, it is evident that he cannot be limited by Congress to such information as that branch may think sufficient for his purposes. In my opinion, *it is entirely com-*

[15] 37 Stat. 415.

225

petent for the President to submit a budget, and Congress can not forbid or prevent it.[16]

Taft proceeded with his plan to prepare and submit a model budget, but Congress took no action on it.

The Budget and Accounting Act

The financial implications of World War I—especially the huge national debt that had to be managed by the Treasury Department—provided the principal force behind passage of the Budget and Accounting Act of 1921.[17] A central purpose of the act was to place responsibility on the President. The House Select Committee on the Budget criticized the existing process on a number of grounds. Budget estimates submitted to Congress represented "only the desires" of the individual departments, establishments, and bureaus. Their requests were not subjected to a "superior revision with a view to bringing them into harmony with each other, to eliminating duplication of organization or activities, or of making them, as a whole, conform to the needs of the Nation as represented by the condition of the Treasury and prospective revenues." No one was responsible. Budget estimates were "a patchwork and not a structure." A great deal of the time of congressional committees was taken up "in exploding the visionary schemes of bureau chiefs for which no administration would be willing to stand responsible." The committee concluded that definite responsibility had to be placed upon the President to subject agency estimates to scrutiny, revision, and correlation.[18]

The 1921 act contained two exceptions to this principle of presidential responsibility. First, he was to set forth in his budget all estimates necessary "in his judgment" except those of the legislative branch and the Supreme Court. In a spirit of comity and

[16] Frederick A. Cleveland, "The Federal Budget," Proceedings of the Academy of Political Science, III, 167-68 (1912-13). Emphasis in original.

[17] Taft's model budget appears at 49 Cong. Rec. 3985 (1913). For evolution of the executive budget from 1789 to 1921, see Fisher, Presidential Spending Power, at 9-35.

[18] H. Rept. No. 14, 67th Cong., 1st Sess. 4-5 (1921).

mutual respect among coequal branches, these estimates are included in the budget without revision. Second, the act prohibited agency officials from submitting appropriations requests directly to Congress, or submitting recommendations on how revenue needs should be met, "unless at the request of either House of Congress." For the most part, then, Congress authorized a newly created Budget Bureau to "assemble, correlate, revise, reduce, or increase the estimates of the several departments or establishments."[19] In 1970 the Budget Bureau became the Office of Management and Budget (OMB).

This structure of presidential responsibility has eroded slowly over time. Budgets not subject to presidential review at the present time include those of the legislative branch and the judiciary, the Federal Deposit Insurance Corporation, the Milk Market Orders Assessment Fund, the Farm Credit Administration, the International Trade Commission, the Federal Reserve System Board of Governors, and a number of privately owned, government-sponsored enterprises.[20] Additional inroads have been made by Congress to circumvent the President and the OMB.

Bypassing the President

Senator Lee Metcalf was concerned about presidential influence on the independent regulatory agencies. In 1971 he introduced legislation to provide that the appropriations requests for certain regulatory agencies be transmitted directly to Congress. Such estimates and requests, reflecting the judgment of the agency concerned, were not to be changed at the direction of any other agency of the executive branch. The bill covered seven agencies: the Civil Aeronautics Board, the Federal Communications Commission, the Federal Maritime Commission, the Federal Power Commission (now the Federal Energy Regulatory Commission), the Federal Trade Commission, the Interstate Commerce Commission, and the Securities and Exchange Commission.

Deputy OMB Director Casper Weinberger, testifying against

---

[19] 42 Stat. 20, sections 201(a), 206, and 207.
[20] OMB Circular No. A-11, §11.1 (June 1981).

the bill, hoped that it would be rejected "speedily and decisively." The effect, he said, would be to remove the seven agencies from the "normal budget controls and unified overall approach to budgeting that has been a vital part of the Government for over 50 years." Having just left his former position as Federal Trade Commissioner, he was in a strong position to argue that any regulatory agency head who did his homework properly, had fortitude, and believed in his budget estimates could expect considerable success in negotiating with the OMB.[21]

Metcalf's bill was not reported from committee. During the next Congress he reintroduced legislation to require the submission of budget estimates directly to Congress. As reported from committee in 1974, the bill was modified to provide that the estimates would be sent *concurrently* to the OMB and to Congress. The President could alter the commissions' requests but would have to include in the budget the commissions' original requests as well as his proposals. The Senate did not act on the bill.[22]

Congress has enacted other types of proposals to weaken OMB control. The Consumer Product Safety Commission, created in 1972, is required to submit its budget concurrently to the OMB and to Congress. In signing the bill, President Nixon said that the provision was "unfortunate and should not be regarded as precedent for future legislation."[23] His prediction hit wide of the mark. Congress adopted the same type of feature in 1973 for the National Railroad Passenger Corporation; in 1974 for the U.S. Railway Association, the Federal Election Commission, the Commodity Futures Trading Commission, and the Privacy Protection Study Commission; in 1975 for the National Transportation Safety Board; and in 1976 for the Interstate Commerce Commission.[24] When the Secretary of Energy seeks funds from

[21] "Regulatory Agency Budgets" (Part 2), hearings before the Senate Government Operations Committee, 92d Cong., 2d Sess. 396-99 (1972).

[22] S. Rept. No. 1319, 93d Cong., 2d Sess. 21-22 (1974).

[23] 86 Stat. 1229, sec. 27 (k) (1) and Public Papers of the Presidents, 1972, at 1050.

[24] In order of listing: 87 Stat. 553, sec. 601(b)(1); 87 Stat. 992, sec. 202 (g)(2), 88 Stat. 1283, sec. 311(d)(1), 88 Stat. 1390-1391, sec. 101(9)(A), and

Congress, he must indicate the amount requested by the Federal Energy Regulatory Commission in its budgetary presentation to the Secretary and to the OMB.[25] Legislation in 1978 directed the Merit Systems Protection Board to submit its budget concurrently to the President and to Congress.[26]

Far more significant from the standpoint of presidential control and the principles of the Budget and Accounting Act is the Trade Act of 1974. It provides that the estimated expenditures and proposed appropriations for the International Trade Commission (formerly the Tariff Commission) shall be included in the President's budget "without revision." Budget watchers on Capitol Hill (including the author) learned of the provision months after enactment. President Ford had made no mention of the provision when he signed the bill.[27]

Another innovation, tucked away in a statute with little fanfare in 1974, related to the Postal Service. For several years President Nixon had recommended about $200 million less each year than the Postal Service requested for third-class mail. Congress responded by changing the procedure for the budget. The requests of the Postal Service for "public service costs" (rural delivery) and "foregone revenue" (subsidies for third-class mail) had to be included by the President "with his recommendation but without revision, in the budget transmitted to Congress under section 11 of title 31."[28]

President Ford placed the Postal Service's request, without revision, in the appendix to the fiscal 1976 budget. Side by side he stated his own recommendations. So far so good. But in the regular budget document he included only his own recommendations, not those of the Postal Service. OMB officials contended that this budget presentation satisfied the requirements of the 1974 legislation. The history of this legislation strongly suggests, however, that Congress wanted the Postal Service's estimates placed

---

88 Stat. 1906, sec. 5(a)(5)(A); 88 Stat. 2170, sec. 304(b)(7); 90 Stat. 60, sec. 311.

[25] 91 Stat. 583, sec. 401(j) (1977).

[26] 92 Stat. 1125, sec. 1205(j) (1978).

[27] 88 Stat. 2011, sec. 175(a)(1) and Wkly Comp. Pres. Doc., XI, 10-11 (1975).

[28] 88 Stat. 288, sec. 3.

in the President's regular budget, not merely in the appendix. When the bill was pending, OMB Director Roy Ash complained that the feature would have the effect of "restricting the President's presentation of the Postal Service's budget. We believe that such a provision is contrary to the sound provisions embodied by Congress in the Budget and Accounting Act."[29]

It is understandable that the OMB hedged a bit by limiting its compliance to the appendix. The 1974 legislation regarding the Postal Service raised profound and troublesome questions about the nature of a President's budget. If the budget is to set forth information in such form and detail "as the President may determine" (31 U.S.C. 11), can Congress require him to include unrevised agency estimates? The concept of a budget, at least since 1921, is synonymous with a President's recommendations. Take away executive judgment and the idea of a budget disappears.

Two other actions deserve notice. In 1978 President Carter vetoed a bill that would have required three Cabinet officers to report to Congress whenever the President's budget requests for certain activities were less than the amounts authorized by Congress, and to explain why the higher amounts were not requested. Carter regarded the requirement as an "unacceptable intrusion" on his obligations and ability to make budget recommendations.[30] In 1981 President Reagan interpreted narrowly a veterans' bill that might have required him to request specific amounts. He dismissed the latter possibility "for it is the President's constitutional duty to make recommendations to Congress of such measures as he judges necessary and expedient."[31]

Through a number of initiatives, Congress has undercut the integrity and responsibility of the President's budget. Thus far the programs involved have been of modest size and located on the fringe of the executive budget: regulatory agencies, private

---

[29] H. Rept. No. 1084, 93d Cong., 2d Sess. 23 (1974). The intent of Congress can be found at 120 Cong. Rec. 14052 (1974) (remarks of Senator McGee); id. at 19805 (remarks of Congressman Gross); and id. at 19805-07 (remarks of Congressmen Wright, Gross, and Derwinski).

[30] Wkly Comp. Pres. Doc., XIV, 1250 (July 10, 1978).

[31] Id., XVII, 1217 (November 3, 1981).

corporations, and the like. But small erosions on the periphery have a way of spreading to the center. This trend is disturbing.

Congress should not prevent the President from articulating his own budget, and yet the federal government has largely retreated from the principles established in 1921. Today the President does not submit a budget of his own making, representing in aggregate and in detail what he believes to be best for the nation. He does not, and cannot, defend the contents. For the most part he presents estimates for programs over which he has no direct control, particularly the entitlement programs (e.g., social security, federal disability, unemployment compensation), interest on the public debt, and other "uncontrollables" that constitute about three-fourths of the budget. "Uncontrollable" is one of the more unfortunate words in our budgetary vocabulary. The budget *is* controllable. Congress and the President simply choose to make it largely uncontrollable. Nothing in the idea of entitlement prevents the President from recommending less than projected outlays and submitting remedial legislation to Congress to change the law.

Under Carter and Reagan, the President's budget seemed at times little more than a ritual. Carter's budget in 1980 was dead the moment it reached Capitol Hill. Several months later he sent up a new budget. Reagan used the budget to great advantage in 1981, cutting deeply into entitlements, reducing taxes, and raising defense spending, but in 1982, 1983, and 1984 his budgets were virtually ignored by Congress, including the Republican-controlled Senate. The link between the President's budget and presidential responsibility seemed all but severed.

Congressional Revision of Estimates

The Budget and Accounting Act provided for an "executive budget" only in the sense that the President initiated the budget and took responsibility for it. The act allowed members of Congress full freedom, either in committee or on the floor, to decrease or increase the President's estimates.

231

The Prerogative to Add

When John J. Fitzgerald, chairman of the House Appropriations Committee, met with the New York constitutional convention in 1915, he expressed support for a procedure in Congress that would make it as difficult as possible for legislators to increase the amounts proposed by the President. He believed that Congress should be prohibited from appropriating any money "unless it had been requested by the head of the department, unless by a two-thirds vote, or unless it was to pay a claim against the government or for its own expenses."[32]

Charles Wallace Collins, whose studies on budget reform provided part of the momentum for the 1921 act, was of a similar mind. In 1916 he published an article that argued for a form of parliamentary government. "Our institutions," he said, "being more nearly akin to those of England, it is to the English budget system that we more naturally look for the purpose of illustration." He noted that Parliament had long ago yielded the initiative in financial legislation to the Cabinet. The budget in England was ordinarily ratified as introduced. A prime factor of the national budget system in America, according to Collins's view, would be "the relinquishing of the initiative in financial legislation to the executive by the Congress. . . . The President would possess the functions of a Prime Minister in relation to public finance. He would take the responsibility for the preparation of the budget. Complementary to this the Congress would yield its power of amendment by way of increasing any item in the budget, and also its power to introduce any bill making a charge upon the Treasury, without the consent of the executive."[33]

Other changes were necessary to complete Collins's scenario. He would have granted members of the Cabinet a seat in the House and a voice (but not a vote) in all legislative proceedings involving the budget. The committee system of making appro-

---

[32] "Budget Systems," Municipal Research, No. 62 (June 1915), at 312, 322, 327, 340. See also William Franklin Willoughby, The Problem of a National Budget 146-49 (1918).

[33] Charles Wallace Collins, "Constitutional Aspects of a National Budget System," 25 Yale L. J. 376 (1916).

priations "would cease." Since the budget bill represented an administrative measure, Congress "should relinquish its power to
add any new item, to increase any item, or to consider any measure which would impose a burden upon the Treasury unless such
a measure had the sanction of the executive."[34]

In 1918 Representative Medill McCormick (strongly influenced by Collins) introduced a number of bills and resolutions
calling for budget reform. He proposed a House budget committee to replace the committees on Ways and Means and Appropriations; it would have power to reduce presidential estimates but not to add to them, unless requested by the Secretary
of the Treasury upon the authority of the President or unless the
committee could muster a two-thirds majority. Members of the
House would be unable to add to the budget bill when it reached
the floor, except to restore what the President had originally requested.[35]

William McAdoo, Wilson's first Secretary of the Treasury, supported a system to prohibit Congress from increasing the President's requests: "let us be honest with ourselves and honest with
the American people. A budget which does not cover the initiation or increase of appropriations by Congress will be a semblance of the real thing."[36] When Secretary of the Treasury Carter
Glass submitted budget estimates in 1919, he said that the budget
"as thus prepared for the President and on his responsibility should
not, as such, be increased by the Congress."[37] David Houston,
the next Secretary of the Treasury, asked Congress in 1920 not
to add to the President's budget unless recommended by the
Secretary of the Treasury or approved by a two-thirds vote.[38]

This version of an executive budget was rejected by the Budget
and Accounting Act. The budget was executive only in the sense
that the President was responsible for the estimates submitted.
It was legislative in the sense that Congress had full power to

[34] Id. at 382-83.
[35] H. Doc. No. 1006, 65th Cong., 2d Sess. (1918).
[36] Annual Report of the Secretary of the Treasury, 1918-19, at 121 (from his
testimony of October 4, 1919 to the House Select Committee on the Budget).
[37] Id. at 117.
[38] David Houston, Eight Years with Wilson's Cabinet, II, 88 (1926).

increase or reduce his estimates. Increases could be made in committee or on the floor, and in either place by simple majority vote. The act did not contemplate in any fashion the surrender of congressional power. It did not make Congress subordinate to the President's plan. In reporting the bill, the House Select Committee on the Budget explained in straightforward language:

> It will doubtless be claimed by some that this is an Executive budget and that the duty of making appropriations is a legislative rather than Executive prerogative. The plan outlined does provide for an Executive initiation of the budget, but the President's responsibility ends when he has prepared the budget and transmitted it to Congress. To that extent, and to that extent alone, does the plan provide for an Executive budget, but the proposed law does not change in the slightest degree the duty of Congress to make the minutest examination of the budget and to adopt the budget only to the extent that it is found to be economical. If the estimates contained in the President's budget are too large, it will be the duty of Congress to reduce them. If in the opinion of Congress the estimates of expenditures are not sufficient, it will be within the power of Congress to increase them. The bill does not in the slightest degree give the Executive any greater power than he now has over the consideration of appropriations by Congress.[39]

Although Congress formally retained the power to increase budget estimates, the President gained an important advantage by shaping the agenda for legislative action. Because Congress works off his budget, a majority is needed to delete funds recommended by the President. This power of initiative has far-reaching implications. In 1982 Congressman Joseph Addabbo, chairman of the House defense appropriations subcommittee, failed on a tie vote (26 to 26) to delete MX production funds. If proponents of the missile system had to *add* the funds to a congressional budget, a tie vote would have gone against the President.

[39] H. Rept. No. 14, 67th Cong., 1st Sess. 6-7 (1921).

Intercameral Strategies for Reductions

Legislative independence from the President's budget could have been asserted through either increases or decreases. The House Appropriations Committee adopted a strategy that favored decreases, creating a tug of war between the two Houses. Decreases, by reducing resources and keeping them scarce, magnified the power of House Appropriations. The effectiveness of the appropriations subcommittees would be measured by how much they could cut the President's budget.[40] Aware of this philosophy, executive agencies padded their budgets in anticipation of cuts.

Contests between the House and the Senate also tilted congressional action toward decreases. House Appropriations would sometimes reduce an agency's budget below what the committee considered reasonable, expecting the Senate to restore some of the funds. The House could then condemn the Senate as profligate and irresponsible in money matters. Said one group of Representatives: "In the past 10 years the Senate conferees have been able to retain $22 billion out of the $32 billion in increases which the Senate added to House appropriations—a two-to-one ratio in favor of the body consistently advocating larger appropriations, increased spending and corresponding deficits."[41] But many of the House "cuts" represented a sophisticated institutional game. One veteran Senate Republican recalled: "Over in the House it's a great thing to economize. They cut out a lot of things because they know very well that when the bill comes over here, we will restore the money. I know—I was in the House. I used to vote to cut all these funds and then come over here and ask my Senators to be sure that the money got back in. We get plenty of that around here."[42]

---

[40] Richard F. Fenno, Jr., Congressmen in Committees 48 (1973). See also Fenno's The Power of the Purse 102-108 (1966). Allen Schick argues persuasively on pages 415-40 of his Congress and Money (1980) that House Appropriations has become a "subdued guardian" of the purse.

[41] Cong. Q. Wkly Rept., July 20, 1962, at 1226, 1238, cited by Jeffrey L. Pressman, House vs. Senate: Conflict in the Appropriations Process 85 (1966).

[42] Fenno, Power of the Purse, at 632.

Impoundment

After Congress completes the appropriations process, further reductions occur when Presidents impound funds. Harry Truman, Dwight Eisenhower, and John Kennedy impounded funds that Congress had added to their defense budgets. Impoundment also affects funds that Congress has added to domestic programs. In signing an agriculture appropriations bill in 1966, President Johnson objected to $312.5 million that Congress had added to his budget request. Rather than veto the bill he simply reduced expenditures for certain items "in an attempt to avert expending more in the coming year than provided in the budget."[43]

On an entirely different order were the impoundments carried out by the Nixon administration. They set a precedent in terms of magnitude, severity, and belligerence. The message from the White House came across without equivocation: congressional add-ons to the President's budget were irresponsible and wholly lacking in merit. Programs were either cut back to the President's request or, in some cases, terminated and dismantled.[44]

The administration justified some of the impoundments on the ground that the President's budget contained requests to rescind (cancel) certain funds. Since the President wanted to rescind the funds, it was reasoned that he should not spend the money until Congress had an opportunity to consider his request. In three rescission cases the federal courts found the administration's rationale totally inadequate. A President's budget was merely a recommendation, the courts noted. The budget had no special standing. What deserved implementation was not a President's budget but a public law.[45] This principle, which the Nixon administration had ignored in its eagerness to alter federal programs, was reiterated many times by federal courts.

In a decision involving the Office of Economic Opportunity,

[43] Public Papers of the Presidents, 1966, II, 981. For defense impoundments see Fisher, Presidential Spending Power, at 161-65.

[44] Fisher, Presidential Spending Power, at 175-201.

[45] National Association of Collegiate Veterans v. Ottina, Civ. Action No. 349-73 (D.D.C. 1973); Minnesota Chippewa Tribe v. Carlucci, Civ. Action No. 628-73 (D.D.C. 1973); National Association of State Universities and Land Grant Colleges v. Weinberger, Civ. Action No. 1014-73 (D.D.C. 1973).

a district court ruled that it was not permissible for the Nixon administration to begin dismembering the OEO simply because the President decided to omit funds for the agency in his budget. The President's budget was "nothing more than a proposal to the Congress for the Congress to act upon as it may please."[46] In another decision, affecting mental health funds, a federal judge noted that the President "does not have complete discretion to pick and choose between programs when some are made mandatory by conscious, deliberate congressional action."[47] The courts denied that the administration could withhold funds as a means of combating inflation.[48]

Only one of these cases reached the Supreme Court. In 1975 the Court decided that the Clean Water Act, despite ambiguities in its language and legislative history, did not permit the President to withhold from allotment and obligation the funds provided by Congress. The basic thrust of the act convinced the Court that Congress had made a firm commitment of substantial sums to build waste treatment plants.[49] The decision turned essentially on questions of statutory interpretation, but important constitutional principles were underscored: the authority of Congress to mandate spending; the President's obligation to carry out the laws; and the legitimacy of court orders to compel presidential action.

In response to the massive impoundments by the Nixon administration, Congress passed legislation in 1974 to limit the President's power. Precisely what the Impoundment Control Act intended is impossible to say. Like many legislative measures, it is a hybrid, representing bits and pieces of previous House and Senate bills plus some imaginative innovations by conferees. There

[46] Local 2677, the American Federation of Government Employees v. Phillips, 358 F.Supp. 60, 73 (D.D.C. 1973).

[47] National Council of Community Mental Health Centers v. Weinberger, 361 F.Supp. 897, 902 (D.D.C. 1973).

[48] State of Iowa ex rel. State Highway Com'n v. Brinegar, 512 F.2d 722 (8th Cir. 1975); State of Minnesota v. Coleman, 391 F.Supp. 330 (D. Minn. 1975); State Highway Commission of Missouri v. Volpe, 479 F.2d 1099 (8th Cir. 1973).

[49] Train v. City of New York, 420 U.S. 35 (1975). See Fisher, Presidential Spending Power, at 184-92.

is enough ambiguity in the act to allow the executive ample room for interpretation.

The Impoundment Control Act requires special messages from the President whenever he proposes to rescind or defer appropriations. To rescind funds, both Houses must complete action on a bill or joint resolution within forty-five days of continuous session. In the case of a deferral, it remains in effect unless one House passes a resolution of disapproval. For rescissions, then, the burden is on the President to obtain the approval of both Houses within a specified period. For deferrals the burden is on one House to veto the President's proposal.[50] Both branches gained new powers. Congress can now curb unilateral presidential actions, while the President for the first time has general statutory authority to impound funds for both routine and policy purposes.

The Supreme Court's decision in *INS* v. *Chadha* (1983), striking down the legislative veto, invalidated the one-House veto for deferrals. Until the Impoundment Control Act is amended to take account of the Court's decision, Congress will have to disapprove deferrals by including language in regular appropriations bills or supplemental appropriations bills. Even before *Chadha* was announced, Congress had begun disapproving deferrals through these appropriations bills.

Congressional understanding would be helped by eliminating reports on routine impoundments, such as the placing of funds in reserve for contingencies and savings (Antideficiency Act impoundments) or pursuant to specific statutory authority (other than the Impoundment Control Act). Congress could then focus on "policy impoundments" that have the effect of furthering administration priorities at the expense of those enacted by Congress. If the President were required to list the congressional add-on amount next to his proposed rescission or deferral, that would provide an early warning signal to Congress and give the administration some pause before discriminating against congressional initiatives. To be even-handed, policy impoundments ought to take into account events *after* passage of an ap-

---

[50] P.L. 93-344, 88 Stat. 332, Title X.

238

propriations bill that cast doubt on the need to spend funds. Such events should discredit not merely congressional add-ons but the President's original budget requests as well.

The Congressional Budget

The model of an executive budget looked appealing to Congress when it considered reform legislation in the early 1970s. The 1921 Act had assumed that presidential control and responsibility would be improved by centralizing the budget process in the executive branch. But advantages for the President need not flow to Congress, given its unique institutional qualities.

The Congressional Budget Act of 1974 anticipated a contest between two budgets: presidential and congressional. The analogy was weak because the President heads an executive branch, fortified by a central budget office. This hierarchical system restricts the size of budget requests as they move upwards from bureaus and departments to the OMB and the President. But there is no head in Congress and no possibility of a central budget office. Congress is inherently decentralized and no amount of procedural innovation can disguise that reality.

The Budget Act of 1974 contained a number of provisions designed to strengthen congressional control. It created Budget Committees in the House and the Senate, established a Congressional Budget Office (CBO) to supply technical support, and required the adoption of budget resolutions to set overall limits on budget aggregates (such as total outlays and revenues) and to permit debate on spending priorities. Because of bicameralism, decentralization, and committee autonomy within Congress, the CBO can never have the institutional strengths of an OMB.

The gap between promise and performance has been awesome, even if technical and procedural complexities help obscure the results of the Congressional Budget Act. Members of Congress praised the new process for exerting a restraining influence on federal spending. Many of the compliments depended on illusion, for behind all the talk of "comprehensiveness" and "accountability" was the fact that the Budget Committees provided a new access point for members who had been rebuffed by authorization and appropriations committees. To gain sufficient votes to pass the budget resolutions, the Budget Committees had to accommodate these spending interests (especially in the House of Representatives). The totals in budget resolutions were set at generous levels, adding a new rationale for higher spending. The Appropriations Committees found it difficult to argue against amendments to increase spending when their bills provided less than the amounts allowed in a budget resolution. The new process therefore encouraged higher spending than would have been tolerated in the past.[51]

The "current services budget," adopted by the 1974 statute, became a handy concept to legitimate annual, automatic increases for inflation. The concept helped shelter federal programs from budget-cutting drives.[52] Other innovations, such as the March 15 reports submitted by authorizing committees, stimulated program advocacy. Forced to issue recommendations early in the year, authorizing and appropriations committees inflated their estimates beyond likely needs. Their behavior allowed the Budget Committees to put together resolutions substantially lower than the sum of the March 15 requests. Members could then claim "savings" through these make-believe reductions. Instead of keeping within the President's aggregates, members voted on generous ceilings in budget resolutions and announced to their constituents that they had "stayed within the budget." *Which* budget was never made clear.

Although the framers of the 1974 statute knew that entitlements and "uncontrollables" constituted the most disturbing pressure for higher spending, entitlements received a preferred status in the Budget Act and were subjected to little discipline. Serious efforts to constrain entitlements were not made until 1980 and 1981.

Action on budget resolutions consumed increasing amounts of time. The problem of a compressed schedule grew worse when Congress decided to use "reconciliation" to control entitlements

[51] Allen Schick, Congress and Money, 313, 330, 469-70, 475-81 (1980).

[52] Id. at 217-18, 261-64, 585; 123 Cong. Rec. 13576 (1977) (remarks of Senator McClure).

and federal spending. Under reconciliation, Congress acts on an omnibus bill to change benefit levels and benefit criteria for social welfare programs. Senator Lowell Weicker voted against reconciliation instructions in April 1981 "because of the precipitate, injudicious way the President's spending reduction package has been considered in this body. We are supposed to be a deliberative body but, instead, we have been a mirror of the administration's program."[53] Members of Congress voted on a massive reconciliation bill with practically no opportunity for amendment and little understanding of its impact on agencies and programs.

Budget resolutions are highly touted as vehicles for centralized, systematic, and coherent legislative action. The Budget Act assumed that members of Congress would behave more responsibly by having to vote explicitly on budget aggregates, facing up to totals rather than deciding in "piecemeal" fashion the spending actions in separate appropriations and legislative bills. In 1974, as now, it was difficult to defend fragmentation, splintering, and decentralization when reformers pressed eagerly for "coordination" and a "unified budget process." But the risks are high when Congress, possessing very different institutional qualities, tries to emulate the President.

Increasing the size of a legislative vehicle—from an appropriations bill to a budget resolution—magnifies the scope of legislative conflict and encourages additional concessions to members. It costs more to build a majority. And when conflict exceeds a certain point in Congress, the result is escapist budgeting. Members become less, not more, responsible.

The omnibus reconciliation act of 1981 appears to be a case where Congress used a centralized process to force budgetary cutbacks. However, the final bill was drafted largely by the OMB and the Reagan administration. The President adroitly used a congressional tool.[54] This mammoth reconciliation bill produced

[53] 127 Cong. Rec. S3317 (daily ed. April 2, 1981).
[54] Jean Peters, "Reconciliation 1982: What Happened?" 14 PS 732 (1981); Cong. Q. Wkly Rept., August 15, 1981, at 1466; House Committee on Appropriations, "Views and Estimates on the Budget Proposed for Fiscal Year 1983" (Comm. Print March 10, 1982), at 12.

so much confusion and conflict that Congress is unlikely to repeat the experiment.

Congress has taken other steps to avoid responsibility for budget aggregates. By the early 1980s it began placing language in the first budget resolution which stated that a second resolution would be triggered in the fall if Congress failed to act by October 1. The figures in the spring resolution, no matter how unrealistic, automatically became the fall resolution. The House of Representatives also used the first budget resolution to avoid a separate vote on the public debt limit. House Rule XLIV, adopted in 1979, lifts the public debt limit from the spring budget resolution and places it in a joint resolution, which is then "deemed" to have passed the House. In effect, the vote on the budget resolutions counts as a vote on the debt limit. Accountability is lost because the public debt limit rarely commands much attention during debate on the budget resolution, and budget resolutions in recent years have been notoriously unrealistic about budget deficits.[55]

Secret Spending

The framers placed in Article I, Section 9, of the Constitution an explicit safeguard for financial accountability: "A regular Statement and Account of the Receipts and Expenditures of all public Money shall be published from time to time." It is surprising that this provision, so essential to democratic budgeting, did not appear in the draft of the Constitution until the final few days. The manner in which it was added clouds its meaning.

The Statement and Account Clause

On September 14, 1787, George Mason proposed that "an Account of the public expenditures should be annually published." Gouverneur Morris objected that publication would be "impos-

---

[55] For further details see Louis Fisher, "The Budget Act of 1974: A Further Loss of Spending Control," in Tom Wander, et al., eds., Congressional Budgeting: Politics, Process, and Power (1984).

sible in many cases."[56] Morris, a supporter of executive authority, probably believed in some element of secrecy and confidentiality. During his service with the Continental Congress he chided
those who assumed that legislative committees could manage the
people's business. The burden fell on the committee chairman,
who at that time performed the role of executive. As Morris
recalled: "Necessity, preserving the democratical forms, assumed
the monarchical substance of business"—that is, the chairman
did the work of the committee. At the Philadelphia convention
he favored executive power, regarding the President as the
"guardian of the people, even of the lower classes, agst. Legislative tyranny." He warned that Congress would "continually seek
to aggrandize & perpetuate themselves."[57] This kind of attitude
does not make for open government.

Rufus King found fault with Mason's proposal: "the term expenditures went to every minute shilling. This would be impracticable. Congs. might indeed make a monthly publication, but it
would be in such general Statements as would afford no satisfactory information." Unlike Morris, King appeared to be concerned about detail and frequency of publication rather than the
need for secrecy.

James Madison proposed to delete "annually" from the motion
and insert "from time to time." The purpose was to give Congress discretion over the timing of the publication instead of
insisting on an arbitrary schedule that might be ignored altogether. Several statements at this point suggest the need for secrecy. James Wilson, supporting Madison, said "Many operations of finance cannot be properly published at certain times,"
and Thomas FitzSimons insisted that it was "absolutely impossible to publish expenditures in the full extent of the term." The
convention accepted Madison's amendment without a dissenting
vote. Mason's proposal, as rewritten, included an accounting for
receipts as well as expenditures, and applied the requirement for
publication to "all public Money."[58]

[56] Farrand, Records, II, 618.

[57] Id. at 52-54. See also Diary and Letters of Gouverneur Morris (Anne Cary
Morris ed.), I, 12.

[58] Farrand, Records, II, 619.

This clause was discussed at the Virginia ratifying convention in 1788. Mason said that the phrase "from time to time" had been added because "there might be some matters which might require secrecy." This explanation indicates that Congress could delay the publication of sensitive material. Farrand records the confusing elaboration by Mason: "In matters relative to military operations, and foreign negotiations, secrecy was necessary sometimes. But he did not conceive that the receipts and expenditures of the public money ought ever to be concealed. The people, he affirmed, had a right to know the expenditures of their money."[59] This position is consistent only if Mason assumed that the cost of secret operations, after some period of time, would be made public.

The Growth of Secret Funding

With such a fragmentary and cryptic record, it would be hasty to conclude that the framers insisted on the publication of every expenditure of the federal government. The men who assembled at Philadelphia had just been through a decade of secret operations in the war against Great Britain. In Federalist 64, drawing on his own experiences, John Jay justified secrecy in the diplomatic area: "It seldom happens in the negotiation of treaties, of whichever nature, but that perfect *secrecy* and immediate *dispatch* are sometimes requisite. There are cases where the most useful intelligence may be obtained, if the persons possessing it can be relieved from apprehension of discovery." Expenditures made public, then, could not reveal the parties involved.

This special need for diplomacy was soon recognized by statute. In 1790 Congress provided the President with a $40,000 account to be used for foreign intercourse. It was left to his judgment to decide the extent to which the expenditures should be made public. Three years later Congress specified that the President could make a certificate of the amount of expenditures in foreign intercourse "he may think it advisable not to specify." A certificate (simply a statement that funds have been spent, but

[59] Id. at III, 326.

providing no details) is regarded as a sufficient voucher for the sums expended.[60]

Confidential funds in diplomatic affairs became the source of a dispute between President Polk and Congress. In an effort to embarrass Senator Daniel Webster, the House of Representatives passed a resolution in 1848 requiring the President to deliver certain State Department records from the period of March 4, 1841, to May 9, 1843. This interval dovetailed nicely with Webster's tenure as Secretary of State. Part of the information requested dealt with confidential funds in foreign intercourse. Polk refused to give the House the information on funding, pointing out that Congress, by statute, had given the President total discretion over the degree to which such funds should be made public. Although it was his practice to settle all expenditures for contingent expenses of foreign intercourse by regular vouchers, he declined to surrender the certificates made by his predecessor.[61]

On another occasion, in 1811, Congress passed a secret statute that gave President Madison $100,000 to take temporary possession of territory south of Georgia. The law was not published until 1818.[62] The only recurrent exception to the Statement and Account Clause throughout the nineteenth century was the President's contingency account in foreign intercourse. By 1899 the account reached the annual amount of $63,000.

The next exception occurred in 1916, just before the United

[60] 1 Stat. 129 (1790), 1 Stat. 300 (1793), codified at 31 U.S.C. 3526(e) (1982). For an unsuccessful effort by a newspaper to examine these expenditures, see Washington Post Co. v. U.S. Dept. of State, 501 F.Supp. 1152 (D.D.C. 1980).

[61] Richardson, Messages and Papers, V, 2281-2286. Secret spending by President Lincoln, for the purpose of paying a spy during the Civil War, was upheld by the Supreme Court in Totten, Administrator v. United States, 92 U.S. (2 Otto.) 105 (1875). In 1974 a district court stated that Totten "is inapplicable to criminal actions and has been modified by a century of legal experience, which teaches that the courts have broad authority to inquire into national security matters so long as proper safeguards are applied to avoid unwarranted disclosures"; United States v. Ehrlichman, 376 F.Supp. 29, 32 n.1 (D.D.C. 1974).

[62] 3 Stat. 471-72. See David Hunter Miller, Secret Statutes of the United States (1918).

States entered World War I. Congress authorized the Secretary of the Navy to make a certificate of expenses for "obtaining information from abroad and at home." Congress added a third unvouchered account in 1935 by giving the Federal Bureau of Investigation a confidential fund of $20,000 (later raised to $70,000).[63] This is an impressive record. From 1789 to 1935— a period of 146 years (or three-quarters of our history as a national government)—Congress departed from the Statement and Account Clause only on rare occasions and for relatively small amounts of money.

The record changed dramatically with the onset of World War II, which had a profound and lasting effect on democratic budgeting. Millions of dollars were given to the President on a confidential basis in order to expedite war production. The atomic bomb, costing billions of dollars, was developed and produced with secret funds. Congress authorized a confidential fund for the newly created Atomic Energy Commission. In quick succession Congress established unvouchered funds for the White House, the Defense Department, the District of Columbia, the Attorney General, the Bureau of Narcotics and Dangerous Drugs, the Secret Service, the Coast Guard, the Bureau of Customs, the Immigration and Naturalization Service, and other agencies.

In 1973 and 1974, prompted by revelations about the Watergate scandal, several of the confidential funds were deleted because they lacked authorizing language. Congress responded by enacting most of the necessary authorizations. It also consolidated some of the smaller confidential funds into larger accounts to provide for better administrative control.[64]

The General Accounting Office Act of 1980 permits the GAO to carry out a limited audit of unvouchered expenditures, although the statute does not cover the CIA and it allows the President to exempt certain sensitive foreign intelligence and law enforcement activities. The basic purpose of the statute is to allow the GAO "to determine whether the expenditure was, in

[63] 39 Stat. 557 (1916), 10 U.S.C. 7231 (1982); 49 Stat. 78 (1935), 28 U.S.C. 537 (1982).

[64] Louis Fisher, "Confidential Spending and Governmental Accountability," 47 G.W. L. Rev. 347 (1979).

fact, actually made and whether such expenditure was authorized by law."[65] Since Congress generally places almost total discretion in the officials who administer confidential funds, it is difficult to conceive of an expenditure that would not be "authorized."

Despite all of these reforms, it is still extremely difficult even to identify the confidential funds authorized by Congress. A researcher must be aware of language (sometimes clear, sometimes opaque) that appears in authorization bills, appropriations bills, and in the United States Code. It is often uncertain whether an account is confidential (unvouchered) or merely discretionary (subject to full GAO audit). These problems could be alleviated by adopting standard language for confidential funds. Appropriations bills should state the amount of the fund, stipulate in explicit language that the account is unvouchered, and provide references to the authorizing law. Appropriation accounts could use this language: "not to exceed [dollar amount] can be used for emergencies and extraordinary expenses, as authorized by [U.S. Code citation], to be expended on the approval or authority of the Secretary, and payments may be made on his certificate of necessary for confidential purposes."

The justifications for unvouchered funds also deserve scrutiny. Law enforcement seems a legitimate reason when confidentiality is used to protect the identity of informers. However, it is possible to disguise identities through the regular voucher system. Other justifications seem weak: the use of unvouchered funds for entertaining foreign dignitaries (e.g., tickets to theaters and sports events, sightseeing tours), gifts, and travel by White House aides. These reasons appear related less to national security than to agency convenience and the desire to minimize agency embarrassment.

The Intelligence Community

Overshadowing other confidential funds, both in dollar amounts and character of operation, are those spent on the U.S. intelligence community. The Central Intelligence Act of 1949 provided several extraordinary features of financial independence. The

---

[65] P.L. 96-226, 94 Stat. 311, sec. 101 (1980); 31 U.S.C. 3524 (1982).

Director of the Central Intelligence Agency may spend funds on a confidential basis, using certificates rather than vouchers. More important, the CIA does not receive a direct appropriation from Congress. Funds are initially appropriated to the Defense Department. The OMB, after being advised of the CIA budget by the Appropriations Committee, approves the transfer of that amount from the Defense Department to the CIA. The act of 1949 authorized the CIA to transfer to and receive from other government agencies "such sums as may be approved" by the OMB for the performance of any "functions or activities" authorized by the National Security Act of 1947.[66]

Precisely what Congress anticipated by "functions or activities" has long been at issue. Covert operations in Laos and Chile, secret funding of Radio Free Europe and Radio Liberty, and subsidies to religious organizations, student groups, and labor unions have all sparked intense controversies about the proper scope of CIA activities. But of direct interest in this chapter is the tension between the Statement and Account Clause and the method used to fund the CIA.

William B. Richardson, a resident of Greensburg, Pennsylvania, asked the federal courts to declare the Central Intelligence Act a violation of the Statement and Account Clause. A series of rulings from 1969 to 1974 ended with the Supreme Court's decision that Richardson lacked standing to maintain his suit.[67] But he picked up some notable support along the way. An appellate court, in 1972, emphasized the importance of the clause in these terms: "A responsible and intelligent taxpayer and citizen, of course, wants to know how his tax money is being spent. Without this information he cannot intelligently follow the actions of

[66] For CIA statutory authority for funding, see 50 U.S.C. 403 (1976). The relationship between Congress, the CIA, and the OMB is discussed in a letter from OMB Director Roy Ash to Senator William Proxmire, April 29, 1974, reprinted at 120 Cong. Rec. 17487-89 (1974). Further discussion on CIA funding appears in Fisher, Presidential Spending Power, at 214-23.

[67] Richardson v. United States, 418 U.S. 166 (1974). Challenges from any citizen, whether as taxpayer under *Richardson* or as plaintiff under the Freedom of Information Act, fail because of lack of standing and the political question doctrine; Halperin v. Central Intelligence Agency, 629 F.2d 144 (D.C. Cir. 1980).

the Congress or of the Executive. Nor can he properly fulfill his obligation as a member of the electorate. The Framers of the Constitution deemed fiscal information essential if the electorate was to exercise any control over its representatives and meet their new responsibilities as citizens of the Republic."[68] Justice Douglas, one of three members to dissent from the Supreme Court's decision, rejected the proposition that Congress, by statute, is at liberty to suspend a constitutional provision. The claim that Congress had the power to read the Statement and Account Clause out of the Constitution was to him "astounding."[69]

Pressure gradually mounted in Congress to publish an aggregate figure for the entire intelligence community budget (perhaps in excess of $10 billion, of which the CIA represents some 10 to 15 percent). Past CIA Directors William E. Colby and James R. Schlesinger, as well as Director Stansfield Turner (appointed in 1977), have agreed that publication of the aggregate figure would not jeopardize national security. What made them uneasy was the political demand for further details and the possibility that trends and "bumps" in the budget totals from year to year might communicate useful information to America's enemies. But as Colby noted on one occasion, the American constitutional system probably requires publication of more information on the CIA budget than might be convenient from the agency's point of view.[70]

In 1976 the House Select Committee on Intelligence (the Pike

[68] Richardson v. United States, 465 F. 2d 844, 853 (3d Cir. 1972), footnote omitted.

[69] United States v. Richardson, 418 U.S. at 200-01. In 1977 an appellate court decided that Congressman Michael J. Harrington lacked standing to bring suit against the use of public funds for illegal CIA activities; Harrington v. Bush, 553 F.2d 190 (D.C. Cir. 1977). In 1976 a federal court held that the Freedom of Information Act exempted disclosure of the CIA budget; Halperin v. Colby, Civ. Action No. 75-676 (D.D.C. June 4, 1976).

[70] "Nomination of William E. Colby," hearings before the Senate Committee on Armed Services, 93d Cong., 1st Sess. 17, 181 (1973); "Nomination of James R. Schlesinger, To Be Secretary of Defense," hearing before the Senate Committee on Armed Services, 93d Cong., 1st Sess. 67-68 (1973); "Nomination of Admiral Stansfield Turner," hearings before the Senate Select Committee on Intelligence, 95th Cong., 1st Sess. 83-84 (1977).

Committee), at the end of its tumultuous existence, recommended "that there be disclosure of the total single sum budgeted for each agency involved in intelligence, or if such an item is a part or portion of the budget of another agency or department that it can be separately identified as a single item."[71] Less ambitious was the conclusion of the Senate study committee on intelligence activities (the Church Committee) to publish the aggregate figure for the intelligence community budget. In voting 8 to 3 for this recommendation, the committee highlighted one of the major objections to secret budgeting: "most Members of Congress and the public are deceived about the appropriations and expenditures of other government agencies whose budgets are inflated to conceal funds for the intelligence community."[72] Sums were not only concealed; they distorted the totals of other appropriations accounts.

President Ford intervened in 1976 to urge the Senate committee to reconsider its decision. He believed that the "net effect of such a disclosure could adversely affect our foreign intelligence efforts and therefore would not be in the public interest." CIA Director George Bush wrote to the Senate Appropriations Committee, agreeing with the President's position.[73] Also during that time, the Senate was in the process of creating a new committee (the Senate Select Committee on Intelligence) which would have jurisdiction over the authorization of intelligence activities. A specific responsibility placed upon this new committee was to study whether disclosure of budgetary figures would be in the public interest. The Senate deferred action while awaiting the committee's recommendation.

In 1977 the Senate Select Committee voted 9 to 8 in favor of disclosing for fiscal 1978 the aggregate amount of funds appropriated for national foreign intelligence activities. CIA Director Turner had testified that neither he nor President Carter objected

[71] H. Rept. No. 833, 94th Cong., 2d Sess. 3 (1976).

[72] S. Rept. No. 755, 94th Cong., 2d Sess. 384 (1976).

[73] "Whether Disclosure of Funds Authorized for Intelligence Activities is in the Public Interest," hearings before the Senate Select Committee on Intelligence, 95th Cong., 1st Sess. 391-94 (1977).

to the publication of this figure.[74] Since that time, however, the Select Committees on Intelligence in the House and the Senate have decided that public disclosure on intelligence budget figures would not be in the public interest. The figures are available on a confidential basis to each member of Congress.[75]

In the twentieth century, Congress and the President added vast new institutional capabilities to the control and management of the budget. Specialists are available in the Office of Management and Budget, the Congressional Budget Office, executive agencies, and congressional committees. Sophisticated, computerized analyses flow in enormous quantities from all sectors, public and private. Yet the federal budget has acquired a life of its own, seemingly immune from year to year adjustments by government officials. The idea of using the national budget to stabilize the economy and compensate for weaknesses in the private market has been all but abandoned. "Fine tuning" the economy is a relic of the Kennedy years. The budgetary estimates of the Johnson, Nixon, Ford, and Carter administrations were increasingly unrealistic, unreliable, and irresponsible. The Reagan administration projected a series of annual budget deficits in the range of $200 billion, a magnitude that financial analysts unanimously deplored. Added to these deficiencies are the billions in confidential and secret funds that are at odds with the constitutional command for "a regular Statement and Account of the Receipts and Expenditures of all public Money [to be] published from time to time." Recent budgetary practices have brought transformation without progress, expertise without mastery, and information without understanding.

[74] S. Rept. No. 274, 95th Cong., 1st. Sess. (1977).
[75] H. Rept. No. 486 (Part 1), 97th Cong., 2d Sess. 2 (1982); S. Rept. No. 379, 97th Cong., 2d Sess. 2 (1982).

8

TREATIES AND EXECUTIVE
AGREEMENTS

American public interest in international agreements has been meager and spasmodic. Geographic isolation, an abundance of natural resources, and a native distrust of "entangling alliances" are some of the inhibiting factors. Occasionally an emotional issue such as the Jay Treaty or the Versailles Treaty has commanded public attention, but for more prosaic subjects it has been difficult to sustain interest.

This general record of apathy is undergoing important changes. The United States now depends heavily on foreign trade, finds itself vulnerable to oil embargoes and other interruptions of essential supplies, experiences price effects from so-called exogenous variables, and sees its currency fluctuating widely because of international pressures. We now seek cooperation on matters that can be resolved only by regional and worldwide compacts. As executive agreements are relied on more frequently as a substitute for the treaty process, creating charges on the Treasury, both Houses of Congress are called upon to scrutinize them with greater care. These events are forcing the House of Representatives to participate on a more equal basis with the Senate.

Treaties

It is commonplace today to assign to the President the leading role in foreign policy and international affairs. But quite late in the deliberations at the Philadelphia convention, the delegates entrusted the predominant voice to the Senate. As late as August 6, 1787, the constitutional draft gave the Senate exclusive power to make treaties and appoint ambassadors. Opposition surfaced, however. By early September the convention decided that the President should make treaties "by and with the advice and consent of the Senate," and should nominate "and by and with the advice and consent of the Senate . . . appoint Ambassadors."[1]

Article II, Section 2, of the Constitution requires that treaties receive the support of "two thirds of the Senators present." A roll-call vote is not necessary (as for veto overrides), nor is there even a requirement that a quorum be present. In 1952, with two Senators on the floor, the Senate gave its advice and consent to the ratification of three treaties. One of the Senators did not even vote. The other, the presiding officer, cast an 'aye" vote and stated that "two-thirds of the Senators present concurring therein, the resolution of ratification is agreed to, and the convention is ratified." A year later Senate Majority Leader Knowland announced that future treaties would be preceded by a quorum call and subjected to "a yea-and-nay vote, at least on the first of a series of treaties." That remains the general practice.[2]

The use of the word "treaty" in a statute does not necessarily mean an international agreement requiring the advice and consent of the Senate. Unless Congress specifically defines the word in that sense, courts may interpret treaties to mean an international agreement concluded between sovereigns without Senate participation.[3]

Negotiation

Does Senate "advice" on treaties apply only to the final product, as fashioned by the President and his assistants, or to the intermediate stages of negotiation as well? Contemporary judgment generally excludes the Senate from any participation in treaty negotiation. The process of drafting and negotiating a treaty is widely regarded as a "presidential monopoly."[4] And yet this con-

---

[1] Farrand, Records, II, 155, 169, 183, 297-98, 392-94, 495.

[2] 99 Cong. Rec. 9231 (1953). See 98 Cong. Rec. 7217-23 (1952) and Carl Marcy, "A Note on Treaty Ratification," 47 Am. Pol. Sci. Rev. 1130 (1953). For contemporary practice, see "Treaties and Other International Agreements: The Role of the United States Senate," a study prepared for the Senate Committee on Foreign Relations, 98th Cong., 2d Sess. 117 (Comm. Print June 1984).

[3] Weinberger v. Rossi, 456 U.S. 25 (1982).

[4] The Constitution of the United States of America: Analysis and Interpretation, S. Doc. No. 92-82, at 481 (1973); Edward S. Corwin, The President 211-12 (1957 ed); United States v. Curtiss-Wright Corp., 299 U.S. 304, 319 (1936).

clusion is contradicted by the Philadelphia debates, the precedents established by the Washington administration, and the practices and understandings developed thereafter.

The Constitution does not divide treaty-making into two distinct and sequential stages: negotiation by the President and approval by the Senate. The President "makes" treaties, by and with the advice and consent of the Senate. The constitutional language in Article II, Section 2, for treaties differs significantly from that used for appointments. For the latter the President "shall nominate, and by and with the Advice and Consent of the Senate, shall appoint Ambassadors." Here the President's authority to nominate is set apart solely as an executive responsibility. This differs from the language for treaties: the President "shall have Power, by and with the Advice and Consent of the Senate, to make Treaties." In this operation the two branches are inextricably linked.

When Washington first communicated with the Senate regarding the appropriate procedure for treaties, he stated that oral communications with the Senate "seem indispensably necessary; because in these a variety of matters are contained, all of which not only require consideration, but some of them may undergo much discussion; to do which by written communications would be tedious without being satisfactory."[5] This policy suggests an active role for the Senate, not a mere yea or nay to what a President submits.

A subsequent communication from Washington underscores the partnership status of the Senate on treaty-making: "In the appointment to offices, the agency of the Senate is purely executive, and they may be summoned to the President. In treaties, the agency is perhaps as much of a legislative nature and the business may possibly be referred to their deliberations in their legislative chamber." Repeatedly he expressed his intention to send "propositions" to the Senate, again implying that the Senate would be invited to make changes and offer recommendations

---

Also see statement by the legal adviser for the State Department in "Congressional Oversight of Executive Agreements—1975," hearings before the Senate Committee on the Judiciary, 94th Cong., 1st Sess. 38 (1975).

[5] The Writings of Washington (Fitzpatrick ed.), XXX, 373.

to treaty drafts.[6] Hamilton, in Federalist 75, observed that the power of making treaties "will be found to partake more of the legislative than of the executive character, though it does not seem strictly to fall within the definition of either of them."

Washington met with Senators on August 22, 1789, to secure their advice and consent to an Indian treaty. The meeting was conducted at an awkward time, putting all parties under considerable strain. The Senate had just rejected Washington's nomination of Benjamin Fishbourn to be naval officer in Georgia. The legislators felt uncomfortable in Washington's presence and disliked having to rely solely on information provided by the Secretary of War, who was present. Conditions in the room—with noisy carriages traveling by—made it difficult to hear what was said. Under these circumstances the Senators decided that they would not commit themselves to any positions that day. Washington, annoyed by the inconvenience, returned two days later and obtained the Senate's consent.[7] He did not repeat the experiment.

It is a misreading of this incident to conclude that henceforth the Senate was excluded from any role in the negotiation process. Washington continued to seek its advice, but through written communications rather than personal appearances. Senators were asked to approve the appointment of treaty negotiators and even to advise on their negotiating instructions.[8] Far from being a "presidential monopoly," the negotiation of treaties has often been shared with the Senate in order to secure legislative understanding and support.[9]

Woodrow Wilson held a different view. As a scholar he urged the President not to consult with the Senate and treat it as an equal partner. Instead, he recommended that negotiations be pursued independently. After these unilateral executive actions,

[6] Id. at 378.

[7] William Maclay, Sketches of Debate in the First Senate of the United States 122-26 (1880).

[8] Thomas M. Franck and Edward Weisband, Foreign Policy by Congress 136 (1979).

[9] Many examples are cited by George H. Haynes, The Senate of the United States, II, 576-602 (1938).

legislative compliance would be compelled by getting the country "into such scrapes, so pledged in the view of the world to certain courses of action, that the Senate hesitates to bring about the appearance of dishonor which would follow its refusal to ratify the rash promises or to support the indiscreet threats of the Department of State."[10] This mousetrap theory of the treaty power had disastrous consequences for Wilson's record in office as well as for international events after World War I. One of his gravest miscalculations was the decision to exclude prominent Senators from the negotiation of the Versailles Treaty. When administrations have chosen to present the Senate with a *fait accompli*, the Senate has retaliated by tacking on amendments, shelving treaties, and rejecting them outright.[11]

A healthier model of Senate-presidential cooperation is supplied by the North Atlantic Treaty. It was foreshadowed by Senate Resolution 239, passed in 1948, calling for "regional and other collective arrangements for individual and collective self-defense." The Senate developed the resolution in close collaboration with the State Department. Between the time of its passage and ratification of the treaty, ranking members of the Senate Foreign Relations Committee consulted with the State Department. The committee as a whole helped formulate the terms of the treaty. Dean Acheson, although he entertained inflated notions of executive prerogatives during his tenure as Secretary of State, stated in 1971 that the treaty process is formally divided into negotiation and ratification stages but "anybody with any sense would consult with certainly some of the members of the ratifying body before he got himself out on the very end of a limb from which he could be sawed off." He recalled that during the negotiations of the North Atlantic Treaty, Senators Thomas Connally and Arthur Vandenburg "were with me all the time,"

[10] Woodrow Wilson, Congressional Government 233-34 (1885). Similar views appear in his Constitutional Government in the United States 77-78 (1908). His constitutional analysis is effectively refuted by Forrest R. Black, "The United States Senate and the Treaty Power," 4 Rocky Mt. L. Rev. 1 (1931) and Richard E. Webb, "Treaty-Making and the President's Obligation to Seek the Advice and Consent of the Senate with Special Reference to the Vietnam Peace Negotiations," 31 Ohio State L. J. 490 (1970).

[11] Franck and Weisband, Foreign Policy by Congress, at 136-37.

while Senator Walter George actually wrote one of the provisions of the treaty.[12]

The substantial overlap between domestic and foreign matters in contemporary times creates the need to include congressional leaders in the negotiation of international agreements and to establish machinery to permit more effective integration of congressional interests.[13] The volatile politics of the Panama Canal Treaty prompted Senate Majority Leader Robert Byrd, Minority Leader Howard Baker, and several other key Senators to visit Panama and negotiate changes in the treaty with General Torrijos and Panamanian officials. These rescue missions might have been averted had President Carter reached out earlier for Senate advice.[14]

Members of both Houses of Congress have become formal participants in the network of international boards and commissions. They attend international conferences and serve as delegates to the North Atlantic Assembly, the Interparliamentary Union, and other interparliamentary groups. They are appointed as U.S. Representatives to the U.N. General Assembly. Through such participation and experience, members of Congress become deeply involved in negotiation. During 1977 and 1978, twenty-six Senators went to Geneva as official advisers to the SALT II negotiating team.[15] Since 1962 it has been the practice of Congress to require that a specific number of Representatives and Senators be accredited as official advisers to the U.S. delegations that negotiate trade agreements.[16]

[12] "Executive Privilege: The Withholding of Information from the Executive," hearing before the Senate Committee on the Judiciary, 92d Cong., 1st Sess. 262-64 (1971). See Richard H. Heindel et al., "The North Atlantic Treaty in the United States Senate," 43 Am. J. Int'l L. 633 (1949).

[13] See Bayless Manning, "The Congress, the Executive and Intermestic Affairs: Three Proposals," 55 Foreign Affairs 306 (1977).

[14] Cecil V. Crabb, Jr., and Pat M. Holt, Invitation to Struggle: Congress, the President and Foreign Policy 77-79 (1980); John Spanier and Joseph Nogee, eds., Congress, the Presidency and American Foreign Policy 92-93 (1981).

[15] I. M. Destler, "Executive-Congressional Conflict in Foreign Policy: Explaining It, Coping With It," in Lawrence C. Dodd and Bruce I. Oppenheimer, eds., Congress Reconsidered 310 (1981).

[16] Robert C. Cassidy, Jr., "Negotiating About Negotiations: The Geneva Multilateral Trade Talks," in Thomas M. Franck, ed., The Tethered Presidency 267-68 (1981).

Private groups are also more active in the negotiation of international agreements. Advisory committees, consisting of representatives from the private sector, serve on dozens of panels in the foreign affairs field. Part of their functions include assisting in the preparation of international negotiations and advising the State Department on positions to take at conferences.[17] State governments, in their search for export trade and foreign investment, maintain direct contact with both private and government officials of foreign countries. This activity is encouraged by the Commerce Department and American embassies and consulates overseas.[18]

The Logan Act

Efforts to protect the President's responsibility for negotiating with foreign nations go back to the Logan Act of 1799. The previous year, after American negotiations with France had foundered, a Philadelphia physician by the name of George Logan set sail for Europe to try his hand at diplomacy. His trip provoked a resolution in Congress directed against private citizens who "usurp the Executive authority of this government, by commencing or carrying on any correspondence with the Governments of any foreign Prince or State." The same Congress that passed the Alien and Sedition Acts gave birth to the Logan Act. It provides for fines and imprisonment to punish American citizens who carry on unauthorized correspondence or intercourse with foreign governments for the purpose of influencing American policy.[19]

Hundreds of individuals have defied this act, but only one has been indicted and he was found not guilty. During the Vietnam

[17] "The Role of Advisory Committees in U.S. Foreign Policy," prepared for the Senate Committee on Foreign Relations, 94th Cong., 1st Sess. 4 (Comm. Print April 1975).

[18] Harold G. Maier, "Cooperative Federalism in International Trade: Its Constitutional Parameters," 27 Mercer L. Rev. 391 (1976).

[19] 1 Stat. 613 (1799); 18 U.S.C. 953 (1982). The Resolution is cited in Annals, 5th Cong. 2489. See Charles Warren, History of Laws Prohibiting Correspondence with a Foreign Government and Acceptance of a Commission, S. Doc. No. 696, 64th Cong., 2d Sess. (1917).

War, pacifist leaders and American office seekers maintained frequent contact with North Vietnam and the peace delegations at Paris. The State Department takes the position that members of Congress may engage in discussions with foreign officials in pursuance of their legislative duties under the Constitution, provided they advise the officials that they have no authority to negotiate on behalf of the United States.[20]

A recent dispute concerned former President Nixon's trip to China in 1976, at the time of the New Hampshire primary. Senator Barry Goldwater said that Nixon had violated the Logan Act and would do the United States a favor by remaining in China. Goldwater announced that the law was passed in recognition that the "unauthorized actions of private individuals have a potential of interfering with and disturbing the ability of the Executive to make and carry out foreign policy, and if it has application to any situation it must be this one."[21] The State Department regarded Nixon's visit as undertaken entirely as a private citizen. The Department was "unaware of any basis for believing that Mr. Nixon acted with the intent prohibited by the Logan Act."[22]

After more than fifty Americans were held hostage in Iran beginning in November 1979, an assortment of American legislators, professors, clergymen, and parents of the hostages traveled to that country to try to negotiate a release. President Carter appeared to support such ventures. In 1979, after American blacks had traveled to the Middle East to talk to Arab and Israeli leaders, he said: "I don't have any authority, nor do I want to have any authority, to interrupt or to interfere with the right of American citizens to travel where they choose and to meet with whom they choose. I would not want that authority; I think it would be a violation of the basic constitutional rights that are precious to our Nation."[23]

His patience snapped during the summer of 1980 when former Attorney General Ramsey Clark attended a conference in

[20] Digest of United States Practice in International Law, 1975, at 749-50.

[21] 122 Cong. Rec. 4216, 4919 (1976); Washington Post, February 26, 1976, at A7:1.

[22] Digest of United States Practice in International Law, 1976, at 75-76.

[23] Wkly Comp. Pres. Doc., XV 1861 (October 10, 1979).

Iran despite a presidential ban. Several members of Congress were outraged by the visit, calling Clark the "Benedict Arnold of the 20th century" and urging the Justice Department to prosecute him for violating the Logan Act and the International Emergency Economic Powers Act.[24] Carter said he was inclined to prosecute Clark and several others who had violated his directive on the travel ban.[25] This statement is attributable to presidential pique, however, and the incident was soon forgotten. Attorney General Benjamin R. Civiletti later announced that it would be "inappropriate" to prosecute Clark in a criminal suit and no action was ever taken in a civil suit.[26]

Jesse Jackson was an active traveler to foreign countries during the Reagan years, visiting with government leaders in Syria, Cuba, Central America, and other regions, often negotiating for the release of U.S. citizens. Jackson's visit to Cuba in 1984 and his talks with Fidel Castro prompted President Reagan to remind reporters that "there is a law, the Logan Act, with regard to unauthorized personnel, civilians, simply going to—or citizens— to other countries and, in effect, negotiating with foreign governments. Now, that is the law of the land." But he said he had no plans to take legal action.[27]

Because the Logan Act is vague in meaning and restricts First Amendment freedoms, it is of doubtful constitutionality.[28] The historical record certainly suggests that the sanctions are too harsh to be applied. As part of its effort to revise and unify the federal criminal code, Congress has considered repealing the Logan Act.

The Role of the House

In 1976 President Ford vetoed a bill that Congress had passed to implement U.S. obligations under a treaty. The bill contained

---

[24] 126 Cong. Rec. H4407-10 (daily ed. June 3, 1980); id. at S6374-76 (June 6, 1980); id. at S6454-58 (June 9, 1980); id. at H4688 (June 10, 1980).

[25] Wkly Comp. Pres. Doc., XVI, 1087-89 (June 10, 1980).

[26] Washington Post, January 8, 1981, at A6:1.

[27] Wkly Comp. Pres. Doc., XX, 975 (July 2, 1984).

[28] Detlev F. Vagts, "The Logan Act: Paper Tiger or Sleeping Giant?" 60 Am. J. Int'l L. 268 (1966), analyzes the act and concludes that it is probably unconstitutional.

a one-House veto which, he said, "would allow the House of Representatives to block adoption of what is essentially an amendment to a treaty, a responsibility which is reserved by the Constitution of the Senate."[29] Ford's assumption that the House is excluded from treaty matters has been contested in the past and is challenged even more so today.

Several delegates at the Philadelphia convention favored a check on treaties by both Houses rather than by the Senate alone. They reasoned that treaties, accorded the status of law under the Constitution, should be approved by Congress as a whole. At one point it was suggested that "no Treaty shall be binding on the U.S. which is not ratified by a law." Madison wondered whether a distinction might not be made between different types of treaties, allowing the President and the Senate to make "Treaties eventual and of Alliance for limited terms—and requiring the concurrence of the whole Legislature in other Treaties." A later proposal, joining the House with the Senate in advising and consenting to treaties, was decisively beaten back with only one state in favor and ten opposed.[30] The Constitution adopted in September reserved the treaty-making power to the President and to the Senate, but the power to make laws and appropriate funds would soon propel the House into an active role in international agreements.

A major dispute developed in 1796 when President Washington notified the House of Representatives that the Jay Treaty had been ratified. Congressman Edward Livingston offered a resolution requesting the President to transmit to the House a copy of the instructions that had been given to the U.S. minister who negotiated the treaty, together with correspondence and other documents relating to the treaty. Five days later he modified the resolution to permit the President to withhold any papers which existing negotiations might render improper to be disclosed. Liv-

---

[29] Wkly Comp. Pres. Doc., XII, 1486 (October 10, 1976). Substantially the same bill (substituting a two-House for a one-House veto) became law the following year; 91 Stat. 308 (1977). See H. Rept. No. 447, 95th Cong., 1st Sess. (1977). President Carter expressed "serious constitutional reservations" about the two-House veto provision; Wkly Comp. Pres. Doc. XIII, 1128-29 (July 28, 1977).

[30] Farrand, Records, II, 392-94, 538.

ingston maintained that the House possessed "a discretionary power of carrying the Treaty into effect, or refusing it their sanction."[31] Congressman Albert Gallatin of Pennsylvania was even more specific. He said that certain powers delegated to Congress by the Constitution, such as the authority to regulate trade, might clash with the treaty-making powers. The House did not have to acquiesce in decisions agreed to by the President and the Senate. The legislative powers specifically delegated to Congress served as limitations on the treaty process; the general power of granting funds constituted yet another restraining force.[32]

After several weeks of debate the House supported Livingston's resolution by a margin of 62 to 37. Washington denied the request for papers and documents by citing a number of reasons, including the need for caution and secrecy in foreign negotiations as well as the exclusive role of the Senate to participate as a member of the legislative branch. Shortly thereafter Congressman Thomas Blount introduced a resolution (adopted 54 to 37), stating that the House of Representatives did not claim any agency in making treaties,

> but that when a Treaty stipulates regulations of any of the subjects submitted by the Constitution to the power of Congress, it must depend, for its execution, as to such stipulations, on a law or laws to be passed by Congress. And it is the Constitutional right and duty of the House of Representatives, in all such cases, to deliberate on the expediency or inexpediency of carrying such Treaty into effect, and to determine and act thereon, as, in their judgment, may be most conducive to the public good.[33]

Some of the issues of the Jay Treaty reappeared during the debate on the Louisiana Purchase. On the basis of a provisional appropriation of $2 million to be applied toward the purchase of New Orleans and the Floridas, the Jefferson administration

[31] Annals of Congress, 4th Cong., 1st Sess. 426-28.

[32] Id. at 437, 466-74.

[33] Id. at 771-82. This language has been adopted on other occasions, such as on April 20, 1871; Hinds' Precedents, II, §1523. See Ivan M. Stone, "The House of Representatives and the Treaty-Making Power," 17 Ky. L. J. 217 (1929).

entered into an agreement with France to buy the whole of Louisiana. Congressional support required not only the advice and consent of the Senate to the treaty, but also funds supplied by both Houses. Accordingly, Jefferson sent copies of the ratified treaty to the House of Representatives and to the Senate, explaining: "You will observe that some important conditions can not be carried into execution but with the aid of the Legislature, and that time presses a decision on them without delay."[34] The House debated at length a resolution requesting from Jefferson certain papers and documents relating to the treaty. Some portions of the resolution were adopted, others rejected. The resolution as a whole went down to defeat, 59 to 57. The House subsequently joined the Senate in passing legislation to enable Jefferson to take possession of the Louisiana Territory.[35]

On other occasions the House has opposed treaties that required appropriations, two examples being the Gadsden purchase treaty with Mexico in 1853 and the Alaskan purchase treaty with Russia in 1867. The need to have support from both Houses for certain treaties was recognized in a reciprocity treaty with the Hawaiian Islands in 1876. A proviso made the treaty dependent on legislative consent by both Houses.[36]

Article I, Section 8, of the Constitution empowers Congress to "regulate Commerce with foreign Nations, and among the several States, and with the Indian Tribes." For nearly a century Congress treated the tribes as independent nations, subject to the treaty-making power of the President and the Senate. The Civil War changed the government's policy to one of assimilation and citizenship. During this time the Office of Indian Affairs came under heavy fire for corruption and maladministration. In response to those developments the House of Representatives began to voice strong opposition to its exclusion from Indian affairs. When the Senate inserted funds in a bill to fulfill treaties it had ratified with the Indians, the House refused to go along. The session expired in 1869 without an appropriation for the

[34] Richardson, Messages and Papers, I, 350-51 (October 21, 1803).
[35] Annals of Congress, 8th Cong., 1st Sess. 385-419; 2 Stat. 245, 247 (1803).
[36] Chalfant Robinson, "The Treaty-Making Power of the House of Representatives," 12 Yale Rev. 191 (1903).

Indian Office. Congress reached a compromise the following session, but the dispute between the two Houses persisted. Finally, an act approved in 1871 contained the following clause: "*Provided*, That hereafter no Indian nation or tribe within the territory of the United States shall be acknowledged or recognized as an independent nation, tribe, or power with whom the United States may contract by treaty . . . ."[37]

In 1880 the House declared that the negotiation of a commercial treaty, fixing the rates of duty to be imposed on foreign imports, would be "an infraction of the Constitution and an invasion of one of the highest prerogatives of the House of Representatives."[38] The commerce power was again at issue a few years later. A commercial treaty with Mexico in 1883 contained a clause making its validity dependent on action by both Houses. The House Ways and Means Committee interpreted the language to mean that the House had a right to a voice in treaties affecting revenue. Although additional conventions were entered into to extend the time available for congressional approval, the House did not support the treaty and it did not take effect.[39] The prerogatives of the House in matters of foreign commerce, tariffs, and revenues have been protected by the use of statutes that authorize reciprocal trade agreements.[40]

Legislation sometimes serves as a direct substitute for treaties. When the Senate failed to ratify a treaty for the annexation of Texas, President Tyler advised the House of Representatives: "The power of Congress is, however, fully competent in some other form of proceeding to accomplish everything that a formal ratification of the treaty could have accomplished . . . ."[41] He laid before the House the rejected treaty, together with all the correspondence and documents that had previously been made

[37] 16 Stat. 566. See U.S. Department of the Interior, Federal Indian Law 138-214 (1958).

[38] Hinds' Precedents, II, §1524.

[39] 24 Stat. 975 (1883), 25 Stat. 1370 (1885), 24 Stat. 1018 (1886), and Hinds' Precedents, II, §§1526-1528.

[40] For the development of reciprocal trade legislation, see Louis Fisher, President and Congress 133-55 (1972).

[41] Richardson, Messages and Papers, V, 2176 (June 10, 1844).

available to the Senate. Instead of having to obtain a two-thirds vote from the Senate, the annexation of Texas was consummated by simple majority votes from both Houses.[42] Hawaii was annexed in 1898 by the same method after Senate opposition prevented action on a treaty. The St. Lawrence Seaway plan, rejected by the Senate in 1934 in treaty form, passed Congress in 1954 as a regular bill.[43] The Carter administration created a stir when it considered submitting strategic arms limitation (SALT) agreements as a joint resolution rather than as a treaty.[44]

During World War II, proposals were put forth to give the House equal treaty-making powers with the Senate. In part this development reflected criticism of the Senate's performance over the previous half century.[45] Members of the House also challenged the traditional arguments offered in support of the Senate's treaty prerogative. In Federalist 64, Jay had claimed that decisions on treaties should be placed in the hands of the Senate, whose members were chosen by the "select assemblies" of state legislatures and would therefore possess greater expertise than members of the House. The force of this argument was diluted after the Seventeenth Amendment subjected Senators to popular election. Jay also argued that the small size of the Senate permitted greater secrecy and dispatch than could be expected of the House. But by 1944 the Senate had grown from twenty-six members to ninety-six, or larger than the original House membership of sixty-five. On the basis of these changes in the political system, the House in 1945 adopted by a vote of 288 to 88 a resolution to amend the Constitution to provide for treaty ratification by a majority of both Houses. Not surprisingly, the Senate took no action on the measure.[46]

[42] 9 Stat. 1 (1845).

[43] For an opinion by Acting Attorney General McGranery in 1946, upholding the legality of an executive agreement made pursuant to a joint resolution (instead of a treaty), see 40 Op. Att'y Gen. 469.

[44] Armen R. Vartian, "Approval of SALT Agreements by Joint Resolution of Congress," 21 Harv. Int'l L. J. 421 (1980); "Treaty Ratification Process and Separation of Powers," hearing before the Senate Committee on the Judiciary, 97th Cong., 2d Sess. (1982).

[45] H. Rept. No. 2061, 78th Cong., 2d Sess. 4-5 (1944).

[46] 91 Cong. Rec. 4326-68 (1945).

But the issue persists. Most recently the House asserted its role in the treaty power with regard to the Panama Canal and Spain. The dispute over the Spanish Bases Treaty of 1976 began as an executive-legislative conflict. The Senate successfully argued that an agreement with Spain over military bases should be accomplished not by executive agreement, as in the past, but by treaty. Having conceded this point to Congress, the administration ran into other difficulties. Members of both Houses objected to language in the treaty that appeared to make mandatory the appropriation of funds over a five-year period. In addition, the administration maintained that the treaty constituted an *authorization* to have funds appropriated. This threatened the jurisdiction of the Senate Committee on Foreign Relations and the House Committee on Foreign Affairs.

Responding to both issues, the Senate Resolution of Advice and Consent contained a declaration that the sums referred to in the Spanish treaty "shall be made available for obligation through the normal procedures of the Congress, including the process of prior authorization and annual appropriations." Although the administration had wanted the treaty to serve as the authorization, the Senate resolution guaranteed congressional involvement for the authorizing and appropriating committees of both Houses. In effect, the Senate Foreign Relations Committee joined with the House Foreign Affairs Committee to give both panels a role in implementing the treaty. Congress adopted legislation in 1976 to authorize the appropriation of funds needed to implement the treaty.[47]

The Spanish Bases Treaty was replaced by an executive agreement in 1982. The agreement stipulates that the supply of defense articles and services are subject to "the annual authorizations and appropriations contained in United States security assistance legislation . . . ." Although the agreement promises support "in the highest amounts, the most favorable terms, and the widest variety of forms," it also conditions such support on what "may be lawful and feasible."[48] In short, negotiators may

[47] 90 Stat. 765, sec. 507; 90 Stat. 2498.

[48] "Agreement on Friendship, Defense and Cooperation Between the United States of America and the Kingdom of Spain," Complementary Agreement Three, Article 2 (signed July 2, 1982).

266

negotiate what they want; what is actually supplied depends on congressional action.

The lesson of the Spanish assistance agreement should be applied broadly. When the Ford administration signed an executive agreement with Turkey in 1976, it earmarked in Article XIX specific sums for defense assistance. President Ford sent Congress draft legislation to implement the agreement, but the measure was never even reported from committee.[49] Draft legislation the next year was again ignored.[50] Instead, Congress continued the existing arms embargo on Turkey until 1978. After the embargo was lifted the Carter administration entered into an executive agreement with Turkey in 1980, without making a specific pledge of economic or military assistance. The United States promised to make its "best efforts" to provide mutually agreed assistance. The level of that assistance depends on annual authorization and appropriation by Congress.

Ever since Theodore Roosevelt "took" Panama in 1903, the United States has been under pressure to compensate other nations for the venture. In 1922 the Thompson-Urrutia Treaty gave Colombia (previous owner of Panama) special canal rights and a cash grant of $25 million as penance for Roosevelt's use of force.[51] The American presence in the Canal Zone remained a problem, causing a riot in 1964 and leading to talks for a new treaty.

The House of Representatives watched these negotiations with growing apprehension. The prospect of surrendering control of the canal raised questions of military needs and national security. But the constitutional interest of the House was twofold: the power to appropriate and the power to cede United States property. Article IV, Section 3, Clause 2 of the Constitution states: "The Congress shall have Power to dispose of and make all needful Rules and Regulations respecting the Territory or other Property belonging to the United States." In 1975, on a floor vote of 246 to 164, the House adopted an amendment to prohibit the use of any funds "for the purpose of negotiating the surrender or relinquishment of any U.S. rights in the Panama

[49] H. Doc. No. 531, 94th Cong., 2d Sess. (1976). Introduced as S.J. Res. 204.

[50] H. Doc. No. 57, 95th Cong., 1st Sess. (1977).

[51] Robert K. Murray, The Harding Era 340-41 (1969)

Canal Zone." Here was an effort not only to exert control over a completed treaty but to influence negotiations as well. In fact, opponents of the amendment contended that it would make further negotiation impossible. As softened by the conference committee and enacted into law, the language read: "It is the sense of the Congress that any new Panama Canal treaty or agreement must protect the vital interests of the United States in the Canal Zone and in the operation, maintenance, property and defense of the Panama Canal."[52]

Advocates of House prerogatives continued to insist that a treaty with Panama, providing for the transfer of American property or the payment of money to Panama, could not be accomplished by the treaty process alone. Congressman Mickey Edwards and fifty-nine other members of the House filed suit, asking the courts to declare illegal President Carter's submission of the Panama Canal Treaties to the Senate. They argued that he had violated their constitutional right to vote on the disposition of U.S. property.

A district court judge in 1978 held that the members did not have standing to challenge the President's action, particularly where legislative solutions were still available to members (both before and after Senate ratification).[53] The D.C. Circuit affirmed this ruling and held that the property clause of the Constitution is not the exclusive method for disposing of federal property. The use of treaties for that purpose is constitutionally authorized.[54]

Even after these setbacks in the courts and the Senate's ratification of the Panama Canal Treaties, opponents had one last opportunity: they could defeat the implementing legislation. Congress had to set up a Panama Canal Commission and enact other implementing mechanisms, but the chief focus fell on the overall cost to the federal government (and therefore to taxpayers). Despite a concerted effort by opponents in the House of Representatives, Congress passed the implementing legislation in 1979.

[52] 89 Stat. 617, sec. 104. See debate at 121 Cong. Rec. 20945-56 (1975).

[53] Edwards v. Carter, 445 F.Supp. 1279 (D.D.C. 1978).

[54] Edwards v. Carter, 580 F.2d 1055 (D.C. Cir. 1978), cert. denied, 436 U.S. 907 (1978).

Treaty Termination

Although the Constitution requires joint action by the President and the Senate for the making of treaties, it does not specifically address the question of treaty termination. The issue was not discussed at the Constitutional Convention. Article V, however, vests treaties with the same domestic status as federal statutes. Treaties may therefore be terminated by subsequent acts of Congress through the regular legislative process. Indeed, some of the early treaties were terminated by statute. Others were terminated by presidental action without prior congressional authorization, by Senate resolutions, and by new treaties.[55]

After President Nixon's overtures to the People's Republic of China (PRC), some members of Congress became concerned that the Carter administration might unilaterally terminate U.S. treaties with the Republic of China (Taiwan), especially the Mutual Defense Treaty of 1954. The treaty of 1954 allowed "either party" to end the pact after giving the other country a year's notice. The treaty did not specify the process by which "a party" would reach that decision. In a bill enacted on September 26, 1978, Congress adopted the following language: "It is the sense of the Congress that there should be prior consultation between the Congress and the executive branch" on any changes affecting the U.S.-Taiwan treaty.[56] Nevertheless, on December 15, 1978, while Congress was out of session, Carter announced his decision to recognize the PRC and to terminate the defense treaty with Taiwan.

Senator Harry F. Byrd, Jr., submitted a Senate resolution stating that it was the sense of the Senate that "approval of the United States Senate is required to terminate any Mutual Defense Treaty between the United States and another nation." On June 6, 1979, the Senate called up for consideration Byrd's resolution. As rewritten by the Senate Foreign Relations Committee, it became the sense of the Senate that U.S. treaties or treaty provisions should not be terminated or suspended by the President without the concurrence of *Congress* (not just of the Senate,

[55] Digest of United States Practice in International Law, 1978, at 734-65.
[56] 92 Stat. 746, sec. 26 (1978).

269

as Byrd had provided). The committee also added a number of exceptions to take account of various circumstances.[57]

Byrd offered an amendment to restore the original language of his resolution. The Senate adopted his amendment, 59 to 35. A colloquy between Byrd and Senator Frank Church established that the resolution would apply only to future actions, not to past terminations. Senator Barry Goldwater later pointed out that the Taiwan treaty would not be terminated, under the one-year notice requirement, until January 1, 1980. The Byrd Amendment, even if modified or clarified by Church, would therefore still apply to the Taiwan treaty.[58]

While the Senate debated Church's amendment to make Byrd's resolution clearly prospective, Goldwater placed in the Congressional Record the decision of District Judge Oliver Gasch handed down earlier that day. Gasch concluded that the power to terminate treaties "is a power shared by the political branches of this government, namely, the President and the Congress." But he also noted that Congress had yet to indicate an intention to assert its prerogatives. Three resolutions were pending in the Senate. Gasch said that only after the Senate or the Congress had taken action to withdraw support from the President's termination would the controversy be ripe for judicial determination.[59]

Senator Church, realizing that his amendment to make the resolution prospective would not have the desired effect (to eliminate the problem of the treaty with Taiwan), withdrew his amendment. Church sharpened the language and resubmitted an amendment stating that the Byrd resolution "shall not apply with respect to any treaty the notice of termination of which was transmitted prior to the date of adoption of this Resolution."[60] The Senate recessed without voting on the Church Amendment or taking final action on the Byrd resolution. Majority Leader Robert Byrd asked Senator Goldwater to draft an alternative amendment, which he did, but Senators Church and Javits found the language unacceptable. Church said he had "no quarrel with

[57] 125 Cong. Rec. 475, 13672 (1979).
[58] Id. at 13705, 13712-13.
[59] Id. at 13707-09.
[60] Id. at 13716. See also 13714 for amendment withdrawal.

the fact that the Senate, by a substantial majority, wishes to make it plain to the President that, in the future, it does not wish the President to attempt to terminate a mutual defense treaty without the concurrence of the Senate."[61]

The inability or unwillingness of the Senate to reach a final vote proved fatal in the effort to protect congressional interests. Judge Gasch's subsequent decision in October 1979 concluded that the historical precedents, taken as a whole, supported the position that the power to terminate treaties is shared by the President and Congress. Gasch reasoned that if the President is without the lesser power to amend a treaty without first receiving the Senate's advice and consent, he could not possess the greater power to annul a treaty. Some form of congressional concurrence was required, either the approval of a majority of both Houses or the consent of two-thirds of the Senate.[62]

His decision was rejected both by the appellate court and the Supreme Court. The D.C. Circuit ruled that the President, in the precise circumstances before the court, was empowered to terminate the Taiwan treaty. The judiciary, it said, was incapable of distinguishing between treaties that could be terminated by the President alone and those that required joint executive-legislative action. It also pointed out that Congress was aware that it possessed strong legislative measures to state its disapproval and "simply did not take those measures." Even had the Senate acted on the Byrd resolution, it was merely a sense-of-the-Senate measure and would not have been legally binding on the President. The court identified the crucial issue: "Congress as a body has chosen not to confront the President directly on the treaty termination."[63]

Acting without oral argument and within days of the scheduled treaty termination, the Supreme Court dismissed Goldwater's complaint. The Justices split along so many lines that their opinions shed little light on how treaty terminations will be handled in the future by the courts.[64] Justice Powell would have

[61] Id. at 15210. See also 15209-11.
[62] Goldwater v. Carter, 481 F.Supp. 949, 963-64 (D.D.C. 1979).
[63] Goldwater v. Carter, 617 F.2d 697, 707, 712, 714 (D.C. Cir. 1979).
[64] Goldwater v. Carter, 444 U.S. 996 (1979).

dismissed the complaint as not ripe for judicial review. He said that the judiciary should not decide executive-legislative conflicts until the two branches reach an impasse. A congressional challenge would have required the Court to resolve the issue. Rehnquist, joined by Burger, Stewart, and Stevens, viewed the matter as a nonjusticiable political question which should never be considered by the courts. Blackmun, joined by White, believed that the Court should have set the case for oral argument and given it plenary consideration. Brennan disagreed that the matter was a political question. He would have given the President the authority to terminate treaties as an incident of his power to recognize foreign governments. Marshall, without writing a separate opinion, concurred in dismissing the complaint.

The question of treaty termination has been pushed to the side only temporarily, ready to resume its prominence when the moment is ripe. Senator Goldwater introduced legislation in 1981 to require a two-thirds affirmative vote in the Senate to terminate defense treaties.[65] Thus far Congress has not acted on this bill or any other clarifying legislation.

Executive Agreements

The precise boundary between treaties and executive agreements has never been defined to anyone's satisfaction. Of course treaties require the advice and consent of the Senate; executive agreements do not. As a second distinction, treaties (unlike executive agreements) may supersede prior conflicting statutes.[66] Otherwise, there is considerable discretion on the part of administration officials to make international compacts either by treaty or by executive agreement. Among the more controversial executive agreements are the destroyers-bases deal with Great Britain in 1940, the Yalta and Potsdam agreements of 1945, the Vietnam peace agreement of 1973, the Sinai agreements of 1975, and

[65] S.J. Res. 31 (1981). See 127 Cong. Rec. S1343 (daily ed. February 17, 1981) and 129 Cong. Rec. S1959 (daily ed. March 1, 1983).
[66] United States v. Schooner Peggy, 5 U.S. (1 Cr.) 103 (1801); memorandum by Monroe Leigh, Legal Adviser to the State Department, October 8, 1975, reprinted at 121 Cong. Rec. 36718-21 (1975).

recent military base agreements with Spain, Diego Garcia, and Bahrain.

Sources of Authority

During the early years of the Republic, executive agreements were carried out under statutory authority. For example, legislation in 1792 authorized the Postmaster General to make arrangements with foreign postmasters for the receipt and delivery of letters and packets.[67] Executive officials entered into reciprocal trade agreements on the basis of statutory authority. Although such agreements lacked what the Supreme Court in 1912 called the "dignity" of a treaty, since they did not require Senate approval, they are nonetheless valid international compacts.[68] Treaties, too, become a source of authority of executive agreements.

The executive branch claims four sources of constitutional authority under which the President may enter into executive agreements: (1) his duty as chief executive to represent the nation in foreign affairs; (2) his authority to receive ambassadors and other public ministers; (3) his authority as commander in chief; and (4) his duty to "take care that the laws be faithfully executed."[69] These powers are so open-ended that Congress may find its own sphere of action constricted because of ambitious executive interpretations. Particularly nebulous are the first, second, and fourth constitutional sources. A more solid case can be made for the commander-in-chief authority, for surely a President may enter into an armistice or cease-fire agreement with a foreign power (subject to Senate action on a peace treaty at a later date). Other reasonable actions by the President as commander in chief include agreements to protect troops, control occupied areas, and carry out military training.

Few would deny that the President has constitutional author-

[67] 1 Stat. 239 (1792).

[68] Altman & Co. v. United States. 224 U.S. 583, 600-601 (1912). For an opinion by Acting Attorney General McGranery in 1946 upholding the legality of an executive agreement made pursuant to a joint resolution, see 40 Op. Att'y Gen. 469.

[69] 11 FAM [Foreign Affairs Manual] 721.2(b)(3) (October 25, 1974).

ity to recognize foreign governments. However, such determinations may involve the settlement of claims that affect other provisions of the Constitution. Recognition of Soviet Russia by President Roosevelt led to the "Litvinov Assignment" in 1933 and subsequent property claims in the courts. In *United States* v. *Belmont* (1937), the Supreme Court unanimously upheld the assignment as a valid international compact.[70] Five years later, in *United States* v. *Pink* (also involving Roosevelt's recognition of the Soviet Union), Justice Douglas declared that the powers of the President in the conduct of foreign affairs "included the power, without consent of the Senate, to determine the public policy of the United States with respect to the Russian nationalization decrees." To Douglas, the President had authority to do more than simply determine which government to recognize. Presidential authority included the power to determine the policy to go with recognition. Objections to the policy or the recognition were to be "addressed to the political department and not to the courts." And yet the judiciary could not sidestep the subject so deftly. Suppose that an executive agreement, affecting private claims, interfered with such constitutional privileges as the due process and just compensation clauses of the Fifth Amendment?[71]

Inevitably the courts were drawn back into the dispute. The executive agreement in the *Belmont* and *Pink* cases represented the exercise of an implied presidential power: recognition of foreign governments. It also involved a federal question: the balancing of interests between the national government and legislation adopted by a state government. The circumstances were unique and narrowly drawn. But the President is not free to enter into executive agreements that violate constitutional provisions. As the State Department concedes, an agreement cannot be "inconsistent with legislation enacted by Congress in the exercise of its constitutional authority."[72] This principle was given substance by the *Capps* decision of 1953, which struck down an executive agreement because it contravened an existing commercial statute with Canada. Imports from a foreign country repre-

[70] United States v. Belmont, 301 U.S. 324 (1937).

[71] United States v. Pink, 315 U.S. 203, 229 (1942). See Note, "United States v. Pink—A Reappraisal," 48 Colum. L. Rev. 890 (1948).

[72] 11 FAM 721.2(b)(3) (1974).

sented foreign commerce "subject to regulation, so far as this country is concerned, by Congress alone."[73]

The timing of these decisions on executive agreements should not be overlooked. *Capps*, as a restriction on executive authority, was handed down less than a year after the *Youngstown* case declared invalid President Truman's seizure of the steel mills. *Belmont*, a ringing affirmation of executive agreements, was decided just five months after Justice Sutherland in the *Curtiss-Wright* case lent his enthusiastic support to presidential prerogatives in external affairs.

Other court decisions have limited the reach of executive agreements. *Seery* v. *United States* (1955) involved an executive agreement in which the United States agreed to pay Austria a flat sum to settle all obligations incurred by United States armed forces. A naturalized American citizen brought suit to recover damages to her home in Austria, which had been used by American troops as an officer's club. The Court of Claims held that the woman was entitled to compensation under the Fifth Amendment: "we think that there can be no doubt that an executive agreement, not being a transaction which is even mentioned in the Constitution, cannot impair Constitutional rights."[74] And in *Reid* v. *Covert* (1957) the Supreme Court declared invalid an executive agreement that permitted American military courts in Great Britain to rely on trial by court-martial for offenses committed by American military personnel or their dependents. The plaintiff fought successfully for the constitutional right to a trial by jury. The Court declared that an executive agreement with a foreign nation could not confer power "on the Congress, or on any other branch of Government, which is free from the restraints of the Constitution."[75]

---

[73] United States v. Guy W. Capps, Inc. 204 F.2d 655, 660 (4th Cir. 1953), aff'd on other grounds, 348 U.S. 296 (1955).

[74] Seery v. United States, 127 F.Supp. 601, 606 (Ct. Cl. 1955).

[75] Reid v. Covert, 354 U.S. 1, 16 (1957). The treaty power is also subject to the restraints found in the Constitution: "It would not be contended that it extends so far as to authorize what the Constitution forbids, or a change in the character of the government or in that of one of the States, or a cession of any portion of the territory of the latter, without its consent," Geofroy v. Riggs, 133 U.S. 258, 269 (1890).

The opportunity for presidential action widens when specific legislation on foreign commerce does not exist. The Nixon administration entered into so-called Voluntary Restraint Arrangements (VRAs) with European and Japanese steel companies as a means of protecting domestic suppliers. Consumers Union took the issue to court, contending that the import quotas encroached upon Congress's authority over foreign trade and violated the Sherman Antitrust Act. In 1973 a district court declined to issue an injunction, as requested by Consumers Union, but urged the administration and the foreign steel companies to reexamine their actions as a possible violation of the Sherman Antitrust Act.[76] The following year an appellate court, dividing two to one, held that although the President could not impose mandatory import quotas without legislative authority, nothing in the Constitution or existing legislation foreclosed voluntary arrangements. The issue of the Sherman Act was vacated after the plaintiffs requested it be dismissed. A lengthy dissent by Judge Leventhal viewed the President's action as a transgression on congressional authority over foreign commerce. Far from being "voluntary," the arrangements on steel were negotiated bilateral understandings that could be enforced by sanctions imposed by the President.[77]

The Iranian hostage crisis of 1979 set the stage for a series of extraordinary actions by President Carter, including the freezing of Iran's assets in America and the suspension of claims pending in American courts. Although the Supreme Court concluded that the first action had statutory support, it found no specific statutory authority for the second. Legal justification was discovered somewhere in the combination of past presidential practices to settle claims by executive agreement, the history of "implicit" congressional approval, and the failure of Congress to contest the Iranian Agreement. The Court strained to uphold an agreement it could not possibly overturn, given the foreign policy

[76] Consumers Union of U.S., Inc. v. Rogers, 352 F.Supp. 1319 (D.D.C. 1973).

[77] Consumers Union of U.S., Inc. v. Kissinger, 506 F.2d 136 (D.C. Cir. 1974), cert. denied, 421 U.S. 1004 (1975). See Michael H. Salisbury, "Presidential Authority in Foreign Trade: Voluntary Steel Import Quotas From a Constitutional Perspective," 15 Va. J. Int'l L. 179 (1974).

implications. It limited the damage of its opinion by confining it to the specific circumstances before the Court.[78] Whether Carter's action becomes a precedent for further expansions of presidential power depends on congressional reactions to future executive initiatives.

Reporting

Prior to 1950, executive agreements were published in the U.S. Statutes at Large. Since that time they have been printed in *Treaties and Other International Agreements*.[79] A number of sensitive agreements, however, were never made known to Congress or to the public. During a Senate hearing in 1972, a State Department official was asked: "Now, you do have some executive agreements in force that are not listed in this publication, do you not?" He replied: "A very small percentage, classified."[80]

The extent of secret executive agreements was carefully documented by the Symington Subcommittee (of the Senate Foreign Relations Committee) during its hearings in 1969 and 1970. Field trips by committee staff uncovered a number of significant agreements that United States administrations had made covertly with South Korea, Thailand, Laos, Ethiopia, and Spain, among others. Congress passed legislation in 1972 to keep itself informed about such agreements. The statute (known as the Case Act) requires the Secretary of State to transmit to Congress within sixty days the text of "any international agreement, other than a treaty," to which the United States is a party. If the President decides that publication of an agreement would be prejudicial to national security he may transmit it to the Senate Committee on

---

[78] Dames & Moore v. Regan, 453 U.S. 654 (1981). See Arthur S. Miller, "*Dames & Moore v. Regan*: A Political Decision by a Political Court," 29 UCLA L. Rev. 1104 (1982). For congressional "support" through acquiescence, the Court relied on Haig v. Agee, 453 U.S. 280, 290 (1981), which upheld the right of the Secretary of State to revoke passports despite the lack of statutory authority.

[79] 64 Stat. 979 (1950).

[80] "Congressional Oversight of Executive Agreements," hearing before the Senate Committee on the Judiciary, 92d Cong., 2d Sess. 284 (1972).

Foreign Relations and the House Committee on Foreign Affairs under an injunction of secrecy removable only by the President.[81]

Over the next few years several Senators protested that the Nixon and Ford administrations had failed to comply with the Case Act. Senator James Abourezk testified that the "administration has admitted to both Senator Case and myself that there are some agreements they do not submit at all under the Case Act."[82] A GAO study in 1976 disclosed that a number of agreements (delicately called "arrangements" by the executive branch) had never been submitted to Congress or even to the Office of Treaty Affairs in the State Department.[83] A Senate study in 1977 discovered that 39 percent of the executive agreements entered into the previous year were submitted after the sixty-day period (171 out of 440). Thirty-five of those were submitted a *year* late.[84]

To improve administrative compliance with the Case Act, Congress passed legislation in 1977 requiring any department or agency of the United States government that enters into any international agreement on behalf of the United States to transmit to the Department of State the text of the agreement not later than twenty days after its signing.[85] A year later Congress broadened the definition of executive agreement to include the text of any "oral international agreement, which agreement shall be reduced to writing."[86]

As a way of avoiding congressional action on a treaty or an executive agreement, the Carter administration discovered a third option: parallel policy statements. On September 23, 1977, ten days prior to the expiration date of SALT I, the United States and the Soviet Union issued statements that they would adhere to SALT I ceilings. Since the statements were issued separately

[81] 86 Stat. 619 (1972), 1 U.S.C. 112b (1982).

[82] "Early Warning System in Sinai," hearing before the Senate Committee on Foreign Relations, 94th Cong., 1st Sess. 6 (1975).

[83] "U.S. Agreements with the Republic of Korea," ID-76-20 (February 20, 1976).

[84] 123 Cong. Rec. 16127 (1977).

[85] 91 Stat. 224, sec. 5 (1977).

[86] 92 Stat. 993, sec. 708 (1978).

278

and unilaterally, the State Department argued that they did not constitute an "agreement" and therefore required no action by Congress.[87]

Congressional Controls

Reporting after the fact provides inadequate protection for Congress. Legislators want to be advised of significant agreements while they are in the process of being negotiated. The State Department's policy for executive agreements is contained in "Circular 175." Language adopted in 1955 (at the height of the Bricker Amendment drive to curb treaties and executive agreements) called for consultation with congressional leaders and committees whenever there was any "serious question" whether an international agreement required adoption as a treaty, a joint resolution, or an executive agreement. Such consultation would be carried out "whenever circumstances permit." The language was changed in 1974, in the face of renewed congressional criticism, by deleting the word "serious." The 1974 version also added the following guideline for choosing between a treaty and an executive agreement: "The extent to which the agreement involves commitments or risks affecting the nation as a whole." The legal adviser to the State Department, speaking in 1972, commented that, "I think nobody questions that agreements which involve a basic political commitment, such as an undertaking to come to the defense of another country if it is attacked, should be cast in the form of a treaty in the constitutional sense."[88]

Three years later the State Department advised a Senate committee that if the President were to make an agreement to establish a military base, Congress might disapprove the involvement and deny any funds for constructing the facility. The administra-

[87] Franck and Weisband, Foreign Policy by Congress, at 152-54.
[88] "Congressional Oversight of Executive Agreements," at 256. For Circular 175 Procedure, the versions of December 13, 1955 and June 6, 1969 are reprinted in those hearings at 289-306, while an amended version of October 25, 1974 appears in "Congressional Oversight of Executive Agreements—1975," hearings before the Senate Committee on the Judiciary, 94th Cong., 1st Sess. 279-301 (1975).

tion witness added: "I have no doubt that Congress has the clear power to withhold funds, and I see no constitutional objection to their doing so, and in fact I think that is the principal safeguard for Congress' role in this difficult area."[89] Theoretically this is possible, but Congress finds it difficult to exercise its power of the purse if doing so means diplomatic embarrassment for the nation and humiliation to the President.

Instead of being politically trapped by executive initiatives, Congress needs an opportunity to pass judgment at an earlier stage when options are still open. Legislation has been introduced to permit Congress to disapprove executive agreements during a waiting period. The emphasis behind this legislation is not so much the desire to veto executive agreements as to compel the executive branch to consult earlier with Congress to avoid a veto. A Senate bill, passed in 1974, provided that executive agreements would go into effect unless Congress passed a concurrent resolution of disapproval within sixty days.[90] The House did not act on the measure. It did not have much application anyway. Section 5 of the bill excluded from its reach "any executive agreement entered into by the President pursuant to a provision of the Constitution or prior authority given the President by treaty or law." Remove these categories and there is little left except agreements entered into subject to subsequent statutory approval. Different legislation was introduced in 1975 to allow for legislative disapproval simply by Senate resolution.[91] This bill was meant to preserve the Senate's prerogative in treaty-making, but there is little likelihood that the House will count itself out of a role in executive agreements. Moreover, the availability of two-House and one-House legislative vetoes has now been eliminated by the Supreme Court's 1983 decision in *INS* v. *Chadha*.[92]

The State Department has opposed legislative efforts to subject executive agreements to congressional approval. It estimates that more than 95 percent of executive agreements ("probably as high as 97 or 98 percent") are pursuant to congressionsl ap-

[89] "Congressional Oversight of Executive Agreements—1975," at 223.
[90] S. Rept. No. 93-1286; 120 Cong. Rec. 36926-28 (1974).
[91] 121 Cong. Rec. 7740-43 (1975).
[92] 103 S.Ct. 2764 (1983).

proval or implementation, or entered into in implementation of treaties.[93] This estimate indicates that the area of congressional concern is a minuscule 2 to 5 percent, but in fact it is considerably larger. An administration may enter into controversial agreements on the basis of highly questionable interpretations of statutes and treaties. Attorney General Jackson upheld the destroyers-bases deal of 1940 partly on statutory authority.[94] The Nixon administration, after entering into an executive agreement with Portugal in 1971 concerning the use of military facilities, contended that the agreement was made pursuant to Article 3 of the North Atlantic Treaty.[95] Subsequently the Senate passed a resolution insisting that the agreement should have been submitted as a treaty.[96]

Also included within the State Department's 95 to 98 percent category are executive agreements requiring congressional implementation. Although in theory it is true that specific amounts for military and economic assistance are subject to congressional action, the general size of a financial commitment might be morally and politically fixed. This situation prevailed in 1975 when the Ford administration entered into the Sinai agreements, promising several billions of dollars in military and economic assistance to Israel and Egypt. The only agreement submitted to Congress for legislative action was an "early warning system" in the Sinai: two hundred American civilian observers who would operate electronic equipment to monitor Israeli and Egyptian military activities.

The administration claimed that the two sets of agreements were legally distinct and that legislative support for the two hundred technicians (at an annual cost of some $10 million) would not constitute an endorsement of the aid package. But hearings by Congress indicated that the two agreements were joined by a

[93] "Transmittal of Executive Agreements to Congress," hearings before the Senate Committee on Foreign Relations, 92d Cong., 1st Sess. 59 (1971).

[94] 39 Op. Att'y Gen. 484, 488-493 (1940).

[95] "Executive Agreements with Portugal and Bahrain," hearings before the Senate Committee on Foreign Relations, 92d Cong., 2d Sess. 7-8, 35-39 (1972).

[96] S. Rept. No. 92-632, 118 Cong. Rec. 6866-6870 (1972).

number of significant strands.[97] Congress added Section 5 to the Sinai agreements, stating that the authority for the technicians "does not signify approval of the Congress of any other agreement, understanding, or commitment made by the executive branch."[98] This was so much whistling in the dark. The political process and momentum compelled Congress to appropriate essentially what the administration requested.

Congress is faced with a delicate situation. It would like to acknowledge that the President has some reservoir of constitutional power to enter into executive agreements, but at the same time limit his ability to commit the nation militarily and financially. A bill introduced in the House in 1975 was specifically aimed at national commitments regarding the introduction, basing, or deployment of armed forces on foreign territory, as well as any military training, equipment, or financial or material resources provided to a foreign country. Such commitments would be subject to a sixty-day waiting period, during which time Congress could disapprove the commitments by passing a concurrent resolution.[99] Legislative vetoes are no longer available as a method of congressional control.

In 1976 the Senate Foreign Relations Committee held hearings on legislation to require that any international agreement involving a "significant political, military, or economic commitment" to a foreign country be submitted to the Senate as a treaty for its advice and consent.[100] The problem with both the House and the Senate bills is their inability to define what is "significant" and worthy of legislative attention.

Rather than rely on omnibus bills intended to monitor broad and ill-defined categories of executive agreements, Congress re-

[97] "Middle East Agreements and the Early Warning System in Sinai," hearings before the House Committee on International Relations, 94th Cong., 1st Sess. (1975); "Early Warning System in Sinai" hearings before the Senate Committee on Foreign Relations, 94th Cong., 1st Sess. (1975).

[98] 89 Stat. 572 (1975).

[99] H.R. 4438: 121 Cong. Rec. 5557-58 (1975) and "Congressional Review of International Agreements," hearings before the House Committee on International Relations, 94th Cong., 2d Sess. (1976).

[100] "Treaty Powers Resolution," hearings before the Senate Committee on Foreign Relations, 94th Cong., 2d Sess. (1976).

tains the power to subject specific classes of agreements to congressional approval. Fishery agreements are regularly forwarded to Congress for legislative action through the regular process, including passage by both Houses and submission of a bill to the President.[101] Certain executive agreements on nuclear energy are handled the same way.[102] The Trade Act of 1974 requires implementing legislation before specific types of agreements can enter into force.[103] Congressional leverage is further strengthened when executive agreements clearly state that the level of U.S. economic and military assistance to the foreign governments depends on annual authorizations and appropriations by Congress. That approach was used with Turkey in 1980 and Spain in 1982, as noted above. Through these specific actions Congress can successively, and successfully, narrow the President's freedom to enter into executive agreements.

[101] For example, see P.L. 98-44, sec. 105, 97 Stat. 217 (1983) and Wkly Comp. Pres. Doc., XX, 94 (January 26, 1984).

[102] Wkly Comp. Pres. Doc., XX, 94-95 (January 26, 1984).

[103] 88 Stat. 1983, sec. 102(e); 88 Stat. 2001, sec. 151 (1974).

9

THE WAR POWER

Members of Congress can point to specific language in the Constitution for their authority to declare war and provide armed forces. More difficult to locate are the legal sources for presidential authority. Largely because of custom and events, Presidents have been able to make war before Congress has had a chance to act. The history of the past two centuries is one of balancing and reconciling the two powers: war-declaring by Congress and war-making by the President.

For constitutional as well as practical reasons, the two activities are supposed to work in concert. The President commands the troops but only Congress can provide them. Congress declares war but depends on the President to wage it. An associate of President Cleveland was once present when a delegation from Congress arrived at the White House with this announcement: "We have about decided to declare war against Spain over the Cuban question. Conditions are intolerable." Cleveland responded in blunt terms: "There will be no war with Spain over Cuba while I am President." A member of Congress protested that the Constitution gave Congress the right to declare war, but Cleveland countered that the Constitution also made him commander in chief. "I will not mobilize the army," he told the legislators. "I happen to know that we can buy the Island of Cuba from Spain for $100,000,000, and a war will cost vastly more than that and will entail another long list of pensioners. It would be an outrage to declare war."[1]

Commander in Chief

Article I, Section 2, of the Constitution makes the President "Commander in Chief of the Army and Navy of the United States, and of the Militia of the several States, when called into the

[1] Robert McElroy, Grover Cleveland, II, 249-50 (1923).

actual Service of the United States." Scholars have long disagreed whether this merely confers a title (commander in chief) or implies additional powers for the President. Justice Jackson underscored the elusive nature of this power by remarking that the commander-in-chief clause implies "something more than an empty title. But just what authority goes with the name has plagued presidential advisers who would not waive or narrow it by nonassertion yet cannot say where it begins or ends."[2] The Justice Department has argued that the President was given the title not because he was expected to be skilled in the art of war but as a means of preserving civilian supremacy over the military.[3]

To some scholars the commander-in-chief clause should be construed narrowly. Raoul Berger writes: "How narrowly the function was conceived may be gathered from the fact that in appointing George Washington Commander-in-Chief, the Continental Congress made sure . . . that he was to be 'its creature . . . in every respect.'" Instructions drafted by John Adams, R. H. Lee, and Edward Rutledge told Washington "punctually to observe and follow such orders and directions . . . as you shall receive from this or a future Congress."[4] Citing these precedents is of little value for at least two reasons. First, they ignore the extensive delegations that the Continental Congress soon found necessary. For example, an order to General Washington in 1775 stated that "whereas all particulars cannot be foreseen, nor positive instructions for such emergencies so before hand given but that many things must be left to your prudent and discreet management, as occurrences may arise upon the place, or from time to time may fall out, you are therefore upon all such accidents or any occasions that may happen, to use your best circumspection."[5] Second, the precedents are from the wrong period. The office of President of 1787 was created as a separate and inde-

---

[2] Youngstown Co. v. Sawyer, 343 U.S. 579, 641 (1952).

[3] 10 Op. Att'y Gen. 74, 79 (1861).

[4] Raoul Berger, Executive Privilege 62 (1974).

[5] Journals of the Continental Congress, II, 101 (1905). See W. Taylor Reveley, III, "Constitutional Allocation of the War Powers Between the President and Congress: 1787-1788," 15 Va. J. Int'l L. 73, 91-93 (1974).

pendent branch, not as a mere agent of Congress (its status under the Continental Congress).

The need to trust in executive judgment and discretion, rather than on the specific instructions drafted for Washington at the start of the Revolutionary War, more accurately represents the understanding of the framers. At the Philadelphia convention they recognized an implied power of the President to "repel sudden attacks." When it was proposed that Congress be empowered to "make war," Charles Pinckney objected that legislative proceedings "were too slow" for the safety of the country in an emergency. He anticipated that Congress would meet but once a year. Madison and Elbridge Gerry moved to insert "declare" for "make," thereby "leaving to the Executive the power to repel sudden attacks." Their motion carried.[6]

Alexander Hamilton appeared to offer a modest definition of commander-in-chief powers. In Federalist 69 he said that the office "would amount to nothing more than the supreme command and direction of the military and navel forces, as first general and admiral of the Confederacy . . . ." But as Washington's military aide during the war, surely Hamilton knew quite well that "command and direction" are more than clerical tasks. They can determine the scope and duration of a war. As the Supreme Court noted in 1850, the President as commander in chief "is authorized to direct the movements of the naval and military forces placed by law at his command, and to employ them in the manner he may deem most effectual to harass and conquer and subdue the enemy."[7]

But what is the power to move forces "placed *by law* at his command"? How much does the President depend upon Congress to provide the authorizations and appropriations necessary for military action? Under the Constitution, it is the responsibility of Congress to raise and support the military forces, to make rules for their regulation, to provide for calling up the militia to

---

[6] Farrand, Records, II, 318-19.

[7] Fleming v. Page, 50 U.S. (9 How.) 602, 614 (1850). Also see the dissenting opinion by Chief Justice Chase—joined by Justices Wayne, Swayne, and Miller—in Ex parte Milligan, 4 Wall. 2 (1866).

suppress insurrections and to repel invasions, and to provide for the organization and disciplining of the militia.

Congress is empowered to declare war, but only five wars have been declared and in only one (the War of 1812) did members of Congress actually debate the merits of entering into hostilities. In all other cases members simply acknowledged that a state of war did in fact exist. For the most part, American troops have fought in "quasi wars" and other operations never blessed by a congressional declaration of war. In two early decisions handed down in 1800 and 1801, the Supreme Court recognized the existence of these limited, partial, and imperfect wars.[8]

Executive Prerogative

Charles McIlwain, tracing the slow and tortuous evolution of constitutionalism, stressed its antagonism to *gubernaculum*: emergency or extraordinary powers available to the executive. Actions taken for "reasons of state" were solely within the king's province. In contrast was the concept of *jurisdictio*, which limited the king's discretion. An early challenge to *gubernaculum* appears in a seventeenth-century speech in Parliament by Sir Benjamin Rudyard: "This by the way I will say of Reason of State, that, in the latitude by which it is used, it hath eaten out almost, not only the laws, but all the religion of Christendom." Another member of Parliament warned that to admit reason of state in a particular situation would "open a gap, through which Magna Charta, and the rest of the statutes, may issue out and vanish."[9]

The idea of *gubernaculum* has survived in the form of the executive prerogative. John Locke anticipated circumstances in which the executive should be free to act in accordance with his own perception of the public good. In governments where the legislative and executive powers are in distinct hands, "the good of the society requires that several things should be left to the discretion of him that has the executive power." Legislators could

---

[8] Bas v. Tingy, 4 U.S. (4 Dall.) 36 (1800); Talbot v. Seeman, 5 U.S. (1 Cr.) 1 (1801).

[9] Charles Howard McIlwain, Constitutionalism: Ancient and Modern 126 (1947).

not foresee, and provide by laws, everything needed by the community. Cases arise where the executive official has to use power "for the good of the society" until legislators can assemble to pass laws. A strict and rigid observance of the laws, Locke reasoned, might do more harm that temporarily vesting in the executive power the responsibility to take action for the community's good. The power to act "according to discretion for the public good, without the prescription of the law and sometimes even against it, is that which is called prerogative." Locke subjected the prerogative to a few general restrictions. It had to be used for the good of the people "and not manifestly against it." But when disputes arose as to whether the power had been properly used, "there can be no judge on earth." The people had no other remedy "but to appeal to Heaven."[10]

A more secular safeguard emerged under the American system. Presidents could take the initiative, in the absence of law or even against it, but had to seek the legislature's sanction. Thomas Jefferson, remembered as a "strict constructionist" and a sharp critic of Hamilton's liberal interpretations of the Constitution, found a need as President to act without specific legislative authority. After Congress had recessed in 1807, a British vessel fired on the American ship *Chesapeake*. Jefferson ordered military purchases for the emergency, reporting his actions to Congress after it convened. "To have awaited a previous and special sanction by law," he wrote, "would have lost occasions which might not be retrieved."[11] He later said that the observance of the written law is a high duty of a public official, but not the highest. The laws of self-preservation and national security claim a higher priority: "To lose our country by a scrupulous adherence to written law, would be to lose the law itself, with life, liberty, property and all those who are enjoying them with us; thus absurdly sacrificing the end to the means." The executive may act outside the law when necessity demands it, explain his actions, and ask the legislature for acquittance.[12]

---

[10] John Locke, Second Treatise on Civil Government, ch. XIV.

[11] Richardson, Messages and Papers, I, 416 (Oct. 27, 1807).

[12] The Writings of Thomas Jefferson (Washington ed.), V, 542-45.

Lincoln followed these procedures in his extraordinary Civil War actions. In April 1861, with Congress in recess, he issued proclamations calling forth state militias, suspending the writ of habeas corpus, and placing a blockade on the rebellious states. When Congress returned he explained that his actions, "whether strictly legal or not, were ventured upon under what appeared to be a popular demand and a public necessity, trusting then, as now, that Congress would readily ratify them."[13] This is precisely what the legislators did. Congress passed an act "approving, legalizing, and making valid all the acts, proclamations, and orders of the President, etc., as if they had been issued and done under the previous express authority and direction of the Congress of the United States."[14]

Under these extraordinary circumstances, Lincoln believed it was more important to preserve than to observe the Constitution.[15] In his message to Congress in 1861, he claimed that the "war power" was his for the purpose of suppressing the rebellion. No choice was left, he said, "but to call out the war power of the Government and so to resist force employed for its destruction by force for its preservation." With "deepest regret" he found the duty of employing the "war power in defense of the Government forced upon him."[16] It was under the "war power" (actually a fusion of legislative and executive powers) that Lincoln took his extraordinary actions to preserve the Union. Congress supported his initiatives, as did a sharply divided Supreme Court in *The Prize Cases*.[17]

Another controversial use of presidential power was by Franklin Roosevelt during World War II. More than 100,000 Japanese (about two-thirds of them natural-born United States citizens) were herded into "relocation centers" after Roosevelt issued an executive order, based in part on "the authority vested in me as

[13] Richardson, *Messages and Papers*, VII, 3225.

[14] 12 Stat. 326.

[15] Norman J. Small, *Some Presidential Interpretations of the Presidency* 34 (1932).

[16] Richardson, *Messages and Papers*, VII, 3224-25, 3232 (July 4, 1861).

[17] 2 Black 635 (1863). See also 12 Stat. 284, 326 (1861) and Edward S. Corwin, *The President* 228-34, 448-53 (1957).

President of the United States, and Commander in Chief of the Army and Navy . . . ."[18] Bitter opposition came from members of the Supreme Court. Justice Murphy, concurring in *Hirabayashi* (1943), said that the initial curfew action against Japanese-Americans "bears a melancholy resemblance to the treatment accorded to the members of the Jewish race in Germany and in other parts of Europe." In spite of such misgivings, a unanimous court nonetheless supported the curfew.[19] *Korematsu* (1944), splitting the Court 6 to 3, upheld the exclusion of Japanese-Americans and their relocation to detention camps. Murphy, one of the dissenters, protested that the exclusion order resulted from an erroneous assumption of "racial guilt" found in the commanding general's report, which referred to all individuals of Japanese descent as "subversives" belonging to "an enemy race" and whose "racial strains are undiluted." Jackson, also dissenting, concluded that "here is an attempt to make an otherwise innocent act a crime merely because this prisoner is the son of parents to whom he had no choice, and belongs to a race from which there is no way to resign."[20]

A third controversial invocation of commander-in-chief powers was by President Truman. In the wake of a labor-management dispute in 1952, he seized the steel mills as part of his effort to prosecute the Korean War. He did so on the basis of authority vested in him as President "by the Constitution and laws of the United States, and as President of the United States and Commander-in-Chief of the armed forces of the United States." The Supreme Court struck down this use of power in a 6 to 3 decision, but there were as many views as there were Justices. Each of the six representing the majority wrote separate opinions. Justice Jackson divided the commander-in-chief power along an outward-inward axis: "I should indulge the widest latitude of interpretation to sustain his exclusive function to com-

---

[18] E.O. 9066, 7 Fed. Reg. 1407 (1942).

[19] Hirabayashi v. United States, 320 U.S. 81 (1943).

[20] Korematsu v. United States, 323 U.S. 214 (1944). See Nanette Dembitz, "Racial Discrimination and the Military Judgment: The Supreme Court's Korematsu and Endo Decisions," 45 Colum. L. Rev. 175 (1945) and Eugene V. Rostow, "The Japanese American Cases—A Disaster," 54 Yale L. J. 489 (1945).

mand the instruments of national force, at least when turned against the outside world for the security of our society. But, when it is turned inward, not because of rebellion but because of a lawful economic struggle between industry and labor, it should have no such indulgence . . . ."[21] This outward-inward distinction would be revived two decades later in cases involving electronic surveillance for national-security purposes (discussed below).

Edward S. Corwin, dean of presidential scholars, held conflicting opinions on the executive prerogative. He maintained that the framers' view of balanced government carried with it "the idea of a *divided initiative in the matter of legislation and a broad range of autonomous executive power or 'prerogative.'* " Yet the scope of that prerogative became the subject of spirited debate in 1951 after President Truman sent troops to Korea without congressional approval. Henry Steele Commager and Arthur M. Schlesinger, Jr., defended his decision. Corwin rebuked the scholars (calling them the "high-flying prerogative men") and denounced the President's action and the justifications that accompanied it.[22] Less than two decades later both Commager and Schlesinger altered their philosophy of executive power, becoming vociferous critics of the claims of President Johnson to conduct the war in Southeast Asia.[23]

[21] Youngstown Co. v. Sawyer, 343 U.S. 579, 645 (1952).

[22] Edward S. Corwin, The President 14 (1957), emphasis in original. He discusses the meaning of "executive power" on pages 3-30. For a defense of Truman's action, see Schlesinger's letter to the New York Times, January 9, 1951 and Commager's article, "Presidential Power: The Issue Analyzed," New York Times Magazine, January 14, 1951. Corwin replied to them in "The President's Power," New Republic, January 29, 1951.

[23] By 1966 Schlesinger was counseling that "something must be done to assure the Congress a more authoritative and continuing voice in fundamental decisions in foreign policy": Arthur M. Schlesinger, Jr., and Alfred de Grazia, Congress and the Presidency 28 (1967). Commager meanwhile had also altered his view, for he told the Senate in 1967 that there should be a reconsideration of executive-legislative relationships in the conduct of foreign relations: "Changing American Attitudes Towards Foreign Policy," hearings before the Senate Committee on Foreign Relations, 90th Cong., 1st Sess. 21 (1967). See also Commager's testimony in "War Powers Legislation," hearings before the Senate Committee on Foreign Relations, 92d Cong., 1st Sess. 7-74 (1971). Schlesinger in 1973 stated

The executive prerogative retains a following, even among those who were bitterly opposed to the Vietnam War. In 1969 the Senate Foreign Relations Committee admitted its ineptitude in the handling of the Gulf of Tonkin Resolution. In the future, the committee counseled, it would be better to have a President take an emergency action he regards as necessary "without attempting to justify it in advance and leave it to Congress or the courts to evaluate his action in retrospect. A single unconstitutional act, later explained or pronounced unconstitutional, is preferable to an act dressed up in some spurious, precedent-setting claim of legitimacy."[24]

"Defensive War"

Throughout the nineteenth century the concept of defensive war was limited mainly to protective actions along the borders of the United States. Naval wars against the Barbary pirates and France stretched those boundaries, but such actions were infrequent. Nevertheless, these conflicts favored presidential power. Hostilities could exist in either a perfect state of war (marked by a declaration from Congress) or an imperfect state of war (more confined and limited in its nature and extent).

President Polk invited war in 1846 by sending troops into disputed territory along the Texas-Mexico border. Two years later the House of Representatives censured him for "unnecessarily and unconstitutionally" starting a war.[25] President McKinley defended intervention in Cuba in 1898 by describing the conflict as "right at our door."[26] These were isolated events, however. Only after World War II did the idea of defensive war take a

---

that the "idea of prerogative was *not* part of presidential power as defined in the Constitution," although it "remained in the back of [the framers'] mind"; The Imperial Presidency 9 (1973), emphasis in original.

[24] S. Rept. No. 129, 91st Cong., 1st Sess. 32 (1969). See also James R. Hurtgen, "The Case for Presidential Prerogative," 7 Toledo L. Rev. 59 (1975); Arthur S. Miller, Presidential Power 200-14 (1977); and Larry Arnhart, "The God-Like Prince: John Locke, Executive Prerogative, and the American Presidency," 9 Pres. Stud. Q. 121 (1979).

[25] Cong. Globe, 30th Cong., 1st Sess. 95 (1848).

[26] Richardson, Messages and Papers, XIII, 6289 (April 11, 1898).

quantum jump, both conceptually and in practice. American bases were dispersed around the globe. Military commitments became imbedded in various defense pacts and treaties, often with little visibility to Congress or the public. No longer did the administration confine the notion of "repelling sudden attacks" to military actions on our continental boundaries. The legal adviser to the State Department offered this scenario in 1966:

> Under the Constitution, the President, in addition to being Chief Executive, is Commander in Chief of the Army and Navy. He holds the prime responsibility for the conduct of United States foreign relations. These duties carry very broad powers, including the power to deploy American forces abroad and commit them to military operations when the President deems such action necessary to maintain the security and defense of the United States. . . .
>
> In 1787 the world was a far larger place, and the framers probably had in mind attacks upon the United States. In the 20th century, the world has grown much smaller. An attack on a country far from our shores can impinge directly on the nation's security.[27]

This idea of a shrinking globe has been part of the conceptual shift behind the enlargement of presidental power. We apply the concept to travel and communication with neutral effect, but constitutionally it shrinks not merely the globe but congressional power as well. In 1962, after the discovery of missile sites in Cuba, President Kennedy announced that the Western Hemisphere ("as far north as Hudson Bay, Canada, and as far south as Lima, Peru") was in danger. The launching of any nuclear missile from Cuba, against any nation in the Western Hemisphere, would be regarded by the administration as "an attack by the Soviet Union on the United States, requiring a full retaliatory response upon the Soviet Union."[28] When President Johnson requested the Tonkin Gulf Resolution two years later, he argued that a threat in Southeast Asia "is a threat to all, and a

---

[27] Dep't of State Bull., LIV, 484 (1966).
[28] Public Papers of the Presidents, 1962, at 485.

threat to us."[29] During the Reagan administration, the State Department justifed the CIA's mining of several harbors in Nicaragua as a legitimate means of self-defense.[30] Often these "defensive actions" are intertwined with explanations that the President must act to protect American lives and property.

Life-and-Property Actions

With neither statutory authority nor a declaration of war, Presidents have used force abroad on many occasions, ostensibly to protect life and property. They have justified their actions on the basis of executive responsibilities they find inherent in the Constitution. Expeditions of this nature number around two hundred, although if the total were to include actions that merely represent a show of force (such as deploying a battleship off a coast) it would be even larger.[31]

The constitutionality of this presidential activity came before a circuit court in 1860. An American vessel had been dispatched to Greytown (now San Juan del Norte), Nicaragua, after an affront to an American diplomat and some property losses suffered by an American firm. When the commander of the ship decided that local authorities had failed to make appropriate amends, he bombarded the town and sent troops ashore to wreak further vengeance. A resident sued for damages to his property. The court, in *Durand* v. *Hollins*, came to the commander's defense: "as it respects the interposition of the Executive abroad, for the protection of the lives or property of the citizen, the duty must, of necessity, rest in the discretion of the President. Acts of law-

[29] Public Papers of the Presidents, 1963-1964, at II, 931.

[30] Cong. Q. Wkly Rept., April 14, 1984, at 835.

[31] J. Terry Emerson, "War Powers Legislation," 74 W. Va. L. Rev. 53 (1972) and his "Constitutional Authority of the President to Use Armed Forces in Defense of American Lives, Liberty, and Property," reprinted at 121 Cong. Rec. 13205-09 (1975). For further details see James Grafton Rogers, World Policing and the Constitution (1945); Background Information on the Use of United States Armed Forces in Foreign Countries, prepared for the House Committee on Foreign Affairs, 91st Cong. 2d Sess. 50-57 (Comm. Print 1970); R. Ernest Dupuy and William H. Baumer, The Little Wars of the United States (1968); and Barry M. Blechman and Stephen S. Kaplan, Force Without War (1978).

less violence, or of threatened violence to the citizen or his property, cannot be anticipated and provided for; and the protection, to be effectual or of any avail, may, not unfrequently, require the most prompt and decided action."[32]

Bland legalese cannot hide the ferocity of the Greytown bombing. A more measured and deliberate policy was promised by legislation in 1868 (still in effect) directing the President to demand from a foreign government the reason for depriving any American citizen of liberty. If it appeared wrongful and in violation of the rights of American citizenship, the President was to demand the citizen's release. If the foreign government delayed or refused, the President could use such means, "not amounting to acts of war," as he thought necessary and proper to obtain the release.[33]

This statute did not put an end to heavy-handed American actions abroad. Theodore Roosevelt, William Howard Taft, and other Presidents have resorted to force not simply for the purpose of protecting American lives and property but to pursue foreign policy objectives. Woodrow Wilson, taking the Greytown bombardment as an acceptable precedent, ordered American forces to occupy Veracruz, Mexico, in 1914. In a message delivered to a joint session of Congress, he stressed the need for immediate action, offering this legal analysis: "No doubt I could do what is necessary in the circumstances to enforce respect for our Government without recourse to the congress, and yet not exceed my constitutional powers as President; but I do not wish to act in a matter possibly of so grave consequence except in close conference and co-operation with both the Senate and the House."[34]

[32] Durand v. Hollins, 4 Blatch. 451, 454 (1860). A description of the bombing appears in Milton Offutt, "The Protection of Citizens Abroad by the Armed Forces of the United States," Johns Hopkins Univ. Studies in Hist. and Pol. Sci., series XLIV, no. 4, at 32-34 (1928).

[33] 15 Stat. 223 (1868); 22 U.S.C. 1732 (1982). It is possible to derive the life-and-property prerogative from the Privilege and Immunity Clause. Justice Miller, in enumerating some of the rights protected by this constitutional provision, included the right to be protected abroad; Slaughter-House Cases, 83 U.S. (16 Wall.) 36, 79 (1872).

[34] Richardson, Messages and Papers, XVI, 7936.

The House acted with alacrity to authorize the use of armed force, but when Senators had the audacity to pause for one day to think about what they were doing, Wilson went ahead and ordered landing operations by the Marines. The following day—two days after his request—Congress passed a joint resolution justifying the President's use of force. This episode, which began with a trivial incident involving U.S. seamen in Tampico, escalated in the bombardment of Veracruz, American occupation for seven months, and the downfall of the Mexican president, Victoriano Huerto. The following year Wilson intervened in Haiti to secure a more acceptable government there, while confiding to his Secretary of State that "we have not the legal authority to do what we apparently ought to do."[35] American troops were to remain in Haiti until 1934.

Recent decades have lengthened the list of life-and-property actions. President Eisenhower sent troops into Lebanon in 1958 "to protect American lives and by their presence there to encourage the Lebanese government in defense of Lebanese sovereignty and integrity."[36] President Johnson intervened in the Dominican Republic in 1965 to prevent what he feared would be a communist takeover, though he later explained that "99 percent of our reason for going in there was to try to provide protection for these American lives and for the lives of other nationals."[37] President Nixon justified his invasion of Cambodia in 1970 on the ground that enemy actions "clearly endanger the lives of Americans who are in Vietnam now and would constitute an unacceptable risk to those who will be there after withdrawal of another 150,000."[38] When the Nixon administration provided support for the South Vietnamese invasion of Laos the following year, the State Department said that the action would

[35] Arthur S. Link, Wilson: The Struggle for Neutrality 536 (1960). For the joint resolution of support for Veracruz action, see 38 Stat. 770 (1914). A vivid account is given by Robert E. Quirk in An Affair of Honor: Woodrow Wilson and the Occupation of Veracruz (1962).

[36] Public Papers of the Presidents, 1958, at 549.

[37] Public Papers of the Presidents, 1965, II, at 616.

[38] Wkly Comp. Pres. Doc., VI, 597 (1970).

"protect American lives."[39] President Ford, as will be described later, used troops for evacuations from Southeast Asia and for the rescue of the *Mayaguez* vessel. President Carter sent troops to Iran in 1980 in an abortive effort to free American hostages. President Reagan dispatched Marines to Grenada in 1983, ostensibly to rescue American students and other U.S. citizens, but Russian and Cuban influence in that region was the overriding motivation.

Contemporary use of force cannot be justified on the basis of gunboat diplomacy and forays into Mexico or the Caribbean a half-century ago. Ratification of the United Nations Charter imposes restrictions on member states that can be ignored only at substantial political cost. Article 2, Paragraph 4 states that all members "shall refrain in their international relations from the threat or use of force against the territorial integrity or political independence of any state, or in any other manner inconsistent with the purposes of the United Nations." There are only two exceptions: the right of individual or collective self-defense against an armed attack (Article 51) and collective action taken by the United Nations to deal with serious disturbances of the peace. Even the Nixon administration, after its intervention in Cambodia in 1970, acknowledged that whatever the practices prior to 1945, adoption of the UN Charter "changed the situation by imposing new and important limitations on the use of armed force."[40] A body of international legal norms has developed since 1945 that constrains the actions of many sovereign nations.

Early drafts of the War Powers Resolution of 1973 (to be discussed later in this chapter) recognized the responsibility of the President to protect life and property. A bill introduced by Senator Jacob Javits in 1971 would have allowed the President to use armed force "to protect the lives and property, as may be required, of United States nationals abroad." Javits later deleted the words "and property" for fear that they might be interpreted

[39] New York Times, February 9, 1971, at 17:6. For a discussion of the constitutional limits when force is used to protect troops, see 65 Am. J. Int'l L. 34-35, 79-80 (1971).

[40] Statement by John R. Stevenson, Legal Adviser to the Department of State, May 29, 1970, reprinted at 64 Am. J. Int'l L. 933, 940 (1970).

in a nineteenth-century sense of protecting American business investments abroad.[41] The rest of the language disappeared in the House-Senate compromise that became law.

This lack of legislative authority, together with other statutory restrictions on the use of force in Southeast Asia, created an awkward and confusing situation in 1975. President Ford asked Congress to clarify the statutory restrictions so that he could evacuate American citizens and foreign nationals from South Vietnam and Cambodia. He gave Congress nine days to act.[42] Instead of trying to act while a presidential timer ticked away, party leaders in Congress should have issued a statement saying that the President had enough authority for the evacuations, provided he used a minimum of force. Ford had already announced that the War Powers Resolution, as he interpreted it, gave the President "certain limited authority to protect American lives. And to that extent, I will use that law."[43] Why then ask Congress for legislative authority? The issue was complicated by the need to rescue foreign nationals as well, but it was politically unreasonable and unrealistic to expect Congress to legislate on such an explosive issue in nine days.

Members agonized for weeks, trying to discover the right language that would give Ford the authority he wanted without leading to military reinvolvement in Southeast Asia. Legislators were whipsawed by conflicting feelings. On the one hand they wanted to relate all military operations to the procedures of the War Powers Resolution. On the other hand they were apprehensive that any legislation, no matter how meticulously drafted, would become anachronous and ambiguous due to the rapidly changing situation in Southeast Asia.

While Congress anguished over the wording of the legislation, Ford went ahead with the evacuations from Cambodia and South Vietnam. In each case he based his action on the President's "executive power" under the Constitution and on his authority

---

[41] "War Powers Resolution," hearings before the Senate Committee on Foreign Relations, 92d Cong., 1st Sess. 35-36, 95-96, 128 (1971).

[42] Wkly Comp. Pres. Doc., XI, 363 (April 10, 1975).

[43] Id. at 329 (April 3, 1975).

as commander in chief.[44] He took these actions before Congress could deliver the "clarifying authority." But even though the evacuations were over, some members of Congress argued that the legislation should be passed. They reasoned that the President had conducted the evacuations within the limitations of the legislation under consideration (although Ford cited only constitutional sources in his reports); Congress should therefore enact the legislation to establish its authority and somehow legalize the President's action. For such legislators the integrity of the War Powers Resolution was at stake. Others, however, believed that the bill was moot because of the evacuations. Passage of the legislation would merely lift the restrictions that barred reintroduction of troops into Southeast Asia. The House, capping three weeks of legislative frenzy, voted down the conference report. This was an ignominious finale to an ill-conceived legislative exercise.[45]

Following these evacuations and Ford's rescue of the *Mayaguez* crew, Senator Thomas Eagleton introduced legislation explicitly recognizing the President's right to protect lives (but not property). It stipulated various conditions limiting this grant of power: the citizens to be rescued would have to be involuntarily held with the express or tacit consent of the foreign government; there would have to be a direct and imminent threat to their lives; the foreign government either could not or would not protect the individuals; and the evacuations would have to take place as expeditiously as possible and with a minimum of force.[46] Eagleton's proposal, along with other amendments to the War Powers Resolution, has not been acted upon by Congress.

Delegated Emergency Powers

The notion of "emergency" is convenient for attracting legislative support, but at such times it is necessary to distinguish between

[44] H. Doc. Nos. 105 and 124, 94th Cong., 1st Sess. (1975).

[45] 121 Cong. Rec. 12752-64 (1975). For a GAO decision, holding that the evacuation of Vietnamese nationals was necessarily incident to the rescue of Americans, see 55 Comp. Gen. 1081 (1976).

[46] 121 Cong. Rec. 15579-82.

genuine emergencies thrust upon the nation and those that develop because of neglect or contrivance. After President Franklin D. Roosevelt had declared thirty-nine emergencies within the space of six years, Congressman Bruce Barton protested: "Any national administration is entitled to one or two emergencies in a term of 6 years. But an emergency every 6 weeks means plain bad management."[47]

Once the nation is engaged in war, the reservoir of presidential power fills rapidly as Congress delegates vast new duties and responsibilities to the executive branch. It is characteristic of this legislation to offer little in the way of guidelines for administrative action, and yet the courts regularly uphold the statutes.[48] Furthermore, these delegations remain in the hands of the President long after hostilities have ended, long after American troops have returned home. Here too the courts defer to the chief executive in determining when a state of war is over.[49]

Other statutes contain latent or dormant authority for the President, ready to spring to life whenever he issues a proclamation declaring the nation to be in a state of emergency. It came as a surprise to many members of Congress in 1971 to learn that the United States had been in a state of declared national emergency ever since March 9, 1933, when President Roosevelt proclaimed an emergency at the time of the banking crisis. Also still in effect were national emergencies proclaimed by President Truman on December 16, 1950 (after China's entry into the Korean War), and by President Nixon on March 23, 1970, and August 15, 1971.

These discoveries prompted the Senate to establish a special committee to study the possibility of terminating the states of declared national emergency. A committee report in 1973 dis-

[47] 84 Cong. Rec. 2854 (1939).

[48] For example, United States v. Bethlehem Steel, 315 U.S. 289 (1942); Bowles v. Willingham, 321 U.S. 503 (1944); Yakus v. United States, 321 U.S. 414 (1944); and Lichter v. United States, 344 U.S. 742 (1947).

[49] For example, United States v. Anderson, 9 Wall. 56 (1870); The Protector, 12 Wall. 700 (1872); Stewart v. Kahn, 11 Wall. 493 (1870); Hijo v. United States, 194 U.S. 315 (1904); Hamilton v. Kentucky Distilleries, 251 U.S. 146 (1919); Commercial Trust v. Miller, 262 U.S. 51 (1923); Chastleton Corp. v. Sinclair, 264 U.S. 533 (1924); and Woods v. Miller, 333 U.S. 138 (1948).

closed that the four proclamations mentioned above had brought to life 470 provisions of federal law. Each statute extended to the President some facet of control over the lives of American citizens. Among other things, he could seize property, organize and control the means of production, institute martial law, control all transportation and communication, and restrict travel.[50]

In 1976 Congress passed the National Emergencies Act to restrict the use of presidential emergency powers. Its general thrust is to terminate emergency authorities two years from the date the act became law (September 14, 1976). In future national emergencies the President has to publish the declaration in the Federal Register. Congress may terminate the national emergency by passing a concurrent resolution. To prevent emergencies from lingering for decades without congressional attention or action, the 1976 legislation includes an action-forcing mechanism. No later than six months after a national emergency is declared by the President, and at least every six months thereafter while the emergency continues, each House of Congress has to meet to consider a vote on a concurrent resolution to determine whether the emergency should be terminated.[51]

The use of a concurrent resolution to terminate a national emergency has been invalidated by the Supreme Court's decision in *INS* v. *Chadha* in 1983. Even the requirement for congressional consideration every six months has been rendered suspect by disuse. Despite the statutory mandate for congressional action, no concurrent resolution was ever introduced, much less acted upon, after President Carter declared a national emergency over the Iranian crisis in 1979. The Senate Foreign Relations Committee and the House Foreign Affairs Committee merely wrote letters to Carter stating that action on a resolution of disapproval was unnecessary.[52]

The National Emergencies Act exempted certain provisions of

---

[50] S. Rept. No. 549, 93d Cong., 1st Sess, iii (1973).

[51] 90 Stat. 1255 (1976). See "The National Emergencies Act (Public Law 94-412), Source Book: Legislative History, Texts, and Other Documents," Senate Committee on Government Operations and Senate Special Committee on National Emergencies and Delegated Emergency Powers, 94th Cong., 2d Sess. (Comm. Print November 1976).

[52] 126 Cong. Rec. 11270-71, 11537 (1980).

law, including Section 5(b) of the Trading With the Enemy Act, originally enacted in 1917. Over the years this provision had been the basis for controlling domestic as well as international financial transactions. Its reach went far beyond trading with the enemy, and it became a source of presidential authority in peacetime as well as wartime. For example, it was under Section 5(b) that President Roosevelt declared a national emergency in 1933 and announced a bank holiday to prevent hoarding of gold. Presidents Johnson and Nixon also invoked this clause to justify other controversial actions.

Legislation in 1977, as passed by Congress, limits the use of the Trading With the Enemy Act to time of war *as declared by Congress*. A second set of powers, more restricted than those available during time of war, would be given to the President upon his declaration of a national emergency in time of peace. The legislation subjects these powers to the procedural restrictions of the National Emergencies Act.[53]

Electronic Surveillance

Another issue of constitutional dimensions concerns wiretapping and electronic surveillance by executive officials without a warrant. How does this practice square with the Fourth Amendment's requirement that a judicial warrant be obtained, upon probable cause, prior to a search and seizure? Various administrations, beginning in the 1920s but especially from the time of Franklin D. Roosevelt forward, have resorted to wiretapping for the purpose of controlling domestic crime and protecting national security. Differing interpretations by all three branches have compounded and confounded the problem.

Section 605 of the Communications Act of 1934 made it a

[53] H. Rept. No. 459, 95th Cong., 1st Sess. (1977) and 123 Cong. Rec. 22473-78 (1977). See "Trading With the Enemy: Legislative and Executive Documents Concerning Regulation of International Transactions in Time of Declared National Emergency," prepared by the House Committee on International Relations, 94th Cong., 2d Sess. (Comm. Print November 1976). Enacted as P.L. 95-223 (1977).

crime to intercept wire or radio communications.[54] This restriction was reinforced by Supreme Court decisions in 1937 and 1939, holding that the statute applied to federal agents and prohibited information obtained by wiretapping from being introduced as trial evidence.[55] In 1940 President Roosevelt, in a directive to his Attorney General, maintained that the decision did not apply to "grave matters involving the defense of the nation."[56] Subsequent actions by Presidents, courts, and Congress left unclear whether the President possessed inherent power to authorize wiretapping and electronic surveillance when needed for national security.[57]

Title III of the Omnibus Crime Control Act of 1968 authorized the use of wiretaps in cases of domestic crimes, but only after the issuance of a judicial warrant based on probable cause. The act did not attempt to cover "national security" wiretaps. Nothing in the 1968 legislation, or in Section 605 of the Communications Act of 1934, was meant to limit the "constitutional power of the President to take such measures as he deems necessary to protect the Nation against actual or potential attack or other hostile acts of a foreign power, to obtain foreign intelligence information deemed essential to the security of the United States, or to protect national security information against foreign intelligence activities."[58] In short, for more than a quarter of a century, Presidents had authorized warrantless surveillance without specific guidelines from Congress or the courts. No one could say with certainty whether the authority was delegated (by implication) or inherent in the President's office.

Of major significance in defining the President's power is the Supreme Court's 1972 holding in *United States* v. *United States District Court* (also known as *Keith*). The Nixon administration

---

[54] 48 Stat. 1103 (1934).

[55] Nardone v. United States, 302 U.S. 379 (1937) and Nardone v. United States, 308 U.S. 338 (1939).

[56] Reprinted in Zweibon v. Mitchell, 516 F.2d 594, 673-674 (D.C. Cir. 1975).

[57] See "Warrantless Wiretapping and Electronic Surveillance," report by the Senate Committees on Foreign Relations and the Judiciary, 94th Cong., 1st Sess. (Comm. Print February 1975).

[58] 82 Stat. 214, 18 U.S.C. 2511(3) (1970).

had approved wiretaps to gather intelligence information deemed necessary to protect the nation from attempts by *domestic organizations* "to attack and subvert the existing structure of the Government." The actions were taken in the name of the President's inherent power to protect national security. The Court, voting 8 to 0, held that Fourth Amendment freedoms cannot be guaranteed if domestic security surveillances are conducted solely at the discretion of the executive branch. For such surveillance to be constitutional, a warrant issued by the judiciary is essential. The Court regarded the case before it as purely a domestic matter, for no evidence existed that the organization was involved, directly or indirectly, with a foreign power. The Court offered no guidance with regard to the President's surveillance power over "the activities of foreign powers, within or without this country."[59]

Before long the federal courts faced a hybrid case that did not fit either the domestic sector (governed by *Keith*) or foreign affairs. The Jewish Defense League (JDL), originally founded to protect Jews in New York neighborhoods, expanded its interests to include the treatment of Soviet Jews and Soviet emigration policies. Tactics of the group ranged from peaceful picketing of the Soviet mission at the United Nations to vandalizing Soviet offices in New York and Washington and bombing Soviet airline offices in New York. The Nixon administration claimed that the JDL, although a domestic organization, threatened the President's conduct of foreign relations. The Justice Department began wiretapping telephone lines, without a warrant, at the JDL's New York office.

In *Zweibon* v. *Mitchell* (1975), a circuit court held that the wiretap on the JDL violated the Fourth Amendment. The court

[59] United States v. United States District Court, 407 U.S. 297, 308 (1972). Some lower courts held that the President did have inherent authority to order warrantless wiretaps for the purpose of gathering foreign intelligence; United States v. Butenko, 494 F. 2d 593 (3d Cir. 1974), cert. denied, sub. nom. Ivanov v. United States, 419 U.S. 881 (1974); United States v. Brown, 484 F.2d 418 (5th Cir. 1973), cert. denied, 415 U.S. 960 (1974); and United States v. Hoffman, 334 F.Supp. 504 (D.D.C. 1971). See also United States v. Clay, 430 F.2d 165 (5th Cir. 1970), reversed by 403 U.S. 698 (1971).

did not accept the general justification of dispensing with warrants in foreign security surveillance. A majority held that warrants were necessary, at least in cases where a domestic organization was neither an agent nor a collaborator of a foreign power.[60] The court also concluded that the executive practice of conducting national security surveillance without a warrant had been supported by statutory interpretations, not by claims of inherent presidential power.

Throughout this litigation on national security wiretaps the courts were telegraphing Congress for assistance. The intent of the Communications Act of 1934 had been the subject of much speculation, as was Title III of the Omnibus Crime Control Act of 1968. Two roads lay open: either define by statute the scope of executive action as a delegated power, or else recognize that the power to wiretap without a warrant derives from Article II of the Constitution.

Congress enacted legislation in 1978 to restrict executive action. The Foreign Intelligence Surveillance Act requires a court order to engage in electronic surveillance within the United States for purposes of obtaining foreign intelligence information. Federal judges, appointed by the Chief Justice, review applications submitted by government attorneys. Consistent with *Zweibon*, the legislation limits surveillance to foreign powers or agents of foreign powers working as members of that power's intelligence network.[61] The seven federal judges who make up the Foreign Intelligence Surveillance Court have never rejected an intelligence agency's request for a wiretap. Over 1,400 applications have been approved. Government officials claim that the prospect of court review acts as a restraint on agency activities that might have been permitted in the past.[62]

[60] Zweibon v. Mitchell, 516 F.2d 594, 614 (D.C. Cir. 1975), cert. denied, 425 U.S. 944 (1976). See Note, "The Fourth Amendment and Judicial Review of Foreign Intelligence Wiretapping: *Zweibon* v. *Mitchell*," 45 G.W. L. Rev. 55 (1976).

[61] 92 Stat. 1783 (1978).

[62] Keenan Peck, "A Court That Never Says No," The Progressive, April 1984, at 18. See also Larry Tell, "The Cloak-and-Dagger Court," National Law Journal, August 10, 1981, at 1.

Wiretaps by the Nixon administration continued to remain an issue in court long after Nixon resigned from office. Morton Halperin, former chief of the National Security Council Planning Group, brought action against Nixon, Attorney General John Mitchell, National Security Adviser Henry A. Kissinger, White House aide H. R. Haldeman, and other federal officials for wiretapping his home telephone. The tap remained in effect for approximately twenty-one months, from 1969 to 1971, as part of the administration's effort to investigate leaks to the press of foreign policy documents and sensitive information. The tap produced no evidence that Halperin was leaking classified data.

In 1976 a district judge held the tap unreasonable under the Fourth Amendment. He found Nixon, Mitchell, and Haldeman liable for damages and without a good-faith defense.[63] He awarded each of the five members of the Halperin family $1 in nominal damages.[64] An appellate court upheld the judgment on the immunity issue, but returned the case to the district court to reconsider the award of only nominal damages and to add Kissinger to the list of liable officials.[65] Halperin's victories in the lower courts were affirmed in 1981 when the Supreme Court deadlocked 4 to 4. Justice Rehnquist, who had worked for Mitchell at the time of the taps, did not vote.[66]

In the case of *Nixon* v. *Fitzgerald* (1982), the Supreme Court recognized an absolute immunity for Presidents sued for civil damages regarding their official acts.[67] In a companion case, the Court adopted a qualified immunity for other executive officials.[68] Based on those two rulings, the district court dismissed Halperin's suits against Nixon and against Kissinger, Mitchell, and Haldeman.[69] Halperin accepted the verdict on Nixon but appealed the decision on the three other officials.

[63] Halperin v. Kissinger, 424 F.Supp. 838 (D.D.C. 1976).
[64] Halperin v. Kissinger, 434 F.Supp. 1193, 1196 (D.D.C. 1977).
[65] Halperin v. Kissinger, 606 F.2d 1192 (D.C. Cir. 1979).
[66] Kissinger v. Halperin, 452 U.S. 713 (1981).
[67] 457 U.S. 731 (1982).
[68] Harlow v. Fitzgerald, 457 U.S. 800 (1982).
[69] Halperin v. Kissinger, 578 F.Supp. 231 (D.D.C. 1984).

The War Powers Resolution of 1973

Because of continuing controversy over the war power, especially as exercised by Lyndon Johnson and Richard Nixon, Congress passed the War Powers Resolution of 1973. After leaving the presidency, Gerald Ford claimed that the War Powers Resolution "seeks by simple legislation to codify the military powers of the President, spelling out exactly what he can and cannot do, and how, and under what circumstances, to defend the United States and its citizens from international danger."[70] This is a good description of what the Senate tried to do, but not of the version that became public law. A review of House and Senate actions helps clarify this point.

Legislative History

In 1970 the House of Representatives conceded a measure of war prerogatives to the President. A war powers resolution, passed by a vote of 289 to 39, recognized that the President "in certain extraordinary and emergency circumstances has the authority to defend the United States and its citizens without specific prior authorization by the Congress." Instead of trying to define the precise conditions under which Presidents may act, the House relied on procedural safeguards. The President would be required, "whenever feasible," to consult with Congress before sending American forces into armed conflict. He was also to report the circumstances necessitating the action; the constitutional, legislative, and treaty provisions authorizing the action, together with his reasons for not seeking specific prior congressional authorization; and the estimated scope of activities.[71] The Senate did not act on the measure.

Both Houses later passed war powers resolutions that went beyond mere reporting requirements. The House of Represent-

[70] Address to the University of Kentucky, April 11, 1977, reprinted at 123 Cong. Rec. 11700-03 (1977). Quoted remark appears at 11701, col. 3.

[71] 116 Cong. Rec. 37398-408 (1970). Passed again the next year under suspension of the rules (requiring two-thirds support), 117 Cong. Rec. 28870-78 (1971).

atives, following its earlier example, did not try to define or codify presidential war powers. It directed the President "in every possible instance" to consult with Congress before sending forces into hostilities or situations where hostilities might be imminent. If unable to do so, he was to report to Congress within seventy-two hours, setting forth the circumstances and details of his action. Unless Congress declared war within 120 days or specifically authorized the use of force, the President had to terminate the commitment and remove the troops. Congress could also direct disengagement at any time during the 120-day period by passing a concurrent resolution.[72]

The Senate attempted to spell out the conditions under which Presidents could take unilateral action. Armed force could be used in three situations: (1) to repel an armed attack upon the United States, its territories and possessions, retaliate in the event of such an attack, and forestall the direct and imminent threat of such an attack; (2) to repel an armed attack against U.S. armed forces located outside the United States, its territories and possessions, and forestall the direct and imminent threat of such an attack; and (3) to rescue endangered American citizens and nationals in foreign countries or at sea. The first situation (except for the final clause) conforms to the understanding developed at the Philadelphia convention. The other situations reflect the changes that have occurred in the concept of defensive war and life-and-property actions.

The Senate bill required the President to cease military action unless Congress, within thirty days, specifically authorized the President to continue. A separate provision allowed him to sustain military operations beyond the thirty-day limit if he determined that "unavoidable military necessity respecting the safety" of the armed forces required their continued use for purposes of "bringing about a prompt disengagement."[73] This effort to codify presidential war powers carried a number of risks. Because of ambiguities in the language, legislation might widen presidential power instead of restricting it. Executive officials could interpret

[72] 119 Cong. Rec. 24653-708 (1973).
[73] Id. at 25051-120.

308

in broad fashion such terms as "necessary and appropriate retaliatory actions," "imminent threat," and "endangered citizens."

The two Houses presented a compromise measure to President Nixon. He vetoed the bill primarily because he regarded it as impractical and dangerous to fix in a statute the procedure by which President and Congress should share the war power. He also believed that the legislation encroached upon the President's constitutional responsibilities as commander in chief. He reminded Congress that the "only way in which the constitutional powers of a branch of the Government can be altered is by amending the Constitution—and any attempt to make such alterations by legislation alone is clearly without force."[74] Both Houses mustered a two-thirds majority to override the veto: the House narrowly (284 to 135), the Senate by a more comfortable margin (75 to 18).[75]

Although the War Powers Resolution of 1973 overcame a veto, it has not survived doubts about its quality and effectiveness. Some of the congressional support for the resolution was based on party politics and the resolution's symbolic value rather than on its contents. Consider the voting record of fifteen members of the House.[76] After voting against the House bill and the conference version, they inconsistently voted to override the veto. If they opposed the legislation because they considered it inadequate or unsound, why vote to make it public law?

This reversal occurred in part because of fear that a vote to sustain might lend credence to the views advanced in Nixon's veto message. Despite serious misgivings about the quality of the bill, some legislators concluded that congressional inaction could be interpreted as a concession to the constitutional claims of Nixon (and Johnson). Other legislators used the override to propel the House toward impeachment of Nixon. One of those who voted against the House resolution and the conference version but then in favor of overriding the veto—Democrat Bella Abzug of New

[74] Public Papers of the Presidents, 1973, at 893.

[75] 87 Stat. 555 (1973).

[76] Representatives Abzug, Drinan, Duncan, Flynt, Harsha, Hechler (W. Va.), Holtzman, Hungate, Landrum, Lott, Maraziti, Milford, Natcher, Stubblefield, and Whitten.

York—advised her colleagues that: "This could be a turning point in the struggle to control an administration that has run amuck. It could accelerate the demand for the impeachment of the President."[77]

Another factor was that Democrats were anxious to override a Nixon veto. Eight times during the 93d Congress he had vetoed legislation; eight times Congress came up short on the override. A number of members looked upon the War Powers Resolution as a vehicle to test congressional power.[78] This attitude was especially tempting in the wake of the Watergate scandals. The "Saturday Night Massacre," which sent Special Prosecutor Archibald Cox, Attorney General Elliot Richardson, and Deputy Attorney General William Ruckelshaus out of the government, occurred just four days before Nixon's veto of the War Powers Resolution. Ten days before the Saturday Night Massacre, Spiro Agnew had heightened the politicized climate by resigning as Vice President.

Analysis of the Bill

The War Powers Resolution sets forth three main procedures: presidential consultation with Congress, presidential reports to Congress, and congressional termination of military action. The purpose of the resolution, according to Section 2(a), is "to insure that the collective judgment" of both branches will apply to the introduction of U.S. forces into hostilities. Yet an examination of other sections, together with executive interpretations and congressional behavior, supplies ample evidence that collective judgment is by no means assured.

The President is to consult with Congress "in every possible instance." This language obviously leaves considerable discretion to the President as to the form and timing of consultation. The Carter administration noted that the President's responsibilities under the sections involving consultation and reporting "have not been delegated, so that the final decision as to whether con-

[77] 119 Cong. Rec. 36221 (1973).
[78] See Thomas F. Eagleton, War and Presidential Power 213-20 (1974).

sultation is possible and as to the manner in which consultations be undertaken or reports submitted rests with the President."[79]

The authors of the resolution did not expect the President to consult with 535 legislators. But whom should he contact? The leadership? The chairmen and ranking members of designated committees? Selected advisers? Should they merely be briefed or does consultation mean a more active role for Congress? The legislative history makes clear that consultation goes beyond simply being informed of a decision. Consultation means that "a decision is pending on a problem and that Members of Congress are being asked by the President for their advice and opinions and, in appropriate circumstances, their approval of action contemplated."[80] However, to participate on equal terms, legislators need the same information made available to the President. Congressman Paul Findley, a House conferee on the resolution, remarked that legislators would have to drop everything during a crisis and remain with the National Security Council to "evaluate the facts as they are perceived and as they may change during this period of time."[81] Congress has yet to organize itself to play a consultative role.

The War Powers Resolution requires that the President, after introducing forces into hostilities, report to Congress within forty-eight hours. Precisely what conditions require a report is unclear from the legislation. If the report is delayed for any reason, so are the mechanisms for congressional control. For example, military action must terminate within sixty days after the report unless Congress (1) declares war or enacts a specific authorization, (2) extends by law the sixty-day period, or (3) is physically unable to meet as a result of an armed attack upon the United States. The President may extend the period by an additional thirty days if he determines that force is needed to protect and

---

[79] 123 Cong. Rec. 21898 (1977).

[80] H. Rept. No. 287, 93d Cong., 1st Sess. 6-7 (1973).

[81] Findley: "War Powers: A Test of Compliance," hearings before the House Committee on International Relations, 94th Cong., 1st Sess. 57 (1975). Congressman Zablocki stated that "it was not the intention of section 3 to expect the President to consult with all 535 members" ("War Powers: A Test of Compliance," at 55).

remove American troops. Congress has two means of control: either a decision not to support the President during the sixty-to-ninety days or passage of a concurrent resolution at any time to direct the President to remove forces engaged in hostilities.

Although the War Powers Resolution states that nothing in it is intended to alter the constitutional authority of the Congress or the President, some members of Congress were concerned that the new procedure had the effect of broadening presidential power. William Green, a Democrat from Pennsylvania, felt that it put a sixty- to ninety-day congressional "stamp of approval" on presidential actions. Bob Eckhardt, a Texas Democrat, argued that for up to ninety days the Congress would provide the President with the "color of authority" to exercise a war-making power.[82]

Section 2(c) appears to restrict the President's exercise of his powers as commander in chief to three situations: a declaration of war, specific statutory authorization, or a national emergency created by an attack on the United States, its territories or possessions or its armed forces. However, the conference report on the resolution explains that the sections on consultation, reporting, and congressional action are *not* dependent on the language of Section 2(c). The restrictive force of the section seems divorced from the procedural steps that follow.[83]

The President may use his own judgment as to when and where to introduce forces into hostilities. He could so firmly commit the nation's forces and prestige during the ninety-day period that Congress would find it politically and militarily impossible to reverse the operation. What begins as marginal or contrived has the potential of deteriorating into a genuine emergency, compelling congressional support. As the sixty- to ninety-day deadline grew near, legislators might "rally 'round the flag" rather than independently debate the wisdom and merits of the President's decision.

[82] 119 Cong. Rec. 36204, 36208 (1973).

[83] H. Rept. No. 547, 93d Cong., 1st Sess. 8 (1973). Section 2(c) is carefully analyed by William B. Spong, Jr., in "The War Powers Resolution Revisited: Historic Accomplishment or Surrender?" 16 Wm. & Mary L. Rev. 823, 837-841 (1975).

Presidential power, nourished by this early support from Congress, could be extended in other ways. Once engaged in hostilities, the President might draw upon his constitutional authority to repel sudden attacks and protect American troops. It might not be possible for Congress to curb such activity by passing a concurrent resolution ordering him to disengage or letting the ninety-day period expire without legislative support. The legal adviser to the State Department told a House committee in 1975 that if the President has the power to put men into combat "that power could not be taken away by concurrent resolution because the power is constitutional in nature."[84] That position has been reinforced by the Supreme Court's decision in *INS* v. *Chadha* (1983), striking down the legislative veto.

Since passage of the War Powers Resolution, administrative officials have stated their belief that the President's power goes beyond protecting American territory and armed forces. The Ford administration argued that there were six other situations in which the President has constitutional authority to introduce armed forces into hostilities: to rescue American citizens abroad; to rescue foreign nationals where such action directly facilitates the rescue of American citizens abroad; to protect U.S. embassies and legations abroad; to suppress civil insurrection; to implement and administer the terms of an armistice or cease-fire designed to terminate hostilities involving the United States; and to carry out the terms of security commitments contained in treaties. The statement from the Ford administration added: "We do not, however, believe that any such list can be a complete one."[85]

Several amendments have been introduced to perfect the War Powers Resolution. One relates to the failure of the resolution to recognize the President's right to rescue endangered citizens (discussed above). Another relies on the appropriations power to fortify congressional control, an issue discussed at the end of this chapter. A third has to do with the fact that the resolution places restrictions only on the President's power to dispatch *armed service personnel* into hostilities. Not covered are activities by ci-

[84] "War Powers: A Test of Compliance," at 91.
[85] Id. at 90-91.

313

vilian combatants and "paramilitary operations." An effort by Senator Eagleton to include such operations within the coverage of the War Powers Resolution was defeated in 1973. Two years later he introduced legislation to make the provisions of the resolution apply to civilian combatants, such as those employed by the CIA in Angola from 1975 to 1976.[86] Congress has yet to act on such legislation.

Military Initiatives from Ford to Reagan

Presidents have submitted a number of reports under the War Powers Resolution, but the manner of the reports and the response by Congress underscores the fact that the resolution is simply a framework for executive-legislative relations. The actual outcome in every case depends on a spirit of comity and good-faith efforts by the President and members of Congress.

On three occasions in April 1975, President Ford reported to Congress the use of military forces to evacuate U.S. citizens and refugees from Vietnam and Cambodia. Typical of these reports under the War Powers Resolution, Ford cited his constitutional authority as Chief Executive and Commander in Chief rather than statutory sources of authority.

After the evacuations from Southeast Asia, the War Powers Resolution was put to a more severe test the following month. The U.S. merchant ship *Mayaguez*, traveling from Hong Kong to Sattahip, Thailand, was seized by Cambodians. Two days later the United States recovered the vessel and its crew, but only after President Ford had ordered air strikes against Cambodia and called upon Marine ground forces. Weeks and months would pass before Congress had an adequate picture of what had taken place.

Nevertheless, on the very day of the recovery, members of Congress rushed forward with glowing words of praise. A spirit of jingoism filled the air. The episode became a "proud new chapter in our history." Members expressed pride in their country and in their President, exclaiming with youthful enthusiasm that it was

---

[86] 121 Cong. Rec. 40884 (1975). See also legislation introduced by Congressman James Scheuer, 122 Cong. Rec. 581 (1976).

"great to be an American."[87] A few members reserved judgment, which was sensible, for no one knew exactly what had happened or why. A legislator could have announced: "I am happy that the crew is back. Unfortunately, many lives were lost in the effort. It is still too early, the facts still too incomplete, for us to make a judgment." Most members, however, felt compelled to outdo one another with words of commendation and jubilation.

As details of the capture trickled in, Ford's action looked less and less appealing. Approximately forty-one Americans lost their lives trying to rescue thirty-nine crewmen. The administration spent little effort probing diplomatic avenues before resorting to force. The quality of military intelligence was not reassuring. The Marines suffered heavy casualties during the assault on Koh Tang Island, under the erroneous impression that the crewmen were detained there. A punitive spirit seemed to infuse the operations. The United States bombed the Cambodian mainland *after* the crew had been released. A 15,000-pound bomb—the largest conventional bomb in America's arsenal—was dropped on a Cambodian island that measured just a few square miles.[88]

Administration leaders suggested that this use of force contained valuable lessons regarding America's determination to meet its international commitments, but the application of this event to future contingencies is hard to envision. Anthony Lewis of the *New York Times* said that for "all the bluster and righteous talk of principle, it is impossible to imagine the United States behaving that way toward anyone other than a weak, ruined country of little yellow people who have frustrated us."[89] An editorial in the *Washington Post* noted with alarm that the use of force by the greatest power in the world against a small country could serve as such a tonic in the nation's capital: "That anyone could find the Mayaguez affair a valid or meaningful guide to

[87] See especially the Congressional Record of May 15, 1975.

[88] "War Powers: A Test of Compliance"; "Seizure of the Mayaguez," hearings before the House Committee on International Relations, 94th Cong., 1st Sess. (1975); and statement by Senator Javits, 121 Cong. Rec. 18312-13 (1975). See also Jordan J. Paust, "The Seizure and Recovery of the Mayaguez," 85 Yale L. J. 774 (1976).

[89] New York Times, May 20, 1975.

the requirements of post-Vietnam foreign policy at other times and places defies common sense."[90]

As for compliance with the War Powers Resolution, there had been little consultation with Congress. Representative Clement Zablocki, principal author of the House version of the War Powers Resolution, said that the administration's effort to consult with Congress was inadequate.[91] Senator Jacob Javits, a leading sponsor of the resolution, also criticized the administration's consultation record.[92] In subsequent hearings the House Committee on International Relations expressed frustration because it could not obtain information from administration officials who were at the center of the decision-making process.[93]

It is difficult to believe that one month after the costly disengagement from Southeast Asia, after the United States had finally broken free from a lengthy and violent war that racked the country, there could be such a celebration of force. What happened to the "deliberative process" of Congress? The independent legislative capability? The promise of closer scrutiny of executive actions? Unless members take the time personally to analyze a President's decision, Congess cannot expect a coequal status or a share in "collective judgment." Instead, legislators will become prematurely associated with a policy they may later find unworthy of support.

In 1980 President Carter reported to Congress on the use of military force in his unsuccessful attempt to rescue American hostages in Iran. In reporting "consistent" with the War Powers Resolution, he relied on the President's authority as Chief Executive and Commander in Chief. Although Carter's effort to consult with Congress was no better than Ford's, there was little

90 Washington Post, May 16, 1975.

91 "War Powers: A Test of Compliance," at vi, and also 81-82, 100.

92 Id. at 61-75 and 121 Cong. Rec. 18312-13 (1975).

93 "Seizure of the Mayaguez," Part 2 at 137, 147-152, and Part 3 at 259-270. See Robert Zutz, "The Recapture of the S.S. Mayaguez: Failure of the Consultation Clause of the War Powers Resolution," 8 N.Y.U. J. Int'l L. & Pol. 457 (1976). In 1980 a federal district judge upheld Ford's action in *Mayaguez* as immune from judicial scrutiny under the political question doctrine; Rappenecker v. United States, 509 F.Supp. 1024 (N.D. Cal. 1980).

criticism from legislators. However, Secretary of State Cyrus Vance resigned to protest the rescue operation.[94]

Military initiatives in 1982 and 1983 by President Reagan in Lebanon highlighted another weakness of the War Powers Resolution. Although hostilities were not merely "imminent" in Lebanon but had actually broken out, Reagan sent in troops without reporting under Section 4(a)(1) of the War Powers Resolution. By merely reporting "consistent" with the resolution, he did not set in motion the clock that would have limited military action to sixty or ninety days unless Congress specifically authorized an extension. Rather than acting under the procedures of the resolution, Reagan deployed troops pursuant to the President's "constitutional authority with respect to the conduct of foreign relations and as Commander-in-Chief of the United States Armed Forces."[95]

Reagan's refusal to trigger the clock meant that Congress had to pass legislation to invoke Section 4(a)(1). In passing this legislation in the fall of 1983, Congress gave the administration authority for eighteen months, deliberately allowing military forces to remain in Lebanon throughout the election year of 1984 without further legislative action. Members supported this massive delegation by reasoning that Reagan, upon signing the bill, would concede the legitimacy of the process established by the War Powers Resolution. Instead, Reagan made it clear that he might continue military operations beyond the eighteen-month period without reauthorization by Congress.[96]

The choice of eighteen months reflected the decision by both branches to remove Lebanon from the legislative calendar for 1984. Neither Congress nor the President wanted to risk trying to reauthorize a shorter period in the midst of a national election. But after members of Congress adjourned for the remainder of 1983, they recognized that the grant of authority for eighteen

[94] Cong. Q. Wkly Rept. May 3, 1980, at 1200.

[95] Wkly Comp Pres. Doc., XVIII, 1232 (September 29, 1982). See also id. at XIX, 1186 (August 30, 1983) for further reporting "consistent" with the War Powers Resolution.

[96] Id. at XIX, 1342 (September 27, 1983); id. at XIX, 1422-23 (October 12, 1983); P.L. 98-119.

months was a mistake. Reagan also realized that public opinion would not sustain military operations over that period. By the spring of 1984 he had withdrawn the Marines from Lebanon. Nevertheless, the events of 1983 illustrated that Congress was willing, in return for short-term political advantages, to forfeit long-term institutional interests and act contrary to a fundamental goal of the War Powers Resolution. The purpose of that statute was to make Congress a coequal partner both in the initiation and continuation of military force.

In the case of El Salvador, President Reagan did not report under any provision of the War Powers Resolution when he sent military advisers to that country in 1981. The State Department claimed that no report was necessary because the Americans were not being introduced into hostilities or imminent hostilities. In 1981, several members of Congress filed a suit charging that Reagan had violated the War Powers Resolution by sending the advisers. Eventually twenty-nine members of the House of Representatives joined the action against Reagan. Arrayed on the opposite side were sixteen Senators and twelve Representatives who supported Reagan and urged that the case be dismissed. The federal judge, confronted by two congressional factions, refused to do the factfinding that would have been necessary to determine whether hostilities or imminent hostilities existed. The judge pointed out that Congress had failed to act legislatively to restrain Reagan.[97]

The Purse and the Sword

Conflicts between Congress and the President over the war power are generally examined by the judiciary at a safe distance; it is

---

[97] Crockett v. Reagan, 558 F.Supp. 893 (D.D.C. 1982), aff'd, 720 F.2d 1355 (D.C. Cir. 1983). In a similar case, eleven members of Congress brought action against President Reagan for his invasion of Grenada in 1983, contending that he violated the power of Congress to declare war. The court declined to exercise its jurisdiction because of the relief available to members through the regular legislative process; Conyers v. Reagan, 578 F.Supp. 324 (D.D.C. 1984). For an excellent postmortem on the War Powers Resolution, see Michael J. Glennon, "The War Powers Resolution Ten Years Later: More Politics than Law," 78 Am. J. Int'l L. 571 (1984).

intensely interested but in no mood to intervene. Deference has reached the point where courts treat the entire area of the "conduct of the foreign relations" as purely political, in no way subject to judicial inquiry or decision.[98] In 1950 the Supreme Court claimed that "it is not the function of the Judiciary to entertain private litigation—even by a citizen—which challenges the legality, the wisdom, or the propriety of the Commander-in-Chief in sending our armed forces abroad or to any particular region."[99]

What is proper deference by the courts in one case may be obsequiousness in another. Actions taken in the name of national security, whether by Congress or the President, can threaten individual freedoms protected elsewhere in the Constitution. As the Supreme Court noted in *Baker* v. *Carr*: "it is error to suppose that every case or controversy which touches foreign relations lies beyond judicial cognizance."[100]

During the Vietnam War the question arose in the federal courts whether Congress, because it appropriated funds for the Defense Department, had sanctioned the President's war policy. A State Department memorandum in 1966 argued that Congress had shown its support for the war policy of the Johnson administration by enacting the necessary appropriations. Defense appropriations constituted "a clear congressional endorsement and approval of the actions taken by the President.[101]

Judge Templar, in *Velvel* v. *Johnson* (1968), rejected the notion that Congress had been forced against its better judgment to appropriate money for military operations in Vietnam. Congress had the power—both political and constitutional—to terminate military action. The court could not "infer that courage is lacking among the members of Congress, should the majority of the elected representatives of the people conclude to take such action."[102] Nor could Judge Dooling, in *Orlando* v. *Laird* (1970), believe that defense appropriations had been "extorted by the

---

[98] Oetjen vs. Central Leather Co., 246 U.S. 297, 302 (1918).
[99] Johnson v. Eisentrager, 339 U.S. 763, 789 (1950).
[100] 369 U.S. 186, 211 (1962).
[101] Dep't of State Bull., LIV, 487 (1966).
[102] 287 F.Supp. 846, 853 (D. Kans. 1968).

exigencies created by presidential seizures of combat initiatives."[103]

Expert witnesses advised the courts that House and Senate rules prohibited major declarations of policy in appropriations bills. The parliamentary process limited substantive legislation to authorization bills. They also pointed out that some members had voted for military appropriations not because they endorsed the war policy but because they felt an obligation to support American soldiers already committed to battle. Initially the courts were unimpressed by this line of argument. As Judge Judd noted in *Berk* v. *Laird* (1970): "That some members of Congress talked like doves before voting with the hawks in an inadequate basis for a charge that the President was violating the Constitution in doing what Congress by its words had told him he might do. ... The entire course of legislation shows that Congress knew what it was doing, and that it intended to have American troops fight in Vietnam."[104]

Members of the judiciary began to backtrack from the proposition that Congress could indirectly endorse a war simply by appropriating funds. Circuit Judge Adams, in 1972, said that such a determination would require the interrogation of legislators regarding the intent behind their votes, followed by a synthesis of the various replies. He concluded that it would be impossible to gather and evaluate such information.[105] Judges Wyzanski and Bazelon, who had earlier accepted appropriations acts as identical with congressional consent, reversed their positions by 1973. They could now no longer be

> unmindful of what every schoolboy knows: that in voting to appropriate money or to draft men a Congressman is not necessarily approving of the continuation of a war no matter how specifically the appropriation or draft act refers to that

[103] 317 F.Supp. 1013, 1018 (E.D. N.Y. 1970). See also Davi v. Laird, 318 F.Supp. 478, 481 (W.D. Va. 1970) and Orlando v. Laird, 443 F.2d 1039, 1042 (2d Cir. 1971).

[104] 317 F.Supp. 715, 724, 728 (E.D. N.Y. 1970). The position of expert witnesses for the plaintiffs appears at 718 and 721. See also DaCosta v. Laird, 448 F.2d 1368, 1369 (2d Cir. 1971).

[105] Atlee v. Laird, 347 F.Supp. 689, 706 (E.D. Pa. 1972).

war. A Congressman wholly opposed to the war's com-
mencement and continuation might vote for the military appropriations and for the draft measures because he was unwilling to abandon without support men already fighting.
An honorable, decent, compassionate act of aiding those already in peril is no proof of consent to the actions that
placed and continued them in that dangerous posture. We
should not construe votes cast in pity and piety as though
they were votes freely given to express consent.[106]

A major appropriations battle occurred in 1973. President
Nixon's basis for military operations in Vietnam seemed to have
disappeared with the signing of a cease-fire agreement in Paris
on January 27, 1973, and the withdrawal of all American troops
by the end of March. The Gulf of Tonkin Resolution had been
repealed by Congress several years earlier. No longer could the
President point to that as authority or cite the need to protect
American soldiers. Yet Nixon continued to maintain a massive
bombing operation in Cambodia. When a supplemental appropriations bill reached the House floor in May, Clarence Long of
Maryland offered an amendment to prohibit the use of any funds
authorized by the bill to support directly or indirectly U.S. combat activities in, over, or from off the shores of Cambodia. The
amendment was adopted, 224 to 172. The Senate passed an even
stronger amendment, forbidding the use of any funds to support
combat activities in Cambodia or Laos (a restriction covering not
only the supplemental funds but funds made available by previous appropriations). The bill presented to Nixon included the
Senate version.[107]

Nixon vetoed the bill, claiming that the "Cambodian rider"
would destroy the chances for a negotiated settlement in Cambodia. He also warned that nine agencies, dependent upon funds

[106] Mitchell v. Laird, 488 F.2d 611, 615 (D.C. Cir. 1973). Wyzanski's earlier
position appears in Massachusetts v. Laird, 327 F.Supp. 378, 381 (D. Mass.
1971). For the ambivalent quality of defense appropriations, see Campen v. Nixon,
56 F.R.D. 404, 406 (N.D. Cal. 1972).

[107] This paragraph, and the following three, are drawn from Louis Fisher,
Presidential Spending Power 110-18 (1975).

in the bill, would soon exhaust their authority to pay the salaries and expenses of their employees. According to his line of reasoning, the wheels of government would grind to a halt if Congress persisted in presenting objectionable statutory language to the President. Congress failed to override.

The issue of the appropriations power was now firmly joined. Congress could argue that the restrictions in the supplemental bill represented an appropriate effort to limit the President's ability to wage war and to commit the nation to vast expenditures. If Nixon refused to acknowledge congressional preeminence in matters of the purse, legislators could have held *him* responsible for the paralysis of agency operations. In this raw, high-noon confrontation, Congress backed off. A revised bill delayed the cutoff of funds from June 30 to August 15, 1973, in effect giving the President freedom to bomb Cambodia for another forty-five days—which is what he did. But at least Congress, by agreeing to the compromise, succeeded in using its power of the purse to conclude military operations is Southeast Asia.

The "August 15 Compromise" aborted several cases that had been working their way through the federal courts. In a decision of July 25, 1973, a federal judge in New York held that Congress had not authorized the bombing in Cambodia. The fact that Congress could not muster a two-thirds majority to override the President's veto should not, he said, be interpreted as an affirmative grant of authority. This decision was later reversed, in part because an appellate court held that the August 15 date did indeed constitute congressional approval of the bombing.[108] In other decisions the courts accepted the compromise date as evidence that the two political branches were no longer in resolute conflict; therefore there was no need for the courts to referee.[109]

If the War Powers Resolution turns into a mere parchment barrier, rendered permeable because of ambiguities in the language, Congress may want to act directly through its legislative authority to control appropriations. The resolution already clar-

---

[108] Holtzman v. Schlesinger, 361 F.Supp. 553, 563-65 (E.D. N.Y. 1973), stayed by the Supreme Court, 414 U.S. 1304, 1316, 1321, before being reversed, Holtzman v. Schlesinger, 484 F.2d 1307, 1313-14 (2d Cir. 1973).

[109] Drinan v. Nixon, 364 F.Supp. 854, 860-61, 864 (D. Mass. 1973).

ifies one point: defense appropriations do not, by themselves, endorse a military policy. Section 8(a) of the resolution states that the authority to introduce armed forces into hostilities, or into situations where circumstances indicate involvement, shall not be inferred from any provision of law—including any provision contained in any appropriations act—unless such provisions specifically authorizes the introduction of troops.

More explicit would be a cutoff of funds, after the sixty- or ninety-day period expires, to prevent the President from resorting to unused balances available to him. Denial of funds could become effective unless Congress specifically authorizes a continuation of the war before the expiration date.[110] Executive officials would probably regard this as an encroachment upon presidential responsibilities, but Congress would be operating from a solid base of constitutional authority. Acting in this manner would give firm meaning to the hope once expressed by Jefferson: "We have already given in example one effectual check to the Dog of war by transferring the power of letting him loose from the Executive to the Legislative body, from those who are to spend to those who are to pay."[111]

The Politics of Comity

The post-Vietnam years underscore the need for the President to reach an accommodation with Congress in foreign policy and national defense. Unilateral actions by the President eventually become counterproductive. To sustain a successful policy, at some point the executive branch must secure the support and cooperation of Congress. As Secretary of State Kissinger noted in 1975: "Comity between the executive and legislative branches is the only possible basis for national action. The decade-long struggle in this country over executive dominance in foreign affairs is over. The recognition that the Congress is a coequal branch of gov-

---

[110] See Michael J. Glennon, "Strengthening the War Powers Resolution: The Case for Purse-Strings Restrictions," 60 Minn. L. Rev. 1, 32-33 (1975); Garry Wooters, "The Appropriations Power as a Tool of Congressional Foreign Policy Making." 50 B.U.L. Rev. 34 (Special Issue 1970).

[111] The Papers of Thomas Jefferson (Boyd ed.), XV, 397.

ernment is the dominant fact of national politics today. The executive accepts that the Congress must have both the sense and the reality of participation: foreign policy must be a shared enterprise."[112]

The President is not the sole voice in foreign affairs. He cannot, or should not, isolate himself from Congress and the general public, dismissing their contributions as narrow, local, or parochial. Patsy T. Mink, after dual careers in Congress and the State Department, warned that it "is folly to believe, as many in the top echelons of State and White House staff sincerely do, that good foreign policy necessarily stands above the pressures of domestic politics and constituent interests. Politics is the art of reconciling and educating, not of avoiding, those interests."[113] For that task the President needs members of Congress to develop and support effective international policies.

Congressional influence depends on its willingness to act and take responsibility. A failure to act creates a vacuum into which Presidents can enter. Executive authority then becomes a function of congressional action and inaction. As Justice Jackson noted in the Steel Seizure Case of 1952, presidential authority reaches its highest level when the President acts pursuant to congressional authorization. His power is at its "lowest ebb" when he takes measures incompatible with the will of Congress. But in between these two categories lay a "zone of twilight" in which Congress neither grants nor denies authority. In such circumstances "congressional inertia, indifference or quiescence may sometimes, at least as a practical matter, enable, if not invite, measures on independent presidential responsibility."[114]

President Carter's termination of the Taiwan defense treaty was not met by an effective challenge from Congress. Justice Powell noted that if Congress "chooses not to confront the President, it is not our task to do so."[115] Carter's actions against Iran, including his freezing of assets and the suspension of claims pending in American courts, was upheld in the courts partly be-

[112] Dep't of State Bull., LXXII, 562 (1975).
[113] Thomas M. Franck, ed., The Tethered Presidency 74 (1981).
[114] Youngstown Co. v. Sawyer, 343 U.S. 579, 637 (1952).
[115] Goldwater v. Carter, 444 U.S. 996, 998 (1979).

cause of congressional acquiescence. Presidents have a freer hand in foreign affairs "where there is no contrary indication of legislative intent and when, as here, there is a history of congressional acquiescence in conduct of the sort engaged in by the President."[116] A lawsuit challenging President Reagan's actions in El Salvador was dismissed by the federal courts partly because Congress had failed to take any legislative action to thwart him.[117]

It has been argued that the War Powers Resolution and other statutory provisions have created uncertainty in the international arena, preventing the President from negotiating effectively with other nations. Foreign leaders supposedly see these legislative constraints as impediments in entering into long-term commitments. But it would be worse for the President to go it alone, acting in isolation without the backing of Congress and public opinion. Other nations should feel more secure to know that the President has consulted closely with congressional leaders in hammering out a policy that is acceptable to both branches.

[116] Dames & Moore v. Regan, 453 U.S. 654, 678-79 (1981).

[117] Crockett v. Reagan, 558 F.Supp. 893 (D.D.C. 1982), aff'd, 720 F.2d 1355 (D.C. Cir. 1983).

10

CONCLUSIONS

The general drift of authority and responsibility to the President over the past two centuries is unmistakable. This trend by itself should not be cause for alarm. More threatening is executive activity cut loose from legislative moorings and constitutional restrictions—presidential action no longer tethered by law. To remain consistent with the Constitution, executive authority and administrative discretion should be directed and channeled by legislative policy.

We will never be able to define with any precision the meaning of executive and legislative, or show where one branch fades and begins to blend into another. Still, the general theory and practice of separated powers can be retained. No one doubts the difference between night and day, or between youth and old age, though we cannot say with certainty where one ends and the other beings.[1]

Over the past decade the Supreme Court has moved away from a functional, practical approach to separated powers and has adopted a doctrinaire, formalistic model. The functional approach was evident in 1974 when the Court rejected Nixon's claim of an absolute power to determine the limits of executive privilege. Instead, the Court emphasized checks and balances and the need for a "workable government."[2] Separation of powers was followed only in the sense of preserving "the essential functions" of each branch.[3]

Three years later, in another case involving Nixon's papers, the Court again viewed separation of powers in practical terms. It rejected the rigid view of the Court in 1935 that the three branches of government must remain "entirely free from the control or

---

[1] See Erwin N. Griswold in "Evaluating Governmental Performance: Changes and Challenges for GAO," a series of lectures delivered at the U.S. General Accounting Office, 1973-1975, at 110.

[2] United States v. Nixon, 418 U.S. 683, 707 (1974).

[3] Id.

coercive influence, direct or indirect, of either of the others"[4] and favored the "more pragmatic, flexible approach" of James Madison in the *Federalist Papers* and of Justice Story.[5] The duty of judges was to inquire into the extent to which a statute prevented the executive branch from accomplishing "its constitutionally assigned functions . . . [and] whether that impact is justified by an overriding need to promote objectives within the constitutional authority of Congress."[6]

However, in three decisions announced in 1982 and 1983, the Court embraced a doctrinaire notion of separated powers. In *Nixon* v. *Fitzgerald* (1982), which upheld an absolute immunity for the President in civil cases, the Court considered the immunity "a functionally mandated incident of the President's unique office, rooted in the constitutional tradition of the separation of powers and supported by our history."[7] The Court expressed concern about the "dangers of intrusion on the authority and functions of the Executive Branch."[8]

In 1982 the Court also struck down a statute that allowed bankruptcy judges to exercise judicial powers without the protections of life tenure and irreducible salaries guaranteed to Article III judges. Although executive departments and independent commissions discharge a multitude of adjudicatory functions and previous court decisions have upheld "legislative courts" (created under Article I), the plurality opinion interpreted the Bankruptcy Act as evidence that powers were about to be accumulated in a single branch.[9] The Court believed that allowing Congress to establish bankruptcy courts under Article I "threatens to supplant completely our system of adjudication in independent Art. III tribunals and replace it with a system of 'specialized' legislative courts."[10] Justice White, dissenting, denied

---

[4] Nixon v. Administrator of General Services, 433 U.S. 425, 441-42 (1977), quoting from Humphrey's Executor v. United States, 295 U.S. 602, 629 (1935).

[5] 433 U.S. at 442.

[6] Id. at 443.

[7] 457 U.S. 731, 749 (1982).

[8] Id. at 754.

[9] Northern Pipeline Co. v. Marathon Pipe Line Co., 458 U.S. 50, 57 (1982).

[10] Id. at 73.

that the Bankruptcy Act represented an attempt by the political branches "to aggrandize themselves at the expense of the third branch or an attempt to undermine the authority of constitutional [Article III] courts in general."[11]

Finally, in *INS* v. *Chadha* (1983) the Court continued to endorse a highly formalistic model of separated powers. In striking down the legislative veto, the Court dismissed as irrelevant its utility for bridging executive-legislative disagreements: "Convenience and efficiency are not the primary objectives—or the hallmarks—of democratic government . . . ."[12] Once again the Court cited the framers' fear of despotism and the possibility of encroachments by one branch on another.[13] Although denying that the branches were "hermetically" sealed from one another, the Court insisted that the Constitution divided governments into "three defined categories, legislative, executive, and judicial," and that the Court was compelled to resist the "hydraulic pressures inherent within each of the separate Branches to exceed the outer limits of its power . . . ."[14]

The Court seemed to go out of its way to present a worst-case scenario. There was nothing in the history of the Bankruptcy Act to suggest that Congress was positioning itself to take over the federal judiciary, and it is simplistic to believe that the legislative veto was merely a device by which Congress hoped to dominate the executive branch. The framers did not object to a sharing or partial intermixture of powers. They were not doctrinaire advocates of a pure separation between branches. They knew that the "danger of tyranny or injustice lurks in unchecked power, not in blended power."[15] To the extent that the Supreme Court adopts unrealistic and impractical concepts of separated powers, its decisions will be largely ignored or circumvented.

In extraordinary situations the President may have to act promptly without clear constitutional or statutory support. Quick action is not a quality or purpose of a legislative assembly. Con-

[11] Id. at 116.
[12] 103 S.Ct. 2764, 2781 (1983).
[13] Id. at 2782-88.
[14] Id. at 2784.
[15] Kenneth Culp Davis, Administrative Law and Government 54 (1960).

gress is essentially a deliberative body. Under extreme conditions it is better to let the President call upon his "prerogative" without claiming the slightest shred of legal support, perhaps even admitting that his action violates the law. The burden is then on him to justify his decision and to rest his case before Congress and the public. Both would be free, after careful examination of the evidence and the circumstances, to render a verdict of exoneration or condemnation.

The precise jurisdictions and fields of operation for Congress and the President will always elude us. Fortunately, the political process has a self-correcting mechanism, although it comes late and after extensive cost. Ambiguities in the Constitution permit one branch to infringe upon another. Generally this encroachment consists of brief raids in and out of the neutral zone. But at some point, after passing beyond a threshold of common sense and prudence, aggressive actions become counterproductive. They trigger revolts, leading to the recapture of ground taken not only in the most recent assault but in earlier offenses as well. It is not true that "let one occupant of the presidency exercise an additional power, and the advantage thus acquired is never abandoned."[16] Consider what happened with impoundment, the pocket veto, reorganization authority, and executive privilege. Power distorted the judgment of the wielder. The moth circled too close to the flame.

Some students of the presidency believe that the problem of executive power can be brought under control by selecting with greater care the person to occupy the Oval Office. To use the classification of James David Barber, we are urged to elect an "active-positive": someone who is energetic at the job and derives enjoyment from the exercise of power.[17] Other political scientists, including Charles Hardin, prefer to cast a skeptical eye on whoever finds himself in the Oval Office.[18] Here I side with Hardin, not to dwell on the dark side of human nature or to encourage a climate of distrust and suspicion, but because it is

[16] Norman J. Small, Some Presidential Interpretations of the Presidency 198 (1932).

[17] James David Barber, The Presidential Character (1972).

[18] Charles M. Hardin, Presidential Power & Accountability 63 (1974).

an illusion to think that a President will have the technical competence, political instinct, and moral character that will permit us to rest easy while he wields power.

To call for "comity" and "consultation" is not enough. The record suggests that this too is an illusion. Representative Paul Findley remarked in 1976 that he had been in Congress for sixteen years, most of that time serving on the House Committee on International Relations. The chairman of that committee, Clement Zablocki, had been in Congress for twenty-eight years. Throughout this period—which spanned Democratic as well as Republican administrations—Zablocki tried to encourage consultation by the executive branch, but Findley was hard put to think of any cases in which consultation actually occurred in advance of an executive decision. It was out of this "rather dismal experience," Findley said, that many members of Congress decided to propose extraordinary remedies for executive agreements, the war power, and other conflicts with the executive branch.[19]

If Congress has strong misgivings about an issue, it should resolve the matter by relying on language in a public law, not by informal understandings with executive officials. In 1977 members of the House were worried about being inundated by reorganization plans sent down by President Carter. OMB Director Bert Lance assured the House Committee on Government Operations that the administration appreciated this concern and would adhere to a reasonable timetable. Congress correctly insisted on specific language in the reorganization act to prohibit more than three plans from being considered before Congress at one time.[20] When in doubt, the legislative policy belongs in the law.

This is a policy of prudence, not paranoia. We need to distinguish between objectives and the means used to attain them. Justice Jackson reminded us of our tendency to ignore funda-

[19] "Congressional Review of International Agreements," hearings before the House Committee on International Relations, 94th Cong., 2d Sess. 150 (1976).

[20] 91 Stat. 30, Sec. 903 (b). "Providing Reorganization Authority to the President," hearings before the House Committee on Government Operations, 95th Cong., 1st Sess. 43-44 (1977).

mentals of government: "The opinions of judges, no less than executives and publicists, often suffer the infirmity of confusing the issue of a power's validity with the cause it is invoked to promote, of confounding the permanent executive office with its temporary occupant. The tendency is strong to emphasize transient results upon policies—such as wages and stabilization—and lose sight of enduring consequences upon the balanced power structure of our Republic."[21] Theodore Sorensen, reflecting on his views of presidential power during and after his service with the Kennedy administration, warned against shortsighted reactions to immediate events and the failure to take into account the longer view: "I understand this error, having committed it myself a decade ago."[22]

The literature on the presidency, after emphasizing for many years such vague qualities as "vigor," "energy," and "persuasion," is now more cautious about the ends to which power may be put and the legal boundaries for presidential action. Commentators are taking into account not merely the exercise of power, directed for whatever purpose the President chooses, but the source of authority, rights secured under the Constitution, and the larger system of checks and balances.[23] Too often in the past the legal basis for action has been ignored in the eagerness for results.

Constitutional precepts are important goals even when they cannot be entirely satisfied. There is no need for dismay because we aim high and fall short. Machiavelli, often portrayed as the father of political expediency, encouraged us to establish high standards:

a prudent man will always choose to take paths beaten by great men and to imitate those who have been especially admirable, in order that if his ability does not reach theirs, at least it may offer some suggestion of it; and he will act like prudent archers, who, seeing that the mark they plan to

---

[21] Youngstown Co. v. Sawyer, 343 U.S. 579, 634 (1952).

[22] Theodore C. Sorensen, Watchmen in the Night xvi (1975).

[23] John Hart, "Presidential Power Revisited," 25 Pol. Stud. 48 (1977). Compare with Richard E. Neustadt, Presidential Power (1960). Neustadt's original text was not changed in the later editions of 1968 and 1976.

hit is too far away and knowing what space can be covered by the power of their bows, take an aim much higher than their mark, not in order to reach with their arrows so great a height, but to be able, with the aid of so high an aim, to attain their purpose.[24]

The framers of the Constitution settled on a single executive in order to foster unity, responsibility, dispatch, expertise, and a national perspective. To an impressive extent the office of the presidency has alleviated many of the defects experienced by the Continental Congress. Yet the qualities originally anticipated of the executive have undergone profound transformations. It is absurd today to think that a President can be a skilled diplomat, military strategist, macroeconomist, energy expert, and domestic innovator, along with all the other heady roles we expect him to play.

Surely it is arbitrary to highlight the unifying quality of the President. Just as easily we can look at the fragmentation of the executive branch and the many groups within it competing for control. Special interests seek representation within the administration just as they do within Congress. In ways similar to a legislature these groups barter with one another and conduct their own form of logrolling. With heartless accuracy, Alfred de Grazia reminded us some time ago that the President is "a Congress with a skin thrown over him."[25] We need to pierce the skin and comprehend the forces underneath.

The President remains responsible for the operation of the executive branch, but often only in a technical and formal sense. Vast areas are subdelegated to remote sectors of the executive branch. Even Presidents and staff assistants with unusual diligence and energy find themselves overwhelmed by the task. Joseph Califano, after serving as an assistant to President Johnson in the area of domestic affairs, recalled that he doubted he ever

[24] Allan Gilbert, trans., Machiavelli: The Chief Works and Others, 1, 24-25 (1965), from The Prince, ch. 6.

[25] Alfred de Grazia, Republic in Crisis 72 (1965). A pioneer in debunking the "superman" image of the President is Thomas E. Cronin; for a recent work see his The State of the Presidency 76-115 (1980).

met, "much less consulted or helped guide, more than one-third of these noncabinet agency and commission heads. Hyperactive as he was, President Johnson met even fewer of them."[26] Congress is frequently advised to confine its activities to "broad policy" questions and leave "day to day" matters to the executive branch. A similar division of labor takes place within the administration. The President is advised to concentrate on broad policy while delegating details to departments and agencies.[27]

Executive officials are often so absorbed by operations, tactics, and short-run goals that they lose sight of national objectives, other than the raising of campaign contributions and the President's reelection. The 1972 campaign was conspicuous for its bartering of the public interest. The Internal Revenue Service, the Federal Bureau of Investigation, the Central Intelligence Agency, and other agencies were used by the White House to violate the constitutional rights of citizens. Raised to high visibility were the administration's relationships with such special interests as International Telephone and Telegraph, milk producers' cooperatives, and grain exporters.[28] Congress is not innocent in such matters, but we are disposed to expect the worst of legislators and at the same time believe in high virtues of the President and his entourage.

Agency officials, even when they have their facts correct, find it difficult to place them in perspective or part company with long-held assumptions and predilections. White House officials, by necessity generalists, may ignore agency expertise when it fails to dovetail with the political needs of the President. Congressional staffers, upon reaching their counterparts in the agencies, sometimes run into this kind of question: "Do you want the official position or the facts?"

The importance of Congress is its capacity for diversity and openness (relative to the executive branch)—the opportunity it gives to express different sentiments, opinions, and values. It is a disorderly operation and disappointing to those who want firm

---

[26] Joseph A. Califano, Jr., A Presidential Nation 23 (1975).

[27] Id. at 49. See also Stephen Hess, Organizing the Presidency (1976).

[28] "The Final Report of the Select Committee on Presidential Campaign Activities," S. Rept. No. 981, 93d Cong., 2d Sess. (June 1974).

direction and quick action. But this free play of ideas, as well as the freedom not to move until the time is right, is essential to democratic government. What is needed from Congress is the daily grind of overseeing administration policies, passing judgment on them, and behaving with confidence as a coequal branch. This takes courage and an understanding of constitutional responsibilities.

Congress may stand against the President or stand behind him, but it should not stand aside as it did year after year during the Vietnam War, looking the other way and occasionally complaining about executive usurpation. There the crucial ingredient was will power, not constitutional power. Congressional influence depends on more than access to information, additional staff, or a revamping of procedure and organization. Congress must be willing to participate actively in questions of national policy, challenging the President and contesting his actions. It cannot be viewed as quarrelsome behavior for Congress to assess presidential action independently. Issues need the thorough exploration and ventilation that only Congress can provide.

This does not mean that a congressional product will necessarily be better than a presidential proposal. It is not a question of preferring one branch over another but of remaining faithful to the form of government embodied in the Constitution. We must learn, especially when the temptation is great, to resist legal shortcuts because "the cause is good." The door is then left open for capricious acts we may deplore. Robert H. Jackson, whose entire career with the federal government lay outside the legislative branch, serving first as Attorney General and later as Associate Justice of the Supreme Court, urged us to hold fast to essentials: "With all its defects, delays and inconveniences, men have discovered no technique for long preserving free government except that the Executive be under the law, and that the law be made by parliamentary deliberations."[29]

[29] Youngstown Co. v. Sawyer, 343 U.S. at 655.

334

THE CONSTITUTION OF THE
UNITED STATES OF AMERICA
(SELECTIONS)

We the people of the United States, in order to form a more perfect Union, establish Justice, insure domestic Tranquility, provide for the common defence, promote the general Welfare, and secure the Blessings of Liberty to ourselves and our Posterity, do ordain and establish this CONSTITUTION for the United States of America.

Article I

SECTION 1

All legislative Powers herein granted shall be vested in a Congress of the United States, which shall consist of a Senate and House of Representatives.

SECTION 2

. . . .

The House of Representatives . . . shall have the sole Power of Impeachment.

SECTION 3

. . . .

The Senate shall have the sole Power to try all Impeachments. When sitting for that Purpose, they shall be on Oath or Affirmation. When the President of the United States is tried, the Chief Justice shall preside: And no Person shall be convicted without the Concurrence of two thirds of the Members present.

Judgment in Cases of Impeachment shall not extend further than to removal from Office, and disqualification to hold and enjoy any Office of honor, Trust or Profit under the United States; but the Party convicted shall nevertheless be liable and subject to Indictment, Trial, Judgment and Punishment, according to Law.

. . . .

SECTION 6

The Senators and Representatives shall receive a Compensation for their Services, to be ascertained by Law [*Ascertainment Clause*], and paid out of the Treasury of the United States. They shall in all Cases, except Treason, Felony, and Breach of the Peace, be privileged from Arrest during their Attendance at the Session of their respective Houses, and in going to and returning from the same; and for any Speech or Debate in either House, they shall not be questioned in any other Place [*Speech or Debate Clause*].

No Senator or Representative shall, during the Time for which he was elected, be appointed to any civil Office under the Authority of the United States, which shall have been created, or the Emoluments whereof shall have been encreased during such time [*Ineligibility Clause*]; and no Person holding any Office under the United States, shall be a Member of either House during his Continuance in Office [*Incompatability Clause*].

SECTION 7

All Bills for raising Revenue shall originate in the House of Representatives; but the Senate may propose or concur with Amendments as on other Bills.

Every Bill which shall have passed the House of Representatives and the Senate, shall, before it become a Law, be presented to the President of the United States [*Presentment or Presentation Clause*]; if he approve he shall sign it, but if not he shall return it, with his Objections to that House in which it shall have originated, who shall enter the Objections at large on their Journal, and proceed to reconsider it. If after such Reconsideration two thirds of that House shall agree to pass the Bill it shall be sent, together with the Objections, to the other House, by which it shall likewise be reconsidered, and if approved by two thirds of that House, it shall become a Law. But in all such Cases the Votes of both Houses shall be determined by Yeas and Nays, and the Names of the Persons voting for and against the Bill shall be entered on the Journal of each House respectively. If any Bill shall not be returned by the President within ten Days (Sundays excepted) after it shall have been presented to him, the Same shall be a Law, in like Manner as if he had signed it, unless the Congress by their Adjournment prevent its Return, in which Case it shall not be a Law.

Every Order, Resolution, or Vote to which the Concurrence of the Senate and House of Representatives may be necessary (except on question of Adjournment) shall be presented to the President of the United States [*Presentment or Presentation Clause*]; and before the Same shall take Effect, shall be approved by him, or being disapproved by him, shall be repassed by two thirds of the Senate and House of Representatives, according to the Rules and Limitations prescribed in the Case of a Bill.

SECTION 8

The Congress shall have Power To lay and collect Taxes, Duties, Imposts and Excises, to pay the Debts and provide for the common Defence and general Welfare of the United States; but all Duties, Imposts and Excises shall be uniform throughout the United States;

To borrow money on the Credit of the United States;

To regulate Commerce with foreign Nations, and among the several States, and with the Indian Tribes;

To establish an uniform Rule of Naturalization, and uniform Laws on the subject of Bankruptcies throughout the United States;

To coin Money, regulate the Value thereof, and of foreign Coin, and fix the Standard of Weights and Measures;

To provide for the Punishment of counterfeiting the Securities and current Coin of the United States;

To Establish Post Offices and Post Roads;

To promote the Progress of Science and useful Arts, by securing for limited Times to Authors and Inventors the exclusive Right to their respective Writings and Discoveries;

To constitute Tribunals inferior to the supreme Court;

To define and punish Piracies and Felonies commited on the high Seas, and Offenses against the Law of Nations;

To declare War, grant Letters of Marque and Reprisal, and make Rules concerning Captures on Land and Water;

To raise and support Armies, but no Appropriation of Money to that Use shall be for a longer Term than two Years;

To provide and maintain a Navy;

To make Rules for the Government and Regulation of the land and naval Forces;

To provide for calling forth the Militia to execute the Laws of the Union, suppress Insurrections and repel Invasions;

To provide for organizing, arming, and disciplining the Militia, and for governing such Part of them as may be employed in the Service of the United States, reserving to the States respectively, the Appointment of the Officers, and the Authority of training the Militia according to the discipline prescribed by Congress;

To exercise exclusive Legislation in all Cases whatsoever, over such District (not exceeding ten Miles square) as may, by Cession of particular States, and the acceptance of Congress, become the Seat of the Government of the United States, and to exercise like Authority over all Places purchased by the Consent of the Legislature of the State in which the Same shall be, for the Erection of Forts, Magazines, Arsenals, dock-Yards, and other needful Buildings;—And

To make all Laws which shall be necessary and proper for carrying into Execution the foregoing Powers, and all other Powers vested by this Constitution in the Government of the United States, or in any Department or Officer thereof.

SECTION 9

. . . .

The privilege of the Writ of Habeas Corpus shall not be suspended, unless when in Cases of Rebellion or Invasion the public Safety may require it.

No Bill of Attainder [*Bill of Attainder Clause*] or ex post facto Law shall be passed.

. . . .

No Money shall be drawn from the Treasury, but in Consequence of Appropriations made by Law; and a regular Statement and Account of the Receipts and Expenditures of all public Money shall be published from time to time [*Statement and Account Clause*].

. . . .

Article II

SECTION 1

The executive Power shall be vested in a President of the United States of America. He shall hold his Office during the Term of four Years, and, together with the Vice-President, chosen for the same Term, be elected, as follows.

. . . .

The President shall, at stated Times, receive for his Services, a Compensation, which shall neither be encreased nor diminished during the Period for which he shall have been elected, and he shall not receive

338

THE CONSTITUTION (SELECTIONS)

within that Period any other Emolument from the United States, or any of them.

Before he enters on the Execution of his Office, he shall take the following Oath or Affirmation:—"I do solemnly swear (or affirm) that I will faithfully execute the Office of President of the United States, and will to the best of my Ability, preserve, protect and defend the Constitution of the United States."

SECTION 2

The President shall be Commander in Chief of the Army and Navy of the United States, and of the Militia of the several States, when called into the actual Service of the United States; he may require the Opinion in writing, of the principal Officer in each of the executive Departments, upon any subject relating to the Duties of their respective Offices, and he shall have Power to grant Reprieves and Pardons of Offenses against the United States, except in Cases of Impeachment.

He shall have Power, by and with the Advice and Consent of the Senate, to make Treaties, provided two-thirds of the Senators present concur; and he shall nominate, and by and with the Advice and Consent of the Senate, shall appoint Ambassadors, other public Ministers and Consuls, Judges of the supreme Court, and all other Officers of the United States, whose Appointments are not herein otherwise provided for, and which shall be established by Law: but the Congress may by Law vest the Appointment of such inferior Offices, as they think proper, in the President alone, in the Courts of Law, or in the Heads of Departments.

The President shall have Power to fill up all Vacancies that may happen during the Recess of the Senate, by granting Commissions which shall expire at the End of their next Session.

SECTION 3

He shall from time to time give to the Congress Information of the State of the Union, and recommend to their Consideration such Measures as he shall judge necessary and expedient; he may, on extraordinary Occasions, convene both Houses, or either of them, and in Cases of Disagreement between them, with Respect to the Time of Adjournment, he may adjourn them to such Time as he shall think proper; he shall receive Ambassadors and other public Ministers; he shall take Care that the Laws be faithfully executed, and shall Commission all the Officers of the United States.

SECTION 4
The President, Vice-President and all civil Officers of the United States, shall be removed from Office on Impeachment for, and Conviction of, Treason, Bribery, or other high Crimes and Misdemeanors.

Article III

SECTION 1
The judicial Power of the United States shall be vested in one supreme Court, and in such inferior Courts as the Congress may from time to time ordain and establish. The Judges, both of the supreme and inferior Courts, shall hold their offices during good Behaviour, and shall, at stated Times, receive for their Services a Compensation which shall not be diminished during their Continuance in Office [*No-diminution Clause*].

. . . .

SECTION 3
Treason against the United States, shall consist only in levying War against them, or, in adhering to their Enemies, giving them Aid and Comfort. No Person shall be convicted of Treason unless on the Testimony of two Witnesses to the same overt Act, or on Confession in open Court.

The Congress shall have Power to declare the Punishment of Treason, but no Attainder of Treason shall work Corruption of Blood, or Forfeiture except during the Life of the Person attained.

. . . .

Article IV

SECTION 3

. . . .

The Congress shall have Power to dispose of and make all needful Rules and Regulations respecting the Territory or other Property belonging to the United States [*Property Clause*]; and nothing in this Constitution shall be so constructed as to Prejudice any Claims of the United States, or of any particular State.

SECTION 4
The United States shall guarantee to every State in this Union a Republican Form of Government, and shall protect each of them against In-

vasion; and on Application of the Legislature, or of the Executive (when the Legislature cannot be convened) against domestic Violence.

. . . .

Article VI

All Debts contracted and Engagements entered into, before the Adoption of this Constitution, shall be as valid against the United States under this Constitution, as under the Confederation.

This Constitution, and the Laws of the United States which shall be made in Pursuance thereof; and all Treaties made, or which shall be made, under the Authority of the United States, shall be the supreme Law of the Land; and the Judges in every State shall be bound thereby, any Thing in the Constitution or Laws of any State to the contrary not withstanding.

The Senators and Representatives before mentioned, and the Members of the several State Legislatures, and all executive and judicial Officers, both of the United States and of the several States, shall be bound by Oath or Affirmation, to support this Constitution; but no religious Test shall ever be required as a Qualification to any Office or public Trust under the United States.

. . . .

Amendments[1]

AMENDMENT I
Congress shall make no law respecting an establishment of religion, or prohibiting the free exercise thereof; or abridging the freedom of speech, or of the press; or the right of the people peaceably to assemble, and to petition the Government for a redress of grievances.

AMENDMENT II
A well regulated Militia, being necessary to the security of a free State, the right of the people to keep and bear Arms, shall not be infringed.

AMENDMENT III
No Soldier shall, in time of peace be quartered in any house, without the consent of the Owner, nor in time of war, but in a manner to be prescribed by law.

[1] The first ten Amendments were adopted in 1791.

THE CONSTITUTION (SELECTIONS)

AMENDMENT IV

The right of the people to be secure in their persons, houses, papers, and effects, against unreasonable searches and seizures, shall not be violated, and no Warrants shall issue, but upon probable cause, supported by Oath or affirmation, and particularly describing the place to be searched, and the persons or things to be seized.

AMENDMENT V

No person shall be held to answer for a capital, or otherwise infamous crime, unless on a presentment or indictment of a Grand Jury, except in cases arising in the land or naval forces, or in the Militia, when in actual service in time of War or public danger; nor shall any person be subject for the same offense to be twice put in jeopardy of life or limb, nor shall be compelled in any criminal case to be a witness against himself, nor be deprived of life, liberty, or property, without due process of law; nor shall private property be taken for public use, without just compensation.

AMENDMENT VI

In all criminal prosecutions, the accused shall enjoy the right to a speedy and public trial, by an impartial jury of the State and district wherein the crime shall have been committed, which district shall have been previously ascertained by law, and to be informed of the nature and cause of the accusation; to be confronted with the witnesses against him; to have compulsory process for obtaining witnesses in his favor, and to have the Assistance of Counsel for his defence.

AMENDMENT VII

In suits at common law, where the value in controversy shall exceed twenty dollars, the right of trial by jury shall be preserved, and no fact tried by jury, shall be otherwise re-examined in any Court of the United States, than according to the rules of the common law.

AMENDMENT VIII

Excessive bail shall not be required, nor excessive fines imposed, nor cruel and unusual punishments inflicted.

AMENDMENT IX

The enumeration in the Constitution, of certain rights, shall not be construed to deny or disparage others retained by the people.

AMENDMENT X

The powers not delegated to the United States by the Constitution, nor prohibited by it to the States, are reserved to the States respectively, or to the people.

. . . .

SUGGESTED READINGS

Chapter 1

BENNETT, WILLIAM J. "The Constitution and the Moral Order," 3 Hastings Const. L. Q. 899 (1976).

BESSETTE, JOSEPH M., AND JEFFREY TULIS, EDS. The Presidency in the Constitutional Order (1981).

BONDY, WILLIAM. "The Separation of Governmental Powers in History, in Theory, and in the Constitution," Studies in History, Economics, and Public Law, vol. V, no. 2 (Columbia University, 1896).

CARPENTER, WILLIAM S. "The Separation of Powers in the Eighteenth Century," 22 Am. Pol. Sci. Rev. 32 (1928).

DRY, MURRAY. "The Separation of Powers and Representative Government," 3 Pol. Sci. Rev. 43 (1973).

FISHER, LOUIS. "The Efficiency Side of Separated Powers," 5 J. Am. Studies 113 (1971).

GLENNON, MICHAEL J. "The Use of Custom in Resolving Separation of Powers Disputes," 64 B.U. L. Rev. 109 (1984).

GWYN, W. B. "The Meaning of the Separation of Powers," Tulane Series in Political Science, vol. IX (1965).

McDOWELL, GARY L., ED. Taking the Constitution Seriously: Essays on the Constitution and Constitutional Law (1981).

PENNOCK, J. RONALD, AND JOHN W. CHAPMAN, EDS. Constitutionalism (1979).

RADIN, MAX. "The Doctrine of the Separation of Powers in Seventeenth Century Controversies," 86 U. Pa. L. Rev. & Am. L. Reg. 842 (1938).

SHARP, MALCOLM P. "The Classical Doctrine of the 'Separation of Powers,'" 2 U. Chi. L. Rev. 385 (1935).

WHEELER, HARVEY. "Constitutionalism," in Fred I. Greenstein and Nelson W. Polsby, eds. Governmental Institutions and Processes 1-91 (1975).

WORMUTH, FRANCIS D. The Origins of Modern Constitutionalism (1949).

WRIGHT, BENJAMIN F., JR. "The Origins of the Separation of Powers in America," 13 Economica 169 (1933).

Chapter 2

ABRAHAM, HENRY J. Justices & Presidents: A Political History of Appointments to the Supreme Court (1974).

CHASE, HAROLD W. Federal Judges: The Appointing Process (1972).

GROSSMAN, JOEL B. Lawyers and Judges: The ABA and the Politics of Judicial Selection (1965).

HARRIS, JOSEPH P. The Advice and Consent of the Senate: A Study of the Confirmation of Appointments by the United States Senate (1953).

JAMES, LOUIS C. "Senatorial Rejections of Presidential Nominations to the Cabinet: A Study in Constitutional Custom," 3 Ariz. L. Rev. 232 (1961).

KATZENBACH, NICHOLAS DE B. "The Roles of Executive and Legislative Branches in Judicial Appointments," New York L. J. (November 3, 1971).

MACKENZIE, G. CALVIN. The Politics of Presidential Appointments (1981).

MORGANSTON, CHARLES E. The Appointing and Removal Power of the President of the United States, reprinted as S. Doc. No. 172, 70th Cong., 2d Sess. (1929).

REZNICK, LOIS. "Temporary Appointment Power of the President," 41 U. Chi. L. Rev. 146 (1973).

Chapter 3

CIRILLO, RICHARD A. "Abolition of Federal Offices as an Infringement on the President's Power to Remove Federal Officers: A Reassessment of Constitutional Doctrines," 42 Ford. L. Rev. 562 (1974).

CORWIN, EDWARD S. The President's Removal Power Under the Constitution (1927).

DONOVAN, WILLIAM J., AND RALSTON R. IRVINE. "The President's Power to Remove Members of Administrative Agencies," 21 Corn. L. Q. 215 (1936).

FISHER, LOUIS. "Congress and the Removal Power," 10 Congress & the Presidency 63 (1983).

FRUG, GERALD E. "Does the Constitution Prevent the Discharge of Civil Service Employees?," 124 U. Pa. L. Rev. 942 (1976).

HART, JAMES. "The Bearing of Myers v. United States Upon the Independence of Federal Administrative Tribunals," 23 Am. Pol. Sci. Rev. 657 (1929).

———. The American Presidency in Action 155-248 (1948).

McBain, Howard Lee. "Consequences of the President's Unlimited Power of Removal," 4 Pol. Sci. Q. 596 (1926).

Miller, Charles A. The Supreme Court and the Uses of History 52-70, 205-210 (1969).

Richardson, Ivor L. M. "Problems in the Removal of Federal Civil Servants," 54 Mich. L. Rev. 219 (1955).

Thach, Charles C., Jr. The Creation of the Presidency 140-165 (1969 ed.).

U.S. Congress. "Power of the President to Remove Federal Officers," S. Doc. No. 174, 69th Cong., 2d. Sess. (1926).

Chapter 4

Barber, Sotirios A. The Constitution and the Delegation of Congressional Power (1975).

Blachly, Frederick F., and Miriam E. Oatman. Administrative Legislation and Adjudication (1934).

Black, Henry Campbell. The Relation of the Executive Power to Legislation (1919).

Bruff, Harold H. "Presidential Power and Administrative Rulemaking," 88 Yale L. J. 451 (1979).

Cash, Robert B. "Presidential Power: Use and Enforcement of Executive Orders," 39 Notre Dame Lawyer 44 (1963).

Chamberlain, Lawrence H. The President, Congress, and Legislation (1946).

Fairlie, John A. "Administrative Legislation," 18 Mich. L. Rev. 181 (1920).

Fisher, Louis. "Delegating Power to the President," 19 J. Pub. L. 251 (1970).

Fleishman, Joel L., and Arthur H. Aufses. "Law and Orders: The Problem of Presidental Legislation," 40 Law & Contemp. Prob. 1 (1976).

Foster, Stephen A. "The Delegation of Legislative Power to Administrative Officers," 7 Ill. L. Rev. 397 (1913).

Harlow, Ralph Volney. The History of Legislative Methods in the Period Before 1825 (1917).

Hart, James. "The Ordinance Making Powers of the President of the United States," Johns Hopkins University Studies in Historical and Political Science, series XLIII, no. 3 (1925).

Hebe, William. "Executive Orders and the Development of Presidential Power," 17 Vill. L. Rev. 688 (1972).

JAFFE, LOUIS, "Delegation of Legislative Power," Ch. 2 of his book, Judicial Control of Administrative Action (1965).

MERRILL, MAURICE H. "Standards—A Safeguard for the Exercise of Delegated Power," 47 Neb. L. Rev. 469 (1968).

NEIGHBORS, WILLIAM D. "Presidential Legislation by Executive Order," 37 U. Colo. L. Rev. 105 (1964).

ROSENBERG, DOUGLAS H. "Delegation and Regulatory Reform: Letting the President Change the Rules," 89 Yale L. J. 561 (1980).

ROSENBERG, MORTON. "Beyond the Limits of Executive Power: Presidential Control of Agency Rulemaking Under Executive Order 12,291," 80 Mich. L. Rev. 193 (1981).

STEWART, RICHARD B. "The Reformation of American Administrative Law," 88 Harv. L. Rev. 1667 (1975).

STROBEL, MARY H. "Delegation and Individual Rights," 56 So. Cal. L. Rev. 1321 (1983).

U.S. CONGRESS. Executive Orders in Times of War and National Emergency, Senate Special Committee on National Emergencies and Delegated Powers, 93d Cong., 2d Sess. (Comm. Print June 1974).

WEEKS, O. DOUGLAS. "Legislative Power Versus Delegated Legislative Power," 25 Geo. L. J. 314 (1937).

Chapter 5

BELLAMY, CALVIN. "The Growing Potential of the Pocket Veto: Another Area of Increasing Presidential Power," 61 Ill. Bar. J. 85 (1972).

BRUFF, HAROLD H., AND ERNEST GELLHORN. "Congressional Control of Administrative Regulation: A Study of Legislative Vetoes," 90 Harv. L. Rev. 1369 (1977).

CLINEBERG, WILLIAM A. "The President's Veto Power," 18 S.C. L. Rev. 732 (1966).

CONDO, JOSEPH A. "The Veto of S. 3418: More Congressional Power in the President's Pocket?" 22 Cath. U. L. Rev. 385 (1973).

COOPER, JOSEPH. "The Legislative Veto: Its Promise and Its Perils," 7 Public Policy 128 (1956).

COOPER, JOSEPH, AND ANN COOPER. "The Legislative Veto and the Constitution," 30 G.W. L. Rev. 467 (1962).

COTTER, CORNELIUS P., AND J. MALCOLM SMITH. "Administrative Accountability to Congress: The Concurrent Resolution," 9 West. Pol. Q. 955 (1956).

CRAIG, BARBARA HINKSON. The Legislative Veto: Congressional Control of Regulation (1983).

ELLIOTT, E. DONALD. "INS v. Chadha: The Administrative Constitution, the Constitution, and the Legislative Veto," Supreme Court Review, 1983, at 125.

FISHER, LOUIS. "A Political Context for Legislative Vetoes," 93 Pol. Sci. Q. 241 (1978).

GIBSON, RANKIN M. "Congressional Concurrent Resolution: An Aid to Statutory Interpretation?" 37 Am. Bar Ass'n J. 421 (1951).

GINNANE, ROBERT W. "The Control of the Federal Administration by Congressional Resolutions and Committees," 66 Harv. L. Rev. 569 (1953).

JACKSON, CARLETON. Presidental Vetoes (1967).

KAISER, FREDERICK M. "Congressional Control of Executive Actions in the Aftermath of the Chadha Decision," 36 Ad. L. Rev. 239 (1984).

KENNEDY, EDWARD M. "Congress, the President, and the Pocket Veto," 63 Va. L. Rev. 355 (1977).

LEE, JONG R. "Presidential Vetoes from Washington to Nixon," 37 J. Pol. 522 (1975).

Note. "The Presidential Veto Power: A Shallow Pocket," 70 Mich. L. Rev. 148 (1971).

————. "The Veto Power and Kennedy v. Sampson: Burning a Hole in the President's Pocket, 69 N.W. U. L. Rev. 587 (1974).

"Pocket Veto Legislation," 29 Record Ass'n Bar of the City of N.Y. 724 (1974).

STRAUSS, PETER L. "Was There a Baby in the Bathwater? A Comment on the Supreme Court's Legislative Veto Decision," 1983 Duke L. J. 789.

U.S. CONGRESS. "Constitutionality of the President's 'Pocket Veto' Power," hearing before the Senate Committee on the Judiciary, 92nd Cong., 1st Sess. (1971).

————. "The Pocket Veto Power," hearing before the House Committee on the Judiciary, 92d Cong., 1st Sess. (1971).

————. "Studies on the Legislative Veto," prepared for the House Committee on Rules, 96th Cong., 2d Sess. (Comm. Print February 1980).

WHITE, HOWARD. "Executive Responsibility to Congress via Concurrent Resolution," 36 Am. Pol. Sci. Rev. 895 (1942).

Chapter 6

BERGER, RAOUL. Executive Privilege (1974).

BISHOP, JOSEPH W., JR. "The Executive's Right of Privacy: An Unresolved Constitutional Question," 66 Yale L. J. 477 (1957).

BRECKENRIDGE, ADAM CARLYLE. The Executive Privilege (1974).

DIMOCK, MARSHALL EDWARD. "Congressional Investigating Committees," Johns Hopkins University Studies in Historical and Political Science, series XLVII, no. 1 (1929).

EBERLING, ERNEST J. Congressional Investigations (1928).

HAMILTON, JAMES. The Power to Probe: A Study of Congressional Investigations (1976).

HAMILTON, JAMES, AND JOHN C. GRABOW. "A Legislative Proposal for Resolving Executive Privilege Disputes Precipitated by Congressional Subpoenas," 21 Harv. J. on Legis. 145 (1984).

HENKIN, LOUIS. "The Right to Know and the Duty to Withhold: The Case of the Pentagon Papers," 120 U. Pa. L. Rev. 271 (1971).

KRAMER, ROBERT, AND HERMAN MARCUSE. "Executive Privilege—A Study of the Period 1953-1960," 29 G.W. L. Rev. 623, 827 (April and June 1961).

MCGEARY, M. NELSON. The Developments of Congressional Investigative Power (1940).

———. "Congressional Investigations: Historical Development," 18 U. Chi. L. Rev. 425 (1951).

MURPHY, JOHN F. "Knowledge is Power: Foreign Policy and Information Interchange Among Congress, the Executive Branch, and the Public," 49 Tulane L. Rev. 505 (1975).

RELYEA, HAROLD C., ED. The Presidency and Information Policy (1981).

ROURKE, FRANCIS E. Secrecy and Publicity (1966).

———. "Administrative Secrecy: A Congressional Dilemma," 54 Am. Pol. Sci. Rev. 884 (1960).

SCHLESINGER, ARTHUR M., JR., AND ROGER BRUNS, EDS. Congress Investigates, 1792-1974 (1975).

U.S. CONGRESS. "Executive Privilege: The Withholding of Information by the Executive," hearing before the Senate Committee on the Judiciary, 92d Cong., 1st Sess. (1971).

———. "Executive Privilege, Secrecy in Government, Freedom of Information" (3 Vols.), hearings before the Senate Committees on Government Operations and the Judiciary, 93d Cong., 1st Sess. (1973).

———. "Impeachment: Selected Materials," compiled by the House Committee on the Judiciary, 93d Cong., 1st Sess. (Comm. Print October 1973).

———. "Impeachment: Miscellaneous Documents," compiled by the Senate Committee on Rules and Administration, 93d Cong., 2d Sess. (Comm. Print August 7, 1974).

———. "Leading Cases on Congressional Investigatory Power," compiled by the Joint Committee on Congressional Operations, 94th Cong., 2d Sess. (Comm. Print January 1976).

YOUNGER, IRVING. "Congressional Investigations and Executive Secrecy: A Study in the Separation of Powers," 20 U. Pitts. L. Rev. 755 (1959).

Chapter 7

FISHER, LOUIS. Presidential Spending Power (1975).

———. "Confidential Spending and Governmental Accountability," 47 G.W. L. Rev. 347 (1979).

———. "The Authorization-Appropriation Process in Congress: Formal Rules and Informal Practices," 29 Cath. U. L. Rev. 51 (1979).

FUTTERMAN, STANLEY N. "Toward Legislative Control of the C.I.A.," 4 N.Y.U. J. Int'l L. & Pol. 431 (1971).

HUZAR, ELIAS. The Purse and the Sword: Control of the Army by Congress Through Military Appropriations, 1933-1950 (1950).

Note. "The CIA's Secret Funding and the Constitution," 83 Yale L. J. 608 (1975).

POWELL, FRED WILBUR. Control of Federal Expenditures: A Documentary History, 1775-1894 (1939).

SCHICK, ALLEN. Congress and Money (1981).

SCHWARTZMAN, BERMAN. "Fiscal Oversight of the Central Intelligence Agency: Can Accountability and Confidentiality Coexist?," 7 N.Y.U. J. Int'l L. & Pol. 493 (1974).

U.S. CONGRESS. "Impoundment of Appropriated Funds by the President," joint hearings before the Senate Committees on Government Operations and the Judiciary, 93d Cong., 1st Sess. (1973).

———. "Analysis of Executive Impoundment Reports," prepared by the Senate Committee on the Budget, 94th Cong., 1st Sess. (Comm. Print February 1975).

———. "U.S. Intelligence Agencies and Activities: Intelligence Costs and Fiscal Procedures (Part 1)," hearings before the House Select Committee on Intelligence, 94th Cong., 1st Sess. (1975).

———. "Whether Disclosure of Funds Authorized for Intelligence Activities is in the Public Interest," hearings before the Senate Select Committee on Intelligence, 95th Cong., 1st Sess. (1977).

WALDEN, JERROLD L. "The C.I.A.: A Study in the Arrogation of Administrative Powers," 39 G.W. L. Rev. 55 (1970).

WILMERDING, LUCIUS, JR. The Spending Power (1943).

Chapter 8

BESTOR, ARTHUR. "Separation of Powers in the Domain of Foreign Affairs: The Original Intent of the Constitution Historically Examined," 5 Seton Hall L. Rev. 529 (1974).

COHEN, RICHARD. "Self-Executing Executive Agreements: A Separation of Powers Problem," 24 Buff. L. Rev. 137 (1974).

GLENNON, MICHAEL J. "The Senate Role in Treaty Ratification," 77 Am. J. Int. L. 257 (1983).

HENKIN, LOUIS. Foreign Affairs and the Constitution (1972).

JOHNSON, LOCH, AND JAMES M. McCORMICK. "Foreign Policy by Executive Fiat," 28 Foreign Policy 117 (1977).

McCLURE, WALLACE. International Executive Agreements (1941).

McDOUGAL, MYRES S., AND ASHER LANS. "Treaties and Congressional-Executive or Presidential Agreements: Interchangeable Instruments of National Policy," 54 Yale L. J. 181, 534 (1945).

MATHEWS, CRAIG. "The Constitutional Power of the President to Conclude International Agreements," 64 Yale L. J. 345 (1955).

MURPHY, JOHN F. "Treaties and International Agreements Other Than Treaties: Constitutional Allocation of Power and Responsibility Among the President, the House of Representatives, and the Senate," 23 U. Kans. L. Rev. 221 (1975).

OHLY, D. CHRISTOPHER. "Advice and Consent: International Executive Claims Settlement Agreements," 5 Cal. West. Int'l L. J. 271 (1975).

ROVINE, ARTHUR W. "Separation of Powers and International Executive Agreements," 52 Ind. L. Rev. 397 (1977).

SLONIN, SOLOMON. "Congressional-Executive Agreements," 14 Colum. J. Transnat'l L. 434 (1975).

STEVENS, CHARLES J. "The Use and Control of Executive Agreements: Recent Congressional Initiatives," 20 Orbis 905 (1977).

TOMAIN, JOSEPH P. "Executive Agreements and the Bypassing of Congress," 8 J. Int'l L. & Econ. 129 (1973).

U.S. CONGRESS. "International Executive Agreements," hearing before the House Committee on Foreign Affairs, 92d Cong., 2d Sess. (1972).

———. "International Agreements: An Analysis of Executive Regulations and Practices," prepared for the Senate Committee on Foreign Relations, 95th Cong., 1st Sess. (Comm. Print March 1977).

———. "Termination of Treaties: The Constitutional Allocation of Power," materials compiled by the Senate Committee on Foreign Relations, 95th Cong., 2d Sess. (Comm. Print December 1978).

———. "Treaties and Other International Agreements: The Role of the

United States Senate," a study prepared for the Senate Committee on Foreign Relations, 98th Cong., 2d Sess. (Comm. Print June 1984).

Chapter 9

FRANCK, THOMAS M., ED. The Tethered Presidency: Congressional Restraints on Executive Power (1981).

FRANCK, THOMAS M., AND EDWARD WEISBAND. Foreign Policy by Congress (1979).

FRIED, JOHN H. E. "War-Exclusive or War-Inclusive Style in International Conduct," 11 Tex. Int'l L. J. 1 (1976).

FRYE, ALTON. A Responsible Congress (1975).

GLENNON, MICHAEL J. "The War Powers Resolution Ten Years Later: More Politics than Law," 78 Am. J. Int'l L. 571 (1984).

HENKIN, LOUIS. Foreign Affairs and the Constitution (1972).

JAVITS, JACOB K. Who Makes War: The President Versus Congress (1973).

JENKINS, GERALD. "The War Powers Resolution: Statutory Limitation on the Commander in Chief," 11 Harv. J. Legis. 181 (1974).

LOFGREN, CHARLES A. "War-Making Under the Constitution: The Original Understanding," 81 Yale L. J. 672 (1972).

MAY, ERNEST R., ED. The Ultimate Decision: The President as Commander in Chief (1951).

REVELEY, W. TAYLOR III. War Powers of the President and Congress (1981).

ROSSITER, CLINTON. The Supreme Court and the Commander in Chief (1951).

ROSTOW, EUGENE V. "Great Cases Make Bad Law: The War Powers Act," 50 Texas L. Rev. 833 (1972).

SMITH, J. MALCOLM, AND STEPHEN JURIKA. The President and National Security (1972).

SOFAER, ABRAHAM D. War, Foreign Affairs and Constitutional Power: The Origins (1976).

SPANIER, JOHN, AND JOSEPH NOGEE, EDS. Congress, the Presidency and American Foreign Policy (1981).

TURNER, ROBERT F. The War Powers Resolution: Its Implementation in Theory and Practice (1983).

U.S. CONGRESS. "The Powers of the President as Commander in Chief of the Army and Navy of the United States," H. Doc. No. 443, 84th Cong., 2d Sess. (1956).

U.S. CONGRESS. "Congress, the President, and the War Powers," hearings before the House Committee on Foreign Affairs, 91st Cong., 2d Sess. (1970).

———. "Documents Relating to the War Powers of Congress, the President's Authority as Commander-in-Chief and the War in Indochina," Senate Committee on Foreign Relations (Comm. Print 1970).

———. "War Powers Legislation," hearings before the Senate Committee on Foreign Relations, 92d Cong., 1st Sess. (1971).

———. "War Powers Legislation, 1973," hearings before the Senate Committee on Foreign Relations, 93d Cong., 1st Sess. (1973).

———. "The War Powers Resolution: Relevant Documents, Correspondence, Reports," House Committee on International Relations (Comm. Print April 23, 1975).

———. "War Powers Resolution," hearings before the Senate Committee on Foreign Relations, 95th Cong., 1st Sess. (1977).

———. "The War Powers Resolution," a special study of the House Committee on Foreign Affairs (Comm. Print 1982).

WILCOX, FRANCIS O. Congress, the Executive, and Foreign Policy (1971).

INDEX OF CASES

INDEX

367

Locke, John, 5-7, 100, 102-03, 287-88
Logan Act, 258-60
Long, Clarence, 321
Lynn, James T., 43

Machiavelli, Niccolò, 331-32
Mack, Richard A., 96-97
Madison, James, xiv, 8, 14, 19, 21, 99, 103, 243, 327; on appointments, 29, 38, 39; appropriations and, 221, 245; on impeachment, 201, 202; on removal power, 61-66; on treaties, 261; veto power and, 143, 144-45, 150; on war power, 286
Magnuson, Warren, 46
Malek, Frederick, 91
Marshall, John, 20, 31, 70-71
Marshall, Thurgood, 117, 119, 272
Martin, Luther, 29
Mason, George, 201, 242-44
Mathias, Charles McC., Jr., 41
McClellan, John, 199
McCormick, Medill, 233
McGarry, John, 51-52
McGee, John, 88
McIlwain, Charles Howard, 287
McKinley, William, 73, 292
McReynolds, James Clark, 70n, 76
Metcalf, Lee, 227
Mink, Patsy T., 324
Mitchell, John, 57, 306
Monroe, James, 149
Montesquieu, 10
Morgan, Arthur E., 79-80
Morris, Gouverneur, 242-43
Morris, Robert H., 46
Morton, Rogers C. B., 209
Moss, John E., 208-09, 219
Murphy, Frank, 290

National Emergencies Act, 301-02
national security, 81-86, 116-17, 215-20, 303-06

Neagle, David, 22-23
Nimmo, Robert P., 97
Nixon, Richard M., 123, 157, 160, 166, 174, 176, 228, 259, 269, 281; appointments by, 33, 40, 56; executive privilege and, 89-90, 207, 213-15, 216-17, 218; impoundment by, 33, 156, 236-37; international trade and, 125-27, 276; legislative power and, 114-15, 132-33; pay increases and, 107; removal power and, 88-89, 91; veto power and, 91, 151-52, 169, 309-10; wage-price controls of, 114-15; war power and, 296-97, 309-10, 321-22; wiretaps and, 303-06
nominations, 28, 31-37, 95-96, 206
nonstatutory controls, 119-23, 183

Office of Management and Budget (Bureau of the Budget), 90-91, 135, 138-39, 161-62, 227-30, 239, 241, 248
Olsen, Arthur J., 39
Otepka, Otto, 96-97

Page, John, 63-64
pardon power, 205-06, 222
pay legislation, 106-08
Pepper, George Wharton, 18
Pertschuk, Michael, 16
Pessen, Edward, 142
Phillips, Howard J., 56
Pierce, Franklin, 71
Polk, James K., 146, 245, 292
Powell, Lewis F., 118n, 178, 271-72, 324
Presentation Clause, 162-63, 179-80, 336-37
Pressler, Larry, 107-08
proclamations, presidential, 125-28, 135, 136-37, 181
Proxmire, William, 88, 132-33

Reagan, Ronald, 45, 168, 207, 260;

Library of Congress Cataloging in Publication Data
Fisher, Louis.
Constitutional conflicts between Congress and the President.

Rev. ed. of: The Constitution between friends. 1978.
Bibliography: p.
Includes indexes.
1. Separation of powers—United States. 2. United States—Constitutional law.
I. Fisher, Louis. The Constitution between friends. II. Title.
KF4565.F57 1985   320.473   83-60462

ISBN 0-691-07680-4 (alk. paper)
ISBN 0-691-02233-X (pbk.)

Louis Fisher is a specialist in American National Government with the Congressional Research Service of the Library of Congress. His book *Presidential Spending Power* (Princeton) received the Louis Brownlow Book Award in 1976 from the National Academy of Public Administration.